JOHN'S GOSPEL
AND INTIMATIONS OF APOCALYPTIC

JOHN'S GOSPEL
AND INTIMATIONS OF APOCALYPTIC

Edited by

Catrin H. Williams and Christopher Rowland

BLOOMSBURY
LONDON • NEW DELHI • NEW YORK • SYDNEY

Bloomsbury T&T Clark
An imprint of Bloomsbury Publishing Plc

50 Bedford Square	1385 Broadway
London	New York
WC1B 3DP	NY 10018
UK	USA

www.bloomsbury.com
Bloomsbury is a registered trade mark of Bloomsbury Publishing plc

First published 2013

© Catrin H. Williams and Christopher Rowland, with Contributors, 2013

All rights reserved. No part of this publication may be reproduced or transmitted in any form or by any means, electronic or mechanical, including photocopying, recording, or any information storage or retrieval system, without prior permission in writing from the publishers.

Catrin H. Williams, Christopher Rowland and contributors have asserted their rights under the Copyright, Designs and Patents Act, 1988, to be identified as Authors of this work.

No responsibility for loss caused to any individual or organization acting on or refraining from action as a result of the material in this publication can be accepted by Bloomsbury Academic or the authors.

British Library Cataloguing-in-Publication Data
A catalogue record for this book is available from the British Library.

ISBN:	HB:	978-0-56761-852-8
	PB:	978-0-56711-910-0
	ePDF:	978-0-56707-195-8
	ePub:	978-0-56746-300-5

Library of Congress Cataloging-in-Publication Data
John's Gospel and Intimations of Apocalyptic / Catrin H. Williams and Christopher Rowland, with Contributors p.cm
Includes bibliographic references and index.
ISBN 978-0-5676-1852-8 (hardcover) – ISBN 978-0-5671-1910-0 (pbk.)

Typeset by Forthcoming Publications Ltd (www.forthpub.com)

CONTENTS

Abbreviations — vii

INTRODUCTION
Christopher Rowland and Catrin H. Williams — ix

Part I
INTIMATIONS OF APOCALYPTIC

INTIMATIONS OF APOCALYPTIC:
LOOKING BACK AND LOOKING FORWARD
John Ashton — 3

JOHN AND THE JEWISH APOCALYPSES:
RETHINKING THE GENRE OF JOHN'S GOSPEL
Benjamin Reynolds — 36

FROM THE APOCALYPSE OF JOHN TO THE JOHANNINE
'APOCALYPSE IN REVERSE': INTIMATIONS OF APOCALYPTIC
AND THE QUEST FOR A RELATIONSHIP
Ian Boxall — 58

GOD'S DWELLING ON EARTH: '*SHEKHINA*-THEOLOGY'
IN REVELATION 21 AND IN THE GOSPEL OF JOHN
Jörg Frey — 79

UNVEILING REVELATION: THE SPIRIT-PARACLETE
AND APOCALYPTIC DISCLOSURE IN THE GOSPEL OF JOHN
Catrin H. Williams — 104

'INTIMATIONS OF APOCALYPTIC':
THE PERSPECTIVE OF THE HISTORY OF INTERPRETATION
Christopher Rowland — 128

Part II
THE GOSPEL OF JOHN AND ITS APOCALYPTIC MILIEU: SATAN AND THE RULER OF THIS WORLD

WHY ARE THE HEAVENS CLOSED?
THE JOHANNINE REVELATION OF THE FATHER
IN THE CATHOLIC-GNOSTIC DEBATE
April D. DeConick   147

THE RULER OF THE WORLD, ANTICHRISTS AND PSEUDO-PROPHETS:
JOHANNINE VARIATIONS ON AN APOCALYPTIC MOTIF
Jutta Leonhardt-Balzer   180

EVIL IN JOHANNINE AND APOCALYPTIC PERSPECTIVE:
PETITION FOR PROTECTION IN JOHN 17
Loren T. Stuckenbruck   200

Part III
JOHN AND APOCALYPTIC: TEXT AND READERS

TEXT AND AUTHORITY IN JOHN AND APOCALYPTIC
Judith M. Lieu   235

THE READER AS APOCALYPTIST IN THE GOSPEL OF JOHN
Robert G. Hall   254

APOCALYPTIC MYSTAGOGY:
REBIRTH-FROM-ABOVE IN THE RECEPTION
OF JOHN'S GOSPEL
Robin Griffith-Jones   274

EPILOGUE
Adela Yarbro Collins   300

Index of References   308
Index of Authors   325

ABBREVIATIONS

AB	Anchor Bible
ABD	*Anchor Bible Dictionary.* Edited by D. N. Freedman. 6 vols. New York, 1992
AGJU	Arbeiten zur Geschichte des antiken Judentums und des Urchristentums
AGSU	Arbeiten zur Geschichte des Spätjudentums und Urchristentums
ANET	*Ancient Near Eastern Texts Relating to the Old Testament.* Edited by J. B. Pritchard. Princeton, 3rd edn, 1969
BAGD	Bauer, W., W. F. Arndt, F. W. Gingrich, and F. W. Danker. *Greek-English Lexicon of the New Testament and Other Early Christian Literature.* Chicago, 2nd edn, 1979
BETL	Bibliotheca Ephemeridum Theologicarum Lovaniensium
BEvT	Beiträge zur evangelischen Theologie
BZNW	Beihefte zur *Zeitschrift für die neutestamentliche Wissenschaft*
CBQ	*Catholic Biblical Quarterly*
CBQMS	Catholic Biblical Quarterly Monograph Series
CCSL	Corpus Christianorum: Series latina. Turnhout, 1953–
CEJL	Commentaries on early Jewish literature
ConBNT	Coniectanea Neotestamentica or Coniectanea Biblica: New Testament Series
CRINT	Compendia Rerum Iudaicarum Ad Novum Testamentum
CSCO	Corpus Scriptorum Christianorum Orientalium. Edited by I. B. Chabot et al. Paris, 1903–
DDD	*Dictionary of Deities and Demons in the Bible.* Edited by K. van der Toorn, B. Becking, and P. W. van der Horst. Leiden, 1995
DSD	*Dead Sea Discoveries*
EKK	Evangelisch-katholischer Kommentar zum Neuen Testament
FRLANT	Forschungen zur Religion und Literatur des Alten und Neuen Testaments
GCS	Die griechische christliche Schriftsteller der ersten [drei] Jahrhunderte
HSM	Harvard Semitic Museum
HUCA	*Hebrew Union College Annual*
HUT	Hermeneutische Untersuchungen zur Theologie
ICC	International Critical Commentary
IEJ	*Israel Exploration Journal*
JBL	*Journal of Biblical Literature*
JJS	*Journal of Jewish Studies*
JSNT	*Journal for the Study of the New Testament*
JSNTSup	Journal for the Study of the New Testament, Supplement Series
JSP	*Journal for the Study of the Pseudepigrapha*
JSPSup	Journal for the Study of the Pseudepigrapha, Supplement Series

JSSSup	Journal of Semitic Studies, Supplement Series
KJV	King James Version
LCL	Loeb Classical Library
LHBOTS	Library of the Hebrew Bible/Old Testament Studies
LXX	Septuagint
MT	Masoretic Text
NA^{27}	*Novum Testamentum Graece*, Nestle-Aland, 27th edn
NHS	Nag Hammadi Studies
NIGTC	The New International Greek Testament Commentary
NovTSup	Novum Testamentum Supplements
NPNF^2	*Nicene and Post-Nicene Fathers, Series 2*
NRSV	New Revised Standard Version
NTABh	Neutestamentliche Abhandlungen
NTOA	Novum Testamentum et Orbis Antiquus
NTS	*New Testament Studies*
OG	Old Greek
OTP	*Old Testament Pseudepigrapha*. Edited by J. H. Charlesworth. 2 vols. New York, 1983
PG	Patrologia graeca [= Patrologiae cursus completus: Series graeca]. Edited by J.-P. Migne. 162 vols. Paris, 1857–1886
QD	Quaestiones disputatae
RB	*Revue biblique*
RGG	*Religion in Geschichte und Gegenwart*. Edited by K. Galling. 7 vols. Tübingen, 3rd edn, 1957–65
RNT	Regensburger Neues Testament
RSV	Revised Standard Version
SANT	Studien zum Alten und Neuen Testaments
SBL	Society of Biblical Literature
SBLDS	Society of Biblical Literature Dissertation Series
SBLSBS	Society of Biblical Literature Sources for Biblical Study
SBS	Stuttgarter Bibelstudien
SJT	*Scottish Journal of Theology*
SNTSMS	Society for New Testament Studies Monograph Series
STDJ	Studies on the Texts of the Desert of Judah
SVTP	Studia in Veteris Testamenti Pseudepigraphica
TANZ	Texte und Arbeiten zum neutestamentlichen Zeitalter
THKNT	Theologischer Handkommentar zum Neuen Testament
ThWNT	*Theologisches Wörterbuch zum Neuen Testament*. Edited by G. Kittel. Stuttgart, 1933–1979
TSAJ	Texts and Studies in Ancient Judaism
TU	Texte und Untersuchungen
TZ	*Theologische Zeitschrift*
WBC	Word Biblical Commentary
WMANT	Wissenschaftliche Monographien zum Alten und Neuen Testament
WUNT	Wissenschaftliche Untersuchungen zum Neuen Testament
YDCL	Yearbook of Deuterocanonical and Cognate Literature
ZNW	*Zeitschrift für die neutestamentliche Wissenschaft und die Kunde der älteren Kirche*
ZTK	*Zeitschrift für Theologie und Kirche*

INTRODUCTION

Christopher Rowland and Catrin H. Williams

In addition to being a remarkable monument to the history of modern scholarship on the Gospel of John, surveying the history of scholarship with that characteristic mix of concise expression and critical nuance, John Ashton's *Understanding the Fourth Gospel* points in many new directions for study. It is one of these new directions, strangely passed over in the reception of Ashton's book, which was at the heart of a colloquium entitled 'John's Gospel and Intimations of Apocalyptic' held at Bangor University in July 2010 and which forms the basis of this present volume of essays. In a memorable chapter in *Understanding the Fourth Gospel*, which had made its impact on so many of the participants at the colloquium, John Ashton integrates new approaches to the study of apocalypticism with major themes of the Gospel of John, so that apocalyptic themes illuminate central theological ideas in the Gospel – and to great effect. What is more, as elsewhere in the book, he manages to capture the nature of what he discerns through striking phrases, which have since become imaginative catalysts for a new perspective. Take, for example, the phrase in the title of this volume, 'Intimations of Apocalyptic'. From any point of view the Gospel of John can hardly be said to be immediately and obviously a fully blown apocalypse; there is no account of a heavenly vision, ascent to heaven, nor, even if one uses widely held understandings of apocalyptic, a final irruption and winding up of history. What there is – and pervasively so – are 'intimations of apocalyptic'. John's Gospel is a text pervaded with themes concerning 'apocalypse', revelation – concerning the meeting of two worlds mediated through the persons and events of this world. It is full of intimations, therefore, for those with eyes to see the apocalypse manifested in the Word become flesh. Like the sun at dawn on a cloudy day which occasionally bursts through the gloom lighting up the sky, the Johannine narrative offers intimations of another world, another reality, without the direct immediate paraphernalia of a theophany so typical of many apocalyptic visions.

Then there is that memorable summary of Ashton's discussion in his chapter on 'Intimations of Apocalyptic'.[1] He writes there of the divine plan having become incarnate, a revelation of 'God's grand design…now being realized', although Jesus' words 'assume the character of a mystery, one whose meaning cannot be grasped until the dawn of a new age, when in a second stage, it will at last receive its authoritative interpretation. Thus the fourth evangelist conceives his own work as an apocalypse – in reverse, upside down, inside out'.[2] Like 'intimations of apocalyptic', Ashton's words brilliantly encapsulate something which is true, not only about apocalyptic, but about the Gospel of John. He brings together the Fourth Gospel and a religious tradition not usually linked with the Gospel in a way that is illuminating of both. In so doing he succeeds in capturing both the difference and the similarity to revelatory themes, which, as Ashton points out in his book, was noticed by Rudolf Bultmann, but all too rarely explored in connection with Judaism, not least because it is the eschatological component of the apocalyptic literature which has attracted most interest.

Of course, in writing thus there *is* a sense in which some forms of revelation are excluded. Rightly have commentators pointed to verses like John 3.13 to suggest that there is an explicit repudiation of claims to visionary ascent, such as those made by Enoch, Abraham, Isaiah, and others in Jewish and early Christian apocalyptic literature. Revelation in John comes not by visionary experience, or rather, it does, but the visionary experience is 'new birth', an epistemological change which enables one, like the man born blind, to see again, to use the words of William Blake, with 'the doors of perception cleansed'. This point needs to be stressed in the face of those who rightly point out that the narrative of the Gospel of John is exactly that – a narrative, not an apocalypse, neither a heavenly journey nor an angelic revelation. Indeed, there is an oft-remarked dearth of such moments in the Gospel of John. The baptism has become less a visionary experience of Jesus as an authentication for the witness of John the Baptist. The solitary voice from heaven in John 12.28 is likewise a sign for the crowds, who mistake the apocalyptic moment just as they misunderstand the 'apocalypse' in Jesus Christ that confronts them. There is a promise, albeit a future one, of revelation for Nathanael of angels ascending and descending (John 1.51) and of

---

1   John Ashton, *Understanding the Fourth Gospel* (Oxford: Oxford University Press, 2nd edn, 2007), pp.307-29. Note that throughout this introduction reference is made to the second edition of Ashton's book.

2   Ashton, *Understanding*, pp.328-29.

new truths revealed by the Spirit-Paraclete (16.13), but the narrative form of the text compels a different understanding of the nature of apocalypse.

There is perhaps some inevitability, reflected in the essays of this volume, about the need to discuss the meaning of apocalyptic and its relationship to a text like the Gospel of John. As indicated above, we have regarded John Ashton's use of apocalyptic as both an inclusive category, not one narrowly related to a particular form of eschatological belief, as is often found in the history of the study of the subject and is still widely current. John Ashton's language not only functions as a heuristic device to stimulate interpretative approaches, but it also resists the attempt to reduce issues in dealing with the apocalyptic character, and indeed setting, of John's Gospel to a decision about whether one considers apocalyptic to be a particular form of eschatology. Few would want to assert similar eschatological convictions as in the book of Revelation. For example, the destiny of the disciples *in heaven* in John 17.25 is very different from *heaven on earth* in Revelation. Also, the symbolic world of Revelation is largely absent from John. However, to focus exclusively on eschatology – which is certainly an important part of the message of the Fourth Gospel – is to concentrate more on the *content* of apocalyptic texts like Revelation rather than on their *genre*. As texts they concern revelation of a variety of issues, of which eschatology is one – though rarely the only – issue, even in the book of Revelation. Thus, while there may be numerous parallels with the book of Revelation in terms of the contents of its symbolic world, its concern to be, in some sense, a text of revelation and about the unique medium for revelation puts the two texts close in their emphasis, and perhaps also in their world of thought.

The study of the Gospel of John and apocalypticism, including the beginnings of Jewish mysticism, has had a chequered history. The pioneer work in this area by Hugo Odeberg is a fragment[3] – a 'torso'[4] – of what might have been completed, suggestive and insightful as it is. From the perspective of modern scholarship, which is more attentive to questions of date and the appropriateness of using sources whose textual evidence is much later than the New Testament for the interpretation of the New Testament, the inclusion of a mass of much later Mandean and Jewish mystical material in Odeberg's commentary, without detailed

---

3 Hugo Odeberg, *The Fourth Gospel Interpreted in its Relation to Contemporaneous Religious Currents in Palestine and the Hellenistic-Oriental World* (Uppsala: Almqvist & Wiksell, 1929).

4 Martin Hengel, *The Son of God: the Origin of Christology and the History of Jewish-Hellenistic Religion* (London: SCM, 1976), p.89.

apologia, would require more explanation today than is offered in his book. The debate about the relationship between the New Testament writings and Jewish mysticism has been carried out by those whose involvement in the normal curriculum of biblical studies has been attenuated for various reasons. Pre-eminently the monograph by Jan-Adolf Bühner, so strangely marginal in Johannine scholarship, and which John Ashton's work has done much to rehabilitate, must have pride of place.[5] The work of Jarl Fossum has also not made the impact one might have expected in the development of the subject.[6] That is why John Ashton's monograph is such a welcome and refreshing contribution to a subject where particular understandings of religious background have dominated. The marginal character of this work on Jewish apocalypticism and mysticism in connection with the Fourth Gospel, at least as far as mainstream Johannine scholarship is concerned, has meant that the strengths and weaknesses of the hypothesis of relating John to apocalypticism and mysticism have not formed part of the wider intellectual discourse of the academy. As we shall see, not all those who would want to argue for 'intimations of apocalyptic' in the Gospel of John want to suggest that there is any direct borrowing from particular works. However, neither the genealogical approach to Johannine antecedents, nor the application of the analogical method to illuminate Johannine themes, has been a regular part of the debate.

This brings us to another important question raised by the relationship of John's Gospel and apocalypticism. Despite John Ashton's resort to parallels from the history of religion in his *Understanding of the Fourth Gospel*, his underlying method has been less about trying to pin down the origin of the Gospel of John by means of a detailed genealogy of the history of a religious tradition, so much as seeking to understand, by resort to these parallels, how one might best comprehend what we find in this remarkable text. His method, therefore, is usually analogical rather than genealogical. Indeed, if we look at his work on the Gospel of John in the light of his attempt to understand Paul through the lens of studies of shamanism,[7] it is a preference for the analogical rather than the

---

5 Jan-Adolf Bühner, *Der Gesandte und sein Weg im 4. Evangelium: Die kultur- und religionsgeschichtlichen Grundlagen der johanneischen Sendungschristologie sowie ihre traditionsgeschichtliche Entwicklung* (WUNT 2/2; Tübingen: Mohr Siebeck, 1977).

6 *The Image of the Invisible God: Essays on the Influence of Jewish Mysticism on Early Christology* (Novum Testamentum et Orbis Antiquus 30; Freiburg: Universitätsverlag, 1995).

7 John Ashton, *The Religion of Paul the Apostle* (New Haven: Yale University Press, 2000).

genealogical which characterizes his method. His essay for this volume bids us to share in a thought-experiment that juxtaposes the Gospel of John with *1 Enoch*, asking us to imagine that the writer of John was immersed in a text like *1 Enoch*. We are asked to see what can be offered in interpretation by juxtaposing two, probably roughly contemporary, texts. Indeed, even if the texts were not contemporary and John not directly dependent, the task of comparison is the necessary mode and the possible pay-off is comparative and illustrative rather than explanatory.

Time and time again in the Gospel of John one comes across passages where the closest textual analogues come from apocalyptic and mystical literature. Whatever our attitude to the dating of some of these sources, the underlying religious ideology makes most sense when interpreted in the light of such material. While one recognizes the ongoing fascination and compulsion for genealogical answers in the history of ideas, for many of us the concern is not to establish that the Gospel of John was part of a mystical sub-culture, so much as to consider the affinities in hermeneutical approach that the fourth evangelist had both with predecessors and successors. Often what appears to be an explicit borrowing on the part of a writer is done so unconsciously that one has the impression that the prophetic or mystical is moving afresh in each generation. This concern is a characteristic rhetoric and trope of the apocalyptic and mystical, for the tracing of close verbal connections suggests that we are dealing with a *theologia perennis*, a recurring body of thought, things that never die but resurface. What is of importance, therefore, is the use of such writings as a heuristic device to understand the Gospel better.

In the opening essay of this volume, John Ashton does nevertheless propose that the most obvious explanation of the striking parallels between John's Gospel and Jewish apocalyptic is that the fourth evangelist was directly acquainted with some of the apocalyptic writings. He points to the Fourth Gospel's many resemblances to the book of Daniel and the older book of *1 Enoch*, using historical imagination to surmise that the fourth evangelist had previously, from within the Essene community, read Daniel and *1 Enoch*. From Daniel he learnt about the disclosure of dreams and visions and about the idea of two ages; to *1 Enoch* he was indebted for several apocalyptic ideas, including the story of Enoch's visionary journey, the separation of the good from the wicked and, in particular, for the idea of new revelation as superior to the Torah.

Taking the lead from John Ashton's description of John's Gospel as 'an apocalypse – in reverse, upside down, inside out', Benjamin Reynolds' essay explores the relationship between John's Gospel and the Jewish apocalypses with reference to issues of genre. He notes that while John's Gospel cannot be defined as an apocalypse, it does fit into what he calls an 'apocalyptic framework'. As far as genre is concerned, Reynolds favours the designation 'apocalyptic Gospel' as a more precise description of the themes and motifs that John's Gospel shares with the Jewish apocalypses.

Two essays seek out 'intimations of apocalyptic' in John's Gospel by addressing the question of its relationship with the book of Revelation. After a brief assessment of linguistic similarities and differences in the two texts and of strands in their reception history that posit familial relationship rather than common authorship, Ian Boxall investigates six pairs of close verbal echoes which point to 'similarities of voice' between the sayings of Jesus in both texts and which raise questions about the role of early Christian prophecy in the development of the Johannine *logia*. In his essay Jörg Frey focuses on a particular motif common to both Johannine texts, namely God's dwelling on earth (John 1.14; Rev 21.3). Tracing the development of *Shekhina* theology from the exilic period to the first century CE, he argues that different types of transmission are attested in the Johannine material: while John's Prologue draws on wisdom traditions to present Jesus as the embodiment of God's presence, the book of Revelation sets the motif of God's dwelling within an eschatological framework.

Catrin Williams takes up John Ashton's proposal that the presentation of the Spirit-Paraclete as revealer-interpreter (John 14.25-26; 16.12-15) is derived from Jewish apocalyptic thought. By examining both conceptual ('remembering/reminding') and verbal (ἀναγγέλλω) parallels linked to the revelation of divine mysteries, she concludes that Jewish apocalyptic tradition sheds light on two aspects of the Spirit's activity: mnemonic illumination of what was previously veiled, and the passing on of revelation that has not yet been disclosed.

With special reference to William Blake's *Illustrations of the Book of Job*, Christopher Rowland discusses how Blake's interpretation of Johannine christology – especially the presentation of Jesus as the revelation of God – anticipates John Ashton's understanding of the Fourth Gospel as an 'apocalypse in reverse'. Additional intimations of apocalyptic relating to other key Johannine themes – such as cross, glory and judgement – are also identified in the Blake corpus.

If the contributions in Part I are largely held together by their interest in the Fourth Gospel's exposition of the theme of revelation, all the three essays in Part II elucidate the connection between the Johannine and apocalyptic worldviews in their understanding of evil. Taking the 'closed heavens' of John's Gospel as her point of departure, April DeConick contends that John 8.44 refers to the Jewish god, the father of the devil ('you are from the father of the devil', 8.44a), who is different from the Father God. Close examination of four Gnostic-catholic disputes about the meaning of John 8.44 leads DeConick to reassess the relationship between 1 John and John's Gospel. The entire letter, it is claimed, is designed to challenge an exposition of John 8 that centres on the literal, and earlier, reading of v. 44 as a reference to the father of the devil.

Jutta Leonhardt-Balzer examines the meaning and function of the various terms used to denote the eschatological enemy in the Johannine writings (the ruler of this world/the evil one, the devil/Satan, Antichrist). Each term has its use in a specific context, but it is proposed that all the terms can be subsumed under the concept of spirit possession. This provides the relevant background for the Johannine references to the eschatological adversary and to the effect of the Holy Sprit; it also calls into question the commonly held view that John's Gospel contains no reference to exorcisms. In his essay Loren Stuckenbruck enquires whether there is anything eschatological or even apocalyptic about the way that evil – as a continuing reality – is combated in John's Gospel and the Johannine Epistles. With particular reference to Jesus' petitions in John 17, Stuckenbruck asks: what is the function of a prayer for divine protection from 'the evil one'? To answer this question, he analyses a series of petitionary prayers for protection in Jewish apocalyptic tradition, especially in writings from the Dead Sea Scrolls; their understanding of the tension between the present age of wickedness and a future age of restoration provides a close link to John's perspective on the persistent reality of the demonic but whose complete destruction will take place in the eschatological future.

The essays in Part III explore how apocalyptic ideas can help to explain the intended function of the text of John's Gospel for its readers and hearers. Judith Lieu compares textual strategies used by John and apocalyptic literature to define and legitimate the 'knowledge' that they profess to reveal. The importance of 'text' for the communication and dissemination of apocalyptic becomes evident from three levels on which its textuality operates: the literary production of the apocalyptic text as 'book'; the text within apocalyptic, including 'heavenly books'; the reinterpretation of scripture in apocalyptic texts. Lieu's analysis of these levels of textuality within apocalyptic is then used as a lens for reflection on the legitimating techniques attested in the Gospel of John.

What are the expectations for the readers of John's Gospel? Robert Hall proposes that the author hopes for readers/hearers who can respond like apocalyptists by uncovering the mysteries that are otherwise hidden or unknowable. As in Mediterranean revelatory literature and in the ancient Jewish and Christian apocalypses, readers of John's Gospel must be open to revelatory experience; through knowledge of the shifting meanings of the Gospel's many and varied riddles – including orthographical realignments – responsive readers can become the beneficiaries of revelatory insight. The essay by Robin Griffith-Jones complements Hall's contribution in that it analyses John's Gospel as a document whose (re-)performance of Jesus' life was designed to function as an apocalyptic event for its audience. Readers and hearers are brought through a 'new birth from above' as a result of their imaginative engagement with the text, while its sequential effect on the audience is suggested by some of its most memorable Johannine features, including the 'I am' pronouncements and the sayings about 'eternal life'. The transformation undergone by seers during their heavenly ascents could, as a result, now be made available to John's 'earthbound' audience.

Finally, Adela Yarbro Collins offers a reflective response to the essays in the form of an Epilogue. Encouraged by the volume's central theme to conduct her own investigation of John as an 'apocalyptic Gospel', she notes how certain apocalyptic motifs, particularly those linked to eschatological expectation, find their proleptic fulfilment in the death and resurrection of the Johannine Jesus. Like the other contributors, Adela Yarbro Collins welcomes the openness of this volume to the possibility of 'intimations of apocalyptic' in John's Gospel – an openness which, we hope, will generate further discussion of the contribution of apocalyptic traditions to our understanding of the Gospel's origins, its emergence from Judaism, and the distinctiveness of its thought-forms.

*****

We are grateful to Bible Society and to the School of Theology and Religious Studies at Bangor University for jointly funding the colloquium at which most of the essays in this volume were first presented and discussed. For their contribution to the organisation of the Bangor colloquium, we would like to thank: Jody Barnard, Gillian Griffiths, Garry Peel, and Hazel Thompson. We are also grateful to Dominic Mattos at Bloomsbury T & T Clark for accepting this volume for publication, and to Jody Barnard for formatting the essays during the early stages of the editing process.

Part I

INTIMATIONS OF APOCALYPTIC

INTIMATIONS OF APOCALYPTIC:
LOOKING BACK AND LOOKING FORWARD

John Ashton

When Catrin Williams paid me the very great honour of offering to organise a colloquium centred on my big book on the Fourth Gospel, she singled out one chapter, 'Intimations of Apocalyptic', as a general title for the colloquium. Readers of the book may remember that its main purpose was to answer in turn what Rudolf Bultmann had recognised as the two great riddles of the Gospel, the first historical, and the second exegetical. The answer the Gospel itself offers (*für sich*) to the second riddle, what is its basic idea, its *Grundkonzeption*, is simply, says Bultmann, that Jesus was sent as the Revealer, and this basic idea furnishes the object of the first riddle: what (*an sich*) is the historical origin of this extraordinary conception – how is it to be explained? Accordingly, after outlining the different sorts of questions that had been raised concerning the Gospel since the close of the eighteenth century, I divided my book into two main parts, the first, *Genesis*, dealing with the historical problem of the Gospel's origins, and the second, *Revelation*, a detailed response to the exegetical question of the Gospel's dominant theme. The chapter entitled 'Intimations of Apocalyptic' opens the second part,[1] and is thus the beginning of my answer to the problem of the Gospel's *Grundkonzeption*.

In his generous and appreciative foreword to the second edition of my book, Christopher Rowland, whom I must also thank for helping to organise the colloquium, first praises me for recognising in the Fourth Gospel the spirit of apocalyptic so characteristic of it. Then, with his uncanny knack for putting his finger on flaws or deficiencies in the work of his friends and colleagues, he goes on: 'Curiously, he [John Ashton] does not pursue what would be the obvious next interpretative step: the

---

1 John Ashton, *Understanding the Fourth Gospel* (Oxford: Clarendon, 1991), pp.383–406.

elucidation of the relationship, whether literary or in terms of a debt to a common world of thought'.[2] In placing my reflections on apocalyptic in the exegetical section of the book, I had omitted to give it any place in the historical section and failed to surmise how the evangelist might have been directly influenced by contemporary apocalyptic thinking. In this essay I propose to take that next interpretative step.

LOOKING BACK

Yet before looking forward I will begin, as Catrin suggested I might when she proposed a title for my own paper, by looking back – looking back at least as far as 1886, when Adolf Harnack (not yet ennobled) gave the Johannine problem its first classic formulation: 'the origin of the Johannine writings is, from the stand-point of a history of literature and dogma, the most marvellous enigma [like Bultmann, Harnack used the word *Rätsel*, riddle] which the early history of Christianity presents'.[3] Looking again at this opinion of Harnack, expressed with such clarity and assurance over 125 years ago, can we honestly say that his enigma has been solved?

Of course there have been many attempts at a solution, often enough by appealing to other branches of early Christianity. The great scholar Wilhelm Bousset, for instance, asserted that John 'stood on Paul's shoulders',[4] and many others have thought it sufficient to resort to the Synoptic tradition. Indeed even today the disciples of Frans Neirynck, still toiling away in the beautiful city of Leuven,[5] seem content to look

---

2   John Ashton, *Understanding the Fourth Gospel* (Oxford: Oxford University Press, 2nd edn, 2007), p.viii.

3   Adolf Harnack, *History of Dogma* (trans. Neil Buchanan; 7 vols.; London: Williams & Norgate, 1894), I, pp.96–7.

4   Wilhelm Bousset, *Kyrios Christos: Geschichte des Christusglaubens von den Anfängen des Christentums bis Irenaeus* (Göttingen: Vandenhoeck & Ruprecht, 5th edn, 1965 [1st edn, 1913]), p.180: '"Johannes" steht allerdings auf den Schultern des "Paulus"'. Harnack had already spoken of John's Christ as 'Pauline', and, as late as 1924, Maurice Goguel writes confidently of 'the dependence of Johannine thought (*le johannisme*) upon Pauline thought' (*Introduction au nouveau Testament*. Vol. 2, *Le Quatrième Évangile* [Paris: Ernest Leroux, 1924], pp.73–4).

5   This was designated 'the Leuven hypothesis' by its proponents. See Gilbert Van Belle's essay, 'Tradition, Exegetical Formation, and the Leuven Hypothesis', in Tom Thatcher (ed.), *What We Have Heard From the Beginning: The Past, Present, and Future of Johannine Studies* (Waco, TX: Baylor University Press, 2007), pp.325–37.

little further than the first three Gospels for explanations of the peculiarities of the fourth. Bultmann himself, who took up Harnack's problem 40 years later, and narrowed it down by restricting it to 'where John's Gospel stands in relation to the development of *early Christianity*', was confident that it cannot be considered to belong to any of the three main branches of doctrinal development in the early Church, namely Hellenistic Christianity (Paul), Jewish-Hellenistic Christianity (*1 Clement*, the Shepherd of Hermas, Hebrews, *Barnabas*), or Palestinian Christianity (the Synoptic Gospels).[6] Some had looked to the Hermetic literature of Hellenism for an alternative influence, notably Richard Reitzenstein, whose ideas were systematically followed through by the Welshman C. H. Dodd, though Dodd carefully avoided categorising this material as a source.[7] Bultmann himself, notoriously, turned to Mandaean Gnosticism for a solution, and although his hypothesis of a revelation-discourse source won few adherents, many scholars since, including C. K. Barrett and Wayne Meeks,[8] have been convinced that there are sufficient elements in the Gospel, especially the picture of the descending/ascending redeemer, to make it reasonable to suppose that there has been some input from Gnosticism.

The suspicion of Gnostic influence, then, survived the collapse of Bultmann's bold and comprehensive solution, but the disappearance of what was in effect a single-source theory led to the alternative proposal that the evangelist had been affected by a wide variety of sources and influences. This particular proposal was often blurred, though, by the substitution of the vague term 'background' for the more precise terms 'sources' and 'influences', and the blurring led to the suggestion that the Gospel might be a syncretic work. Syncretism is such a loose and baggy word that it can be used to cover practically everything and, consequently, explain practically nothing. 'Is it not possible', asks George MacRae, 'that the Fourth Evangelist may have tried deliberately to incorporate a diversity of backgrounds into the one gospel message precisely

---

6   Rudolf Bultmann, 'Die Bedeutung der neuerschlossenen mandäischen und manichäischen Quellen für das Verständnis des Johannesevangeliums', *ZNW* 24 (1925), pp.100–46 (100–101 [my emphasis]).

7   C. H. Dodd, *The Interpretation of the Fourth Gospel* (Cambridge: Cambridge University Press, 1953).

8   See C. K. Barrett, *The Gospel According to St John: An Introduction with Commentary and Notes on the Greek Text* (London: SPCK, 2nd edn, 1978), pp.38–40, 65–6; Wayne A. Meeks, 'The Man from Heaven in Johannine Sectarianism', *JBL* 91 (1972), pp.44–72 (44–6).

to emphasize the universality of Jesus?'[9] – a wild suggestion (how does one incorporate a background?) which is at the same time a confession of ignorance. Much more fruitful, as it turned out, and more widely adopted, was a very different approach that involved the study of the history of particular themes and concepts characteristic of the Gospel. What partisans of both these approaches had in common was their rejection of Bultmann's insistence upon the need of a single overriding explanation of what he saw as a Gnostic myth taken over and purified by the evangelist.[10] Accordingly, scholars in increasing numbers took the path of seeking out the origins of individual themes or traditions.[11]

Following the lead of Siegfried Schulz, who in 1957 had published four short studies of the traditions lying behind the themes of Son of Man, Son, Paraclete and the Return of Jesus,[12] many distinguished scholars adopted his suggested method of *Themageschichte* and wrote important books or essays on a wide variety of other topics. Here I can only point to those from which I myself have derived most benefit. First

---

9   George W. MacRae, 'The Fourth Gospel and *Religionsgeschichte*,' *CBQ* 32 (1970), pp.13–24 (15).

10   One of Bultmann's pupils, Luise Schottroff, swallowed Bultmann's ideas almost whole; see Luise Schottroff, *Der Glaubende und die feindliche Welt: Beobachtungen zum gnostischen Dualismus und seiner Bedeutung für Paulus und das Johannesevangelium* (Neukirchen–Vluyn: Neukirchener, 1970). The only major scholar to agree with Bultmann that the theological problems of the Gospel could only be resolved by singling out a specific sector of early Christianity was another of his pupils, Ernst Käsemann; see his *The Testament of Jesus: A Study of the Gospel of John in the Light of Chapter 17* (London: SCM, 1968), p.3. Käsemann points to the heady atmosphere of early Christian 'enthusiasm', and speaks (without proof or argument) of the development of hymns that 'described Jesus as a pre-existent heavenly being whose earthly existence was but a stage of a journey to take him back to heaven' (21). Frustratingly, he does not actually name a single one of these hymns, but presumably he was thinking of the Logos-hymn in the Prologue, which he certainly regarded as pre-Johannine, and of hymns such as that in the letter to the Philippians (Phil 2.6-11) and in 1 Tim 3.16, a little hymn which, starting as it does by applying the word 'mystery' to Christ, is tantalisingly close to much in the Fourth Gospel – but its origins are no less obscure.

11   At the relevant point in his large work [see n. 16 below] Jörg Frey points out that what he calls *die realgeschichtlichen Feststellungen* that Bultmann had largely brushed aside (*ausgeklammert*) could not remain suppressed indefinitely: *Die johanneische Eschatologie 1: Ihre Probleme im Spiegel der Forschung seit Reimarus* (WUNT 96; Tübingen: Mohr Siebeck, 1997), p.156.

12   Siegfried Schulz, *Untersuchungen zur Menschensohn-Christologie im Johannesevangelium: Zugleich ein Beitrag zur Methodengeschichte der Auslegung des 4. Evangeliums* (Göttingen: Vandenhoeck & Ruprecht, 1957).

and foremost Wayne Meeks's *The Prophet-King*,[13] which opens with a perceptive discussion of the issues raised by the by-then general rejection of Bultmann's theories. The following year saw the publication of Peder Borgen's 'God's Agent',[14] a truly seminal article which was followed up nine years later by Jan-Adolf Bühner's equally seminal work on the Divine Emissary.[15] Twenty years after this, not least but, appropriately, last, came Jörg Frey's impressively large study of eschatology.[16] Well, not quite last, because I must not forget Catrin Williams's excellent treatment of the I-am sayings, which, right at the end of the century, rounded off some forty years of fruitful study of Johannine themes.[17]

And yet – and yet – however far we were to extend this list, there is one theme we would search for in vain, the one that Bultmann had rightly singled out as the Gospel's *Grundkonzeption*, the theme of *revelation*. No doubt there is an obvious reason for this omission, namely that the word itself does not occur in the Gospel.[18] But the same is true of eschatology, which did not prevent Frey from writing three large volumes on that topic. So, between the interstices of what might have looked like a tightly woven net covering all the interlocking themes of John's elaborate Christology, the biggest theme of all had slipped

---

13   Wayne A. Meeks, *The Prophet-King: Moses Traditions and the Johannine Christology* (NovTSup 14; Leiden: E. J. Brill, 1967).

14   Peder Borgen, 'God's Agent in the Fourth Gospel', in Jacob Neusner (ed.), *Religions in Antiquity: Essays in Memory of Erwin Ramsdell Goodenough* (Studies in the History of Religions [Supplements to Numen] 14; Leiden: E. J. Brill, 1968), pp. 137–48.

15   Jan-Adolf Bühner, *Der Gesandte und sein Weg im 4. Evangelium: Die kultur- und religionsgeschichtlichen Grundlagen der johanneischen Sendungschristologie sowie ihre traditionsgeschichtliche Entwicklung* (WUNT 2/2; Tübingen: Mohr Siebeck, 1977).

16   Jörg Frey, *Die johanneische Eschatologie* (WUNT 96, 110, 117; 3 vols.; Tübingen: Mohr Siebeck, 1997–2000).

17   Catrin H. Williams, *I am He: The Interpretation of 'Anî Hû' in Jewish and Early Christian Literature* (WUNT 2/113; Tübingen: Mohr Siebeck, 2000). It should perhaps be added that historical-critical studies began to tail off in the 1980s, yielding place to narrative criticism. This, if one includes its epigones, such as reader-response criticism, continues to dominate Johannine studies to this day (at any rate in the greater part of the English-speaking world).

18   Except in the quotation from Isa 53.1 in John 12.38. The words 'wisdom' and 'mystery' are also absent, both of which figure prominently in Jewish apocalypses to denote the object of revelation. The only book I know devoted to this theme, Gail M. O'Day's, *Revelation in the Fourth Gospel: Narrative Mode and Theological Claim* (Philadelphia: Fortress, 1986), ignores the history-of-traditions aspect completely.

through undetected.[19] Somehow or other, throughout the upsurge of Johannine studies that began in the 1960s, both of Bultmann's key questions were lost sight of until I drew attention to them twenty years ago and gave what I still believe to be more or less the right answer to the second riddle. But what of the first?

Among the Jewish sources scoured by scholars during these years for possible influences on John there is a noticeable neglect of apocalypses,[20] largely because the term 'apocalypse' was confused during most of this period with the futuristic eschatology that John, for the most part, abandons in favour of what he calls 'eternal life'. Had the theme of revelation been selected for the kind of close history-of-traditions scrutiny that had been directed to other themes, some attention would have had to be paid to the apocalypses, whose distinguishing mark, after all, is their inclusion of new revelations that do not figure in the Hebrew Bible. Indeed one could argue (as I did in my book) that the Fourth Gospel actually fits quite snugly into John Collins's widely accepted definition of an apocalypse as 'a genre of revelatory literature with a narrative framework, in which a revelation is mediated by an otherworldly being to a human recipient, disclosing a transcendent reality which is both temporal,

---

19 An honourable exception to this generalisation is Ignace de la Potterie's paper, 'L'arrière-fond du thème johannique de vérité', in Kurt Aland *et al.* (eds.), *Studia Evangelica 1: Papers Presented to the International Congress on "The Four Gospels in 1957" held at Christ Church, Oxford, 1957* (Texte und Untersuchungen 73; Berlin: Akademie-Verlag, 1959), pp.277–94, where he demonstrates, from a study chiefly of *1 Enoch*, the Book of Wisdom, and the Dead Sea Scrolls that, *contra* Bultmann and Dodd, the true background of John's concept of truth is Jewish wisdom and apocalyptic. Significantly, however, this study is seldom if ever mentioned in American, British or German scholarship. In 1963 Ignace de la Potterie published a modified and simplified Italian version, which I translated for my collection *The Interpretation of John* (London: SPCK, 1986), pp.53–66. Here he goes so far as to say that the contrast between 'in parables' and 'plainly' in John 16.25 'shows that we are actually in the literary genre of apocalyptic' (62).

20 They are absent, for instance, from the otherwise comprehensive survey of various genres of Jewish writings among which Wayne Meeks, in a well-known article, studied the implications of Jesus' question to Pilate: '"Am I a Jew?" – Johannine Christianity and Judaism', in Jacob Neusner (ed.), *Christianity, Judaism and Other Greco-Roman Cults: Studies for Morton Smith at Sixty* (Studies in Judaism in Late Antiquity 12; Leiden: E. J. Brill, 1975), pp.163–86. Once again, however, de la Potterie's article, 'L'arrière-fond' (see n. 19 above), is an honourable exception. There are two other exceptions, both already mentioned: Schulz's *Untersuchungen* and Bühner's *Der Gesandte*, discussed below in a brief appendix.

insofar as it envisages eschatological salvation, and spatial insofar as it involves another, supernatural world'.[21]

There is not a perfect fit, because although the 'stranger from heaven' claims in the Gospel to speak of heavenly as well as earthly things (3.14), these heavenly things have nothing in common with the extraordinary disclosures of the typical apocalypse. What is more, the properly eschatological salvation promised in many apocalypses for the end of time is conceived by the fourth evangelist as the immediate reward of faith in Jesus.[22] It has to be said, then, that between the Gospel and apocalypses, as we normally think of them, there are significant differences. I argued that the Gospel is the reverse of an apocalypse, since its revelations concern events that have already taken place in the world below, not heavenly occurrences foreshadowing what is to come to pass later on earth.

In putting forward these suggestions I had been greatly influenced by J. Louis Martyn's pioneering little book, *History and Theology in the Fourth Gospel*.[23] One of Martyn's central insights, summed up neatly as 'the two-level drama', had been anticipated, though expressed less colourfully, in a paragraph by another great New Testament scholar, Nils Alstrup Dahl, where he reflects on the words 'the hour comes and is now' (4.23):

> The point of the formula is not simply to state the eschatological character of the present hour; it serves, rather, to visualize the relation between the 'time' of the earthly ministry and the 'time' of the church; in spite of the temporal distance, there is an essential identity. What is present in the time after the ascension was anticipated in the life of Jesus, and the witness borne to his historical ministry is, therefore, at the same time a testimony to his presence here and now. It would be as false to stress only the identity of the qualified time and dehistoricize the Gospel as it would be to stress only the diversity of the chronological time and give a historicizing, biographical interpretation of the Gospel.[24]

---

21   John J. Collins, *The Apocalyptic Imagination: An Introduction to the Jewish Matrix of Christianity* (New York: Crossroad, 1984), p.4 (see Ashton, *Understanding* [1st edn], pp.384–5).

22   Bultmann avoids the evangelist's own term for this reward, that is to say 'life', or 'eternal life', replacing it with his own rebarbative coinage, 'eschatological existence'.

23   J. Louis Martyn, *History and Theology in the Fourth Gospel* (New York: Harper & Row, 1968).

24   Nils A. Dahl, 'The Johannine Church and History', in W. Klassen and G. F. Snyder (eds.), *Current Issues in New Testament Interpretation: Essays in Honour of Otto A. Piper* (London: SCM, 1962), pp.124–42 (128).

Dahl's powerful insight into the evangelist's double perspective lies behind both Martyn's theory of the two-level drama in much of the Gospel (which he expressly compares with apocalyptic) and my own elaboration of this theory in my book, where, parting company from Martyn slightly, I add to his two stages the further idea (also drawn from apocalyptic) of two ages.[25] What Dahl calls 'chronological time' Martyn characterises by the German word *einmalig*, adding in a note that 'the reader will not go far wrong if he renders my use of *einmalig* by the expression "once upon a time"'.[26] In my own preferred distinction of two levels of understanding this corresponds to what I call the *story* level, a term that avoids the fairy-tale associations of 'once upon a time'. Yet Martyn's subsequent explanation of his two-level drama is admirably clear:

> John handles the temporal distinction between the two stages in a way quite different from that which is characteristic of Jewish apocalyptic. The initial stage is not the scene of 'things to come' in heaven. It is the scene of Jesus' life and teaching. Its extension into the contemporary level 'speaks to' current events not by portraying the immediate future, but by narrating a story which, on the face of it, is about the past, a story about Jesus of Nazareth... John's two stages are past and present, not future and present.[27]

Despite what might have seemed strong reasons for pushing my enquiry directly into the shadowy realm of apocalyptic, I did not do so at the time. Now, however, I am convinced that just as the most obvious explanation of John's use of the gospel form is that he had some acquaintance with at least one of the Gospels that preceded his own, so the most obvious explanation of the remarkable parallels to which I drew attention in my 'Intimations of Apocalyptic' chapter is that the evangelist was acquainted with one or more apocalyptic writings and, more generally, with what Christopher Rowland calls their 'world of thought'. Towards the beginning of the *Genesis* part of my book I had proposed that the fluid model of rivers or sources of tradition should be replaced with the

---

25 Ashton, *Understanding* (1st edn), pp.387–91.
26 Martyn, *History and Theology*, p.29 n.22.
27 *History and Theology*, pp.136–7. Equally novel and important is Martyn's brilliant re-imagining of the clash between the Jesus-faction and the Moses-faction that has found expression in John 9, and his successful explanation of how the relations of the Jesus-group with those we might call the hardliners in the synagogue are reflected in numerous passages of the Gospel. This aspect of his work, however, relates to the *Genesis* rather than to the *Revelation* section of my own book.

static image of soil or earth, better to suggest the rich loam of the unorthodox or dissenting Jewish tradition within which 'the message concerning Jesus was planted and in which it continued to thrive'.[28] But it is clearly open to Rowland to retort, 'Then why didn't you pick up a spade and start to dig?'

LOOKING FORWARD

Theme and Genre

How should we proceed? Not, evidently, by looking for instances of the *words* 'reveal' and 'revelation' in apocalyptic literature; they are absent from the Fourth Gospel and are not particularly common in apocalypses either. But in apocalyptic, as in the Fourth Gospel, the *concept* of revelation is everywhere in evidence, which is why, of course, we call these writings apocalypses in the first place. Rowland's challenge was to elucidate the relationship between the Fourth Gospel and apocalyptic, 'whether literary or in terms of a debt to a common world of thought'.[29] In practice there cannot be much difference between these, because all that we know about the common world of thought comes from the literature. Within the literature, however, besides the theme or themes of revelation just mentioned, there are also the generic resemblances (generic in the sense of 'belonging to a genre'). At least in theory generic resemblances provide the stronger argument, because a resemblance to the deep structures of a particular genre is less likely to be sheerly fortuitous than the sharing of a theme or group of themes, which might well be common currency in works emanating from groups or communities living alongside one another in city or countryside.[30] This is why, in the

---

28 Ashton, *Understanding* (1st edn), p.128.
29 *Understanding* (2nd edn), p. viii.
30 In the chapter on dualism in *Understanding* (1st edn, pp.205–37), I based my suggestion that the evangelist was a convert from Essenism on the close correspondence between the light/darkness motif in the Gospel and in the Community Rule at Qumran (pp.235–7). The chief weakness of this argument is that a comparable dualism is by no means confined to these two writings, and, in response to objections from other scholars, I withdrew this suggestion in the second edition of the book (*Understanding* [2nd edn], p.393 n.14). But I am now inclined to return to my original suggestion. See James Charlesworth's recent comments on this topic in his wide-ranging essay, 'The Fourth Evangelist and the Dead Sea Scrolls: Assessing Trends over Nearly Sixty Years', in Mary L. Coloe and Tom Thatcher (eds.), *John,*

chapter of my book that gave the present volume and the present essay its title, I focused upon the *generic* resemblances between apocalyptic and the Fourth Gospel. Yet although in theory it is possible to distinguish between generic and thematic resemblances, some of the most important and significant *themes* of apocalyptic – revelation, mystery, wisdom, truth – are so intimately bound up with the essential characteristics of the *genre* that discussing them apart would result in tedious and awkward repetitions.

Judgement

The one exception to this generalisation – judgement – may seem an unlikely choice for inclusion in an argument stressing the Fourth Gospel's debt to apocalyptic. Indeed it may seem paradoxical to the point of perversity to single out judgement in this way, because John clearly believed that the judgement of God is indistinguishable from the judgement that individual men and woman pass on themselves when they respond positively or negatively – as the case may be – to the message of Jesus, and it is not confined to God's end-of-time condemnation of the wicked. It is John's so-called realised eschatology (expressed most succinctly in 3.17-18) that has led scholars to overlook apocalyptic as a possible source for his main ideas. There are other instances, however, in which the fourth evangelist showed himself quite prepared to turn accepted dogmas upside down, such as Jesus' shockingly venomous response to the Jews' assertion that Abraham was their father: 'You are of your father the devil' (8.44). His handling of the theme of judgement, though less shocking, is just as bold. Convinced as he was that God's judgement upon mankind was already manifested in the way people responded to the message of Jesus, the fourth evangelist, whilst retaining the heavy emphasis upon judgement evident in so many apocalyptic writings (above all, the *Epistle of Enoch*), placed the *time* of judgement in the present and not in the hereafter.

It may be said that the sharp division between the righteous and the wicked, the good guys and the bad guys, is everywhere to be seen in Second Temple Judaism. The *War Scroll* at Qumran is evidence enough that other writings besides apocalypses may be dualistic throughout. We cannot be sure, therefore, exactly where John got his sense of moral

Qumran, and the Dead Sea Scrolls: Sixty Years of Discovery and Debate (Early Judaism and Its Literature 32; Atlanta: SBL, 2011), especially pp.165–72. I will return to this question below.

dualism. More significant perhaps is the generally neglected theme of cosmic conflict deftly picked out by Judith Kovacs, who starts by highlighting the texts in the Fourth Gospel in which Jesus speaks of 'the ruler of this world' (12.31-32; 14.30-31; 16.8-11). Taken together, these sayings 'suggest that the Fourth Evangelist sees the death, resurrection and ascent of Jesus as the turning point in the conflict between God and the forces of evil'.[31] She then proceeds to argue that the references in these texts to 'casting out' and to judgement 'are part of a more general theme of cosmic conflict, central to Johannine dualism', adding that 'the parallels in apocalyptic texts, which, unlike Gnostic texts, clearly antedate the Fourth Gospel, have remained largely unexplored'.[32] Her next step is to consider some of these apocalyptic texts, starting with the opening of *1 Enoch*, which plunges straightaway into a prophecy of cosmic conflict that culminates in a divine act of judgement (1.2-5), and continues with the story of 'the Watchers' and their leader Azazel, another tale of cosmic conflict (10.1-22). Other texts she adduces in this connection include the *War Scroll* at Qumran (1.15-19), the *Testament of Moses* (which predicts the demise of the devil, the punishment of the nations, and the destruction of their idols [10.1, 7]), and Ezra's vision of one 'like a figure of a man' (*4 Ezra* 13.2-11). Kovacs next highlights 'the way the Gospel combines forensic imagery with images of battle' (12.31; 16.11),[33] and stresses how this resembles what we find in apocalyptic texts such as the opening of *1 Enoch* already mentioned, *1 En.* 55.4, where there is a second allusion to the judgement upon Azazel, and other passages in *4 Ezra* (12.33; 13.39). She also points to 'a similar juxtaposition of combat and forensic images' in Daniel 7–12.[34] It seems reasonable to conclude that the decisive victory over God's great adversary, which the fourth evangelist saw to have been brought about through the death of Jesus, is a motif for which he was indebted to apocalyptic. But, once again, he could have found it in Daniel, the main source of his identification of Jesus with the Son of Man.[35]

31 Judith L. Kovacs, '"Now Shall the Ruler of This World be Driven Out": Jesus' Death as Cosmic Battle in John 12:20–36', *JBL* 114 (1995), pp.227–47 (231).
32 Kovacs, 'Ruler of This World', p.235.
33 Kovacs, 'Ruler of This World', p.238.
34 Kovacs, 'Ruler of This World', p.239.
35 See Benjamin E. Reynolds, *The Apocalyptic Son of Man in the Gospel of John* (WUNT 2/249; Tübingen: Mohr Siebeck, 2008); John Ashton, 'The Johannine Son of Man: A New Proposal', *NTS* 57 (2011), pp.508–29. In the chapter of *Interpretation* in which he expresses the alternative view that Ps. 79 (80) is a more likely scriptural basis for the Johannine Son of Man than Daniel 7 (p.245 n.1), C. H. Dodd makes no mention of John 5.27, although he cites it in full a few pages later (p.256).

Comparison and Debt

This brings us to the delicate question of comparison and debt. Even to raise this question is almost inevitably to invite the accusation of parallelomania, as Samuel Sandmel called the common assumption that every resemblance implies a debt.[36] This tricky issue cannot be fully treated here. Suffice it to say that, in what follows, I shall point to so many resemblances between the Fourth Gospel and two other writings – the Book of Daniel and *1 Enoch* – that it will appear unreasonable to deny a debt on the part of the fourth evangelist to either of these.

Rudolf Bultmann, the only scholar to have offered a comprehensive solution to Harnack's riddle, maintained that it is a mistake to look for the origins of the Gospel's central ideas independently of one another: 'for John's language is a whole, and it is only in this whole that each individual term gets its meaning (*seine feste Bestimmung*)'.[37] But this assumption has often been questioned. Jörg Frey has shown that it was just that – no more than an assumption. Only when Reitzenstein began to look for the origins of the Gospel in some form of oriental Gnosticism did the idea of a single source take hold.[38] Yet the traditions-history pursuit of individual themes has done nothing to further the solution of the big riddle. I suspect that there was never any strong conviction that it would really do so: scholars were frightened off by the thunderous collapse of Bultmann's grand edifice, and simply averted their gaze from the problem he had so signally failed to solve. One who did just glance at it was Ernst Käsemann, who, as we have seen, contented himself with the vague assertion that the origins of the Fourth Gospel were to be sought somewhere in the heady atmosphere of early Christian enthusiasm. His contemporary, C. H. Dodd, sidestepped the problem by asserting that any search for the evangelist's sources and influences is misguided and futile. This was an evasion, not a solution; yet Dodd made it clear that, in his view, the dominant influence upon John was the type of religious thought represented by what he called 'the higher religion of Hellenism: the Hermetic literature' – the title of the second chapter of his book.[39]

---

36 Samuel Sandmel, 'Parallelomania', *JBL* 81 (1962), pp.1–13.
37 Rudolf Bultmann, 'Johanneische Schriften und Gnosis', *Orientalische Literaturzeitung* 43 (1940), pp.150–75 (154).
38 See Ashton, *Understanding* (2nd edn), p.388; Jörg Frey, 'Licht aus den Höhlen? Der "johanneische Dualismus" und die Texte von Qumran', in Jörg Frey and Udo Schnelle (eds.), *Kontexte des Johannesevangeliums* (WUNT 175; Tübingen: Mohr Siebeck, 2004), pp.117–203 (170–1).
39 Dodd, *The Interpretation of the Fourth Gospel*, pp.10–53.

Evidently if there were any obvious answer, it would have been found long ago. But, unlike the Synoptic Problem (where the failure to find a satisfactory answer is surely consequent upon the equally evident failure to find a satisfactory question), it cannot be said that Harnack's riddle rests upon a misconception. I, like Bultmann, do assume that a comprehensive answer is required, not however, unlike him, because of any notable consistency in the *language* of the Gospel, but because of the innumerable echoes and intimations of apocalyptic *thought*, which entitle us, I believe, to infer a deep acquaintance on the part of the fourth evangelist with one or more apocalyptic *writings*.

The Book of Daniel

It would be preposterous to picture the fourth evangelist (whom, from now on, I shall call John) scrolling through the book of Daniel in a search for proof texts. He must have read it from beginning to end. In what follows I shall be making the more questionable assumption that he read it from within an Essene community (which it is convenient to call Qumran). In guessing John's responses to what he read, I cannot of course claim anything like certainty; but my surmises will always be possible and often, I hope, probable.

As he read Daniel,[40] John's interest must have been aroused by a number of features in the first six chapters, especially the unusual powers of the eponymous hero of the book. After the introductory chapter it becomes clear that Daniel's main role was that of an exceptionally gifted interpreter of dreams and visions. This had been stressed as early as the first chapter, which concludes with the statement that Daniel and his three companions, 'in every matter of wisdom and understanding', were ten times better than King Nebuchadnezzar's troop of hired magicians (1.20). So it comes as no surprise that when, at the beginning of ch. 2, the king's men are summoned to interpret[41] some especially nasty dreams

---

40   Worth mentioning is the fact that the total of eight manuscripts of the book of Daniel discovered at Qumran exceeds the Qumran finds for most books of the Hebrew Bible. See Peter W. Flint, 'The Daniel Tradition at Qumran', in Craig A. Evans and Peter W. Flint (eds.), *Eschatology, Messianism, and the Dead Sea Scrolls* (Grand Rapids: Eerdmans, 1997), pp.41–60. (The same is true of *1 Enoch* and *Jubilees*.)

41   Hebrew: להגיד; OG, Theodotion: ἀναγγεῖλαι. *Contra* NRSV ('tell'); see also John J. Collins, *Daniel: A Commentary on the Book of Daniel* (Hermeneia; Minneapolis: Fortress, 1993), p.148. Eventually, it is true, the king is *told* (by Daniel) what he had seen (vv. 31-35), but what the king is asking for here is an interpretation. In

that the king had been having, they find themselves in total disarray and attempt to bluster their way out: the gods alone can offer the interpretation he is demanding (2.11). John noticed the constant, almost wearisome, repetition of the expression 'expound the interpretation'. The Hebrew equivalent of the Aramaic word פשרא ('interpretation') was familiar to him because of its frequent occurrence in the novel readings (which we now call *pesharim*) of biblical prophetic texts in the Qumran library; though it did not occur to him that it might have been the very text he had just been reading that prompted the Qumran teacher to offer a number of bold new interpretations of his own.

One particular parallel, however, did cause him to stop and think. Daniel's explanation of the king's vision extended far into the future: indeed it concerned 'a kingdom which shall never be destroyed' and 'will stand for ever' (2.44). He had prefaced his account of the vision by telling the king that 'there is a God in heaven who reveals mysteries' and has made known to the king 'what will be in the latter days' (2.28: באחרית יומיא). This reminded John of the assertion of one of his own teachers concerning a passage in Habakkuk that God had told him (the prophet) to write what was going to happen to the last generation, הדור האחרון (1QpHab 7.2). He would reflect deeply upon this idea. Prophecies could have a relevance long after the time when they were first uttered.

John enjoyed the stories that follow for what they are: tales well told – the escape from the fiery furnace in ch. 3, the sinister story of Nebuchadnezzar's horrible punishment in ch. 4, so terrifyingly depicted by

---

the context of something mysterious or not understood, the hiphil of נגד, like its Aramaic equivalent החוי (the haphel of חוי), means 'to expound' or 'to interpret', not 'to tell'. The first occurrence of this meaning in Daniel is in 2.2 (Hebrew); the second, where the object of the verb is פשרא ('interpretation'), is in 2.4 (Aramaic): 'Tell your servants the dream and we will expound the interpretation'. Including v. 2, and allowing for the occasional substitution of הודיע ('make known') for החוי, the term occurs more than a dozen times in ch. 2, mostly with פשרא as its object, but twice (vv. 27, 29) with רז (mystery), a word that crops up in many different documents of the Dead Sea Scrolls. (See too Dan 5.7, 8, 12, 15-17, the writing on the wall.) The Old Greek has half-a-dozen different renderings of החוי, besides ἀναγγέλλειν. Theodotion is more consistent, translating החוי as ἀναγγέλλειν and הודיע as γνωρίζειν. The importance of this for the Fourth Gospel is that ἀναγγέλλειν is used of the Paraclete (16.13); see Ashton, *Understanding* (1st edn), pp.423–4. (This footnote opens by correcting a small mistranslation in John Collins's text of Daniel. I want to close it by acknowledging that the discussion of Daniel that follows would have been impossible, even unthinkable, without the aid of Collins's magnificent commentary.)

William Blake; in ch. 5 there is the vivid evocation of Belshazzar's feast that fired the imagination most remarkably of Rembrandt, and then, much later, of William Walton. Finally, in ch. 6, we have the account of Daniel's deliverance from the lions' den – unforgettable, surely, at any rate if one has the well-known negro spiritual, 'Didn't my Lord deliver Daniel', ringing in one's head.

The last of these stories is set in the reign of the otherwise unknown Darius the Mede. Chapter 7 moves back to the first year of his predecessor, Belshazzar. Now it is Daniel's turn to have alarming dreams (7.15) and to find himself unable to interpret them on his own. From being the protagonist in a series of stories, he has suddenly begun to write in his own person. The first of his dreams, which opens with the spectacle of four terrifying beasts, continues with a brilliant evocation of Ezekiel's vision of the *merkavah*, the divine chariot, the throne of the Ancient of Days (7.9-10), and this is immediately followed by the appearance, with the clouds of heaven, of a man-like figure, an angel (7.13-14). John had already wondered about the angelic figures who had flashed in and out of the two tales of deliverance earlier in the book, the mysterious fourth man in the fiery furnace (3.25), whose appearance was 'like a son of the gods' (לבר־אלהין) – a divine being – and the angel sent by God to shut the mouths of the lions in their den (6.22). But here was a different and altogether superior being, the recipient of 'dominion and kingdom' that had hitherto been reserved to God alone. It is as if, John reflected with surprise, the insistence in the earlier chapters on the power and might of God (2.20-22, 47; 3.33 [= OG 4.2-3]; 4.34-35; 6.26) was simply paving the way for a quite extraordinary transference of all authority to this man-like figure in the clouds. (He could not know, of course, how important a role this figure was to play in his own later thinking.)

Alarmed and mystified by this vision, Daniel 'approached one of those who stood there and asked him the truth concerning all this' (7.16). One of the phrases used in the earlier chapters of the interpretation of Nebuchadnezzar's dreams is now applied to a truly heavenly vision: the bystander, says Daniel, 'made known to me the interpretation of these things' (7.16). As he read what the interpreting angel said about the beasts, John began to suspect that what was presented as a prophecy was really a summary of the reigns of three mighty kings who, though said to be about to 'arise out of the earth' (7.17), were already long dead – plus a fourth, represented by the most terrible of the beasts, who grew a horn that 'made war with the Holy Ones, and prevailed over them, until the Ancient of Days came, and judgement was given for the Holy Ones of the Most High, and the time came when the Holy Ones received the kingdom' (7.21-22). This suspicion was soon confirmed by the specific interpretation of 'the ram with two horns' in the next chapter as the kings of Media and Persia, and the he-goat as the king of Greece (8.20-21). The idea of a story about the past that was nevertheless represented as prophecy about the future stuck in John's mind. What impressed him above all, however, was the parallel between all that went on in heaven, in the vision itself, and what was to transpire on earth (for the word 'earth' appears in 7.17, right at the beginning of the interpretation). It was almost as if the heavenly events were somehow ushering in their earthly analogues.

Yet the vision was not solely about the past, for right at the end of ch. 7, after the ravages of Antiochus, of whom it was prophesied that 'he shall wear out the Holy Ones of the Most High, and shall think to change the times and the law' (7.25), came the concluding promise: 'And the kingdom and the dominion and the greatness of the kingdoms under the whole heaven shall be given to the people of the Holy Ones of the Most High; their kingdom shall be an everlasting kingdom, and all dominions shall serve and obey them' (7.27). Well, thought John ruefully, since he regarded himself, like the rest of the Qumran community, very much as belonging to 'the people of the Holy Ones', that will be the day!

Daniel had to wait a further two years before his next vision (8.1), which also involved visionary beasts representing real kings, though the kingdoms of three of these, unlike the earlier ones, are actually named – Media, Persia and Greece (8.20-21) – and the fourth, the bold-faced king, is clearly Antiochus Epiphanes (8.23-25). At some point (8.17) the seer is told that his vision is 'for the time of the end', recalling a passage from Habakkuk, one of the Qumran community's favourite prophets, some of whose words are actually cited in the *pesher*: 'For there is still (עוד) a vision (חזון) concerning the appointed time (למועד), it hastens to its end (לקץ) and will not lie (ולא יכזב)' (Hab 2.3, quoted in 1QpHab 7.5-6). This message concludes with the solemn declaration: 'the vision of the evenings and the mornings which has been told is true; but seal up the vision, for it pertains to many days hence' (8.26). More than many days, thought John, many years! Daniel, so secretive hitherto, had at last revealed his secret – admitting that what he was writing then, just after he had these visions, would not be understood until long afterwards. The real meaning of all this would strike John years later, as he in his turn wrote an account of Jesus' words and deeds that had much greater significance for him and his own contemporaries than it did for those who actually saw what Jesus did and heard what he said.

As John read on, the history became clearer. Chapter 9, which (like ch. 6) is set in the first year of the reign of Darius the Mede, is mostly concerned with a prayer of repentance and supplication. The last three chapters are taken up with a vision of another remarkable angel who himself takes on the role of interpreter, and tells Daniel that he has come to make him understand what is to befall his people in the latter days. 'For the vision is for days yet to come' (10.14). So once again, thinks John, reading this, the seer was to be told of events whose significance would only emerge much later. And in fact the angel then promises to tell Daniel 'what is inscribed in the book of truth' (10.21), and almost immediately afterwards (11.2) declares: 'I will expound the truth to you' (אמת אגיד לך), using the same word and the same verb form that was used by King Nebuchadnezzar when demanding an explanation of his dreams at the beginning of ch. 2. 'The truth', the remarkable revelation that follows, a more or less accurate prediction (!) – covering nearly four centuries – of the history of Near Eastern monarchies from Cyrus King of Persia to Antiochus Epiphanes, is a mysterious truth disclosed by an angelic being to a human seer. But now, reflected John, what the seer was about to hear was much more than the interpretation of a dream: this was a truth, inscribed in 'the book of truth', that required an angel messenger for its full disclosure.

In what follows, the extent and nature of the crimes of Antiochus are fully spelled out (11.36-39). Then comes the prophecy of his defeat (11.40-45) and the further promise of the arrival of 'Michael, the great prince, who has charge of your people' (12.1). John shared the hopes of the author of the *War Scroll* that the Kittim (a.k.a. Romans), already mentioned at 11.30, would, with the help of the Prince of Light (1QM 13.10) – who, he was sure, was the angel Michael – be comprehensively defeated. Before that, however, there would be a time of great tribulation, 'such as never has been since there was a nation till that time' (12.1).[42] Yet this terrible threat is straightaway followed by the extraordinary prophecy that some of those sleeping in the dust of the earth would awake to eternal life (לחיי עולם, 12.2-3). Later the concept of resurrection (not explicit in Daniel) became important to John for quite different reasons, and he himself was to transform, quite drastically, the concept of eternal life cherished by the Qumran community. Next comes the emphatic command, 'You, Daniel, shut up the words; and seal the book, until the time of the end' (12.4), and a final goodbye, 'Go your

---

42 The Greek word for tribulation, θλῖψις, regularly occurs in the eschatological discourses of the Synoptic Gospels; see Mark 13.19, 24 and parallels; cf. 1 Thess 1.6; 3.3, 7; 2 Thess 1.4, 6. It is also found in John 16.21, 33.

way, Daniel, for the words are shut up and sealed until the time of the end' (12.9). Reaching the end of the book, John would carry with him a memory of this constantly repeated theme: not for now but for much later.

One last emphatic contrast he would also remember, between the wise and the wicked, who are divided by an unbridgeable gulf: 'none of the wicked shall understand; but those who are wise shall understand' (12.10). The wise are the *maskilim* – the title assumed by the teachers of the Qumran community. As it is used here at the end of the book, this word constitutes an *inclusion*; the same word is applied to Daniel and his companions right at the beginning, where, besides other great qualities, they are said to be משכילים בכל־חכמה, proficient in all wisdom (1.4).

Living as he did in the Qumran community, John had one source of consolation that was unavailable to the author of the book of Daniel. This was the sense its members shared of the proximity of the angels. In the hymn of praise appended to the *Community Rule*, John remembered, there is a remarkable assurance about all that 'God has given to his chosen ones as an everlasting possession', for 'he has caused them to inherit the lot of the Holy Ones; he has joined their assembly to the Sons of Heaven to be a Council of the Community' (1QS 11.7-8). Sinners would be purified so as to be 'united with the sons of your truth and partake of the lot of your Holy Ones' (1QH 19.11-12; cf. 1QH 11.21-23; 14.12-14; 4Q181.3-4; 4Q418.81). John recalled how relieved he was to know himself free from the kind of physical blemish that would have prevented him from taking his place among the men of renown of the assembly, 'for the holy angels are among their congregation' (1QSa 2.8-9); and long afterwards he would remember something he had read in which the final destiny of the wicked was contrasted with a promise to the good – that they would be counted 'as a congregation of holiness in service for eternal life and [sharing] the lot of his holy ones…each man according to the lot which he has cast…for eternal life (לחיי עולם)' (4Q181.3-4; cf. CD 3.20; 1QH 4.15; 5.12).

John had learned a lot from Daniel, first the idea of a mysterious dream or vision that could not be understood without the aid of an interpreter, an idea confirmed and strengthened in the second half of the book by the appearance of a number of interpreting angels: the bystander (7.16), Gabriel (8.15-17; 9.20-23), one with the appearance of a man (10.10-21). Stress is laid early on in the book upon God as a revealer of mysteries (2.22, 47), but the mysteries are small ones, and the wisdom attributed to Daniel (1.4) is a mantic wisdom whose only resemblance to the revealed wisdom of the true apocalypse lies in the word itself. John also took away with him the idea of two ages, in the first of which even the seer himself failed to understand, for understanding was reserved for a later age. And he got the sense too of a strong link between heavenly and earthly events, the latter not just foreseen but also foreshadowed by what was seen to take place above in a vision or dream.

1 Enoch

At least three of the five writings gathered together to form the book we now know as *1 Enoch* are likely to have been known to John, not because he cites or even alludes to them, but simply because they were so widely available at Qumran.[43] Scholars often tend to assume that the writers they study have read everything that might interest them in all that was written in the past. But in the ancient Near East parchment was an expensive item, and this is a highly unlikely supposition. Not all books, not even all the books of the Bible, will have been readily available to everyone.[44] We know from the Dead Sea Scrolls, however, that the books of Enoch were highly prized and widely read. We can be sure of this not just because of the great number of Aramaic manuscripts found, in fragmentary form, at Qumran, but because *1 Enoch* is so often cited or alluded to in a variety of other different writings, such as *Jubilees* and the *Damascus Document*, the *Aramaic Levi* document, the *Wisdom of Solomon*, and even the book of Daniel. Later we find it quoted by Jude and (probably) alluded to in 1 Peter. The big exception is

---

43 J. T. Milik, the first editor of the Aramaic fragments of *1 Enoch*, found five scrolls with fragments of Book 1 (chs. 1–36), four of Book 3 (chs. 72–82), four of Book 4 (chs. 83–90) – separate from the rest – two of Book 5 (chs. 91–107 [108]), but none of Book 2 (chs. 37–71). See *The Books of Enoch: Aramaic Fragments of Qumrân Cave 4* (Oxford: Clarendon, 1976).

44 See Julio Trebolle-Barrera, 'Qumran Evidence for a Biblical Standard Text and for Non-Standard and Parabiblical Texts', in Timothy H. Lim *et al.* (eds.), *The Dead Sea Scrolls in Their Historical Context* (Edinburgh: T. & T. Clark, 2000), pp.89–106. (I owe this reference to Graeme Auld.) 'In addition to ideological or theologically driven considerations, which were doubtless the weightiest', says Michael Stone, 'the expense and labour of hand-copying a book must…have served as a winnowing factor. Books that had to be hand-copied were presumably considered important and worthwhile enough (for content, for function, or for some other reason) to justify the expense and effort' (*Ancient Judaism: New Visions and Views* [Grand Rapids: Eerdmans, 2011], pp.8–9). In general this observation concerning the Second Temple period as a whole must also be true of Qumran; though, as in mediaeval monasteries, there will have been trained scribes at Qumran who spent most of their time copying manuscripts of books valued by the community.

the section of *1 Enoch* known as the *Parables of Enoch* (chs. 37–71), not represented at Qumran by even a single fragment: whatever its date we cannot be sure that it was available to any of the New Testament writers.⁴⁵ However, the many parallels, both thematic and generic, between John and *1 Enoch* do make it probable that John, like many others, had read and been influenced by the older book.

The superscription (1.1) makes one thing clear from the outset: the author sees his vision as a blessing that will result in the discomfiture of his enemies and the salvation of the righteous. In the verse that really begins the book (1.2) the writer, already named as Enoch, is said to have taken up – what? The Aramaic word מתל (Hebrew: משל) means, I believe, something spoken or written that contains comparisons or correspondences. In some contexts it refers to a parable, in others to a proverb. The significant correspondence in what follows is between heaven and earth; but since the Aramaic (4QEnᵃ 1i) is actually a plural, it may refer here to all the correspondences that follow in the next 36 chapters (the *Book of the Watchers*). The same verse makes it clear that the book is concerned with revelations, both of seeing and of hearing. The author asserts that he understood what he saw and heard, but nevertheless declares, as Daniel was to do later, that he is speaking for a generation that is still far off (1.2). So even in these few introductory verses there is much for John to absorb and recall. Yet these calm prefatory words do nothing to prepare for the thunderclap that follows, declaring the dissolution of the cosmos no less startlingly than Richard Strauss's *Also sprach Zarathustra* (in Stanley Kubrick's reading) announces its constitution.

In ch. 2 Enoch contrasts the ordered universe – heaven and earth, summer and winter, seas and rivers – with the disorder and disobedience of the wicked. A terrible sentence is pronounced on them all, whereas

---

45 Milik advanced the 'inevitably hypothetical' opinion that the *Book of Parables* was conceived on the model of the Sibylline oracles (circulating around the year 270 CE or shortly afterwards), which he saw as a Christian production (*The Books of Enoch*, pp.89–107). Other scholars have rejected both his suggestion of Christian influence and his very late dating, yet there is still no agreement on the date. In successive articles in a recent publication edited by Gabriele Boccaccini, *Enoch and the Messiah Son of Man: Revisiting the Book of Parables* (Grand Rapids: Eerdmans, 2007), David Suter and Michael Stone argued for different dates, Suter maintaining 'that we are not yet in a position to rule out a date after the destruction of Jerusalem' (p.443), Stone judging that 'we will not be far wrong if we put it in the latter part of the first century BCE, or somewhat later' (p.449). The fact that no fragments of the *Parables* were found at Qumran is not in itself proof that the book was not there. However, it is unsafe to suppose that John had access to this work.

'wisdom will be given to all the chosen, and they will all live' (5.8). Chapter 6 begins the story of 'the watchers, the sons of heaven', and their villainous deeds, which include the revelation of skills and secrets to mankind, including forbidden mysteries (8.2; 9.6; 10.7). Enoch was told to say to the watchers, 'You were in heaven and no mystery was revealed to you; but a stolen mystery you learned' (16.3), that is, 'the mystery that the watchers told and taught their sons' (10.7). John would never forget the account of Enoch's vision of his own ascent into heaven in ch. 14, or his later journey throughout the cosmos, accompanied by seven angels informing him of the significance of all he saw. Two of these, first Uriel (21.5) and later Michael (25.1), inquire of Enoch, 'Why do you wish to learn the truth?', referring to heavenly mysteries that he could not understand without their help. As he reflected on Enoch's need of an interpreting angel, John thought of Daniel, as indeed he had when reading the summary of Enoch's commission that opens ch. 14: 'The book of the words of truth' (*1 En.* 14.1; cf. 13.10; Dan 10.21–11.1).

What then did John take away from this first part of *1 Enoch*? A memory of the Great Holy One's descent to earth, of the light shining upon the righteous, and, in this early proclamation of the theme of judgement that would resonate through the whole book, the uncompromising separation of the good and the wicked; a recollection too of the evil intransigence of the watchers, and a realisation that it could be wrong to impart mysteries to mankind. He also remembered the story of Enoch's visionary journey, with its detailed description of the heavenly chariot.

The conclusion to the *Book of the Watchers* comes in chs. 81–82 of the present book, where the theme of revelation is especially prominent. First, Enoch himself is invited to look on some heavenly tablets, to read what is written on them and learn every detail (81.1); and then, as the seven accompanying angels set him down in front of the door of his house, they order him to make everything known to Methuselah, his son. He is given a year to teach his sons (81.6), and he addresses Methuselah in the following terms:

> All these things I recount and write for you, and all of them I have revealed to you... Keep, my son Methuselah, the books of the hand of your father, that you may give them to the generations of eternity. Wisdom I have also given to you and to your sons...that they may give to all the generations until eternity this wisdom that surpasses their thought...and they will incline their ears to learn this wisdom (82.1-3).[46]

---

46   For this translation, see George W. E. Nickelsburg, *1 Enoch 1: A Commentary on the Book of 1 Enoch, Chapters 1–36; 81–108* (Hermeneia; Minneapolis: Fortress, 2001), p.333.

The *Book of Dreams* (chs. 83–84, 85–90) is very different from the *Book of the Watchers*.[47] Moreover, since Enoch identifies himself as an antediluvian, indeed a pre-historic figure, each and every event of human history that he sees or dreams actually occurred long after he saw and predicted it. Here is an especially clear example of the two stages of revelation: the progression from the delineation of a hidden mystery to its eventual disclosure.[48]

The last book, the *Epistle of Enoch* (chs. 101–108) is dominated by the theme of judgement. No reader could possibly miss this, but John was most interested in the conclusion of the *Epistle* itself (104.9–105.2), which is complicated by the ambiguity of the Aramaic word קושט. George Nickelsburg points out that this term (which he spells קשטא) can mean either truth or righteousness[49] (though perhaps 'rightness' is closer than 'righteousness'). What is important, however, is that Enoch is here putting forward his own writings as a further revelation, in addition to 'the words of the Holy One', also called 'the words of truth' (104.9). The passage opens with a warning against falsifying these (alternative expressions for the Mosaic Law), and continues by issuing the same warning in relation to Enoch's own writings, a source of joy to the righteous (his own community). This is how, in Nickelsburg's translation, the passage begins:

> Do not err in your hearts or lie, or alter the words of truth, or falsify the words of the Holy One, or give praise to your errors. For it is not to righteousness that all your lies and all your error lead, but to great sin. And now I know this mystery, that sinners will alter and copy the words of truth, and pervert many, and lie and invent great fabrications, and write books in their own names.
>
> Would that they would write all my words in truth (in their names), and neither remove nor alter these words, but write in truth all that I testify to them. And again I know a second mystery, that to the righteous and pious and wise my books will be given for the joy of righteousness and much wisdom (104.9-12).[50]

---

47 Since the Aramaic manuscripts of the so-called *Astronomical Book* or *Book of Luminaries* (chs. 72–82) contain none of the material of the other four books, this book may not have been read alongside the others until it came to be included in the whole collection. So, apart from the final two chapters, which form a conclusion to the *Book of the Watchers*, I omit the *Book of Luminaries* here (as Nickelsburg does from the first part of his commentary).

48 See Ashton, *Understanding* (1st edn), pp.392–4.

49 The ambiguity is confined to the three concluding verses (104.13–105.2). Although Nickelsburg expresses a preference for 'righteousness' in his commentary (*1 Enoch 1*, pp.534–5), he retains 'truth' in the translation (p.531).

50 Nickelsburg, *1 Enoch 1*, p.531.

Insofar as he sees his own books, and not 'the words of truth', as the source of joy, Enoch is apparently rating his own revelations as superior to the Torah, in a fashion reminiscent of the Johannine Prologue (1.17). (And we shall see that he attributes temporal precedence to these also.) He also knows a double mystery, concerning the fate, first of sinners, and then of 'the righteous and pious and wise'.

What follows (chs. 106–108) is a kind of appendix to all that precedes: the story of the birth of Noah. Lamech, alarmed by the weird appearance of his new-born son, runs to his father Methuselah for counsel. Methuselah's response is to turn to his own father, Enoch, explaining that he is doing so 'because from the angels you have the exact facts and the truth' (106.12). Once again, coming as they do from a heavenly source, these are no ordinary facts, and this is no ordinary truth. As Nickelsburg points out, in no fewer than six passages in this final section of *1 Enoch*, 'the author attests with an oath that he has learned from the heavenly tablets God's hidden purpose to recompense the righteous' (cf. 98.1, 4, 6; 99.6; 103.1-4; 104.1).[51] The fifth on this list is particularly explicit: 'And now I swear to you, the righteous, by the glory of the Great One, and by his splendid kingship and his majesty I swear to you, that I know this mystery. For I have read the tablets of heaven, and I have seen the writing of what must be…'. There could be no clearer claim than this to be the privileged recipient of heavenly mysteries.

Racing through the books of Daniel and *1 Enoch*, I have deliberately focused on the four features especially characteristic of apocalyptic that I singled out in *Understanding* for the purpose of demonstrating the peculiar affinity of the Fourth Gospel with this particular genre: mystery (the two ages), visions and dreams (the two stages), riddle (insiders and outsiders) and correspondence (above and below).[52] The future author of that Gospel, I suggested, though perhaps unlikely to have paid them particular attention at the time, will have had these characteristics stored somewhere in his memory bank, and after becoming a follower of Jesus will have brought them to bear upon the stories concerning Jesus that had helped to convert him to his new faith.

---

51 Nickelsburg, *1 Enoch 1*, p.521.
52 Ashton, *Understanding* (1st edn), pp.387–405.

Revealed Wisdom in Second Temple Judaism

Since it is in their attitude to *revealed wisdom* that the various currents of thought flowing through Second Temple Judaism can best be distinguished from one another,[53] before turning to the Fourth Gospel I want to consider some apocalyptic writings that represent these attitudes, concluding with *1 Enoch*.

Looking at the various sects and groupings in Second Temple Judaism, we can easily see that the most significant difference between them is in their attitude to the Jewish Law; the most important question in this connection is how far any particular group is prepared to welcome additional revelations beside and besides the Torah. Any attempt to range these must begin with Deuteronomy. Those whom we now call the deuteronomists had suppressed, with some success, a much more ancient wisdom tradition. For these stalwart upholders of the Law there is no mystery about what God has revealed and what he requires of his people: it is all readily available in the Torah – 'This commandment which I command you this day is not too hard for you, neither is it far off. It is not in heaven, that you should say, "Who will go up for us to heaven, and bring it to us, that we may hear it and do it?"…But the word is very near you; it is in your mouth and in your heart, so that you can do it' (Deut 30.11-14). The belligerent tone of this proclamation is best explained as an aggressive rejection of claims that divine revelations either had been or would be passed on to others by a seer who had to ascend to heaven to receive them; for 'the secret things belong to the Lord our God; but the things that are revealed belong to us and to our children for ever, that we may do all the words of this law' (Deut 29.29).

According to an earlier tradition there had been an ascent and a vision: 'Moses and Aaron, Nadab, and Abihu, and seventy of the elders of Israel went up, and they saw the God of Israel' (Exod 24.9-10). Deuteronomy

---

53 See the important article of George W. E. Nickelsburg: 'Revealed Wisdom as a Criterion for Inclusion and Exclusion: From Jewish Sectarianism to Early Christianity', in Jacob Neusner and Ernest S. Frerichs (eds.), *"To See Ourselves As Others See Us": Christians, Jews, "Others" in Late Antiquity* (Chico, CA: Scholars Press, 1985), pp.73–91. One might argue that the definition of apocalyptic should be revised so as to include revealed wisdom as a necessary category. Such a revision would mean excluding the book of Daniel from the list, because the mantic wisdom attributed to Daniel in the first half of the book has nothing whatever to do with the revealed wisdom of apocalyptic; and this, comprising as it does the themes of truth and mystery, is also absent from the second half. Most scholars are likely to fight shy, however, of taking such a drastic step.

denies this: 'You came near', says Moses to the people, 'and stood at the foot of the mountain [but did not go up], while the mountain burned with fire to the heart of heaven, wrapped in darkness, cloud, and gloom. Then the Lord spoke to you out of the midst of the fire; you heard the sound of words, but saw no form; there was only a voice' (Deut 4.11-12). And the author cleverly reinforces this denial of any sight of God by offering it as the explanation of the first of the Ten Commandments: 'since you saw no form on that day that the Lord spoke to you at Horeb out of the midst of the fire, beware lest you act corruptly by making a graven image for yourselves, in the form of any figure, the likeness of male or female...' (4.15-16). It is reasonable to suppose, therefore, that the belief that others besides Moses himself had ascended (to heaven) to receive a revelation belongs to an ancient wisdom tradition that the deuteronomists were anxious to contain.[54]

We can put the point even more strongly: the deuteronomists drained the rich expression 'wisdom and understanding' of most of its richness and limited what was left to the law: keep and do these statutes and ordinances, Moses enjoins his hearers, 'for that will be your wisdom and understanding in the sight of the peoples' (Deut 4.6). Whatever wisdom and understanding those other peoples could claim, it could never begin to match the statutes and ordinances that Moses was about to set before the people of Israel (4.8); nor should they look to any other source for wisdom and understanding.

The principles of the deuteronomists were eagerly seized on and followed up by Ben Sira, who saw wisdom as a terebinth or vine, taking root among the people of Israel, where she gracefully spread her branches (24.16-17). Seduced by the charm of his poetry, one can easily overlook the way he effectively disarms and domesticates wisdom in the course of his work. He repeats the well-known saying that the fear of the Lord is the beginning of wisdom (1.14), but he also says that it is her root and her crown (1.18, 20). He tells us of the lover of wisdom that 'she will reveal her secrets to him' (4.18). But this is misleading, for he concludes by identifying the fruits of the tree of wisdom with 'the book of the covenant of the Most High God, the law which Moses commanded us as an inheritance for the congregation of Jacob' (24.23). In fact, like the deuteronomists, he has no time for mysteries: 'hidden wisdom and unseen treasure, what advantage is there in either of them?' (20.30). No

---

54 See Margaret Barker's innovative (and often deliberatively provocative) *The Older Testament: The Survival of Themes from the Ancient Royal Cult in Sectarian Judaism and Early Christianity* (London: SPCK, 1987), especially chs. 2 (Wisdom) and 5 (Deuteronomy).

doubt Ben Sira thought of his own position as traditional and safe. But we must not be fooled into believing that any tendency this author might find threatening was as novel and subversive as he might wish to represent it.

Greek Baruch, whose language, as he eulogises wisdom (for which his word is φρόνησις), is redolent of a certain wistful nostalgia, is on the face of it very different from Ben Sira. Nostalgia is not quite the right word, because at the end of his beautiful song the wisdom he has just extolled, the remote and inaccessible wisdom of Job's great hymn (Job 28), now re-named knowledge (ἐπιστήμη), is suddenly, in an extraordinary and, it has to be said, totally unconvincing switch of register, handed over by God to Jacob/Israel; subsequently, from this time on, 'she appeared upon earth, and lived among men' (Bar. 3.37 [38]). But how, and in what form? The answer (the same as Ben Sira's) comes in the next verse, the first of the following chapter: 'She is the book of the commandments of God, and the law that endures for ever' (4.1). And as such she is a source of life to all who hold fast to her.

This wisdom, now transformed into the law, is of course different from the esoteric knowledge that is the subject-matter of the apocalypses, which requires another, very special revelation, one that sometimes follows precisely the kind of ascent that is denied in Deuteronomy. The name given to this knowledge, wisdom, is the same, but though initially remote, this other wisdom, unlike that of Job's hymn, is not in principle inaccessible. We have to do then with at least three kinds of wisdom: first, the utterly remote, known only to God; secondly, the newly revealed wisdom of the apocalypses; and, thirdly, the readily available wisdom spelled out in frequently platitudinous aphorisms in what we call the wisdom literature. (There is also a fourth kind, the evil wisdom purveyed by the wicked angels in *1 Enoch*.)

The first thoroughgoing apocalyptist I want to summon to testify is Syriac Baruch, who is interesting for many reasons. Very much to the left of Ben Sira, because he unashamedly announces new revelations, he is nevertheless desperately keen to proclaim his allegiance to the law; he has no doubt that the present ills of his people are the penalty for their disobedience. So although in one respect he challenges the exclusivity of the die-hard conservatives, in another respect he ranges himself alongside them as a champion of the law. As God tells him: 'Man would have had excuse for not understanding my judgement, if he had not been given the law, and I had not instructed him in understanding' (*2 Bar.* 15.5). This is one of a number of passages (cf. 32.1; 46.5; 48.22, 38, 40, 47; 54.14; 59.2, 11; 66.5; 84.2-5, 8-9; 85.14) in which the seer speaks of the law in parallelism either with wisdom herself or, as here, with one of her synonyms ('understanding'); so it could be argued that, like Ben Sira and Greek Baruch, Syriac Baruch identifies wisdom with the law.[55] But this is obviously not so, for the bulk of the book consists of new visions and new interpretations. On the other hand Baruch betrays no sense that he is anywhere breaking any taboo, or acting in a way that might provoke the anger or disapproval of his fellow Jews. (In this respect he differs from the New Testament writer he most resembles: the evangelist Matthew.)

Next I want to consider Baruch's contemporary, the author of the writing we know as *4 Ezra*. Scholars are agreed that these two are closely linked (though the nature of the link is disputed), but they could hardly be more different in the attitude they take towards their own revelations. True, Ezra continues to respect and prize the law (as is indicated even by his choice of pseudonym: Ezra the Scribe); but by including his own secret revelations among those that God disclosed to Moses on Sinai, and yet asserting that they are still to be kept secret *after* the publication of the twenty-four books that already had scriptural authority, he is effectively asserting the absolute superiority of his own new revelations. Indeed the last instruction Ezra receives from God is, 'Make public the twenty-four books that you wrote first and let the worthy and the unworthy read them; but keep the seventy that were written last, in order to give them to the wise among your people. *For in them are the springs of understanding, the fountains of wisdom, and the river of knowledge*' (14.45-47). Wisdom, that is to say the wisdom that has yet to be revealed, will be found in books that include the one we have just finished reading, the written version of Ezra's own revelations.

From the perspective I am taking here, Enoch is the furthest to the left on the religious spectrum. Although not directly critical of the law, he does his best to deflect the attention of his readers from it, because he is convinced that his own revelations are far more important. In this respect the opening section of the *Animal Apocalypse* (85.3–89.38), which covers most of the Pentateuch from Genesis to Deuteronomy, is especially significant. With the help of Nickelsburg's commentary[56] I was able to reckon that *1 Enoch* devotes 29 verses (85.3–89.9) to the antediluvian period – from the creation of Adam to the death of Noah (Gen 2–9), that is to say eight chapters of the biblical text; the next snippet (89.10-12), from the death of Noah to the beginnings of Israel,

---

55 'Your law is life', he says to God, 'your wisdom the true guide' (38.2; cf. 44.13; 48.24; 77.16).

56 Without it I would be unable to make head or tail, hoof or horn, of this cryptic text.

takes a mere three verses to cover 27 whole chapters (Gen 10–36), a huge leap; there follow a further 26 verses (89.13-38), mostly concerned with the events of Exodus, but actually covering the rest of the Pentateuch to the end of Deuteronomy.[57] So Enoch, fascinated by the early part of Genesis, which of course contains his own story, has relatively little interest in the Patriarchs. His interest in Abraham is confined to the fact that, as 'the plant of righteousness' (93.5), he is the ancestor of the Chosen People, but he has nothing to say about the Abrahamic covenant; moreover when he comes to the great events of the book of Exodus he omits any reference to Sinai. From the *Animal Apocalypse* alone, which constitutes most of just one of the five books in the Enochic corpus, one might conclude that the author is distancing himself from any tendency to restrict the traditions of Judaism to the Law and from attaching too much significance to the figure of Moses; in fact there are only two further references to the Sinaitic covenant and the Law of Moses in the book. The first of these occurs a little later in a single verse of the *Apocalypse of Weeks* ('a covenant for all generations', 93.6). The other, at the end of the *Epistle of Enoch*, where Enoch's own revelations are implicitly given precedence over the Law, I have already discussed (104.9-12).

The conviction that Enoch had little interest in the Mosaic Law is reinforced when we turn to the rest of the work, and in particular when we see the importance of the concept of wisdom, which, as Nickelsburg points out, occurs at key points in the corpus as a designation for the corpus itself. The whole process began when Enoch himself, who lived in antediluvian times, long before the patriarchs and prophets, ascended to heaven to receive wisdom, then descended, wrote it in books, and handed these over to his son, Methuselah. Right at the beginning of the book, after describing himself as 'a righteous man whose eyes were opened by God', the author declares that he 'had the vision of the Holy One and of heaven, which he showed me' (1.2), alluding no doubt to his experience of a *merkavah* vision, described in detail in chs. 14–15. When he came down from heaven he wrote his account of his visions and their interpretation, and, at the end of the third part of the corpus, the *Book of the Luminaries* (chs. 72–82), in a passage that really belongs to the conclusion of the *Book of the Watchers*, he addresses his son, Methuselah: 'All these things I recount and write for you, and all of them I have

---

57   The remaining 77 verses (89.39–90.38) cover what is left of the history of Israel and Judah up to the famous account of the birth of the endlessly discussed white bull (90.37) widely associated with the Messiah.

revealed to you, and I have given you books about all these things. Keep...the books of the hand of your father, that you may give them to the generations of eternity. Wisdom I have also given to you and to your sons, and to those who will be your sons, that they may give to all the generations until eternity this wisdom that surpasses their thought' (82.1-2; cf. 104.12-13). (And I have argued above that the word 'truth' is also employed occasionally in *1 Enoch* to denote the kind of knowledge that is reserved for initiates.)

In the last quarter of the first century CE (which, like most scholars, is when I assume that the fourth evangelist lived and worked), there was an ongoing debate between the traditionalists who asserted that the Torah was not just mandatory but definitive, and those who, for whatever reason, thought otherwise; it is clear that the fourth evangelist was deeply involved in this debate. Even Bultmann acknowledges that John 5 and 9 'reflect the relation of early Christianity to the surrounding hostile (in the first place Jewish) world',[58] a truth that lies at the heart of Lou Martyn's very different approach to the Gospel. Some apocalyptists – at any rate Syriac Baruch – attempted to keep a foot in both camps. So did some Christians – certainly Matthew.

The extreme and revolutionary wing of the Christian movement, which eventually prevailed, is well represented by the fourth evangelist. In his attitude to the new revelation brought by Jesus he sets himself and his community apart from those he calls 'the Jews'. If we consider the simple fact that the Jews' opposition to Jesus consists of nothing more or less than their refusal to accept a message put forward as a radical alternative to the Mosaic Law, we can see not only how this anticipates the clear break between Judaism and Christianity that came to characterise what we now call the Common Era, but also, looking back, how it is foreshadowed in the refusal of the deuteronomists and their successors to accept any revelation except that mediated by Moses.

The John who composed the Fourth Gospel has one belief that he shares with the John who composed the book of Revelation: the belief in a new revelation that completely supersedes the old. The second John made use of the abundant material he found in what we now call the Old Testament. The first John, I believe, had a model for his own powerful conviction that the revelation that Jesus had come to bring was 'the truth', something that could no longer be claimed for the message of Moses. This model was Enoch. He, alone among the apocalyptic writers

---

58 Rudolf Bultmann, *The Gospel of John: A Commentary* (trans. George R. Beasley-Murray; Oxford: Basil Blackwell, 1971), p.239.

of the Second Temple, believed that his own revelations were superior to the Mosaic Law. He, not Moses, was the one who ascended to heaven and saw God. He, not Moses, was the true recipient of heavenly secrets, frequently summed up as wisdom, and wrote them down in a book to be read by his descendants. If, as I think likely, the fourth evangelist read this book, then Enoch's sheer effrontery may well have inspired him to make similar claims on behalf of his own hero.[59]

To sum up, and to return to Christopher Rowland's challenge that I look for 'a common world of thought', I propose the Jewish world of the late first century, following the fall of the temple, when 'the disciples of Moses', as John calls them, had to confront a variety of groups prepared to challenge the supremacy of Moses and to resist the conviction of these disciples of Moses that the Torah was God's final word – a world of thought, that is to say, in which what divided the opposing parties was the question of the source and nature of God's revelation.

Among these groups were champions of Enoch, whose apocalyptic writings were widely dispersed, and whose astonishing *chutzpah* in claiming that he, not Moses, was the true intermediary between heaven and earth must have emboldened anyone thinking along the same lines, in particular John the evangelist, who found in his works a structural model or pattern for his own. So in all likelihood, besides a general debt to 'a common world of thought', he owed a particular debt, a literary debt, to this apocalyptic writer. Just as John's use of the gospel form is most easily explained if we suppose that he actually knew one of the other Gospels in written form, so the structural resemblances of his Gospel to the apocalypses is most easily accounted for if we suppose him to have been acquainted with at least one of these – and I have argued that *1 Enoch* is the most likely candidate.

Conclusion

Introducing his admirable study of St Paul, Calvin Roetzel writes of the necessity of guesswork in any exploration of Paul's life, and of the historical imagination required to deal with the gaps in the text, 'understood in the broadest sense to include not just Paul's written words but also the culture, social world, and political realities surrounding

---

59 Yet when, thinking primarily of Moses, he came to deny that anyone else, apart from the Son of Man, had ascended to heaven (3.13), he must surely have intended to exclude Enoch's claims also.

them'. To his own question, 'Why run the risk of falsification through an appeal to historical imagination?', his first answer is, 'because there is no alternative'.[60]

If this is true of Paul, how much truer is it of John? In the twentieth century the four answers that have been given to Harnack's great riddle have all demanded an exercise of historical imagination. Bultmann pictured a convert from Gnosticism, constantly re-reading a number of highly complex texts that he had retained from his first allegiance, and systematically purging them of their mythical impurities. Dodd imagined a sophisticated Greek, originally immersed in the religious thought of the Hermetica and never entirely freed from its influence. Käsemann, almost casually, pointed to 'early Christian enthusiasm'. In the first edition of *Understanding* I myself went further, suggesting, though with insufficient evidence and argument, that John was a convert from Essenism.

Once we accept, however, as virtually all scholars do nowadays, that John, like Paul, Mark, Matthew, and most early Christians, was a convert from Judaism, it is eminently reasonable to ask, 'From what branch or group or sect?' Whereas Luke (whose imaginative reconstruction of Paul's life rapidly became canonical) could plausibly imagine his hero seated at the feet of Gamaliel (Acts 22.3), the same could scarcely be said of John. He is surely less likely to have come from among the Pharisees, with their absolute insistence upon the primacy of the Law of Moses, or from the Sadducees, with their emphasis on the priesthood and the Temple, and their denial of resurrection, than from a branch of Judaism that was already at odds with 'the high priests and the Pharisees' (one of the standard terms that John would use to refer to the adversaries of Jesus), and had already broken away from the Temple.

I have now no qualms, therefore, in picturing John as a convert from Essenism. In this essay I have taken a step further, imagining him as a novice at Qumran, which he left, still a relatively young man, in 68 CE, during the war of independence against Rome, when the whole community was forcibly disbanded. Nor is there any intrinsic implausibility in supposing, as I have done, that he was already predisposed to the possibility of new revelations. In this regard I will add one final point. In a recently published article[61] I have argued for a close analogy between the

---

60 Calvin J. Roetzel, *Paul: The Man and the Myth* (Edinburgh: T. & T. Clark, 1999), p.1.
61 John Ashton, '"Mystery" in the Dead Sea Scrolls and the Fourth Gospel', in Mary L. Coloe and Tom Thatcher (eds.), *John, Qumran, and the Dead Sea Scrolls: Sixty Years of Discovery and Debate* (Atlanta: Society of Biblical Literature, 2011), pp.53–68.

Qumranian concept of the רז נהיה, 'the mystery of what is coming to pass', and the Johannine Logos. This too, as I had argued a quarter of a century earlier, really means God's plan for the world.[62] On embracing a new revelation, the good news concerning Jesus, John could see that the mystery that he had suspected long before to have a value independent of the Mosaic Torah, was at last coming to pass in Jesus.

The first comprehensive solution to Harnack's most marvellous enigma was put forward in a lecture by Rudolf Bultmann in 1923.[63] What I have just written is the second. Will it be received any better than the first?

Appendix:
The Contribution of Jan-Adolf Bühner

I have said that the debt of the Fourth Gospel to apocalyptic was universally overlooked until I drew attention to it myself in *Understanding*. There is one important exception, however, to this generalisation.[64] This is the remarkable study of Jan-Adolf Bühner, *Der Gesandte und sein Weg im 4. Evangelium*, especially the third and final part, headed 'Die religionsgeschichtlichen Voraussetzungen der johanneischen Sendungschristologie' (pp. 269–421), in which he advances the thesis that an apocalyptic Son-of-Man tradition formed the first layer of John's Christology, subsequently overlaid by a Mission and Son Christology whose tradition history he had studied in the second part of his book: 'Die kulturgeschichtlichen Voraussetzungen der johanneischen Sendungschristologie' (pp. 117–267).

Taking Bühner's book up again thirty years after I first read it, I found myself wondering if I ever actually got as far as the final part. Certainly I have no recollection of it. (Or is it that, as sometimes happens when one is dealing with material one is not yet ready to take in, my eyes had slid uncomprehendingly over an argument that at the time I could not fully understand or perhaps not fully accept?)[65]

---

62 John Ashton, 'The Transformation of Wisdom: A Study of the Prologue of John's Gospel', *NTS* 32 (1986), pp.161–86.
63 Rudolf Bultmann, 'Die Bedeutung der neuerschlossenen mandäischen und manichäischen Quellen fur das Verständnis des Johannesevangeliums', *ZNW* 24 (1925), pp.100–146 (100 n.1).
64 Apart from Ignace de la Potterie.
65 References to Bühner's work by other scholars are few and far between. His name is missing (from a list of well over 200) in more than 30 pages of 'works cited' in a collection of articles published in 2007: Tom Thatcher (ed.), *What We Have Heard From the Beginning: The Past, Present, and Future of Johannine Studies*

In this third part Bühner makes the following assertion: 'It has been widely observed in scholarship that ancient layers of the Gospel of John are rooted in apocalyptic tradition'.[66] He alludes directly to Siegfried Schulz's *Untersuchungen*, but evinces no interest in Schulz's contention that the fourth evangelist is indebted to the *Parables of Enoch*,[67] and continues with the comment that 'nevertheless the inner connection of this [apocalyptic] tradition and its themes with *Christology* has been completely overlooked'. This is his own major concern, and he observes that 'one can still detect signs that for his Christological outline of the descent and ascent of the emissary, John has drawn among other things upon the picture of a prophet's visionary ascent (*ein anabatisch-visionäres Prophetenbild*)'.[68]

So here is a scholar who believes that John's Christology is best explained on the hypothesis that there was a tradition that Jesus himself was a visionary seer who, like Moses, had ascended a mountain where he received privileged revelations that he then descended to communicate to others – a bold hypothesis indeed, but one which, I am now convinced, should not be dismissed out of hand.[69]

(Waco, TX: Baylor University Press, 2007). Other missing names are those of Hugo Odeberg and Jürgen Becker.

66 Bühner, *Der Gesandte und sein Weg*, p.374.

67 We have already observed that, since the publication of J. T. Milik's 1976 edition of the Aramaic fragments of the books of Enoch in Qumran cave 4, it cannot be assumed that the *Book of Parables* was composed early enough for John to have known it.

68 Bühner, *Der Gesandte und sein Weg*, pp.374–5.

69 This is not the place to expatiate upon the very considerable merits of Bühner's book or to criticise the small but significant weaknesses in his argument. I have built upon some of his insights in my aforementioned article, 'The Johannine Son of Man: A New Proposal'.

JOHN AND THE JEWISH APOCALYPSES:
RETHINKING THE GENRE OF JOHN'S GOSPEL

Benjamin Reynolds

1. Introduction

Although the Gospel of John is clearly one of the Four Gospels, it has also been likened to apocalyptic literature. As in the Jewish apocalypses, John's Gospel is permeated with the theme of revelation and mystery and with ascents and descents between earth and heaven. Jesus the Logos descends from heaven and makes known the Father to those on earth. He can reveal the heavenly things (τὰ ἐπουράνια) because he has come from above and will return to where he was before, and his presence on earth makes possible a vision of God the Father. John Ashton[1] and Christopher Rowland[2] have argued for seeing John's Gospel as similar to apocalyptic literature and have explained what that might mean for 'understanding the Fourth Gospel'.[3] However, not all scholars are open to such a connection between apocalyptic literature and John's Gospel. For example, with reference to John 1.51, Douglas Hare states: '…the use of such grotesque, apocalyptic imagery as [the Son of Man as a ladder] is not characteristic of the Fourth Gospel'.[4] Despite disagreements such as these, the Gospel of John is more closely connected with the Jewish apocalypses than the presence or absence of angels, thrones, tours of

---

1   John Ashton, *Understanding the Fourth Gospel* (Oxford: Oxford University Press, 2nd edn, 2007). Note that throughout the present study, unless otherwise noted, references are to the *second* edition of Ashton's book.

2   Christopher Rowland and Christopher R. A. Morray-Jones, *The Mystery of God: Early Jewish Mysticism and the New Testament* (CRINT 12; Leiden: Brill, 2009).

3   See the earlier work of Hugo Odeberg, *The Fourth Gospel: Interpreted in Its Relation to Contemporaneous Religious Currents in Palestine and the Hellenistic-Oriental World* (Chicago/Uppsala: Argonaut, 1929).

4   Douglas R. A. Hare, *The Son of Man Tradition* (Minneapolis: Fortress, 1990), p.83.

heaven, visions of hell, climactic judgement scenes, and other such 'apocalyptic imagery' would indicate.

In this essay I will compare the Jewish apocalypses[5] and the Gospel of John. I will address the definition of 'apocalypse', highlight the Gospel's apocalyptic framework, note the ways in which John is not an apocalypse, and conclude with a proposal for describing John's genre. The questions I am seeking to answer include: 'What is the relationship between John and the Jewish apocalypses?' and 'How can that relationship best be described in terms of the genre of the Gospel of John?' John Ashton has explained John's Gospel as 'an apocalypse – in reverse, upside down, inside out'.[6] With great respect for Ashton and Rowland, I contend that this description, while elegant and provocative, lacks precision when a comparison is made between John's Gospel and the Jewish apocalypses.

Admittedly, both Ashton and Rowland have acknowledged that they do not intend for the designation 'apocalypse in reverse' to function as a precise description of the Gospel of John's relationship with the genre of 'apocalypse'.[7] However, because Ashton's explanation is the only description that has been given, it rightly serves as the starting-point for any discussion of 'intimations of apocalyptic' in John.[8] If Ashton's description is not intended to be exact, is it possible to describe the relationship with more precision? And what might a more accurate description look like?

Now, in pursuing the answers to these questions, I am in significant agreement with John Ashton and Christopher Rowland, and I want to stress that I see this discussion as an in-house debate amongst those who view John's Gospel as having some relationship with apocalyptic

---

5   Due to issues of space and scope, only the Jewish apocalypses will be addressed. Examination of the early Christian apocalypses in comparison with the Gospel of John is an important area for further study. For descriptions of Jewish and Christian apocalypses, see John J. Collins (ed.), *Apocalypse: The Morphology of a Genre* (Semeia 14; Atlanta: Scholars Press, 1979). See also Adela Yarbro Collins (ed.), *Early Christian Apocalypticism: Genre and Social Setting* (Semeia 36; Decatur: Scholars Press, 1986).

6   Ashton, *Understanding*, p.329. See also Rowland, *The Mystery of God*, pp.123–31.

7   They did so in response to this paper as well as in following private conversations at the Bangor colloquium. For Christopher Rowland the designation 'apocalypse in reverse' serves as a kind of heuristic device or metaphor to denote the effect of John's Gospel on its readers/hearers.

8   See, for example, the various titles of papers from the Bangor colloquium in this volume.

literature. I assume that no one would classify the Gospel as an apocalypse, but there may be various ways to explain this relationship and the similarities shared by John and the Jewish apocalypses. Even Ashton, in his second edition of *Understanding the Fourth Gospel*, states that to include the Gospel of John in the definition of apocalypse 'stretches the genre somewhat but perhaps not to breaking point'.[9] Thus, I may well come to a conclusion with which Ashton and Rowland will agree. Either way, my intention is to clarify some of the issues of genre surrounding the relationship between the Gospel of John and apocalyptic literature.

2. Of Apocalypses, Apocalyptic and Definitions

Entering into discussions of genre poses a number of problems, not the least of which is the fact that the term 'genre' and genre definitions are scholarly constructs and are always unstable. Any definition of a genre such as 'apocalypse' must recognise the porous and nebulous nature of these abstract constructs. However, if we do not begin from *a* definition of some kind, abstract or not, there is no clarity concerning what we are discussing. In this regard, the defining of genres in general is, in my opinion, a necessary exercise; however, at the same time, we must constantly remind ourselves that the border between what is on the inside of the genre and what is outside is in reality a border of our own making.

For the purpose of this essay, therefore, defining the terms 'apocalypse' and 'apocalyptic' is important for clarifying John's relationship with apocalyptic literature. What does it mean to say that the Gospel of John is 'an apocalypse – in reverse, upside down, inside out'? What would it mean to say that it is an 'apocalypse' proper? While we may prefer to avoid the need to define terms, some clarity is required with regard to what we mean by 'apocalypse' and, therefore, by a 'reversed apocalypse'.

Unfortunately, and unsurprisingly, defining the words 'apocalyptic' and 'apocalypse' is not without its challenges. First, a survey of scholarly use reveals an inconsistency in the use of the terms.[10] In biblical studies, there is a tendency in some circles for 'apocalyptic' to refer mainly to eschatology, even though eschatology is not always a feature

---

9   Ashton, *Understanding*, p.7.

10   Richard E. Sturm, 'Defining the Word "Apocalyptic": A Problem in Biblical Criticism', in Joel Marcus and Marion L. Soards (eds.), *Apocalyptic and the New Testament: Essays in Honor of J. Louis Martyn* (JSNTSup 24; Sheffield: Sheffield Academic, 1989), pp.16–48.

of apocalypses. For instance, Jesus' message of the kingdom has been likened to 'apocalyptic' because of the hope in a cosmic overthrow of the world's present condition,[11] and 'apocalypticism' has been associated with an 'imminent expectation' or a 'cosmic drama of the end'.[12] Second, popular uses of the words 'apocalyptic' and 'apocalypse' most often refer to cataclysmic, end-of-the-world scenarios.[13] These difficulties of scholarly confusion and popular meaning, along with others, contribute to the inconsistency of meaning in the use of the terms 'apocalyptic' and 'apocalypse'.

A helpful starting-point in attempting to clarify the confusion in the scholarly discussion is the definition of 'apocalypse' by the SBL Genres Project. This definition, primarily advocated by John Collins, states that an apocalypse is:

> a genre of revelatory literature with a narrative framework, in which a revelation is mediated by an otherworldly being to a human recipient, disclosing a transcendent reality which is both temporal, insofar as it envisages eschatological salvation, and spatial insofar as it involves another, supernatural world.[14]

This definition has received criticism of various kinds,[15] but, for the purposes of discussing the Gospel of John and the Jewish apocalypses, John Ashton's critique of the definition is the most relevant.[16]

Ashton's concern seems to be the way in which the Gospel of John fits this definition of apocalypse 'snugly' while 'it is obviously *not* an apocalypse'.[17] He rightly notes the importance of clarifying the difference

---

11 Rudolf Bultmann, *Theology of the New Testament* (trans. Kendrick Grobel; 2 vols.; New York: Charles Scribner's Sons, 1951/1955), I, pp.4–6.

12 See Ernst Käsemann, *The Testament of Jesus: A Study of the Gospel of John in the Light of Chapter 17* (trans. Gerhard Krodel; Philadelphia: Fortress, 1968), p.13, cf. p.72.

13 The website www.apocalypticmovies.com provides information about films that portray catastrophic events that threaten to destroy the world or actually do destroy the world. This website also lists post-apocalyptic films which take place after such 'apocalyptic' events.

14 John J. Collins, *The Apocalyptic Imagination: An Introduction to Jewish Apocalyptic Literature* (Grand Rapids: Eerdmans, 2nd edn, 1998), p.5.

15 See especially the critique by David Hellholm, 'The Problem of Apocalyptic Genre and the Apocalypse of John', *Semeia* 36 (1986), pp.13–64.

16 For a brief overview of 'apocalyptic', see the introductory essay in David E. Aune, *Apocalypticism, Prophecy, and Magic in Early Christianity: Collected Essays* (Grand Rapids: Baker Academic, 2008), pp.1–12.

17 Ashton, *Understanding*, p.309 (emphasis original).

between prophecy in the Old Testament and the mediation of revelation in apocalypses and the importance of discussing the relevance of the milieu of the apocalyptic literature. He also argues that the mode of apocalyptic revelation should be specified – a vision or dream needing interpretation, or heavenly ascent.[18] Although the mode of the revelation may be distinctive of apocalypses, not all apocalypses include the modes of vision, dream, or heavenly ascent. In *4 Ezra*, for example, an angel at times meets Ezra even when he does not appear to be in a visionary state (5.31; 7.1; cf. 4.1). In *Jubilees*, Moses goes up Mt. Sinai to meet God in the more or less literal sense of climbing the mountain. While the *Book of the Luminaries* and the *Apocalypse of Weeks* imply heavenly journeys, there is no explicit reference to these journeys.[19] These four examples of apocalypses suggest that specifying the mode of revelation in a definition of 'apocalypse' should be done with caution.[20] However, as Ashton's objection indicates, more clarity might be beneficial as long as it is not overly specific. Thus, I suggest emending the SBL definition so that it states that the heavenly mediation to the human recipient is 'often, though not always, through visions, dreams, or an ascent to heaven'.

A further aspect of Ashton's critique of the SBL definition of 'apocalypse' is that eschatology 'is not a constant or a necessary feature of apocalyptic writing'.[21] Since he gives no further explanation of this criticism, I can only assume that Ashton disagrees with the part of the SBL definition that refers to 'eschatological salvation'. Ashton is correct that eschatology, in the sense of a climactic judgement at the end of the world, does not make up the content of all apocalypses.[22] Clearly, this

---

18   Ashton, *Understanding*, p.310.

19   See Collins, *Apocalyptic Imagination*, p.60. The implication of heavenly journeys in the *Book of the Luminaries* and the *Apocalypse of Weeks* may be seen in *1 En.* 81.5; 93.2; see George W. E. Nickelsburg, *1 Enoch 1: A Commentary on the Book of 1 Enoch, Chapters 1–36; 81–108* (Hermeneia; Minneapolis: Fortress, 2001), pp.340, 443.

20   John J. Collins, 'Introduction: Towards the Morphology of a Genre', *Semeia* 14 (1979), pp.1–20 (11), contends that the phrase referring to the mediation of revelation by an otherworldly figure in the definition of 'apocalypse' includes the various modes of revelation.

21   Ashton, *Understanding*, p.309.

22   John Ashton, *Understanding the Fourth Gospel* (Oxford: Clarendon, 1st edn, 1991), p.384, notes that Käsemann speaks of 'apocalyptic' in the way that he himself speaks of eschatology. He cites Käsemann, 'On the Subject of Primitive Christian Apocalyptic', in *New Testament Questions of Today* (London: SCM, 1969), pp.108–37 (109 n. 1): 'It emerges from the context that almost throughout I speak of primitive Christian apocalyptic to denote the expectation of an imminent Parousia'.

sort of eschatology concerns some apocalypses (e.g. *Parables of Enoch, 2 Baruch*), but the phrase 'eschatological salvation' in the SBL definition is explained by Collins to refer to 'personal eschatology', that is, what happens to the righteous and the wicked when they die.[23] If we understand 'eschatological salvation' as *'personal* eschatological salvation', rather than purely cataclysmic, end-time eschatology, it may be possible to allow the definition to stand. Ashton and Rowland are correct to point out the lack of this sort of eschatology in all of the Jewish apocalypses. However, the Jewish apocalypses do appear to be concerned with the salvation of the righteous and the wicked. This is a concern for personal eschatology without reference to 'apocalyptic' imagery, angels, thrones, books, or the destruction of the world.

Taking into account Ashton's comments concerning the mode of revelation and the milieu of writing, the following definition of 'apocalypse' is an emended version of the one previously suggested:

> a genre of revelatory literature with a narrative framework, in which a revelation is mediated by an otherworldly figure to a human recipient *often, though not always, through visions, dreams, or an ascent to heaven,* disclosing a transcendent reality which is both temporal, insofar as it envisages *personal* eschatological salvation, and spatial insofar as it involves another, supernatural world, *'and an apocalypse is intended to interpret present, earthly circumstances in the light of the supernatural world..., and to influence both the understanding and the behavior of the audience by means of divine authority'*.[24]

See Michael E. Stone, 'Lists of Revealed Things in the Apocalyptic Literature', in Frank M. Cross, Werner E. Lemke, and Patrick D. Miller Jr. (eds.), *Magnalia Dei: The Mighty Acts of God. Essays on the Bible and Archaeology in Memory of G. Ernest Wright* (Garden City: Doubleday, 1976), pp.414–52.

23 Collins, 'Morphology', p.9. Collins argues that 'personal afterlife' is one of the most 'consistent' aspects of the apocalyptic genre. However, it should be noted that elsewhere Collins appears to take the view that apocalypses contain cataclysmic eschatology. See idem, 'From Prophecy to Apocalypticism: The Expectation of the End', in John J. Collins (ed.), *The Encyclopedia of Apocalypticism. Vol. 1, The Origins of Apocalypticism in Judaism and Christianity* (New York: Continuum, 1998), pp.129–61.

24 The italics indicate additions to the SBL definition. The latter half of the definition is the emendation suggested by Adela Yarbro Collins ('Introduction: Early Christian Apocalypticism', *Semeia* 36 [1986], pp.1–11 [7]) to address the question of apocalyptic milieu; however, the ellipsis indicates where I have removed the phrase 'and of the future' because of the concerns over eschatology discussed above. See Benjamin E. Reynolds, *The Apocalyptic Son of Man in the Gospel of John* (WUNT 2/249; Tübingen: Mohr Siebeck, 2008), p.16.

Having established a working definition of 'apocalypse', and keeping in mind that it also remains a scholarly construct, this essay will now focus on the ways in which the Gospel of John fits the framework of an 'apocalypse' and yet offer reasons why it is not an 'apocalypse'.

3. The Gospel of John's Apocalyptic Framework

The Gospel of John can be described as having the framework of an apocalypse in that it coheres in a surprising way with our working definition of 'apocalypse'. The Gospel is a narrative that reveals mysteries about God and his Son. It begins with an otherworldly figure descending from heaven and mediating the revelation of heavenly things (3.12-13) to human recipients (1.11, 50-51); the revelation includes making known the Father (1.18) and the transcendent reality of heaven. Jesus, the otherworldly figure, is clearly from heaven and has descended to earth (1.1-2, 18; 3.13, 34; 9.33; 17.5). The gap between heaven and earth is bridged through the opening of heaven and the Son of Man connecting heaven and earth (1.51).[25]

The revelation mediated by Jesus discloses the personal eschatological salvation that is possible through belief in him (3.16; 14.6). The temporal aspect of this salvation has its own Johannine peculiarity since there is a present connotation to judgement and salvation (3.17-18; 9.39), yet their future consummation is also envisaged (5.28-29; 6.39-40; 14.1-3). The revelation that Jesus gives is written down and testified by a human recipient (1.14; 2.11; 21.24).

Further, like most apocalypses, the Gospel of John places earthly events in heavenly perspective (1.1-5; 3.13, 31; 6.27-35, 62; 9.33, 39; 13.33; 17.1-5; 20.17). And the call to believe through the actions of Jesus is surely a call to the audience to respond to authoritative revelation as the one who speaks and does what he has seen and heard from the Father. Therefore, given that the Gospel fits this particular definition and framework of an apocalypse and shares numerous themes with the Jewish apocalypses,[26] it would seem that, in many respects, the Gospel of John should be considered an apocalypse.[27]

---

25 Udo Schnelle, *Das Evangelium nach Johannes* (THKNT 4; Leipzig: Evangelische Verlagsanstalt, 2nd edn, 1998), p.56.

26 It can be argued that the Gospel of John shares the following themes with Jewish apocalypses: the opening of heaven (John 1.51 with *2 Bar.* 22.1; *T. Levi* 2.6; *T. Ab.* A 7.3; *Apoc. Ab.* 19.4; *Apoc. Zeph.* 10.2; Rev 4.1-2; 19.11); ascent or descent of an otherworldly figure or human recipient (John 3.13; 6.62 with *1 En.* 14.8;

4. Why John's Gospel is Not an Apocalypse

Although the Gospel shares the framework of an apocalypse, meeting the key features of our working definition of 'apocalypse', John Ashton is correct to say that the Gospel of John is not an apocalypse.[28] Five reasons will be offered below which indicate that the Gospel of John diverges from the genre of 'apocalypse', regardless of the Gospel's apocalyptic framework and shared similarities with Jewish apocalypses. The first four reasons pertain to John's presentation of Jesus as the otherworldly mediator who becomes a human being, who is the content of the revelation, who is one with God, and who is crucified, buried, and raised. The fifth reason addresses the fact that the revelation of the Johannine Jesus has multiple human recipients, which raises questions concerning pseudepigraphy and the authorship of the Gospel.

4.1. The Mediator as a Human Being

Like the Jewish apocalypses, the Gospel of John is set within a narrative framework in which an otherworldly figure mediates revelation to a human recipient. One element where John's Gospel diverges from the normal apocalyptic plot relates to the character of the otherworldly being. In the Jewish apocalypses, the mediator figure is commonly an angel. It is the angel Gabriel who interprets Daniel's vision (Dan 8.15-26). Uriel teaches Enoch about the heavenly luminaries in the *Book of the Luminaries* (*1 En.* 72–82). In the *Testament of Abraham* it is Michael

---

T. Levi 2.6-7; *T. Ab.* A 10.1); the revelation of heavenly things (John 1.18; 3.12-13 with *T. Ab.* A 11-14); the vision of God (John 12.41; 14.9 with Rev 4–5; *1 En.* 14.8-23; *Apoc. Ab.* 18); the vision of God in the heavenly temple (John 2.21; 12.41 with *1 En.* 14); judgement and the Son of Man (John 5.27; 9.39 with Dan 7.9-12; *1 En.* 62; *T. Ab.* A 11-13; *Apoc. Ab.* 22.3-5; *3 Bar.* 15–16; cf. *Apoc. Zeph.* 6.17; 10.11); double resurrection of the righteous and the wicked (John 5.28-29 with *1 En.* 51.1-5; *4 Ezra* 7.28-36; *2 Bar.* 50.2–51.4; Rev 20.5-6, 11-14); the importance of the written record of revelation (John 20.30-31; 21.24 with *1 En.* 68.1; 81.6; 82.1; 83.8-10; *2 En.* 23.3-6; 40.1-12; *2 En.* J 68.2; Rev 1.11; *Jub.* 1.5, 7, 26; 2.1; *4 Ezra* 14.44-46; *2 Bar.* 50.1; cf. 77.12–87.1). These themes deserve more explanation, but, for now, this footnote will have to suffice.

27   Ashton (*Understanding*, p.7) states: 'Provided that we understand eschatological in the sense that Bultmann employs this word (i.e. as referring to what the Gospel calls life) and admit that Jesus really did speak, as he claims to have done, of "heavenly things" (3.12), this [the SBL definition of apocalypse] fits the Fourth Gospel to a T'.

28   Ashton, *Understanding*, p.309.

who leads Abraham on his heavenly journey. Phanael takes Baruch into the heavens and discloses heavenly mysteries to him (*3 Bar.* 2.1, 5), and the unnamed 'angel of the presence' reveals the law to Moses in *Jubilees*. In contrast, it is not an angel who descends and reveals the heavenly mysteries in the Gospel of John, but rather Jesus, the Logos, the Son of God.

Some scholars have argued that the Gospel of John presents an angelomorphic Christology, particularly in 1.51, where the angels of God are said to ascend and descend on the Son of Man.[29] One of the more obvious similarities between the Johannine Jesus and angels is that both are sent by God and reveal messages from God.[30] However, while there are similarities, the significant difference between Jesus and the otherworldly mediators of the Jewish apocalypses is that the heavenly figure of John's Gospel becomes human – 'the Word became flesh and dwelt among us' (1.14). In the Jewish apocalypses, the angelic mediators remain angels and do not become like those to whom they reveal the heavenly mysteries.[31]

An example of this difference can be seen in the episode from the *Testament of Abraham* where Michael ('the commander-in-chief') is directed by God to descend and tell Abraham that he is about to die (A 1.5). Michael is so overcome by Abraham's hospitality and righteousness that he ascends to heaven and announces to God that he cannot inform the patriarch of his impending death (A 4.6). God commands Michael to return and to eat whatever Abraham puts in front of him. A dream given to Isaac will allow Michael to announce Abraham's death through the interpretation of the dream. Michael's response to this plan reveals his concern about the food. As angels do not eat food, he asks what he is to do with the food that Abraham will put in front of him (A 4.9). God tells Michael that he will send a spirit upon him that will devour whatever he puts into his mouth (A 4.10). After Michael

---

29 See Charles A. Gieschen, *Angelomorphic Christology: Antecedents and Early Evidence* (AGJU 42; Leiden: Brill, 1998), pp.270–93; Jarl E. Fossum, *The Image of the Invisible God: Essays on the Influence of Jewish Mysticism on Early Christology* (NTOA 30; Göttingen: Vandenhoeck & Ruprecht, 1995), pp.135–51.

30 Gieschen, *Angelomorphic Christology*, pp.284–6; Robert H. Gundry, *Jesus the Word According to John the Sectarian* (Grand Rapids: Eerdmans, 2002), pp.13–14.

31 Kevin P. Sullivan, *Wrestling with Angels: A Study of the Relationship Between Angels and Humans in Ancient Jewish Literature and the New Testament* (AGJU 55; Leiden: Brill, 2004), pp.37–83, especially 82–3. See Martha Himmelfarb, *Ascent to Heaven in Jewish and Christian Apocalypses* (Oxford: Oxford University Press, 1993), pp.70–1.

descends, the devouring spirit does its work and 'the commander-in-chief' interprets Isaac's dream (A 7.8-12). What is clear from this episode is that angels are not human and therefore do not eat.[32]

In John's Gospel, the human Jesus does eat and drink, even though he is a heavenly mediator sent by God. He does not eat or drink when the disciples return with food (4.31-34), although their expectation is that Jesus can, and will, eat. He reclines at table with Lazarus (12.2), has dinner with his disciples (13.2), and drinks the sour wine from the cross (19.29).[33] The fact that Jesus is a human being *and* the heavenly emissary is a significant difference between John and the Jewish apocalypses, given that an apocalypse is partly defined in terms of an otherworldly figure mediating revelation to a human recipient. In John, the otherworldly figure has become a human being like the recipients to whom he reveals the heavenly mysteries.[34]

4.2. The Mediator as the Content and Centre of the Revelation

A second significant difference between the Gospel of John and Jewish apocalypses is that in the Gospel the otherworldly figure is also the content of the revelation. To describe this as the merging of Message and Messenger[35] or Jesus as Revealer and Revelation[36] captures the sense of the assimilation that moves the Gospel of John beyond the bounds of texts belonging to the genre of 'apocalypse'. Revelation in the Jewish apocalypses never focuses on the angelic figure. Angels interpret dreams and visions, speak messages from God, and transport seers into heaven, but they are never the content of the revelation. They do not take centre stage; rather, they direct attention away from themselves to what is revealed.

---

32 In Tob. 12.19, Raphael claims that he never ate anything. A vision made it appear as though he ate. See Sullivan, *Wrestling with Angels*, pp.179–95.

33 There are indications that even the resurrected Jesus eats food (21.13-15).

34 With regard to John 3.13, Ashton contends that Jesus is an angel *and* a seer. He states (*Understanding*, p.258): 'The blinding realization that in Jesus angel and seer are one and the same marks one of the most significant advances in the whole history of Christian thought: its ramifications are endless'. Ashton appears to be referring to Jesus as seer because of his descent from heaven and role in revealing the mysteries that he has seen in heaven. Jesus' descent–ascent pattern is partly what Ashton sees as the reversal of apocalyptic seers' typical ascent–descent pattern. However, while some seers ascend to heaven and then descend, it is not true of all. Some seers remain on earth, and angels descend and disclose revelation to them, as Jesus does in John's Gospel. See below for further discussion.

35 Gundry, *Jesus the Word*, p.14.

36 See Bultmann, *Theology*, II, p.66.

By contrast, the heavenly mediator figure in John's Gospel directs people to God, but it is only through belief in Jesus that people can receive eternal life or come to the Father (14.6). The focus on Jesus' identity (chs. 7–9), on his words and works (4.34; 5.36; 8.26, 28), and on the necessity of belief in him for salvation (3.16; 20.30-31), highlight the way in which the heavenly emissary in John is the centre and content of the revelation that he himself brings.

Two additional features in the Gospel of John underscore this important difference. First, the otherworldly figure is the Son of Man, the one who has the authority to judge (5.27). In the Jewish apocalypses in which a son of man figure appears, the mediator is the one who discloses or interprets a vision of the son of man (cf. *1 En.* 62 with 71.14; *4 Ezra* 13). The angel is not part of the vision, nor is the angel confused with any of the figures in the vision.[37] Secondly, the Johannine Jesus receives glory (12.23; 13.31-32). Angels in the Jewish apocalypses do not typically receive glory, nor do they come close to the status of the heavenly mediator as presented in John's Gospel.[38] These features highlight the important difference between the Gospel and the apocalypses in that the heavenly emissary in John is the content and focus of the revelation. This is something that does not occur in the Jewish apocalypses.

4.3. The Mediator as One with God

The third indication that the fourth evangelist is not writing an apocalypse proper is the oneness that Jesus, the mediator figure, shares with God. In the Jewish apocalypses, angelic mediators are messengers of God and speak the words of God. Notably, in *Jubilees* and *4 Ezra* it is often difficult to determine whether God or the angelic mediator is speaking.[39] In addition, in the *Apocalypse of Abraham* the angel Yahoel bears the divine name (10.3, 8) and is described in terms suggestive

---

37 In the *Parables of Enoch*, we do find the interesting possibility that the human recipient (or seer) of the revelation (Enoch) is the son of man figure of his vision (70.1; 71.14). See Daniel C. Olson, 'Enoch and the Son of Man in the Epilogue of the Parables', *JSP* 18 (1998), pp.27–38.

38 Even Yahoel, in *Apoc. Ab.* 10.3-17, is not glorified or worshipped even though he is given the divine name. Yahoel worships God along with Abraham (17.2). See Larry W. Hurtado, *One God, One Lord: Early Christian Devotion and Ancient Jewish Monotheism* (London: T&T Clark/Continuum, 2nd edn, 1998), pp.81–2; Christopher Rowland, *The Open Heaven: A Study of Apocalyptic in Judaism and Early Christianity* (New York: Crossroad, 1982), p.103.

39 *4 Ezra* 5.31, 38-56; 6.11-16, 30-32; 7.1-17; *Jub.* 1.22, 26, 27; 2.1; 6.20, 32; 33.18; 50.1-2. See Ashton, *Understanding*, pp.291–2.

of divine attributes (11.1-6).[40] Christopher Rowland contends that even though Yahoel has divine attributes and bears the divine name, 'the figure is clearly an angel'.[41]

Like the angels in these apocalypses, the Johannine Jesus is clearly an otherworldly mediator of heavenly revelation and thus a messenger and agent of God.[42] For this reason, similarities between Jesus and the angelic mediators are to be expected. However, John presents a oneness between Jesus and the Father that extends beyond the role of the otherworldly mediators in the Jewish apocalypses. Jesus says, 'I and the Father are one' (10.30; cf. 17.22). Jesus does what God does: he judges, he gives life (5.19-24), and he works on the Sabbath (5.17). Jesus is accused of making himself equal with God (5.18). He claims the divine name 'I Am' (8.28), and he says that he has come in his Father's name (5.43; 17.11; cf. 12.28). Jesus has the glory of the only begotten of the Father (1.14); God and Jesus are glorified in one another (13.31-32; also 12.41). Not only was the Logos with God, the Logos was God (1.1).[43] Ernst Käsemann states: 'In unique dignity as the Father's "exegete" (1.18), he surpasses everyone else who may otherwise have been sent'.[44]

The mediator figures of the Jewish apocalypses primarily disclose or interpret revelation. They point away from themselves to the content or meaning of what is revealed. The mediator in John's Gospel directs attention to himself because he is the revelation.

4.4. The Mediator as Crucified, Buried, and Raised

A further difference between the Jewish apocalypses and John's Gospel is almost too obvious to mention. Unlike the otherworldly mediators in the Jewish apocalypses, Jesus suffers death by crucifixion, is buried, and is raised to life on the third day. In Johannine language, this is the

---

40   See Gieschen, *Angelomorphic Christology*, pp.76–8, 277–8, who also cites *Prayer of Joseph* 9; *1 En.* 69.15; *3 En.* 12.5. See also Rowland, *Open Heaven*, pp.94–113; Ashton, *Understanding*, pp.281–98.

41   Rowland, *Open Heaven*, p.103; Sullivan, *Wrestling with Angels*, p.82.

42   See Peder Borgen, 'God's Agent in the Fourth Gospel', in *Philo, John, and Paul: New Perspectives on Judaism and Early Christianity* (Brown Judaic Studies 131; Atlanta: Scholars Press, 1987), pp.171–84.

43   See Richard Bauckham, *Jesus and the God of Israel: God Crucified and Other Studies on the New Testament's Christology of Divine Identity* (Grand Rapids: Eerdmans, 2008), pp.46–50.

44   Käsemann, *Testament*, p.11.

lifting up and glorification of Jesus.[45] Nothing like death or suffering happens to the otherworldly mediators in the Jewish apocalypses,[46] and, as mentioned above, no angel receives glory as does the Johannine Jesus. Although this aspect relates to some of the previously mentioned differences (i.e. Jesus' humanity), the death, burial, and resurrection of Jesus mark a stark contrast between the Gospel of John and the Jewish apocalypses.

4.5. Multiple Human Recipients and Pseudonymous Authorship
In the Jewish apocalypses a human being receives the revelation. While such individuals are well-known figures from Israel's past, including Enoch, Moses, Abraham, Baruch, Ezra, and Levi, each Jewish apocalypse names only one figure as the recipient of the heavenly mysteries. In contrast, the fourth evangelist portrays the revelation as being received by more than one human figure, as the Gospel's opening verses make clear: 'Jesus came to his own but his own did not receive him' (1.11). Again, a few verses later, the evangelist writes '*we* have seen his glory' (1.14), implying that the glory of the Word become flesh was seen by more than one person (cf. 21.24). In 2.11 there is further evidence for multiple recipients of the revelation: 'Jesus revealed his glory and *his disciples* believed in him'. And in 1.51 Jesus speaks to Nathanael using the second person plural: 'you will see (ὄψεσθε) heaven opened and the angels of God ascending and descending on the Son of Man'. In addition, Jesus tells Thomas: καὶ ἀπ' ἄρτι γινώσκετε αὐτὸν καὶ ἑωράκατε αὐτόν ('and from now on you [pl.] know him [the Father] and you [pl.] have seen him', 14.7). The Johannine revelation is clearly revealed to a broader group and not one individual. The receipt of the heavenly revelation by more than one figure is a subtle but noteworthy difference between the Gospel of John and Jewish apocalypses.[47]

At the same time, the Gospel itself is described as the testimony of one figure, the disciple whom Jesus loved (13.23; 19.26; 20.2; 21.7, 20). Without delving deeply into the authorship debate, the Beloved Disciple is probably among those who claim to have seen Jesus' glory (note the

45 Raymond E. Brown, *The Gospel According to John* (AB 29/29A; 2 vols.; New York: Doubleday, 1966–70), I, p.146; Josef Blank, *Krisis: Untersuchungen zur johanneischen Christologie und Eschatologie* (Freiburg: Lambertus-Verlag, 1964), p.267.

46 Note that the mediator in Dan 10 was opposed by the prince of the kingdom of Persia (v. 13).

47 Note *T. Ab.* A 7.8-12, where Michael interprets Isaac's dream to Isaac, Abraham, and possibly to Sarah; however, Abraham is the only one taken on the tour of heaven.

plural 'we' in 1.14; cf. 12.37-43); he testifies to the events of Jesus' passion (19.35; 20.8) and writes down what he has seen (21.24; cf. 19.35; 20.30-31). This may suggest a singular human recipient of the revelation. However, the Beloved Disciple is clearly one of many disciples to have received and seen Jesus' revelation, and there is no mention of him experiencing a heavenly ascent, a dream, or a vision. Further, unlike most Jewish apocalypses (cf. Rev 1.9), the author of John's Gospel is unnamed. Jewish apocalypses are typically pseudonymous and the reason for this, in all likelihood, is to lend authority to the revelation.[48] On the whole, therefore, there are significant differences between John and the Jewish apocalypses with regard to the recipients of the heavenly revelation and pseudonymous authorship.[49]

4.6. Summary

Although the Gospel of John corresponds closely to our working definition of an apocalypse, it is, nevertheless, not an apocalypse. The Gospel may fit the framework of an apocalypse and share motifs with the Jewish apocalypses, but the usual cast of characters in the apocalypses do not match those found in the Gospel. Jesus is no mere angelic messenger. Instead, as mediator of the revelation, he is also the centre of the revelation, is one with the source of the revelation, and is a human being, even one who suffers death, like those to whom he discloses the revelation. This merging of apocalyptic characters bursts the wineskins of the genre of 'apocalypse'.

In addition, a comparison between pseudonymous authors of Jewish apocalypses and the Beloved Disciple raises an interesting area for further study, although, as far as the definition of apocalypse is concerned, the revelation in John's Gospel is disclosed to multiple human recipients rather than to a single recipient. These differences in the function of

---

48 See Rowland, *Open Heaven*, pp.61–70; Collins, *Apocalyptic Imagination*, pp.39–40, 270–1; Loren T. Stuckenbruck, 'Apocrypha and Pseudepigrapha', in John J. Collins and Daniel C. Harlow (eds.), *The Eerdmans Dictionary of Early Judaism* (Grand Rapids: Eerdmans, 2010), pp.143–62 (154–56).

49 In the Jewish apocalypses, the great heroes of Israel are associated with seeing the heavenly mysteries and reporting what they have seen. Now, although the author is unnamed, the designation 'the disciple whom Jesus loved' apparently functioned as a referent to a specific person who was most likely known to the first hearers and readers of the Gospel. Further study is needed, but does the designation 'Beloved Disciple' function as a pseudonym similar to those of the Jewish apocalypses? Or might the veiled anonymity of the author function as some sort of compromise between the pseudonymity of the Jewish apocalypses and the anonymity of the Gospels?

otherworldly mediator and human recipient imply that the Gospel does not conform to the definition of an apocalypse. The framework of 'apocalypse' is still visible but the cast of characters in the apocalyptic plot – the otherworldly figure, human recipient, revelation and God – merge together in the person of Jesus.

5. Questioning John's Gospel as 'Apocalypse in Reverse'

John Ashton argues that, rather than an apocalypse proper, 'the fourth evangelist conceives his own work as an apocalypse – in reverse, upside down, inside out'.[50] It appears that Ashton perceives the Gospel of John to be an apocalypse reversed and upside down primarily because the revelation takes place on earth. He states, 'There is no divine plan first disclosed to a seer in a vision and then repeated in earthly terms. The divine plan itself – the Logos – is incarnate: fully embodied in the person of Jesus. It is his life that reveals God's grand design of saving the world, a design now being realized, lived out, by the community'.[51] This position is echoed by Christopher Rowland: 'Heavenly visions of God are not what is on offer in the Fourth Gospel, for claims to see God must be regarded as claims to see Jesus. The Gospel of John is indeed "an apocalypse in reverse".'[52]

The view that John's Gospel is 'an apocalypse in reverse' therefore appears to rely on two points: (1) the Gospel of John has no *heavenly* vision of God by a seer and (2) the vision of God is given in, of, and through the life of the earthly Jesus, the Logos made flesh. If we understand apocalypses primarily in terms of heavenly ascents and throne room visions, describing John's Gospel as 'an apocalypse in reverse' makes perfect sense. However, an apocalypse has not been defined as such in this essay. Rather, an apocalypse has been defined as a narrative that focuses on heavenly revelation mediated by an otherworldly figure to a human recipient. In my opinion, designating the Gospel of John as

---

50 Ashton, *Understanding*, pp.328–9. To repeat (see above), although I recognise that Ashton's comment is more of a turn of phrase than a technical description, I think that it can be misleading if it is taken even somewhat literally. Further, this description still leaves open the question of how to describe the relationship between the Gospel of John and the Jewish apocalypses.

51 Ashton, *Understanding*, p.328, also pp.528–9.

52 Rowland, *Mystery of God*, p.131, and 'Apocalyptic, Mysticism, and the New Testament', in Hubert Cancik *et al.* (eds.), *Geschichte–Tradition–Reflexion: Festschrift für Martin Hengel zum 70. Geburtstag. I: Judentum* (Tübingen: Mohr Siebeck, 1996), pp.405–30 (426).

'an apocalypse in reverse' is not the best way to explain the similarity of John with the Jewish apocalypses, and this for two reasons. First, not all Jewish apocalypses narrate visions of heaven or ascents to heaven, even though the revelation may often be mediated in these ways. And secondly, the embodiment of the vision of God in a human being seems less like an inversion and more like an innovation. I will address these two points in turn.

5.1. Apocalypses without Heavenly Ascents or Visions of Heaven

Two of the Jewish apocalypses, *4 Ezra* and *2 Baruch*, do not speak of heavenly ascents; nor do they include visions of God. The seer is grounded on earth and the otherworldly mediator descends to earth to answer Ezra's and Baruch's prayers and questions. In fact, *4 Ezra* seems to refute ascent speculation, making the claim that God cannot be reached (8.21), while the angel Uriel clarifies the impossibility of descent to hell or ascent to heaven (4.8).[53]

Of greater interest is *Jubilees*. At first glance, one might not think to include this text in the list of Jewish apocalypses, since it does not contain the strange visionary imagery or heavenly ascents that the word 'apocalypse' often conjures in the imagination. *Jubilees* has even been called a 'borderline case for the apocalyptic genre'.[54] The text recounts Israel's history from creation to Moses and strongly emphasises the importance of keeping the law and of obeying God's commands; as such, *Jubilees* would seem to be closer to the biblical account in Exodus, were it not for its framework.[55] The text begins with Moses going up Mt. Sinai to receive the law and speaks of the glory of the Lord dwelling on the mountain. However, once Moses is on the mountain, what he is told – the history of Israel from creation until Moses' own day – is described as revelation. *Jubilees* 1.4 states: 'And the Lord revealed to him both what (was) in the beginning and what will occur (in the future), the account of the division of all the days of the Law and the testimony' (cf. 1.27-29).[56]

---

53 See Rowland, *Mystery of God*, p.126; Michael E. Stone, *Fourth Ezra: A Commentary on the Book of Fourth Ezra* (Hermeneia; Minneapolis: Fortress, 1990), pp.80–1, 272–3. Note that the *Testament of Abraham* has examples of both heavenly descent by an otherworldly mediator and ascent by a human seer.

54 Collins, *Apocalyptic Imagination*, p.83. See also John C. Endres, *Biblical Interpretation in the Book of Jubilees* (CBQMS 18; Washington, D.C.: The Catholic Biblical Association of America, 1987), pp.4–5.

55 See Rowland, *Open Heaven*, pp.51–2.

56 All translations of *Jubilees* are from O. S. Wintermute, 'Jubilees', *OTP*, vol. 2.

The similarity with prophetic literature is apparent; however, *Jubilees* qualifies as an apocalypse because it is a narrative in which heavenly revelation is mediated by an otherworldly figure (whether 'the angel of the presence' or God himself) to a human recipient (Moses). The aspect of 'personal eschatological salvation', which is not connected to a cataclysmic, end-time judgement, is noticeable in the emphasis on righteous living through the keeping of the law (*Jub.* 6.17-22; 13.26; 15.25-27; 32.10-15; 33.10-14; 49.1–50.13). Although *Jubilees* lacks heavenly ascents and visions and is located on the borderline of the genre, it is still classified as a Jewish apocalypse.[57] Like the Gospel of John, *Jubilees* is a revelatory narrative that takes place on earth, and it portrays the otherworldly mediator as appearing on earth. Thus, I do not find it entirely helpful to use the earthly location of John's Gospel in order to describe it as 'an apocalypse in reverse'. Some apocalypses depict revelation as being given on earth and do not contain heavenly ascents or throne room visions.[58] These features do not necessarily intimate that the apocalyptic framework has been reversed.

5.2. The Embodiment of Revelation as Indication of an Inverted Apocalypse?

Ashton also seems to ground his view that John's Gospel is 'an apocalypse in reverse' on the fact that God's revelation is embodied in the human person of Jesus. My understanding of what Ashton is describing is as follows: it is in Jesus' earthly life, specifically in his actions and words, that the revelation of the heavenly mystery of God's salvation takes place. The revelation is not mediated through a heavenly ascent or a vision in which a human seer attempts to view the heavenly mysteries. Ashton states: 'Thus the fundamental paradox consists in the identification of a man, Jesus, with a heavenly being whose message has nothing to do with the things of earth. The form is apocalyptic but…the destiny of Jesus is the reverse of an apocalypse. This, not some esoteric mystery disclosed to a seer or dreamer, is the true revelation.'[59] As I understand it,

---

57 Collins, *Apocalyptic Imagination*, p.83; Rowland, *Open Heaven*, pp.51–2.

58 The earthly location of apocalyptic revelation is typical of historical apocalypses (including *2 Baruch, 4 Ezra, Jubilees,* Apocalypse of Weeks) in contrast to the obvious heavenly location of revelation as depicted in ascent apocalypses. Historical apocalypses are part of the genre of apocalypse, but they focus more on visions and do not contain heavenly ascents. See Collins, *Apocalyptic Imagination*, pp.6–7.

59 See Ashton, *Understanding*, p.529.

Ashton describes John's Gospel as 'an apocalypse in reverse' because Jesus' destiny ends in heaven and not as a seer returning to earth. Furthermore, Ashton sees the Gospel as a reversed apocalypse because 'the true revelation' is the heavenly revelation embodied on earth in the person of Jesus.

Essentially, Ashton seems to argue that the inverted pattern of descent–ascent (rather than ascent–descent), as well as the embodiment of the heavenly revelation in a human being, are the reasons why John's Gospel should be called an apocalypse 'in reverse, upside down, inside out'. However, if this is the case, we are again confronted with the reality that revelation occurring on earth does not mean that John is an apocalypse in reverse (cf. *Jubilees, 4 Ezra, 2 Baruch*, Daniel). Further, the embodiment of the revelation in the person of Jesus is not the inversion or reversal of an apocalypse. What we have in the Gospel of John is too much of an innovation to be called an 'apocalypse' or even 'an apocalypse in reverse'. The embodiment of the revelation of God in a human being is unlike anything encountered in the Jewish apocalypses, even in reverse.[60] The framework found in John's Gospel is not inverted but rather has been transformed on the inside. While Ashton has rightly noted the existence of a relationship between John's Gospel and the genre of 'apocalypse', to call the Gospel 'an apocalypse in reverse' seems to be an imprecise description of its relationship with the Jewish apocalypses.

John's Gospel fits the framework of an apocalypse in several key points of the definition of 'apocalypse',[61] but the differences between the Gospel and the Jewish apocalypses have more to do with the merging of characters and plot twists than with the overall plot.[62]

---

60 Although this is not directly connected to the revelation disclosed in heavenly ascents, some scholars have noted the apparent transformation of human seers into angels following their ascents: Levi's priesthood in the *Testament of Levi*, Enoch called 'that son of man' in *1 En.* 71, and Enoch becomes angelic in *2 En.* 22.9-10. See Himmelfarb, *Ascent to Heaven*, pp.37, 40, 45–6; Sullivan, *Wrestling with Angels*, pp.85–141.

61 See Ashton, *Understanding*, p.7.

62 As Jörg Frey suggested in response to the reading of the present study at the Bangor colloquium, the reason for these differences is likely due to Johannine Christology and not to some conscious or unconscious attempt by the author to distance the Gospel from the Jewish apocalypses.

6. The Gospel of John as 'Apocalyptic Gospel'

Although in some ways John's Gospel appears to fit within the definition of 'apocalypse', there are enough differences to prevent it from being classified in this way. At the same time, the Gospel's similarities with the genre of apocalypse indicate some sort of connection with it. For the lack of something more elegant than 'apocalypse in reverse', I suggest that John is better described as an 'apocalyptic Gospel'. This description may not be exciting or provocative, but it more precisely describes the relationship between the Jewish apocalypses and the Gospel of John.

John is, first and foremost, a Gospel. Although John is clearly different from Matthew, Mark and Luke, the four Gospels have more in common with each other than they do with most other literature.[63] Leaving aside the discussion concerning the origin of the gospel genre,[64] the Gospels do exhibit similarities with Graeco-Roman biography;[65] however, they also place great emphasis on proclamation, something that is generally absent from biography.[66] At its simplest, a gospel may be defined as a narrative about Jesus' life that proclaims the 'good news' of salvation that comes through faith in Jesus.[67] Robert Guelich thus concludes his important essay by stating: 'The Gospels are a literary genre whose form and content consist of, to use Mark's words, the "gospel of Jesus Messiah, Son of God"'.[68]

---

63   Ashton, *Understanding*, p.24, agrees with this. See also Robert Guelich, 'The Gospel Genre', in Peter Stuhlmacher (ed,), *The Gospel and the Gospels* (repr., Grand Rapids: Eerdmans, 1991; WUNT 28 [Tübingen: Mohr Siebeck, 1983]), pp.173–208. Craig S. Keener, *The Gospel of John: A Commentary* (2 vols.; Peabody, MA: Hendrickson, 2003), I, p.33, states: 'Whatever else may be said about the Fourth Gospel's genre, it must fall into the same broad category as the Synoptics'.

64   For this, see Lawrence M. Wills, *The Quest of the Historical Gospel: Mark, John and the Origins of the Gospel Genre* (London: Routledge, 1997).

65   Richard A. Burridge, *What Are the Gospels? A Comparison with Graeco-Roman Biography* (SNTSMS 70; Cambridge: Cambridge University Press, 1992); Keener, *Gospel*, pp.29–34. Cf. Ashton, *Understanding*, pp.24–7, who notes the parallels with *bioi* but questions whether *bioi* is a sufficient description of the Gospels' genre.

66   See Ashton, *Understanding*, p.355; Martin Hengel, *The Four Gospels and the One Gospel of Jesus Christ: An Investigation of the Collection and Origin of the Canonical Gospels* (trans. John Bowden; London: SCM, 2000), pp.141–57.

67   See Willem S. Vorster, 'Gospel, Genre of', *ABD*, II, pp.1077–9; Guelich, 'Gospel Genre', pp.206–7.

68   Guelich, 'The Gospel Genre', p.208. See his discussion on p.206 for how the four canonical Gospels relate to the non-canonical gospels.

The Gospel of John clearly fits the literary genre called 'gospel' in that it is a narrative about Jesus' life and proclaims the good news about him.[69] Of all the four Gospels, John has one of the clearest and strongest calls for belief in Jesus (20.30-31). John's proclamation, or shall we say, revelation of Jesus consists not only of Jesus' words but also his actions.[70]

Describing John's Gospel as an 'apocalyptic Gospel' is an attempt to underscore the framework, motifs, and themes that it shares with the Jewish apocalypses. In this sense, the definition of the adjective 'apocalyptic' in this essay is being aligned with the literary genre and with the content of apocalypses. Despite the popular usage of the word 'apocalyptic' and its inconsistent use in scholarly circles, this is the best way to define the term.[71] At the same time, not all items in apocalypses can or should be called 'apocalyptic'. This point is well made by Michael Stone in his essay 'Lists of Revealed Things', in which he documents the types of things that are revealed in apocalypses and how they are not necessarily of otherworldly character.[72] Unfortunately, this is a point which continually needs to be made, since, for example, in a recent essay the Greek letters *alpha* and *omega* were described as 'apocalyptic letters'.[73] The meaning of the adjective 'apocalyptic' should be anchored to the genre of 'apocalypse', not to any one specific apocalypse.

As a Gospel, John is a narrative about Jesus that proclaims the good news of salvation that comes through him. As an apocalyptic Gospel, John's narrative fits the framework of an apocalypse and makes use of numerous themes found in Jewish apocalypses. The Gospel of John does

---

69   Again, it should be kept in mind that definitions of 'genre', as with 'apocalyptic', are scholarly constructs; however, at the same time, defining our terms is useful and I would argue necessary for any meaningful discussion.

70   See Ashton, *Understanding*, p.529. Cf. Bultmann, *Theology*, II, pp.65–8; Gail R. O'Day, *Revelation in the Fourth Gospel: Narrative Mode and Theological Claim* (Philadelphia: Fortress, 1986), especially p.94.

71   Klaus Koch, *The Rediscovery of Apocalyptic* (Studies in Biblical Theology 22; London: SCM, 1972), p.35; John J. Collins, 'Genre, Ideology and Social Movements in Jewish Apocalypticism', in *Seers, Sibyls and Sages in Hellenistic-Roman Judaism* (Leiden: Brill, 2001), pp.25–38 (27). See also Michael E. Stone, 'Apocalyptic Literature', in Michael E. Stone (ed.), *Jewish Writings of the Second Temple Period* (CRINT 2.2; Philadelphia: Fortress, 1984), pp.383–441.

72   Stone, 'Lists of Revealed Things', especially pp.435–9. Also Rowland, *Open Heaven*, p.37.

73   John Herrmann and Annewies van den Hoek, 'Apocalyptic Themes in the Monumental and Minor Art of Early Christianity', in Robert J. Daly (ed.), *Apocalyptic Thought in Early Christianity* (Grand Rapids: Baker Academic, 2009), pp.33–80 (36 and 44).

not merely proclaim the good news of Jesus; it reveals the Father and the way to him through an otherworldly figure who has descended to earth to make the Father known. The heavens have opened in order for this revelation to take place. Human witnesses have seen this revelation and have testified to it.

7. Conclusion

The Gospel of John reveals obvious links with the genre of 'apocalypse'. An otherworldly figure descends and discloses heavenly secrets to human recipients. These heavenly things involve the salvation of humanity and unveil information about the relationship between heaven and earth, and, more particularly, about God and the righteous.

Although the Gospel shares this affinity with Jewish apocalypses and appears to fit the definition of 'apocalypse', John is not an apocalypse. The Gospel of John's otherworldly figure is merged with other apocalyptic characters. Jesus is not only a mediator, but also the content and centre of the revelation that he brings. Jesus is also more than a mediator in that he is glorified; he is the Son of Man with authority to judge, and, most significantly, he is one with God. In another twist in the apocalyptic plot, Jesus the otherworldly mediator has become a human being who, as a human, lives, dies, is buried, and raised. Moreover, in John's Gospel the revelation is mediated to multiple human recipients. These differences highlight the transformation of the central plot typical of an apocalypse in such a way that the Gospel no longer fits the genre of apocalypse.

Despite the differences between the Gospel of John and the Jewish apocalypses, they are somehow related. Referring to John as an 'apocalypse in reverse' – even when used as a rhetorical turn of phrase – is, I think, misleading, in that this description does not take into account those Jewish apocalypses that depict otherworldly figures descending to earth, that speak of revelation being given on earth, or that portray human recipients who do not leave earth nor who have visions of God. The subtle but significant differences between John's Gospel and the Jewish apocalypses keep the Gospel from being declared a full-fledged apocalypse. Rather, John is first a Gospel, but an apocalyptic Gospel in whose narrative framework of an apocalypse can be detected. John's Gospel is not so much an apocalypse reversed, inside out, upside down, but an apocalypse that is shaken, stirred, and inserted into a Gospel.

To call the Gospel of John an 'apocalyptic Gospel' may not be elegant, but I contend that it offers a more precise description of its revelatory portrayal of the life, work, and passion of Jesus set, as it is, within an apocalyptic framework.

From the Apocalypse of John to the Johannine 'Apocalypse in Reverse': Intimations of Apocalyptic and the Quest for a Relationship

Ian Boxall

1. Introduction

In his Foreword to the second edition of *Understanding the Fourth Gospel*, Christopher Rowland poses the following challenge: 'once one has found the apocalyptic key to the Gospel of John, there is the crucial Johannine question about the relationship to the *revelatory* text in the New Testament, the Apocalypse'.[1] Rowland is quite aware that the two are very different texts: 'The gospel is a book of witness to the unique and definitive emissary from the world above, whereas the Apocalypse is a book of prophecy'. Yet, having identified 'intimations of apocalyptic' in that apparently most un-apocalyptic of New Testament books, the old question of its relationship with the book of Revelation emerges once again. What, if anything, is the relationship between our John ('the evangelist') and the shadowy figure whom John Ashton calls 'the other John' (the seer of Patmos)?

As previous attempts to address this question reveal, the types of possible relationship are diverse. Many have undertaken, with varying degrees of sophistication, to describe the similarities and differences in style, grammar and subject-matter between the two New Testament writings, and I will touch on the details only briefly here.[2] For a minority,

---

1 Christopher Rowland, 'Foreword', in John Ashton, *Understanding the Fourth Gospel* (Oxford: Oxford University Press, 2nd edn, 2007), p.viii.
2 See, e.g., Henry B. Swete, *The Apocalypse of St John* (London: Macmillan, 1906), pp.clxxviii–clxxxi; R. H. Charles, *A Critical and Exegetical Commentary on the Revelation of St John* (ICC; 2 vols.; Edinburgh: T. & T. Clark, 1920), I, pp.xxix–l, cxvii–clix; Pierre Prigent, *Commentary on the Apocalypse of St. John* (trans. Wendy Pradels; Tübingen: Mohr Siebeck, 2004), pp.36–50.

their common features have been sufficient to urge a revival of the traditional view that the Fourth Gospel and the Apocalypse share a common author,[3] a position already queried in the third century by Bishop Dionysius of Alexandria. (The arguments about authorship have been well-rehearsed in critical commentaries on the Apocalypse.) Others have attempted a *via media* between common authorship and no relationship, whether C. K. Barrett's hypothesis of a Johannine school (in which the evangelist, the presbyter of the epistles, and the final editor of the Apocalypse were all pupils of John, the apostle and apocalyptic visionary), or Oscar Cullmann's looser Johannine 'circle', or Raymond Brown's distinctive Johannine community.[4] Still others have resorted to a more general explanation of dependence on common traditions; Otto Böcher, for example, considers the possibility of shared origins in a Judaeo-Christian *prophetisch-apokalyptisch* movement which had emigrated to Asia Minor from Palestine.[5] Again, I do not propose to discuss the merits and weaknesses of these hypotheses in detail,[6] nor set out a detailed rival reconstruction of my own.

The aim of the present study is rather more modest: to explore whether the quest for a relationship between the Apocalypse of John and the Johannine 'apocalypse in reverse' remains a fruitful one, and what kinds of questions we should be asking if we decide it does, particularly in the light of John Ashton's recent work. It will involve a brief examination of the similarities and differences between these two Johannine writings, a consideration of some strands in the reception history of the two texts

---

3 E.g. Grant R. Osborne, *Revelation* (Baker Exegetical Commentary on the New Testament; Grand Rapids: Baker Academic, 2002), pp.2–6.

4 E.g. C. K. Barrett, *The Gospel According to St John* (London: SPCK, 2nd edn, 1978), pp.61–2, 133–4; Oscar Cullmann, *The Johannine Circle* (New Testament Library; London: SCM, 1976); Raymond E. Brown, *The Community of the Beloved Disciple* (London: Geoffrey Chapman, 1979). Culpepper traces the roots of the Johannine 'school' hypothesis to David Friedrich Strauss and Ernest Renan (R. Alan Culpepper, 'Guessing Points and Knowing Stars: History and Higher Criticism in Robert Browning's "A Death in the Desert"', in Abraham J. Malherbe and Wayne A. Meeks [eds.], *The Future of Christology: Essays in Honor of Leander E. Keck* [Minneapolis: Fortress, 1993], pp.53–65 [58]).

5 Otto Böcher, 'Johanneisches in der Apokalypse des Johannes', *NTS* 27 (1980–1981), pp.310–21 (319).

6 For a positive assessment of the Johannine 'school' hypothesis, drawing upon comparative analysis of recognised schools in the ancient world, see R. Alan Culpepper, *The Johannine School: An Evaluation of the Johannine-School Hypothesis Based on an Investigation of the Nature of Ancient Schools* (SBLDS 26; Missoula: Scholars Press, 1975).

which arguably have a bearing on a solution to this question, and a particular proposal about where the closest point of contact between the Gospel and Revelation might be located.

2. Intimations of Apocalyptic

But I begin with John Ashton's *Understanding the Fourth Gospel*, and particularly the section entitled 'Intimations of Apocalyptic'. For at least in modern critical scholarship, the supposed 'non-apocalyptic' character of the Gospel has often been a major reason for drawing a wedge between it and the book of Revelation, especially when 'apocalyptic' has been straightforwardly identified with a particular form of future eschatology rather than the revelation of heavenly mysteries.[7] If one rather stresses, as does Ashton, four intimations of apocalyptic – the two ages, the two stages, insiders and outsiders, correspondence – within the Fourth Gospel, then the poles may not appear so far apart. Although very different in form, such that the seer of Patmos is caught up into heaven to receive the revelation, the Apocalypse too can be seen to utilise the two ages motif in a manner not dissimilar to the Gospel of John: the mystery hidden in the life of Jesus (or in his life and death, alluded to in symbolic language throughout: e.g. Rev 1.1, 5, 7, 18; 2.8; 5.5-6, 9, 12; 11.8; 12.5, 11; 13.8; 22.16; possibly also 6.2 and 19.13)[8] has subsequently been explained with terrifying clarity to a privileged follower decades after the event. Alternatively, one might stress the role of John of Patmos as a kind of 'Teacher of Righteousness', penetrating into the mysteries of his prophetic predecessors Ezekiel and Daniel now unambiguously opened up for the last days.[9]

There is an interesting footnote to this juxtaposition in an early medieval commentary on the book of Revelation (albeit connected with a

---

7   Ashton, *Understanding* (2nd edn), p.308.

8   The first horseman at Rev 6.2 has often been understood since earliest times as a visionary description of Christ's proclamation of the gospel (cf., e.g., Matt 4.17). The 'blood' on the garment of the Divine Warrior at 19.13 could be interpreted as Christ's own blood, shed on the cross. The echoes of Christ's life and death are increased if we understand the phrase μαρτυρία 'Ιησοῦ as a subjective genitive, referring to the testimony which Jesus himself bore.

9   For the suggestion that John's relationship to his community is akin to that between the Teacher of Righteousness and the community of Qumran, see David Hill, 'Prophecy and Prophets in the Revelation of St John', *NTS* 18 (1971–72), pp.401–18 (415).

belief in the common authorship of all the Johannine writings), which found its way into Western medieval hagiography, liturgy and devotion. According to this line of interpretation, which also overlaps to some extent with the apocalyptic 'two stages', there was an intimate connection established between what John 'saw' while resting on the Lord's breast at the Last Supper, and the 'opening of the heavens' on the island of Patmos. In other words, the heavenly mysteries revealed to John on Patmos came to be understood as an outworking, an intensification of the divine insight granted to the Beloved Disciple already at the supper, and later expounded in different form in his Gospel.[10]

Nor is Revelation without the apocalyptic two stages, although, when compared to apocalypses such as Daniel and *4 Ezra*, the explicit elucidation of shadowy visions is confined to a minimum (e.g. Rev 1.20; 13.18; 17.7-18), as is the role of the *angelus interpres* (10.1; 11.1; 17.1; 19.9; 21.9; cf. the role of one of the 24 elders at 5.5; 7.13-17). The insider/outsider division is maintained in Revelation's distinction between the followers of the Lamb and the Beast respectively, even if, on the one hand, the revelation is theoretically open to all rather than sealed up to remain the preserve of the 'wise', and, on the other, there is a certain blurring of the boundaries within the seven churches themselves (e.g. 2.2, 14, 20; 3.1, 15). Finally, if we are looking for correspondence, the book of Revelation has it aplenty. John's privileged vantage point provided by access into the heavenly throne-room (4.1), and the heavenly visions seen there, offer him a unique lens through which to interpret the realm below.

One might object, of course, that these are precisely the features one would expect to find in two works inspired by the same apocalyptic tradition. At the very least, however, it does begin to answer the claims of some scholars that Revelation itself has been mis-catalogued as an 'apocalypse',[11] bringing the two books closer together in the process. But are there clearer indications that the two texts are tapping into this tradition in ways sufficiently similar to justify talk of a 'relationship'?

---

10 On this see, e.g., Jeffrey F. Hamburger, *St John the Divine: The Deified Evangelist in Medieval Art and Theology* (Berkeley: University of California Press, 2002), p.131; Annette Volfing, *John the Evangelist and Medieval German Writing: Imitating the Inimitable* (Oxford: Oxford University Press, 2001), p.74.

11 E.g. Jürgen Roloff, *Revelation* (A Continental Commentary; Minneapolis: Fortress, 1993), pp.5–7.

3. Two Johannine Texts?

To begin to lay the groundwork, we now turn to another immediate objection, which springs from the ambiguity of the internal evidence of the Apocalypse and the Gospel. A brief survey of recent scholarship might lead us to doubt whether this quest for a relationship between the two is in fact a worthwhile enterprise. After all, Richard Bauckham's important collection of essays on the Apocalypse, *The Climax of Prophecy*, contains just nine references to the text of John's Gospel, in a volume of over 500 pages.[12] From the side of Fourth Gospel studies, a recent collection of papers on the Gospel of John, from a conference in memory of Raymond Brown, contains only four references to the book of Revelation (and these not in the main text but found in one single footnote).[13] This concurs with the view of the later Brown himself. In his posthumously published revised introduction to the Fourth Gospel, Brown no longer believed, as he had in the original edition of his commentary, that Revelation should be brought into play in consideration of Johannine theology.[14] Finally, we have John Ashton's own assessment in *Understanding the Fourth Gospel*: 'According to tradition the book of Revelation shares a common author with the Fourth Gospel: the apostle John. But in language, form, style, and content the two works are utterly different.'[15]

Moreover, as for the kinds of explanation that presuppose a Johannine community or circle, have not these been effectively demolished by another book edited by Bauckham, the 1998 collection *The Gospels for All Christians*?[16] Suffice it to say here that, however important a corrective the Bauckham volume has been, it has been met with some pretty robust criticisms, and for many the hypothesis of a 'Community of the

---

12 Richard Bauckham, *The Climax of Prophecy: Studies on the Book of Revelation* (Edinburgh: T. & T. Clark, 1993), p.505.

13 John R. Donahue (ed.), *Life in Abundance: Studies of John's Gospel in Tribute to Raymond E. Brown* (Collegeville: Liturgical, 2005), p.132 n.53. These are all references to 'living water': Rev 7.17; 21.6; 22.1, 17.

14 Raymond E. Brown, *An Introduction to the Gospel of John* (ed. Francis J. Moloney; New York: Doubleday, 2003), p.225 n.19.

15 Ashton, *Understanding* (2nd edn), p.307.

16 Richard Bauckham (ed.), *The Gospels for All Christians: Rethinking the Gospel Audiences* (Edinburgh: T. & T. Clark, 1998). See, however, the responses of Philip F. Esler, 'Community and Gospel in Early Christianity: A Response to Richard Bauckham's *Gospels for All Christians*', *SJT* 51 (1998), pp.235–48; David C. Sim, 'The Gospels for All Christians? A Response to Richard Bauckham', *JSNT* 84 (2001), pp.3–27.

Beloved Disciple' (to adopt Raymond Brown's phrase) continues to have life in it.

But what can be said in response to Ashton's claim that 'in language, form, style, and content' the Fourth Gospel and the book of Revelation are 'utterly different'? On the one hand, there are indeed striking differences in style, grammar and syntax (including the tell-tale use of particles, conjunctions and adverbs), and in vocabulary. This has been significantly reinforced by the stylometric analysis carried out by Anthony Kenny, which provides fairly conclusive evidence against common authorship.[17]

As for the differences in vocabulary, Elisabeth Schüssler Fiorenza's famous 1976 article on the Quest for the Johannine School[18] follows H. B. Swete in its observation that there are just eight words that are shared only by the Apocalypse and the Fourth Gospel in the New Testament.[19] By contrast, she notes, Revelation shares 43 words with Paul, and almost the same number with Luke.

Schüssler Fiorenza's article is a good example, however, not only of how ambiguous the evidence actually is, but even more of how certain kinds of statistical analysis can be highly misleading. First, the letters of Paul comprise a much larger body of comparative evidence than the Fourth Gospel (61 chapters in the undisputed Paulines alone). Secondly, Schüssler Fiorenza's conclusion overlooks words and themes found also in other parts of the New Testament which are used both by the Gospel and Revelation (Swete himself notes that of the 913 words used in the Apocalypse, 416 are also found in the Gospel),[20] as well as the frequency of their occurrence.

---

17 Anthony Kenny, *A Stylometric Study of the New Testament* (Oxford: Clarendon, 1986), pp.76–9.

18 Elisabeth Schüssler Fiorenza, 'The Quest for the Johannine School: The Book of Revelation and The Fourth Gospel', in her *The Book of Revelation: Justice and Judgment* (Minneapolis: Fortress, 2nd edn, 1998), pp.85–113. Schüssler Fiorenza summarises previous attempts to retain the Johannine connection: (1) difference of genre; (2) chronological development; (3) complementary theologies; (4) the secretary hypothesis. She goes on to describe how (4) has developed into the theory of a 'Johannine school' or 'circle'.

19 ἀρνίον, Ἑβραϊστί, ἐκκεντεῖν, κυκλεύειν (in FG [John 10.24], found only in B), ὄψις, πορφυροῦς, σκηνοῦν, φοῖνιξ (Swete, *Apocalypse*, p.cxxii). Frey has δέκατος (Rev 21.20; John 1.39; cf. Rev 11.3) instead of κυκλεύειν (Jörg Frey, 'Erwägungen zum Verhältnis der Johannesapokalypse zu den übrigen Schriften des Corpus Johanneum', in Martin Hengel [ed.], *Die johanneische Frage: Ein Lösungsversuch, mit einem Beitrag zur Apokalypse von Jörg Frey* [WUNT 67; Tübingen: Mohr Siebeck, 1993], pp.326–429 [341]).

20 Swete, *Apocalypse*, p.cxxii.

Indeed (as Jörg Frey and Pierre Prigent among others have reminded us),[21] despite the differences, some of these common features are quite striking and theologically significant, and should not be underplayed by overconcentration on differences of language or the ambiguity of statistical analysis. Indeed, Prigent helpfully separates off theological similarities from the more problematic issues of language in order to bring some clarity to the debate. Shared terminology includes: λόγος as a Christological term; bride/bridegroom imagery; the attribution to Jesus of 'I am' sayings; the phrase 'water of life' or 'living water'; the regular use of words to do with life (ζωή), witness/testimony (μαρτ- root), conquering (νικᾶν), and keeping (τηρεῖν).[22] Now is not the time for a systematic review of the complex evidence of vocabulary, style and theological perspective which has led scholars to very different conclusions over this question.[23] We shall, however, come back to a particular group of common features in due course.

4. Strands from Revelation's Reception History

For now, however, I want to pick up on another invitation posed by Christopher Rowland in his Foreword to the second edition of Ashton's *Understanding*: to explore the potential of *Wirkungsgeschichte* for illuminating the text. Although Rowland has in mind also the wider 'effective history' of John in art and music as well as literary texts, the two strands I want to mention briefly are literary, and relate to the history of the reception of the Apocalypse rather than of the Gospel.

The first comes from that most famous dissenter from the patristic consensus of a single author for Revelation and John's Gospel. Most critical commentaries on the Apocalypse make reference to Dionysius of Alexandria's challenge to Johannine authorship of the book as early as the third century.[24] Although not denying the canonical status of

---

21 Frey, 'Erwägungen', pp.341–6; Prigent, *Apocalypse*, pp.36–50. See also Otto Böcher, 'Das Verhältnis der Apokalypse des Johannes zum Evangelium des Johannes', in J. Lambrecht (ed.), *L'Apocalypse johannique et l'Apocalyptique dans le Nouveau Testament* (BETL 53; Gembloux: J. Duculot/Leuven: Leuven University Press, 1980), pp.289–301.

22 Prigent, *Apocalypse*, pp.41–50. For a more substantial list of common features, see Böcher, 'Verhältnis', pp.295–301.

23 For a good discussion, see Swete, *Apocalypse*, pp.cxxi–cxxv, clxxix–clxxxi.

24 See also Dimitris Kyrtatas, 'The Transformations of the Text: The Reception of John's Revelation', in Averil Cameron (ed.), *History as Text: The Writing of Ancient History* (London: Duckworth, 1989), pp.154–5.

Revelation – 'it is', he wrote, 'the work of a holy and inspired man' (ἁγίου ... καὶ θεοπνεύστου, Eusebius, *Hist. eccl.* 7.25.7)[25] – Dionysius was one of the first to draw a wedge between the Fourth Gospel and 1 John on the one hand, and Revelation on the other, initially one suspects on exegetical grounds (his opposition to the literal millennialism of his fellow Egyptian Nepos). The reasons he gives include stylistic and linguistic differences (he accuses John of Patmos of using 'barbarous idioms' and 'solecisms'), and differences of vocabulary:

> But the Apocalypse is different from these writings and foreign to them; not touching, nor in the least bordering upon them; almost, so to speak, without even a syllable in common with them (ἀλλοιοτάτη δὲ καὶ ξένη παρὰ ταῦτα ἡ 'Αποκάλυψις, μήτε ἐφαπτομένη μήτε γειτνιῶσα τούτων μηδενί, σχεδόν, ὡς εἰπεῖν, μηδὲ συλλαβὴν πρὸς αὐτὰ κοινὴν ἔχουσα, *Hist. eccl.* 7.25.22).

Dionysius' last comment is in fact a gross exaggeration, as the above discussion makes clear, even though his general conclusions are cited approvingly by scholars.

What is sometimes overlooked by such scholars (and this is my first reception-historical point) is the fact that Dionysius nevertheless seems to want to *retain* a definite link between the two texts. He posits, first of all, a familial relationship between the fourth evangelist (whom he took to be the apostle John) and the 'other John' who wrote Revelation:

> But I am of the opinion that there were many with the same name as the apostle John, who, on account of their love for him (οἳ διὰ τὴν πρὸς ἐκεῖνον ἀγάπην), and because they admired and emulated him, and desired to be loved by the Lord as he was, took to themselves the same surname (καὶ τὴν ἐπωνυμίαν τὴν αὐτὴν ἠσπάσαντο), as many of the children of the faithful are called Paul or Peter (*Hist. eccl.* 7.25.14).

One such person may have been John Mark of Jerusalem; the other, Dionysius speculates, was John the author of Revelation. Secondly, he utilises the tradition of the two μνήματα of John in Ephesus to distinguish between the two authors:[26] 'But I think that he was some other one

---

25 Gustave Bardy (ed.), *Eusèbe de Césarée, Histoire ecclésiastique: Livres V–VII. Texte grec, Traduction et Notes* (Sources Chrétiennes 41; Paris: Les Éditions du Cerf, 1955), pp.206–7 (English translation from *NPNF*²).

26 Eusebius also made use of this tradition, which he merged with a passage from Papias, in order to argue, as Dionysius does here, for two individuals called John (*Hist. eccl.* 3.39.1-7).

of those in Asia; as they say that there are two monuments in Ephesus, each bearing the name of John' (*Hist. eccl.* 7.25.16). The historical value of this tradition is not important. What is striking is that Dionysius, who was intent on smashing apart the well-established tradition of common authorship, should nevertheless want to maintain not only geographical proximity between the two authors (an Ephesus connection), but also a degree of personal admiration and familial attachment of one for the other. He can hardly be adduced, as he often is, as a supporter of *no* relationship.

Though he is not explicit, Dionysius could be read as implying that Revelation is later than the Gospel, written by a disciple emulating the work of his mentor. My second reception-historical point, however, is that when the respective order of the two books is discussed by patristic authors, one often finds the reverse chronological sequence, especially by those who hold to a single author. The Apocalypse was written first, and then the Gospel as the pinnacle of the Johannine output, and, by implication, the more mature reflection. Hippolytus, for example,[27] writes that John first composed the Apocalypse on Patmos, and then the Gospel on his return to Asia. Hippolytus is commenting here on Rev 10.11, where John is told by the mighty angel that he must 'prophesy again about many peoples and nations, languages and kings'. The prophecy, he claims, is none other than the Fourth Gospel itself, uttered to the people of Asia and then written in a book. This is a fascinating claim in itself, for it apparently identifies the Fourth Gospel with the heavenly scroll that John devours at this point.

Similarly, Epiphanius, a fourth-century bishop of Salamis, has John receiving the Apocalypse on Patmos (surprisingly, in the very early reign of the emperor Claudius), before writing his Gospel many years later when over the age of ninety (*Pan.* 51.12.2, 33.9). The same order is found in two early Gospel Prologues, both of which were popularised by their regular inclusion in Latin manuscripts of the Gospels:

> postmodum Iohannes apostolus descripsit primum revelationem in insula Pathmos, deinde evangelium in Asia (*'Anti-Marcionite Prologue' to Luke*).[28]

---

27   As reconstructed from the twelfth-century commentary of Dionysius bar Salibi: Pierre Prigent, 'Hippolyte, commentateur de l'Apocalypse', *TZ* 28 (1972), pp.391–412; Pierre Prigent and Ralph Stehly, 'Les fragments du *De Apocalypsi* d'Hippolyte', *TZ* 29 (1973), pp.313–33.

28   *Der Lukasprolog* I, lines 19-20: Jürgen Regul, *Die antimarcionitischen Evangelienprologe* (Vetus Latina 6; Freiburg: Verlag Herder, 1969), pp.30–1.

hoc autem evangelium scripsit in Asia, posteaquam in Pathmos insula apocalypsin scripserat, ut, cui in principio canonis incorruptibile principium in genesi, et incorruptibilis finis per virginem in apocalypsi redderetur, dicente Christo: Ego sum α et ω (*Monarchian Prologue to John*, attributed to Priscillian, d. 386).[29]

I mention this tendency to place Revelation early in the Johannine trajectory because it represents an early hunch about chronological order, which concurs with a tendency among a number of contemporary scholars, who arrive at it via quite different routes, and without presupposing common authorship.[30] Does placing Revelation early in the Johannine trajectory prove to be a better way of explaining both the similarities and the differences? To give just one example, does it help explain Revelation's polemical language of the 'synagogue of Satan' (Rev 2.9; 3.9) spoken by an author still wanting to retain for himself the title Ἰουδαῖος? Here we have not the full-blooded Johannine use of Ἰουδαῖοι ('Jews' retains its positive sense), although signs of an irreconcilable fissure are beginning to break out, and persecution instigated by the synagogue appears to be a genuine threat.

5. Six Examples

It is time now to return to the text of the Apocalypse, and to its similarities with the Fourth Gospel. There are a number of places where remarkable verbal echoes come to the surface, challenging the assertion of Dionysius of Alexandria that Revelation almost lacks 'even a syllable' in common with the Gospel and 1 John. To illustrate the point, I want to focus on six pairs of verses (in each pair one from the Apocalypse and one from the Gospel), where commentators have noted such similarities.[31] Some of these are more in terms of grammatical structure than

---

29 Regul, *Die antimarcionitischen Evangelienprologe*, p.43.

30 R. H. Charles concludes, in his 1919 Schweich Lectures on the Apocalypse: 'John [the Seer] was clearly connected in some way with the author of the Gospel and Epistles. Either these two Johns belonged to the same religious circle in Ephesus, or more probably the author of the Gospel and Epistles was in some manner a pupil of John the Seer, though master and pupil took very different directions, as is not unusual in such cases' (R. H. Charles, *Lectures on the Apocalypse* [The Schweich Lectures 1919; London: Humphrey Milford, Oxford University Press, for the British Academy, 1923], pp.72–3).

31 For most of these, see Ben Witherington III, *Revelation* (New Cambridge Bible Commentary; Cambridge: Cambridge University Press, 2003), p.3.

vocabulary, some a combination of both. While not all by themselves may convince, they are often striking for their peculiarities, and I hope a cumulative case will begin to emerge.

1. The first example is the unusual juxtaposition of the verb δύναμαι with βαστάζειν, which occurs only twice in the New Testament (Rev 2.2 and John 16.12):

οἶδα τὰ ἔργα σου καὶ τὸν κόπον σου καὶ τὴν ὑπομονήν σου, καὶ ὅτι **οὐ δύνῃ βαστάσαι** κακούς, καὶ ἐπείρασας τοὺς λέγοντας ἑαυτοὺς ἀποστόλους εἶναι καὶ οὐκ εἰσὶν καὶ εὗρες αὐτοὺς ψευδεῖς.

I know your works: your labour and your steadfastness; and that **you cannot bear** evil people, but have tested those who call themselves 'apostles' – but are not – and have found them to be liars (Rev 2.2).

Ἔτι πολλὰ ἔχω λέγειν ὑμῖν, ἀλλ' **οὐ δύνασθε βαστάζειν** ἄρτι.

I still have many things to say to you, but **you cannot bear** them now (John 16.12).

Admittedly, in the two passages the phrase has slightly different connotations: in Revelation it refers to an inability of Ephesian Christians, or rather their angel, to tolerate evil people (a good thing), whereas in the Gospel it describes the inability of the disciples to bear or receive the unveiling of riddles until the Spirit comes (a temporary deficiency). Nevertheless, the grammatical sense of the phrase is the same in both texts.

2. Both John and Revelation share the language of 'receiving from my Father' (λαμβάνω παρὰ τοῦ πατρός μου), tapping into a common Christological motif. At Rev 2.27-28 it is used of the Son of Man's authority to rule or shepherd with an iron sceptre, which he shares with 'the one who conquers'. In John 10.18 it refers to Christ's authority to lay down his life and take it up again, received as a command from the Father. In this second passage, like its parallel in the Apocalypse, shepherding also provides the wider context, for it comes in the middle of the Good Shepherd discourse. This picks up on a theme common to both, the identification of Christ the Shepherd as the Lamb (Rev 7.17; John 1.29, 36):[32]

---

32 Cf. John 19.14, 31, where the death of the paschal lamb provides the interpretative key to the passion of Christ. Schüssler Fiorenza claims that the fact that Rev 2.27-28 is dependent for its vocabulary on Ps 2 (cf. Isa 40.11; *Pss. Sol.*

καὶ ποιμανεῖ αὐτοὺς ἐν ῥάβδῳ σιδηρᾷ ὡς τὰ σκεύη τὰ κεραμικὰ συντρίβεται, ὡς κἀγὼ **εἴληφα παρὰ τοῦ πατρός μου**, καὶ δώσω αὐτῷ τὸν ἀστέρα τὸν πρωϊνόν.

He will shepherd them with an iron rod, as clay vessels are shattered, as **I also have received from my Father**; and I will give him the bright morning-star (Rev 2.27-28).

οὐδεὶς αἴρει αὐτὴν ἀπ' ἐμοῦ, ἀλλ' ἐγὼ τίθημι αὐτὴν ἀπ' ἐμαυτοῦ· ἐξουσίαν ἔχω θεῖναι αὐτήν, καὶ ἐξουσίαν ἔχω πάλιν λαβεῖν αὐτήν· ταύτην τὴν ἐντολὴν **ἔλαβον παρὰ τοῦ πατρός μου**.

No one takes it from me, but I lay in down of my own will. I have authority to lay it down, and I have authority to take it up again; this commandment **I have received from my Father** (John 10.18).

3. The next pairing utilises the verb τηρεῖν with the preposition ἐκ to describe divine protection from a threat (Rev 3.10; John 17.15). Not only is the verb a favourite one for the Johannine corpus,[33] these two verses represent the only two occurrences of the phase τηρεῖν ἐκ in the New Testament:

ὅτι ἐτήρησας τὸν λόγον τῆς ὑπομονῆς μου, κἀγώ **σε τηρήσω ἐκ** τῆς ὥρας τοῦ πειρασμοῦ τῆς μελλούσης ἔρχεσθαι ἐπὶ τῆς οἰκουμένης ὅλης πειράσαι τοὺς κατοικοῦντας ἐπὶ τῆς γῆς.

Because you have kept the word of my steadfastness, I also will **keep you from** the hour of testing which is about to come upon the whole inhabited world, to test those who make their home on the earth (Rev 3.10).

οὐκ ἐρωτῶ ἵνα ἄρῃς αὐτοὺς ἐκ τοῦ κόσμου, ἀλλ' ἵνα **τηρήσῃς αὐτοὺς ἐκ** τοῦ πονηροῦ.

I do not pray that you remove them from the world, but that you **keep them from** the Evil One (John 17.15).

4. A fourth example is the use of the phrase ἔχειν μέρος, not simply meaning 'to have a share' or 'portion', but in the specific sense of sharing in eschatological salvation. In Rev 20.6 it comes in the context of

---

17.40-43) means that the metaphor of shepherding is quite different from that in the Gospel (Schüssler Fiorenza, 'Quest', p.99). This is not so clear, however. On the Shepherd/Lamb juxtaposition in Revelation and John, see Frey, 'Erwägungen', pp.390–2.

33   Of the 70 New Testament occurrences of the verb, 18 appear in the Fourth Gospel, seven in 1 John and eleven in the Apocalypse (Prigent, *Commentary*, p.40 n.170).

a beatitude, blessing the one who participates in the first resurrection, that is, in the millennial reign of the martyrs. In John 13.8 it describes the 'part' in Christ offered to Peter if he allows Jesus to wash his feet, a passage with strong baptismal echoes:

μακάριος καὶ ἅγιος **ὁ ἔχων μέρος** ἐν τῇ ἀναστάσει τῇ πρώτῃ· ἐπὶ τούτων ὁ δεύτερος θάνατος οὐκ ἔχει ἐξουσίαν, ἀλλ' ἔσονται ἱερεῖς τοῦ Θεοῦ καὶ τοῦ Χριστοῦ καὶ βασιλεύσουσιν μετ' αὐτοῦ χίλια ἔτη.

Blessed and happy is the one who **has a share** in the first resurrection; over such people the second death has no authority; but they will be priests for God and the Christ and they will reign with him for a thousand years (Rev 20.6).

λέγει αὐτῷ Πέτρος· οὐ μὴ νίψῃς τοὺς πόδας μου εἰς τὸν αἰῶνα. ἀπεκρίθη αὐτῷ ὁ Ἰησοῦς· ἐὰν μὴ νίψω σε, οὐκ **ἔχεις μέρος** μετ' ἐμοῦ.

Peter said to him, 'You will never wash my feet'. Jesus answered him, 'unless I wash them, you do not **have a share** with me' (John 13.8).

The only other New Testament passage where the phrase occurs is at Luke 11.36,[34] referring to a body which is full of light, having no share in darkness.

5. The Apocalypse and the Gospel both make use of an unusual Semitic phrase combining the verb 'to do' with an abstract noun, in this case either 'a lie' (Rev 22.15)[35] or 'the truth' (John 3.21, a phrase found elsewhere in the Johannine corpus at 1 John 1.6):

ἔξω οἱ κύνες καὶ οἱ φάρμακοι καὶ οἱ πόρνοι καὶ οἱ φονεῖς καὶ οἱ εἰδωλολάτραι καὶ **πᾶς ὁ φιλῶν καὶ ποιῶν ψεῦδος**.

Outside are the dogs, the sorcerers, the fornicators, the murderers and the idolaters, and everyone who loves and **practises a lie** (Rev 22.15).

ὁ δὲ **ποιῶν τὴν ἀλήθειαν** ἔρχεται πρὸς τὸ φῶς, ἵνα φανερωθῇ αὐτοῦ τὰ ἔργα ὅτι ἐν Θεῷ ἐστιν εἰργασμένα.

The one who **practises the truth** comes to the light, in order that it might be seen that his works have been done in God (John 3.21).

---

34 εἰ οὖν τὸ σῶμά σου ὅλον φωτεινόν, μὴ ἔχον μέρος τι σκοτεινόν, ἔσται φωτεινὸν ὅλον ὡς ὅταν ὁ λύχνος τῇ ἀστραπῇ φωτίζῃ σε.

35 David E. Aune, *Revelation 17–22* (WBC 52C; Nashville: Thomas Nelson, 1998), p.1224. Aune points to a parallel in the Greek version of *1 En.* 99.9: τὰ ψεύδη ἃ ἐποιήσατε.

6. Our final example is a shared invitation to the thirsty to come (ἐρχέσθω), and either to 'receive the water of life freely' (λαβέτω ὕδωρ ζωῆς δωρεάν, Rev 22.17), or 'to drink' (καὶ πινέτω, John 7.37):

Καὶ τὸ πνεῦμα καὶ ἡ νύμφη λέγουσιν· Ἔρχου. καὶ ὁ ἀκούων εἰπάτω· Ἔρχου. καὶ **ὁ διψῶν ἐρχέσθω**, ὁ θέλων **λαβέτω ὕδωρ ζωῆς** δωρεάν.

The Spirit and the Bride say, 'Come!' Let the one who hears say, 'Come!' **Let the one who drinks come**, let the one who wants to **receive the water of life** freely (Rev 22.17).

Ἐν δὲ τῇ ἐσχάτῃ ἡμέρᾳ τῇ μεγάλῃ τῆς ἑορτῆς εἱστήκει ὁ Ἰησοῦς καὶ ἔκραξεν λέγων· Ἐάν τις **διψᾷ ἐρχέσθω** πρός με **καὶ πινέτω**.

On the last day of the Feast, the great day, Jesus stood and cried out, '**If anyone thirsts, let him come** to me **and drink**' (John 7.37).

These parallel phrases also flag up another similar phrase, 'the water of life' or 'the spring of the water of life', in the Apocalypse (7.17; 21.6) which recalls the Johannine riddle ὕδωρ ζῶν, 'fresh water' or 'living water' (John 4.10, 13-14; 7.38, which John Ashton equates with 'revelation'),[36] and the related phrase 'spring of water' (John 4.14). In Revelation 22, although the Old Testament antecedent is Isa 55.1, with its threefold invitation to 'Come!', the vocabulary is much closer to that of John.[37]

6. The Voice of the Johannine Jesus?

The examples from the Gospel are all sayings of the Johannine Jesus, perhaps unsurprising given the space devoted to discourses and dialogues in the Gospel of John. In contrast to the rather talkative Christ of the Fourth Gospel, however, the Jesus of the book of Revelation is remarkably taciturn. The notable exception is chs. 2–3, where the 'one like a son of man' utters divine oracles, through the mouthpiece of his prophet John, to the angels of the seven churches. Elsewhere, the voice of the risen Lord breaks through only rarely.[38]

---

36 Ashton, *Understanding* (2nd edn), p.338.
37 Isaiah 55.1 reads (NRSV): 'Ho, everyone who thirsts, come to the waters; and you that have no money, come, buy and eat! Come, buy wine and milk, without money and without price'.
38 For example, in the repeated 'I am coming soon' (ἰδοὺ ἔρχομαι ταχύ) in Rev 22.6-21; or some of the 'I am' sayings which permeate the book (Rev 1.17; 22.13, 16).

This makes it all the more striking that, of the six passages just explored from the Apocalypse, three are plainly on the lips of the exalted Son of Man (Rev 2.2, 27-28; 3.10) in his message to the angels of the seven churches, that section of Revelation in which Jesus is at his most garrulous. The literary context of a fourth (22.15) makes it, at least by implication, also a saying of the risen Jesus, who has begun speaking in v. 12 and who is not interrupted by the Spirit and the Bride until v. 15.[39]

Of the remaining two sayings, one (Rev 22.17) comes in the context of a solemn liturgical dialogue, in which the final invitation to the thirsty to 'come' and take freely from the water of life could be spoken by Christ himself.[40] A similar phrase at Rev 21.6 – 'The one who is thirsty I will allow to drink without charge from the spring of the water of life' – is spoken by the one seated on the throne, and Jesus is certainly involved in the dialogue elsewhere in this chapter (22.20b). Finally, Rev 20.6 is one of the seven beatitudes found throughout the book (the others occurring at 1.3; 14.13; 16.15; 19.9; 22.7, 14). The speaker of these beatitudes, though ambiguous, seems to have a heavenly origin (the second beatitude at 14.13 is dictated to John by an unnamed heavenly voice). That Christ may be the speaker at 20.6 is not unlikely, given that two other beatitudes in Revelation are immediately preceded by words of Jesus: ἰδοὺ ἔρχομαι ὡς κλέπτης (Rev 16.15; cf. Matt 24.43; Luke 12.39; 1 Thess 5.2; 2 Pet 3.10; Rev 3.3); καὶ ἰδοὺ ἔρχομαι ταχύ (Rev 22.7).[41]

These findings can be combined with two further sets of evidence. First, there are Revelation's six distinctive 'I am' sayings, which represent another body of parallels with the discourses of John's Gospel.[42] Certainly there are differences from the 'I am' sayings of the Gospel, in content as well as in speaker. In Revelation, although four of these six

---

39 Ian Boxall, *The Revelation of St John* (Black's New Testament Commentaries: London: Continuum; Peabody, Mass.: Hendrickson, 2006), p.317.

40 Ugo Vanni places Rev 22.17e-20a on the lips of John as narrator ('Liturgical Dialogue as a Literary Form in the Book of Revelation', *NTS* 37 [1991], p.363). However, given that this narration is envisaged as taking place in a liturgical setting, the voice of 'John' has an authority on a par with the one on whose behalf he speaks, and is itself spoken by a 'lector' who also takes the roles of Christ and the angel.

41 The 'Johannine echo' at Rev 20.6 means that not all the examples can be attributed to David Aune's hypothetical second edition of Revelation, essentially involving the addition of Rev 1.1-6; 1.12b–3.22; 22.6-21 (David E. Aune, *Revelation 1–5* (WBC 52A; Dallas: Word, 1997), pp.cxx–cxxxiv).

42 On these, see Frey, 'Erwägungen', p.400.

are uttered by Christ (1.17; 2.23; 22.13, 16), the remaining two (1.8; 21.6) are spoken by 'the one seated on the throne'. Nevertheless, the shared phenomenon is striking.

Second, the wider context of Revelation's use of τηρεῖν (found in our third example above) is pertinent to the discussion. Particularly striking are the 'Johannine sounding' phrases within which John of Patmos uses this verb, such as 'keep my word' and 'keep my works', as well as the more theocentric 'keep the commandments of God'. Of the eleven occurrences of τηρεῖν in Revelation, five are spoken by Jesus in the messages to the seven churches (2.26; 3.3, 8, 10 [×2]), while another three are found within the beatitudes (1.3; 16.15; 22.7, the latter two immediately preceded by words of Jesus). Of the remainder, 12.17 is a narratorial comment about those who 'keep the commandments of God and hold the testimony of Jesus'; 14.12 is an interjection (apparently from heaven) issuing a call for the endurance for the saints, 'those who keep the commandments of God and hold fast to the faith of Jesus'; 22.9 is spoken by the interpreting angel.

In other words, some of the closest echoes of the Fourth Gospel in the Apocalypse are found on the lips of the exalted Jesus, and of other heavenly beings. Of course, what has been offered here is not an exhaustive study of the Johannine echoes in the Apocalypse. Nor does it take into account those other examples, admittedly not quite so numerous, of sayings in Revelation which echo Synoptic sayings of Jesus: the repeated 'Let the one who has an ear, listen...' in the messages to the seven churches (e.g. Rev 2.7; cf. Matt 13.9; Mark 4.23; Luke 14.35), or the interjection 'Look, I am coming like a thief!' at Rev 3.3 and 16.15 (cf. 1 Thess 5.2; Matt 24.43; Luke 12.39; 2 Pet 3.10).[43]

But it does raise a set of questions worthy of further exploration. In considering the question of a relationship between Revelation and John's Gospel, is it a fruitful avenue to pay particular attention to the sayings and auditions? In other words, to what extent does the Christ of the Apocalypse speak with the accents of the Johannine Jesus? Or, to pose the question differently, following the preferred order of some patristic authors, are there echoes of the Christ of Revelation in the words of Jesus in the Fourth Gospel? True, in appearance Revelation's Christ is very different. He comes with the full panoply of apocalyptic imagery, with hair dazzling white and eyes like flames of fire, or in the

---

43 See, e.g., Richard Bauckham, 'Synoptic Parousia Parables and the Apocalypse', *NTS* 23 (1976–77), pp.162–76.

guise of a terrifying victorious Lamb, or on a white horse with armies at his disposal. But the apocalyptic form of Revelation should not disguise the similarities of voice, any more than the choice of the gospel genre should obscure the Fourth Gospel's profound indebtedness to the apocalyptic tradition.

Two related questions also emerge. The first is one of origins: if there is indeed a relationship between the *logia* of Revelation and the Fourth Gospel, how are we to envisage it? Second, can we conclude anything from these parallel sayings about the chronological sequence of the two texts? I will develop these two questions in order.

First, regarding the question of the relationship between the sayings of the Johannine Jesus and 'Johannine accents' in the Apocalypse, it is important to begin by reminding ourselves that we are talking of resemblances at a verbal and syntactical level. I have hinted only briefly at those many other points in Revelation where links have been detected with the Johannine tradition. Sometimes, they are verbal similarities, as is the case with the sayings just discussed. In other cases, different vocabulary is used in a similar fashion: the famous case being the shared Christological motif of the Lamb, where the Gospel and Revelation use two different Greek words, ἀμνός and ἀρνίον respectively.

In still other cases two passages may be juxtaposed where a deeper train of thought belies the almost total lack of verbal similarity. There is, for example, hardly any overlap in vocabulary between John's metaphor of the pregnant woman in John 16.21-22 and the dream vision in Revelation 12 of the pregnant woman clothed with the sun. There is, therefore, no question of a literary relationship. Yet for all their differences, in form, style and language, there are remarkable similarities. Both interpret the woman as a symbol for a vulnerable community: in the Gospel, the community of disciples experiencing grief in the 'little while' between the death and resurrection of Jesus; in the Apocalypse, the heavenly personification of God's people, experiencing the birth-pangs as the messianic age begins to dawn. In both, then, there is a Christological focus, which is brought all the more closer if we follow some commentators in interpreting the 'birth' of Revelation's male child, who is immediately caught up to God and to his throne, as his death and exaltation. Both, moreover, are set within the context of threatened persecution, and both passages use the language of victory (and the same verb νικᾶν) as something already achieved by Christ.

7. Hearing Heavenly Voices

But let us return to the sayings. One possible avenue might be to explore the role of early Christian prophecy in the emergence or development of Johannine sayings.[44] John of Patmos presents himself as a prophet, and one of the functions of the Spirit in Revelation is as the 'Spirit of prophecy' (Rev 19.10). The messages to the seven churches in chs. 2–3 take the form of prophetic oracles, introduced with the formal phrase 'Thus says...'. John Ashton has himself hinted at what this avenue might look like, by imagining the existence of a 'Johannine prophet', or occasionally of plural 'prophets'. He reminds us, for example, that the leader(s) of the community in Brown's 'second stage' might be fruitfully envisaged as apologists and preachers, or possibly prophets.[45] Or, referring to Martyn's 'middle period', he can talk of a 'prophet' in the community's midst, 'speaking in the name of Jesus and offering new insights into who he was and what he represented'.[46] Further, he points to the Gospel's distinctive 'Amen' and 'I am' sayings as possible utterances of the Johannine prophet.[47]

In other words, Ashton opens the door to prophetic activity within the community playing at least some role in the formation of the distinctive Johannine discourses. Given their concentration in the words of heavenly voices, might the 'Johannine resemblances' in the Apocalypse also be early examples of this shadowy Johannine prophetic activity?

However, we should not rule out the apocalyptic dimension too quickly. Hearing heavenly voices is also an apocalyptic motif, whether of God himself (*1 En.* 14.24; 55.1; 62.1; *2 En.* 9.15; *Apoc. Ab.* 9.1-3), angelic mediators (*1 En.* 80.1; *2 En.* 9.9) or unidentified celestial speakers (*1 En.* 40.2-3; *Ascen. Isa.* 7.4; 10.1; *2 Bar.* 22.1). Moreover, the oracular prophecy of Revelation 2–3 is itself located in the context of an apocalyptic vision, that of 'one like a son of man'. The narrative setting for this vision provides some hints as to what the process here might have been:

---

44 On Revelation as a prophetic book, see Hill, 'Prophecy'; also David E. Aune, *Prophecy in Early Christianity and the Ancient Mediterranean World* (Grand Rapids: Eerdmans, 1983), pp.274–88.
45 Ashton, *Understanding* (1st edn), p.164.
46 Ashton, *Understanding* (1st edn), p.172.
47 Ashton, *Understanding* (1st edn), pp.182–9.

> I, John, your brother and fellow-sharer in the tribulation and the kingdom and the perseverance in Jesus, was on the island called Patmos on account of the word of God and the testimony of Jesus. I was in the Spirit [*or* fell into ecstasy] on the Lord's day, and I heard behind me a loud voice like the sound of a trumpet, saying, 'Write what you see in a book and send it to the seven congregations...' (Rev 1.9-11a).

If we take seriously the claim made here that this highly complex work is nevertheless rooted in actual visionary experience, then a number of possibilities follow. First, the setting for the vision is a spiritual trance 'on the Lord's day'. At the very least, John of Patmos locates his inaugural vision on the day when fellow Christians in the seven churches would be gathered for worship. But one should not rule out the possibility that John's vision is itself received in a liturgical context. Here another reception-historical point may be pertinent. For whereas in the Western imagination John is a sole exile on a deserted island – think, for example, of the paintings by Botticelli, Memling, and Velázquez – the Eastern tradition (typified most fully in the fifth-century *Acts of John by Prochorus*) depicts John as the leader of a fledgling Christian community, and receiving his revelation, in the company of Prochorus his scribe, after a careful preparation involving prayer and fasting. Byzantine icons since at least the eleventh century typically present John and Prochorus together, the former in ecstasy as he dictates the opening words of the Fourth Gospel. The Western view certainly has no greater support from the text of Revelation, and the Eastern alternative has the benefit of verisimilitude, given what can be ascertained about the population of Patmos in the first century CE.[48] This raises the question as to what activities John the seer might have engaged in as preparation for his visions and auditions 'on the Lord's day'.[49]

The preceding argument may be combined with broader evidence pointing to a careful and systematic study of and meditation upon certain biblical texts, akin to the importance of texts such as Ezekiel 1 for later Jewish mystics. Recent studies have noted how prophetic texts such as Daniel, and especially Ezekiel, were particularly formative for the author of Revelation, with Ezekiel's book even providing a structure for John's

---

48 On the connections between Patmos and Miletus, and the evidence for a thriving resident population, see, e.g., H. D. Saffrey, 'Relire l'Apocalypse à Patmos', *RB* 82 (1975), pp.385–417.

49 See, e.g., Christopher Rowland, *The Open Heaven: A Study of Apocalyptic in Judaism and Early Christianity* (London: SPCK, 1982).

visionary work.[50] Given the Christian character of Revelation, we might also ask about the extent to which meditation upon the Christian story, including sayings of Jesus, was part of this complex process.

Perhaps this is a warning against driving too sharp a wedge between apocalyptic and prophecy, at least in an early Christian context. Paul's discussion in 1 Corinthians 12–14 shows that both prophecy and apocalyptic revelations could occur within the context of the same liturgical assembly (1 Cor 14.26-33). Moreover, while Paul lists the role of prophet among the gifts of the Spirit, he provides no separate category for apocalypticist. If Paul also provides evidence for a liturgical setting for the reception of revelations, the Apocalypse may broaden that out to suggest that the revelations were themselves the fruit of careful preparation and sustained contemplation, not least on the scriptures and their true meaning in the light of Christ.

To return to the second question: do these parallels in the sayings material suggest anything about the chronological order of the two works? We can only give a tentative answer, but two initial points may be made. The first is that the 'Johannine-sounding' sayings of Revelation are not universally Christocentric in the way in which they are in the Fourth Gospel. Some are reserved for the lips of 'the one seated on the throne', still others for lesser heavenly beings such as interpreting angels. While one must avoid the assumption that Christology always develops in a linear fashion, this may provide one piece for evidence in support of the Apocalypse representing a 'more primitive' stage of the tradition.

The second point is that Revelation is more heaven-focused and future-focused, with little interest in the earthly Jesus. Heaven has not yet come to earth in the way in which it has in the Fourth Gospel, and it is true that it retains a greater focus on future eschatology. Nevertheless, some qualification is called for. On the one hand, John's vision of the heavenly throne-room in the Apocalypse reveals the victory which has already been achieved through the death and resurrection of the slaughtered Lamb, including his earthly testimony, and this somewhat overshadows the visions of the End. On the other, John Ashton has reminded us of the two levels on which the sayings of Jesus in the Gospel function, moving us away from preoccupation with Jesus as he was to reveal the deeper meaning of his sayings in the light of the definitive interpretation offered by the Spirit-Paraclete.

---

50   E.g. Michael D. Goulder, 'The Apocalypse as an Annual Cycle of Prophecies', *NTS* 27 (1981), pp.342–67; Ian Boxall, 'Exile, Prophet, Visionary: Ezekiel's Influence on the Book of Revelation', in Henk J. de Jonge and Johannes Tromp (eds.), *The Book of Ezekiel and its Influence* (Aldershot: Ashgate, 2007), pp.147–64.

8. Conclusion

Where has all this brought us? On one level, not very far, particularly for those who were expecting a more robust attempt at locating the seer of Patmos firmly within a specific stage in the history of the Johannine Community. But it seems to me that there are too many imponderables to justify such a reconstruction, although there are some indications that a location earlier rather than later in the tradition best fits the evidence for Revelation. Nevertheless, a number of avenues have opened up for further exploration. One is to examine more systematically the connection between the two texts at the level of sayings, particularly a comparison of the voice of the heavenly Jesus of the Apocalypse with that of the heaven-come-to-earth Jesus of the Fourth Gospel. Related to that is the study of heavenly voices more broadly, in their various forms, as an apocalyptic motif. Secondly, further study could profitably be done on the implications for Apocalypse–Gospel relationships of the mechanics of Jewish and early Christian visionary experience, particularly in a communal, liturgical context. But at the very least for now, I hope that I have sketched out a scenario whereby the prophet-seer of Patmos might be regarded not as a wolf, not even as a hired hand, but as a fully paid-up member of the Johannine sheepfold, perhaps even one of the original sheep.

GOD'S DWELLING ON EARTH: '*SHEKHINA*-THEOLOGY' IN REVELATION 21 AND IN THE GOSPEL OF JOHN

Jörg Frey

It is with great pleasure that I accept the invitation to honour John Ashton, one of the most insightful Johannine scholars of our days. His comprehensive work *Understanding the Fourth Gospel* amply demonstrates his mastery of the Johannine problems and of the various scholarly attempts to solve them.[1] In view of my own work on eschatology in the Johannine tradition,[2] I found it interesting to observe how perceptively John Ashton deals with the relics and traces of early Christian (and Jewish) apocalyptic thought in the Fourth Gospel. The apocalyptic background of the Johannine writings has often been downplayed or neglected, both in German scholarship, due to the impact of Rudolf Bultmann's hermeneutics, and in British scholarship, under the influence of the work of C. H. Dodd. It is only more recently that the apocalyptic background of certain motifs in the Fourth Gospel, such as the heavenly abodes (John 14.2-3),[3] the I-am-Sayings,[4] or the Johannine Son of Man,[5] has been considered more extensively.

---

1 John Ashton, *Understanding the Fourth Gospel* (Oxford: Clarendon, 1991); see also John Ashton, *Understanding the Fourth Gospel* (Oxford: Oxford University Press, 2nd edn, 2007).

2 Jörg Frey, *Die johanneische Eschatologie* (WUNT 96, 110, 117; 3 vols.; Tübingen: Mohr Siebeck, 1997, 1998, 2000), and 'Eschatology in the Johannine Circle', in Gilbert Van Belle, Jan G. van der Watt, and Petrus Maritz (eds.), *Theology and Christology in the Fourth Gospel: Essays by the Members of the SNTS Johannine Writings Seminar* (BETL 184; Leuven: Peeters, 2005), pp.47–82. See also my collection of essays in *Die Herrlichkeit des Gekreuzigten: Studien zu den Johanneischen Schriften I* (ed. Juliane Schlegel; WUNT 307; Tübingen: Mohr Siebeck, 2013).

3 See Frey, *Eschatologie*, III, pp.134–53.

4 See Catrin H. Williams, *I Am He: The Interpretation of 'Anî Hû' in Jewish and Early Christian Literature* (WUNT 2/113; Tübingen: Mohr Siebeck, 2000).

In the present essay I will follow the path of what John Ashton calls 'Intimations of Apocalyptic',[6] by discussing one motif that is used, albeit in a quite different manner, in both the Fourth Gospel and Revelation. Having addressed the question of the relationship between Revelation and the other writings of the Johannine Corpus in a lengthy article several years ago, I will first give a brief sketch of the problems and my proposals before revisiting the topic by focusing on the motif of God's dwelling on earth, the *Shekhina*, as adopted in Revelation 21 and in the Gospel of John, especially in John 1.14.[7]

1. The Gospel and the Apocalypse: Glimpses on 'Johannine Questions'

In an essay written in 1992 and published as an extensive complement to Martin Hengel's *Johannine Question* in its enlarged, and significantly modified, German version,[8] I addressed the issue of possible historical or traditio-historical links between Revelation and the other works of the Johannine Corpus, especially the Fourth Gospel. In my opinion, the most widespread view – that Revelation was written by an unknown prophet

---

5 See Benjamin E. Reynolds, *The Apocalyptic Son of Man in the Fourth Gospel* (WUNT 2/249; Tübingen: Mohr Siebeck, 2008).

6 Thus especially in the chapter on 'Intimations of Apocalyptic' in Ashton, *Understanding* (2nd edn), pp.305–29.

7 See the more extensive discussion of John 1.14 in Jörg Frey, 'Motive der Einwohnung Gottes in der Christologie und Tempelmetaphorik des Johannesevangeliums: Joh 1,14, die "*Schekhina*-Theologie" und die johanneische Erzählung', in Bernd Janowski and Enno Edzard Popkes (eds.), *Das Geheimnis der Gegenwart Gottes: Zur Schechina-Vorstellung in Judentum und Christentum* (WUNT; Tübingen: Mohr Siebeck, forthcoming).

8 Jörg Frey, 'Erwägungen zum Verhältnis der Johannesapokalypse zu den übrigen Schriften des Corpus Johanneum', in Martin Hengel, *Die johanneische Frage: Ein Lösungsversuch, mit einem Beitrag zur Apokalypse von Jörg Frey* (WUNT 67; Tübingen: Mohr Siebeck, 1993), pp.326–429. Interestingly, the article remained somewhat overlooked, especially in the English-speaking world, because Hengel's important monograph was already widespread in its shorter English version (Martin Hengel, *The Johannine Question* [trans. John Bowden; London: SCM; Philadelphia: Trinity, 1989]); as a result, the enlarged German version was less noticed. My 'appendix', which had grown out of debates with my esteemed academic teacher from reading the proofs of the English version, was only included in that German version. Notably, Hengel himself modified his view at some points according to the suggestions I made in that part of his book.

named John, who was unrelated to the author or authors of the other 'Johannine' writings – is not satisfactory. A connection certainly exists between the inscriptions of the five works ascribed to 'John' – the Gospel, the Epistles, and Revelation – because there is no evidence that these five inscriptions point to different figures all named 'John'.[9] Furthermore, all the inscriptions are read as a reference to the Apostle John, the son of Zebedee, although this enigmatic figure was most probably not the author of any of the Johannine writings.

The first clear attestation of Revelation is by Justin Martyr (*Dial.* 81.4), who attributes the work to the Apostle John,[10] with whom the Gospel and the Epistles are also linked quite early, certainly some time before Irenaeus, possibly already by Justin.[11] The five works that form the (wider) 'Johannine Corpus', at least in their canonical shape, claim to be authored or, at any rate, authorised by one and the same figure called John, although the name 'John' only occurs in the text of Revelation, notably in its 'framing' parts (1.1, 4, 9; 22.8).

The inscriptions are, of course, often regarded as later additions to the text of the respective works, although – especially in the case of the Fourth Gospel – such an addition should not be considered as having occurred at a much later stage, if, as Martin Hengel has shown, the 'book titles' became necessary as soon as more than one gospel writing was available in a community.[12] Thus we might even assume that the superscription to the Fourth Gospel had already been added when the work was edited together with its 'appendix', ch. 21, in order to be distributed among various communities.[13] Despite its historical problems, the attribution of the Gospel to the Apostle John could easily be adduced from its narrative design. The riddle of the anonymous disciple in John 1.40 calls

---

9   Cf. Frey, 'Erwägungen', pp.327–9.

10   Cf. David E. Aune, *Revelation 1–5* (WBC 52A; Dallas: Word, 1997), pp.l–liii.

11   Cf. Charles E. Hill, *The Johannine Corpus in the Early Church* (Oxford: Oxford University Press, 2004), p.344. On the use and attribution of the Fourth Gospel in the second century, see Hengel, *The Johannine Question*, pp.1–23; idem, *Die johanneische Frage*, pp.9–95; furthermore Titus Nagel, *Die Rezeption des Johannesevangeliums im 2. Jahrhundert* (Arbeiten zur Bibel und ihrer Geschichte 2; Leipzig: Evangelische Verlagsanstalt, 2000).

12   See Martin Hengel, *Studies in the Gospel of Mark* (London: SCM, 1985), pp.64–88, 162–83.

13   Thus Hengel, *The Johannine Question*, p.74; also Udo Schnelle, *Das Evangelium nach Johannes* (THKNT 4; Leipzig: Evangelische Verlagsanstalt, 3rd edn, 2004), p.346.

for decipherment, and although this figure is not explicitly identified with the Beloved Disciple, the readers are implicitly invited to draw that conclusion and to identify the Beloved Disciple – against the background of Mark's story of the calling of the disciples – with John, the son of Zebedee.[14] Thus the title, the 'Gospel according to John', already suggests such an attribution, although the real author or tradition-bearer behind the Gospel is probably a different person.

For the Johannine Epistles and Revelation the situation is even more difficult, because we cannot determine as precisely (as for the Fourth Gospel) when the inscriptions were added. None of the Johannine Epistles mentions any 'John', and only the two smaller epistles include the enigmatic attribution to 'the Elder' (2 John 1; 3 John 1). Given that the two minor epistles – whose text comprised not more than one papyrus sheet – were probably transmitted only together with the first epistle, we must assume a very close connection between all three, at least for the time when they were edited and distributed. If, moreover, there are no compelling linguistic reasons for distinguishing between the author of the smaller epistles and the first epistle, we may conclude that all three epistles were written by an authoritative teacher in Asia Minor who was simply called 'the Elder'. The only candidate for a more precise identification of that figure is the so-called 'Presbyter John' mentioned by Papias of Hierapolis,[15] and it is a plausible inference that this significant tradition-bearer was actually the author of the Johannine Epistles. However, the inscriptions of the epistles do not refer to Presbyter John but simply to 'John', and it can be assumed that, from the beginning, these inscriptions were understood to be in close relation with the inscription of the Fourth Gospel. Consequently, the epistles, which were most probably edited as a complement to the Gospel, were read at a relatively early stage as the writings of John, the son of Zebedee; hence, the historical figure of the 'Elder' John, who acted as teacher and

---

14 Cf. especially Hartwig Thyen, *Das Johannesevangelium* (HNT 6; Tübingen: Mohr Siebeck, 2005), pp.133–4. For the argument that John (even in chs. 1–20) presupposes at least Mark and is to be read against a Markan background, see Jörg Frey, 'Das Vierte Evangelium auf dem Hintergrund der älteren Evangelientradition. Zum Problem: Johannes und die Synoptiker', in Thomas Söding (ed.), *Johannesevangelium – Mitte oder Rand des Kanons? Neue Standortbestimmungen* (QD 203; Freiburg: Herder, 2003), pp.60–118. See also Hengel, *The Johannine Question*, pp.70–1, 75, 95, 102; Richard Bauckham, 'John for Readers of Mark', in idem (ed.), *The Gospel for All Christians: Rethinking the Gospel Audiences* (Grand Rapids: Eerdmans, 1998), pp.147–71.

15 Eusebius, *Hist. eccl.* 3.39.4; cf. Hengel, *The Johannine Question*, pp.24–30.

tradition-bearer in Asia Minor, was fused quite early with the foundational figure of the Apostle John, who may have suffered martyrdom much earlier[16] and whose presence in Asia Minor is far from certain.

I cannot enter here into the discussion as to whether the Johannine Epistles were written after or even before the Gospel; in any case, they are linked very closely with the Gospel, both linguistically and thematically. We may even speculate that the author of the epistles is actually the real authority behind the Gospel, so that the fusion between the image of the 'Elder' John and the Apostle John happened in the process of the composition of the Gospel, especially by means of the enigmatic narrative figure of the anonymous disciple in John 1 and the Beloved Disciple. From John 21 we can see that the Beloved Disciple, who is said to be 'the one who has written this' (21.24), is not a merely fictional figure but is probably a witness and tradition-bearer who died at some point before the composition of John 21 (cf. 21.22-23). The editors from his school took up the rumour that he might 'stay forever', that is, live until the end of times, but they corrected it in the sense that he would now 'stay forever' in his testimony.

Within the larger framework of such a reconstruction, as originally developed by Martin Hengel in *The Johannine Question*, I got the impression that the most difficult and still unsolved riddle can be outlined as follows: relatively early, long before Irenaeus, all five works of the 'Johannine Corpus' were linked together by the idea that all of them had been composed by the same author ('John'), despite their very different theology and significant variations in language and style.[17] Therefore, in my 1992 essay I examined the relationship between Revelation and the other writings belonging to the Johannine corpus. To provide a thorough investigation of that relationship, I undertook a comparative analysis of the language of Revelation and the Fourth Gospel – their vocabulary, phraseology, syntax, possible Semitisms – and of shared motifs and theological parallels between the two works. The results concerning the language were quite clear: because of significant

---

16   Cf. the traditions about John's death at the hands of the Jews, mentioned by Hengel, *The Johannine Question*, pp.158–9 n.121, and, more extensively, in idem, *Die johanneische Frage*, pp.88–92. It is quite plausible that these traditions were later pushed aside by the overwhelming tradition about the aged Apostle John in Ephesus. But for this reason they deserve even more historical consideration.

17   For Revelation and the Gospel, this was already clearly stated by Dionysius, the third-century bishop of Alexandria, whose philological analysis (which is, of course, theologically motivated by his opposition to Revelation's chiliasm) is quoted in Eusebius, *Hist. eccl.* 7.25.22-23. See Frey, 'Erwägungen', p.359.

differences in style, syntax and use of particles, common authorship must be excluded with a high degree of probability.[18] Nevertheless, there are several common motifs and traditions which may point to connections somewhere in the Johannine tradition, such as the sayings on the 'living water', the I-am-Sayings (cf. Rev 1.8, 17; 2.23; 21.6; 22.13, 16), the notion of an intimate relationship between Father and Son and, respectively, between God and the Lamb, the use of λόγος as a Christological title (John 1.1, 14, 18; Rev 19.13) and even the 'antichrist' tradition (2 John 7; 1 John 2.18; cf. Rev 13). However, the precise application of these motifs differs between Revelation and the other Johannine writings.[19] A tentative clue to solving the *aporia* could be the observation that some 'Johannine' elements in Revelation occur most frequently in the framing chapters (Rev 1–3 and 21–22), which probably mark the final stage of composition. From that observation I concluded that Revelation was possibly edited within the context of the (late) Johannine School or by a final editor/redactor influenced by Johannine ideas and language. Given that the name 'John' also only appears within that 'redactional' framework, I proposed that Revelation should be read as a kind of 'Johannine' *pseudepigraphon*, ascribed to the figure of (the Elder) 'John' from Asia Minor, who, in my view, was the real author of the Epistles and perhaps the Gospel (apart from ch. 21). The setting of the vision at Patmos (Rev 1.9-11) might be an ideal scene or possibly draws on the tradition that the Ephesian teacher John had been to Patmos at some point in the past.

Of course, within the discourse of Christianity in Asia Minor, which had been influenced by Pauline tradition as well as by the Johannine School, Revelation represents a distinctive voice in comparison with the views expressed in the other Johannine writings. It takes a radically different stance on matters of eschatology[20] and, in particular, towards the urban and provincial culture under Roman rule.[21] Moreover, within

---

18   See all the linguistic details in Frey, 'Erwägungen', pp.336–82 (summary on pp.380–2).

19   See the detailed comparison in Frey, 'Erwägungen', pp.383–415.

20   On the eschatology of Revelation, see now my extensive discussion in Jörg Frey, 'Was erwartet die Johannesapokalypse? Zur Eschatologie des letzten Buchs der Bibel', in Jörg Frey, James A. Kelhoffer, and Franz Tóth (eds.), *Die Johannesapokalypse: Kontexte – Konzepte – Rezeption* (WUNT 287; Tübingen: Mohr Siebeck, 2012), pp.473–552.

21   On the relevance of the imperial cult, see my article: 'The Relevance of the Roman Imperial Cult for the Book of Revelation: Exegetical and Hermeneutical Reflections on the Relation between the Seven Letters and the Visionary Main Part

the framework of the historical reconstruction sketched above, it could even be a voice within the debate about the further development of the Johannine School during the first decades of the second century.

I cannot pursue here the question as to whether Revelation is actually a 'Johannine' *pseudepigraphon*, posthumously attributed to the leading figure of the Johannine circle in Asia Minor. I will rather focus on one motif or concept that was mentioned but not investigated in my earlier essay,[22] *God's dwelling* or *'tabernacling'* 'among us' or 'among his people'. As this concept is adopted by both the Fourth Gospel and Revelation, a comparison of its application in the two works should shed new light on their theological relationship.

2. John 1.14 and Revelation 21.3:
The Vocabulary and the Concept of the *Shekhina*

As is well known, the concept of the *Shekhina* is employed in the Prologue of John's Gospel: 'For the word became flesh and *tabernacled* (ἐσκήνωσεν) among us' (John 1.14). The same word or word stem is also used twice, albeit differently, in Rev 21.3. In the narration of the vision of the New Jerusalem descending from heaven it is said: 'I heard a loud voice from the throne: "Behold the *tabernacle* (ἡ σκηνή) of God is among people, and he will tabernacle (σκηνώσει) with them, and they will be his people, and God himself will be with them as their God"'. I use this uncommon translation to highlight the fact that Revelation uses the same Greek verb σκηνόω as in John 1.14 and also the noun σκηνή, which can mean 'dwelling' or 'tent' or, more precisely, the wilderness tabernacle of ancient Israel; the tabernacle was the provisional pattern for the temple of Solomon, the place where the Lord or – according to other traditions – his name, should dwell on earth.

This motif provides an ideal case for comparison, because in both instances the same Greek word σκηνόω (John 1.14; Rev 21.3) is utilized. This verb is also found in three other passages in Revelation, twice with the simple meaning of dwelling on earth (12.12) or in heaven (13.6), but in Rev 7.15 to convey the notion of God's 'tabernacling' among or 'above' (ἐπί) the group of redeemed humans who stand in front of the divine throne. Of all the New Testament writings, the verb σκηνόω is

of the Book', in John Fotopoulos (ed.), *The New Testament and Early Christian Literature in Greco-Roman Context: Studies in Honor of David E. Aune* (NovTSup 122; Leiden: Brill, 2006), pp.231–55.
22 Cf. Frey, 'Erwägungen', p.392.

only attested in these two texts. Equally significant is the use of the noun σκηνή. Apart from Rev 21.3 it is employed twice in Revelation to signify God's heavenly dwelling, which is blasphemed by the beast (13.6) and is revealed in the heavenly vision in Rev 15.5. As far as the other New Testament writings are concerned, the term is frequent in Hebrews, often denoting the heavenly sanctuary (Heb 8.1-2; 9.11). It is also found in the Synoptic transfiguration accounts (Matt 17.4; Mark 9.5; Luke 9.33) to denote the 'tents' that Peter wishes to make on the mountain, once in Luke 16.9 for the eternal 'dwellings', as well as in Acts for the tabernacle in the wilderness (Acts 7.44)[23] and – in the quotation of Amos 9.11 – the 'hut' of David (Acts 15.16). Notably, the words are not used by Paul and in the other epistles. In Paul's letters, the composite verb ἐπισκηνόω occurs once, to describe the experience of God's power overshadowing human weakness (2 Cor 12.9). However, this concept differs markedly from the notion of God's dwelling within the believer, as it is expressed in Rom 8.9 with regard to the Spirit (using the verb οἰκέω), or in Gal 2.20 with regard to Christ (with the verb ζάω).

John 1.14 and Rev 21.3 are therefore comparable because of their common use of the same Greek word, which is not only rare in the New Testament but strongly related to the biblical idea of God's dwelling in the 'tabernacle' in the wilderness, or later in the Jerusalem temple, or – more spiritually – in his people. Moreover, in view of the wider variety of New Testament concepts used to express God's presence on earth – in the community of believers or within a single believer (in Christ or in the Spirit)[24] – the concept of his dwelling or 'tabernacling' in the midst of his people is only attested in the Gospel of John and the Revelation of John. These two writings are thus to be singled out for comparison so that the mutual relationship of their respective adoption of the concept can be explored.

With all due caution, this concept can be described as God's dwelling or *Shekhina* on earth. In using this term, I follow the lead of the Tübingen Old Testament scholar Bernd Janowski, who has described and analysed the development of what he calls a '*Shekhina*-theology' from the period of the Babylonian exile through the Second Temple period to

---

23 Acts 7.43 uses the same word to polemicize against Israel's worship in the 'tent' of the pagan deity Moloch; this is contrasted with the worship of the desert generation in the true tabernacle.

24 See now the work by Manuél Ceglarek, *Die Rede von der Gegenwart Gottes, Christi und des Geistes: Eine Untersuchung zu den Briefen des Apostels Paulus* (Europäische Hochschulschriften: Theologie 911; Frankfurt am Main: Peter Lang, 2011).

the Johannine Prologue.[25] Of course, the Hebrew abstract noun שכינה is only attested after 70 CE, when the *Shekhina* becomes a technical term in Rabbinic theology and in the Targums.[26] After the destruction of the temple, the term *Shekhina* is used to express God's continuing covenantal faithfulness or the continuing election of Israel in a period when the locus of God's presence on earth has been destroyed or is inaccessible to Jews.[27] Nevertheless, as these later *Shekhina*-traditions evidently draw on a number of biblical and post-biblical traditions about God's dwelling in the 'tabernacle', the temple, and among the Israelites, it is possible to assign the label '*Shekhina*-theology' even to these traditions.

3. The Tradition of God's 'Tabernacling' in the Midst of his People and its Diverse Types of Transmission

A theology of God's dwelling within his people, based on the use of the Hebrew word שכן, was developed during the period of the Babylonian

---

25 Bernd Janowski, '"Ich will in eurer Mitte wohnen": Struktur und Genese der exilischen Schekina-Theologie', in idem, *Gottes Gegenwart in Israel: Beiträge zur Theologie des Alten Testaments* (vol. 1; Neukirchen-Vluyn: Neukirchener, 1993), pp.119–47; idem, 'Schekhina', *RGG*[4] 7.1274–5; idem, 'Gottes Weisheit in Jerusalem: Sirach 24 und die biblische *Schekina*-Theologie', in Hermann Lichtenberger and Ulrike Mittmann-Richert (eds.), *Biblical Figures in Deuterocanonical and Cognate Literature* (YDCL 2008; Berlin: de Gruyter, 2009), pp.1–29. See also idem, 'Die Einwohnung Gottes in Israel: Eine religions- und theologieschichtliche Skizze', in Bernd Janowski and Enno Edzard Popkes (eds.), *Das Geheimnis der Gegenwart Gottes*.

26 See especially Arnold M. Goldberg, *Untersuchungen über die Vorstellung von der Schekhinah in der frühen rabbinischen Literatur: Talmud und Midrasch* (SJ 5; Berlin: de Gruyter, 1969). See further Peter Kuhn, *Gottes Selbsterniedrigung in der Theologie der Rabbinen* (SANT 17; Munich: Kösel, 1968); Hanspeter Ernst, *Die Schekhîna in rabbinischen Gleichnissen* (Judaica et Christiana 14; Bern: Peter Lang, 1994); Clemens Thoma, 'Gott wohnt mitten unter uns: Die Schekhina als zentraler jüdischer Glaubensinhalt', *Freiburger Rundbrief* 14 (2007), pp.82–5. With regard to the New Testament, see Joseph Sievers, '"Where Two or Three…": The Rabbinic Concept of Shekhinah and Matthew 18:20', in Eugene J. Fisher (ed.), *The Jewish Roots of Christian Liturgy* (New York: Paulist, 1990), pp.47–61 (revised German version: '"Wo zwei oder drei…": Der rabbinische Begriff der Schechina und Matthäus 18,20', in *Das Prisma. Beiträge zur Pastoral, Katechese und Theologie* 17, no. 1 [2005], pp.18–29, where all references to the Targums are omitted).

27 Clemens Thoma, 'Schekhina', in Jakob J. Petuchowski and Clemens Thoma (eds.), *Lexikon der jüdisch-christlichen Begegnung* (Freiburg: Herder, 1989), pp.352–6 (352).

exile.²⁸ Ezekiel 43.7 promises the enduring presence of God in the restored and ideal temple of Jerusalem, which is called the place where God wants to 'dwell in the midst of the people of Israel forever'. In the conclusion to the passage this promise is repeated: 'I will dwell in their midst forever' (43.9).²⁹ Here we have the Hebrew verb שׁכן, which is rendered in the Septuagint by the composite verb κατασκηνόω (καὶ κατασκηνώσω ἐν μέσῳ αὐτῶν τὸν αἰῶνα), that is, a verb derived from the stem σκην- which matches the consonants of the Hebrew שׁכן.³⁰ According to this probably exilic (or early post-exilic) text, Yahweh will dwell not merely in the renewed sanctuary, but notably in the midst of the Israelites forever.

As Janowski has pointed out, this exilic and post-exilic *Shekhina*-concept differs from the Deuteronomic and Deuteronomist tradition, where the verb שׁכן is also used, but only to denote Yahweh as having deposited his *name* in the temple in Jerusalem. This idea is found, for instance, in the frequent formula that God has chosen (or, in the fiction of Deuteronomy, 'will choose') a place for his name to dwell.³¹ A cautious distinction is made between Yahweh and his name, with only the name having a presence or dwelling in the temple. Earlier concepts, developed when the temple still existed, obviously avoided the idea of God himself dwelling in the temple. Its destruction and the crisis of the exile stimulated reflections about the relationship between the temple and the Lord, both in retrospection and in lament,³² as well as in ideas of restoration and hopes for the ideal future.

A first example of the new ideas that developed after the destruction of the temple is the Deuteronomistic comment about the sanctification of the sanctuary in 1 Kgs 8.31-51, which identifies heaven as the real place

---

28 For the following passages, cf., generally, Janowski, '"Ich will in eurer Mitte wohnen"'.

29 ושכנתי בתוכם לעולם. On the structure of the vision in Ezek 43.1-11, see Janowski, '"Ich will in eurer Mitte wohnen"', pp.124–5.

30 It is interesting to observe that the LXX translators sometimes chose, where possible, a Greek equivalent to the Hebrew words according to similarity in spelling or sound. Another example is the frequent rendering of the Hebrew אהב by the Greek ἀγαπάω. Notably, σκηνόω is used very rarely in the LXX, and only once (3 Kgdms 8.12) to refer to God's dwelling in the darkness. The other passages which use שׁכן are rendered by rather different verbs, probably because the LXX translators were hesitant to express the idea of God's dwelling or tabernacling on earth. This subject deserves a separate investigation.

31 See Deut 12.11; 14.23; 16.2, 6, 11; 26.2; Neh 1.9; cf. Jer 7.12; Ezra 6.12; cf. Janowski, '"Ich will in eurer Mitte wohnen"', p.128 n.38.

32 E.g. the lament in Ps 74.2: 'Remember Mt. Zion, where you have dwelt'.

of Yahweh's rest (1 Kgs 8.39, 43, 49), not the earthly house where he merely allowed his name to dwell. Yahweh is not bound to the temple; he is not limited at all to this dwelling-place, and it is simply his name (i.e. the possibility to pray to his name) that characterizes the earthly sanctuary.[33]

The experience of crisis and judgement could, however, also inspire hope for the renewed presence of the Lord, as is promised in the addition to the account of the building of Solomon's temple in 1 Kgs 6.12-13: 'If you walk in my statutes and obey my rules and keep all my commandments and walk in them, then I will establish my word with you, which I spoke to David your father, and *I will dwell among the children of Israel* and will not forsake my people Israel'.[34] Interestingly, the same phrase is encountered in the Priestly codex (Exod 25.8) where the erection of the 'tabernacle' is commanded in order that Yahweh will 'dwell in the midst' (ושכנתי בתוכם) of his people. This is then repeated in the climactic divine speech of Exod 29.43-46:[35]

> There I will meet with the people of Israel,
> and it shall be sanctified by my glory.
> I will consecrate the tent of meeting and the altar.
> Aaron also and his sons I will consecrate to serve me as priests.
> I will dwell among the people of Israel and will be their God.[36]
> And they shall know that I am Yahweh their God, who brought them out of the land of Egypt
> that I might dwell among them.
> I am Yahweh their God.

The sanctuary in the wilderness, the tent or 'tabernacle', is the place where Yahweh will dwell among the Israelites. This speech does not mention obeying the commandments, nor the cult, but simply the encounter between God and his people; the ultimate reason for this is that he is the Lord, the God of the Israelites, and they are his people. In this passage in Exodus 29 we find a combination of four elements: the verb שכן, the first part of the covenantal formula ('I will be their God'), the revelation formula ('they shall know that I am Yahweh [כי אני יהוה] their God'), and God's glory (כבוד). With the temple in ruins, exilic

---

33 Cf. Janowski, '"Ich will in eurer Mitte wohnen"', pp.130–1. According to Janowski, 'Shekhina', p.1274, this is the earliest attestation of the *Shekhina*-theology in the Hebrew Bible.
34 Cf. Janowski, '"Ich will in eurer Mitte wohnen"', pp.134–6.
35 Cf. Janowski, '"Ich will in eurer Mitte wohnen"', pp.138–40.
36 The Hebrew reads: ושבנתי בתוך בני ישראל והייתי להם לאלהים.

theology developed the notion that Yahweh does not simply dwell in a house or in the temple, but resides in heaven and in the midst of his people. Thus, with this concept, the universal and 'covenantal' dimensions have merged. The pattern of the wilderness tabernacle functions as the 'ideal' sanctuary, and it can also serve as a model for the eschatological hope of future communion between God and his people. God's 'tabernacling' in the midst of his people becomes, as a result, a central eschatological idea.

Before turning to the two New Testament texts that draw on such a biblical *Shekhina*-theology, attention can be drawn to the fact that the pattern, as developed in the Priestly codex and in the book of Ezekiel, was later developed into a number of quite diverse types that converge in some way or other in the New Testament.[37]

(a) A first type can be found in Zech 2.14-15 (= Vulgate and KJV: 2.10-11):[38] 'Sing and rejoice, O daughter of Zion, for behold, I come and I will dwell in your midst (ושכנתי בתוכך), declares the LORD. And many nations shall join themselves to the LORD in that day, and shall be my people. And I will dwell in your midst, and you shall know that the LORD of hosts has sent me to you.' The idea of Yahweh's 'tabernacling' in the midst of his people is linked here to the eschatological expectation of his coming, and to the universalised view of the nations coming to Zion and joining God's people. This marks an important step towards the eschatological reception of this concept in the New Testament.

There is a less universalistic sub-type in Joel 4.17 (LXX and KJV: 3.17) where it is said: 'So you shall know that I am the LORD your God, *who dwells in Zion*, my holy mountain. And Jerusalem shall be holy, and strangers shall never again pass through it.' Joel 4.20-21 then adds: 'But Judah shall be inhabited forever, and Jerusalem to all generations. I will avenge their blood, blood I have not avenged, for the LORD dwells in Zion.' The idea of Yahweh dwelling in Zion seems to be a common theme in post-exilic religious poetry, as the end of Psalm 135 shows: 'Blessed be the LORD from Zion, he who dwells in Jerusalem!'

(b) A reception of the *Shekhina*-concept, in which the temple motif is given particular emphasis, can be found in the *Temple Scroll* from Qumran. This pre-sectarian text adopts and reinforces the holiness concept from Ezekiel 40–48, linking it with the idea of the square-shaped sanctuary and developing an ideal or eschatological view of the holy people around the holy place. In 11QT^a 29.7-8a it is said: 'I shall accept them and they shall be my people and I will be for them forever. I will

---

37 Thus Janowski, '"Ich will in eurer Mitte wohnen"', p.145.
38 See also Zech 8.3, 8.

tabernacle with them forever and ever.'[39] This passage links the bipartite covenant formula with the notion of God's eternal dwelling with his people.[40] Another closely related passage (that refers back to Ezek 3.26-28) is *Jub.* 1.17: 'I will build my sanctuary in their midst, and *I will dwell with them*, and I will be their God and they will be my people'. This concept of God's dwelling with his people is more clearly eschatological and linked to a new sanctuary.[41]

(c) There is a third, very important, reception or transformation of the idea of divine dwelling in the later wisdom tradition, most prominently in Sirach 24.[42] In the self-praise of Wisdom, which is already identified with the divine Torah, it is said: 'Then the Creator of all things gave me a command, and my Creator chose the place for my tent. He said, "Make your dwelling in Jacob, and in Israel receive your inheritance"' (Sir 24.8).[43] Wisdom comes from the realm of God (cf. Sir 24.3) and enters the realm of the world – more precisely Israel – where it finds its 'resting-place' (24.7) and its heritage. The biblical motifs of 'rest' (מנוחה) and heritage (נחלה) are now combined with the idea of 'dwelling',[44] originally developed to denote God's presence in the temple or among his people. In the verses that follow, Wisdom narrates her own story: 'In the holy tent I ministered before him, and so I was established in Zion. Thus in the beloved city he gave me a resting-place, and in Jerusalem was my domain. I took root in an honoured people, in the portion of the Lord, his heritage' (Sir 24.10-12).[45]

Sirach 24 is the most important example of the sapiential transformation of the *Shekhina*-theology. Apart from the terms ἀνάπαυσις (v. 7) / κατάπαυσις (v. 11) and κληρονομία (vv. 7, 12) / κατακληρονομέω (v. 8), the text uses both the noun σκηνή and the verb κατασκηνόω (v. 8). Explicitly referring to the holy tent in the wilderness and to the holy city of Jerusalem, it interprets the tradition of God's 'tabernacling' on earth as the presence of his wisdom, which has found a resting-place on earth in the place of God's temple.

39   For the translation, with some modifications, see Geza Vermes, *The Complete Dead Sea Scrolls in English* (London: Penguin, 2004), p.201.
40   Notably, the *Temple Scroll* refers to God's people as a whole, not to a 'sectarian' part of it. Other texts from the post-biblical period stress God's presence with a particular group or part of the people, e.g., the righteous (cf. *T. Jud.* 25.3).
41   In *Jub.* 1.29 reference is also made to a sanctuary in the 'new creation'.
42   On this, see Janowski, 'Gottes Weisheit in Jerusalem', pp.10–21.
43   The Greek reads: ὁ κτίσας με κατέπαυσεν τὴν σκηνήν μου καὶ εἶπεν ἐν Ιακωβ κατασκήνωσον καὶ ἐν Ισραηλ κατακληρονομήθητι.
44   Thus Janowski, 'Gottes Weisheit in Jerusalem', p.18.
45   Translation NRSV.

(d) A fourth pattern can be found in Philo, *On Dreams* 1.148-49, where Lev 26.12 is applied to God's dwelling in the human soul, so that finally the soul is 'a house of God, a holy temple'.[46] Here, the wise human being becomes a temple, the dwelling-place of God.

As already noted, it is only after the destruction of the temple that the Hebrew word שכינה (*Shekhina*) becomes a technical term for the divine presence.[47] Both in Rabbinic texts and the Targums, *Shekhina* frequently serves as a substitute for the divine name or for God himself and as a complement to clarify the manner of the divine presence.[48] In the early Targum *Neofiti*, the term *Shekhina* occurs more rarely, but usually in combination with 'glory', as, for example, in the frequent rendering of the biblical expression 'the glory of the Lord' as 'the glory of the *Shekhina* of the Lord'.[49] *Shekhina* is also used forty times in *Neofiti* in connection with the verb 'to dwell';[50] the technical term thus enters the passages mentioned above about God's dwelling in the midst of his people.[51] However, the Targumic parallels are more relevant for the explanation of New Testament themes (such as the term λόγος in John) than for the reception of the biblical tradition of God's 'dwelling' with his people, which can be adequately explained from the other lines of transmission already noted.[52]

46 Cf. also Philo, *On Rewards and Punishments* 123.

47 Apart from the literature mentioned above, see the helpful collection of Targumic passages in John Ronning, *The Jewish Targums and John's Logos Theology* (Peabody: Hendrickson, 2010), pp.50–62, and, from a leading specialist of Targumic literature, Martin McNamara, *Targum and Testament Revisited: Aramaic Paraphrases of the Hebrew Bible: A Light on the New Testament* (Grand Rapids: Eerdmans, 2nd edn, 2010), especially pp.148–54. See also Andrew Chester, *Divine Revelation and Divine Titles in the Pentateuchal Targumim* (TSAJ 14; Tübingen: Mohr Siebeck, 1986), pp.313–24.

48 McNamara, *Targum and Testament Revisited*, p.150, on Targum Onqelos: 'So whenever the biblical text expresses God's lingering or moving about in any particular place via the preposition *tôk* ("in the midst of"), *qereb* ("near"), *ʿim* ("with"), the Targum adds *šekinta*'.

49 Cf., e.g., *Tg. Neof.* Exod 16.6-7; Exod 19.17, 20 (see McNamara, *Targum and Testament Revisited*, p.153).

50 McNamara, *Targum and Testament Revisited*, p.153.

51 Thus *Tg. Neof.* Exod 29.45-46: 'so that the Glory of my *Shekhina* might dwell among them' (cf. McNamara, *Targum and Testament Revisited*, p.153), or *Tg. Zech.* 2.5: 'I will make my *Shekhina* dwell in her midst' (cf. Ronning, *The Jewish Targums*, p.60).

52 We can thus omit a discussion about the precise date of the Targums, which are commonly held to have been written or shaped much later than 70 CE, although some oral traditions probably go back to the Second Temple period. See, however,

From the sapiential pattern it is a mere small step to the Johannine Prologue, which is profoundly influenced by wisdom theology, whereas the *Shekhina*-motif in Revelation draws on the eschatological type of transmission. We will now briefly examine these two New Testament texts and their respective reception of the motif of God's dwelling on earth or in the midst of his people.

4. God's Tabernacling on Earth in Jesus (John 1.14) and Jesus as the Place of the Divine Presence in the Fourth Gospel

I cannot, in the present context, enter the wider discussion about the Johannine Prologue and its interpretative problems.[53] In my view the Prologue, in its present form, is deliberately designed as a reading instruction for the Gospel and provides major clues for the interpretation of the subsequent Gospel story. I view with scepticism the numerous reconstructions of an allegedly pre-Johannine 'Logos hymn', because they remain altogether hypothetical and uncertain. A valid interpretation of John 1.14 should be developed from the text as transmitted, not on the basis of a hypothetical 'original' poem or hymn.

Of the various suggestions regarding the Prologue's structure – dipartite, tripartite, or concentric – I prefer a tripartite structure as suggested, for example, by Michael Theobald in his landmark investigation of the Prologue, which also appears in slightly modified form in his commentary.[54] According to Theobald's analysis, the three syntactical

McNamara, *Targum and Testament Revisited*, p.148, who refers to 2 Macc 14.35, 'a temple for your habitation' (ναὸν τῆς σῆς σκηνώσεως), suggesting that the use of the Greek abstract noun could already point to some Jewish liturgical development in the direction of the use of the abstract expression *Shekhina*. But since 2 Maccabees is composed in Greek and probably in the Diaspora, it is difficult to draw conclusions about Palestinian Jewish liturgy. It is significant that the term occurs only twice in the Mishnah (*m. 'Abot* 3.3 and 3.6), thus the technical use of the term in the Targums seems to be a post-70 CE phenomenon.

53   For further remarks, see Jörg Frey, 'Heil und Geschichte im Johannesevangelium: Zum Problem der ‚Heilsgeschichte' und zum fundamentalen Geschichtsbezug des Heilsgeschehens im vierten Evangelium', in Jörg Frey, Stefan Krauter, and Hermann Lichtenberger (eds.), *Heil und Geschichte* (WUNT 248; Tübingen: Mohr Siebeck, 2009), pp.459–510 (491–7). A more extensive discussion of the relevance of the *Shekhina*-motif for the interpretation of John 1.14 will be given in my article mentioned above (n.7).

54   Michael Theobald, *Die Fleischwerdung des Logos. Studien zum Verhältnis des Johannesprologs zum Corpus des Evangeliums und zu 1 Joh* (NTAbh 20;

units (vv. 1-5, 6-13, 14-18) all start with a certain 'beginning'[55] and end in the presence of the community of believers. The light that 'shines in the darkness' (v. 5: present tense!), and the children of God who believe in his (Jesus') name (vv. 12-13), reflect the situation of the community, as does the solemn confession that 'we saw his glory' (v. 14) and 'received grace upon grace' (v. 16). This means that John 1.14 marks the beginning of the Prologue's final section, in which the 'we'-group of witnesses confess to having received grace and truth in Jesus and contemplate the glory of the eternal word (v. 14b) and the image of the invisible God (v. 18) in him.

The tradition-historical background of the Prologue is formed primarily from wisdom theology.[56] Apart from the references to the creation account and its later receptions,[57] and particularly to the revelation on Mt. Sinai (Exod 33–34) in vv. 14-18,[58] the tradition of Israelite wisdom generally serves to explain the Prologue. In later wisdom theology, the (creative) word of God, his Torah given to Israel, and his wisdom are closely associated with each other, while Wisdom (or God's creative word) is envisioned as pre-existent and as a figure that has entered the earthly realm, found its place in Israel, and communicated itself to human beings.

The closest parallels to the Johannine Prologue can be found in Sirach 24, according to which Wisdom 'came forth from the mouth of the Most High' (Sir 24.3; cf. John 1.1), and had its dwelling in the highest heavens

---

Münster: Aschendorff, 1988); see also idem, *Im Anfang war das Wort: Textlinguistische Studie zum Johannesprolog* (SBS 106; Stuttgart: Katholisches Bibelwerk, 1983), and now his commentary, *Das Evangelium nach Johannes. Kapitel 1–12* (RNT; Regensburg: Pustet, 2009).

55 Verse 1 marks the 'absolute' beginning of God's eternity 'before' creation, v. 6 marks the historical beginning of Jesus' ministry (with John the Baptiser), and v. 14 points, mythologically, to the 'individual' beginning of Jesus as the 'incarnate' logos, thus 'replacing' any kind of birth story (which is unnecessary for John).

56 See the thorough investigation by Craig A. Evans, *Word and Glory: On the Exegetical and Theological Background of John's Prologue* (JSNTSup 89; Sheffield: JSOT, 1993); on the wisdom tradition, see particularly Hartmut Gese, 'Der Johannesprolog', in idem, *Zur biblischen Theologie: Alttestamentliche Vorträge* (BEvT 78; Munich: Kaiser 1977), pp.152–201, and also Martin Hengel, 'The Prologue of the Gospel of John as the Gateway to Christological Truth', in Richard Bauckham and Carl Mosser (eds.), *The Gospel of John and Christian Theology* (Grand Rapids: Eerdmans, 2008), pp.265–94.

57 See Evans, *Word and Glory*, pp.77–9; cf. extensively Masanobu Endo, *Creation and Christology: A Study on the Johannine Prologue in the Light of Early Jewish Creation Accounts* (WUNT 2/149; Tübingen: Mohr Siebeck, 2002).

58 See Evans, *Word and Glory*, pp.79–83.

(Sir 24.4) before receiving the command from the creator of all things: 'Make your dwelling in Jacob' (Sir 24.8: ἐν Ιακωβ κατασκήνωσον). The parallel expression, ἐν Ισραηλ κατακληρονομήθητι (Sir 24.8), makes it clear that the idea of the tent (σκηνή) does not imply that this dwelling in Israel is restricted to a limited period of time. It is, rather, a heritage, and this biblical motif (from the notion of inheriting a piece of land) clearly implies duration. Furthermore, the somewhat un-Greek expression κατέπαυσεν τὴν σκηνήν μου, which should be translated as 'he made my tent as a resting-place for me',[59] confirms that the wisdom of the creator should receive an enduring place of rest in the tabernacle of the wilderness and then in the temple of Jerusalem.

Wisdom received a resting-place and ἐξουσία (Sir 24.11; cf. John 1.12) among the honoured people (24.12: ἐν λαῷ δεδοξασμένῳ; cf. John 1.11). Its branches were of glory (δόξα; cf. John 1.14) and grace (χάρις) (24.16; cf. John 1.16). These expressions are, moreover, linked to the law that Moses commanded (Sir 24.23; cf. John 1.17) and of which it is said: 'It shines forth instruction like light' (ὁ ἐκφαίνων ὡς φῶς παιδείαν, Sir 24.27). Indeed, all the central terms of the Prologue (or closely related terms) already occur in Sirach 24 (ἀρχή, κατασκηνόω and σκηνή, ἐξουσία, δόξα, χάρις, νόμος, γινώσκειν, φωτίζειν, φῶς). Only the term λόγος is missing and, of course, any idea of 'incarnation', which is the *proprium* of the Johannine Prologue as compared with Sirach 24.[60]

We can now focus on John 1.14 and describe the implications and relevance of the adoption of the *Shekhina*-motif in the Johannine context:

And the Word became flesh
and dwelt among us,
and we have seen his glory,
glory as of the only Son from the Father,
full of grace and truth.

Καὶ ὁ λόγος σὰρξ ἐγένετο
καὶ ἐσκήνωσεν ἐν ἡμῖν,
καὶ ἐθεασάμεθα τὴν δόξαν αὐτοῦ,
δόξαν ὡς μονογενοῦς παρὰ πατρός,
πλήρης χάριτος καὶ ἀληθείας.

---

59 See Gese, 'Johannesprolog', p.182 n.15, who suggests that the un-Greek wording, which is difficult to translate, is a literal rendering of the Hebrew phrase *hinnîᵃh miškanî*, which is to be translated as 'made my tent as a resting-place'.

60 Of course, numerous other texts from the sapiential tradition could be mentioned, while Sir 24 also possesses parallels in the subsequent gospel narrative. But these links are not relevant for the present purpose and can be left aside here.

Syntactically, v. 14 forms the beginning of a new section in the Prologue. After the long ending of v. 13, the words καὶ ὁ λόγος resume the beginning (v. 1), thereby leading the text to its climax. For the first time the first person plural is used: the logos 'tabernacled' among *us*, and *we* saw his glory. This is the testimony of the community of believers, a testimony that dominates the final section of the Prologue.

Verse 14 itself is structured into five *stichoi*, of which the first two are closely related and linked by a common subject (ὁ λόγος),[61] whereas the third *stichos*, 'and we saw his glory', introduces a new subject that is explained and continued in the final two *stichoi*. This means that the expression ἐσκήνωσεν ἐν ἡμῖν is the first and most immediate explanation of the much-debated phrase ὁ λόγος σὰρξ ἐγένετο. It also elucidates the paradoxical idea that the *divine* logos 'became' flesh. This phrase is enigmatic as it remains unclear whether the divine and eternal λόγος is perceived to undergo change (and thus to enter the realm of human changeability), or whether it should be understood in terms of the appearance of divine beings, a well-known phenomenon in the Graeco-Roman world. The only clue provided by the Gospel is the phrase immediately linked to the reference to the 'incarnation', that is, the notion of the λόγος 'tabernacling' or dwelling 'among us', which points back to the image of God's dwelling in the tabernacle in the wilderness.

The 'tabernacle' imagery also provides a connection with the notion of the revelation of God's glory, as expressed in the third *stichos*. In the 'tabernacle' God's glory was revealed (Exod 40.34). The motif of the tent and the 'tabernacling' divine λόγος is, therefore, a unique way to characterize, in advance, the person of the incarnate Jesus as the place where God's word and glory become visible among humans. Of course, the immediate background of the Prologue – and the idea of the 'tabernacling' λόγος – is the sapiential motif of Wisdom 'tabernacling' in Zion or in Israel as presented in Sirach 24. But the context of John 1.14, with its references to the revelation of God at Mt. Sinai, also alludes to earlier stages of the biblical *Shekhina*-tradition as reflected, for example, in Exodus 25–40.

From the very beginning of the Gospel, already in its provisional reading instruction, the earthly Jesus – the main protagonist of the subsequent narrative – is immersed in the light of the biblical revelation of God's glory in the holy tent or temple. This is designed as the place of encounter between heaven and earth, between God and his people. Jesus – most notably, the earthly and incarnate one – is God's definitive

---

61 Thus Gese, 'Johannesprolog', p.168.

dwelling-place on earth. In other words, he is God's *Shekhina*. In the work and way of the incarnate one, ultimately in his death, and in the image of the (risen) crucified one, the Father himself is revealed (John 1.18) or made visible for those who believe (14.7, 9).

Although the verb σκηνόω does not occur elsewhere in the Gospel, the idea conveyed in the Prologue is matched by the use of the temple theme in the Johannine narrative.[62] Quite consistently, Jesus or his body are metaphorically described as a temple. In an allusion to Jacob's vision at Bethel, Jesus is equated with the place where God's house was to be found (John 1.51). In John 2, Jesus' prediction about the destruction and rebuilding of the temple is explained in a profound way for the Johannine readers: 'He spoke about the temple of his body' (2.21). Through his presence, the search ceases for the right place of worship, as does the antagonism between the traditional holy places of Mt. Gerizim and Jerusalem (4.23). The saying in John 7.37-39 implies that it is from *his* body that the rivers of living water shall flow (cf. Ezek 47). As the invisible Father has been made visible in him, Jesus – or his body – represents, or even replaces, the temple as the place of God's salvific presence.

In the Johannine Prologue this theme is phrased briefly, and slightly differently, through the biblical tradition of the wilderness 'tabernacle', though transmitted through the post-biblical sapiential tradition. The Johannine community thus confesses that, in Jesus, the λόγος 'became' flesh insofar as, in Jesus, the divine λόγος dwelt or 'tabernacled' among us, revealing his divine glory and truth.

In contrast to the reception of the *Shekhina*-motif elsewhere in the New Testament (Rev 21.3), John 1.14 (and the whole Gospel) conceives of God's presence on earth – his dwelling among his people – as an event that has already taken place in Jesus, in the revelation of the Father through him (1.18) and, ultimately, in the image of the crucified one in which the Father's eternal love is revealed. Even after Jesus' 'departure' (i.e. in the post-Easter community), this presence continues as a spiritual presence, mediated through the Spirit-Paraclete (14.16-17) and individually experienced as the abiding presence of Jesus and of the Father with those who love him and keep his words (14.23). In this respect, John comes close to the individualized type of God's 'dwelling' adopted by Philo, although the bodily aspect has not been completely omitted.

---

62 See especially Johanna Rahner, *'Er sprach aber vom Tempel seines Leibes': Jesus von Nazaret als Ort der Offenbarung Gottes im vierten Evangelium* (BBB 117; Bodenheim: Philo, 1998); Mary L. Coloe, *God Dwells with Us: Temple Symbolism in the Fourth Gospel* (Collegeville: Liturgical, 2001).

Even in post-Easter times, it is the narrated earthly Jesus who is the image of the Father and the 'place' where humans find God's salvific presence. It is therefore significant that, at the end of the Gospel (20.24-29), the signs of his crucifixion cause Thomas to believe and to confess climactically, 'My Lord and my God' (20.28).

In marked contrast to the other dominant tradition in late post-exilic times, there is virtually no hint in John of a future revelation of God's glory or future communion between God and his people. The reception of the biblical *Shekhina*-motif is clearly selective. Later in the Gospel there is some hope for the disciples' communion with the exalted Jesus at the place 'where he is' (14.3; 17.24) and for a future vision of his 'glory' (17.24), but the biblical and post-biblical expectation of God's presence on earth, his dwelling among his people, appears to be definitively fulfilled in the appearance of Jesus, the 'tabernacling' word.

5. God's Dwelling with his People in the New Jerusalem (Revelation 21.3) and the Hope for Eschatological Communion with God

The reception of the *Shekhina*-motif in John 1.14 differs significantly from the adoption of the same motif in Rev 21.3. In the book of Revelation it is completely embedded within an eschatological framework, in the vision of the New Jerusalem descending from heaven in the new creation. Without entering into a discussion of the interpretative problems of Revelation,[63] I will highlight only a few aspects of the context and literary design of this vision. It seems clear to me that Rev 21.1–22.5 represents an eschatological image rather than an image of the present

---

63 See my earlier article, Jörg Frey, 'Die Bildersprache der Johannesapokalypse', *ZTK* 98 (2001), pp.161–85, and especially my 'Was erwartet die Johannesapokalypse?' On Rev 21, see, apart from the commentaries, Unyong Sim, *Das himmlische Jerusalem in Apk 21,1–22,5 im Kontext biblisch-jüdischer Tradition und antiken Städtebaus* (Bochumer Altertumswissenschaftliches Colloquium 25; Trier: WVT, 1996); Daria Pezzoli-Olgiati, *Täuschung und Klarheit: Zur Wechselwirkung zwischen Vision und Geschichte in der Johannesoffenbarung* (FRLANT 175; Göttingen: Vandenhoeck & Ruprecht, 1997), pp.161–86; Peter Söllner, *Jerusalem, die hochgebaute Stadt: Eschatologisches und himmlisches Jerusalem im Frühjudentum und im frühen Christentum* (TANZ 25; Tübingen: Francke, 1998), especially pp.188–261; Pilchan Lee, *The New Jerusalem in the Book of Revelation* (WUNT 2/129; Tübingen: Mohr Siebeck, 2001), and the important article by Celia Deutsch, 'Transformation of Symbols: The New Jerusalem in Rv 21,1–22,5', *ZNW* 78 (1987), pp.106–26.

reality of the church. Although the various visionary images of Revelation do not line up to form a coherent sequence of 'events', the appearance of the 'bride' – the New Jerusalem – seems to presuppose the fall of the 'harlot' (19.7), that is, the fall of the Roman empire, which is the principal future expectation expressed in the text. The image of the New Jerusalem draws heavily on a number of traditions from the Hebrew Bible (especially Ezek 40–48 and Isaiah) and post-biblical interpretations,[64] but also subjects them to substantial modification. This is most obvious when the square shape of the temple, as depicted in Ezekiel's temple vision and in the *Temple Scroll* from Qumran, is altered into a gigantic cube (Rev 21.16-17) whose measurements go far beyond human imagination; particularly fanciful is the idea of the twelve doors supposedly attached to the cube. Most clearly Rev 21.1 states that the New Jerusalem is part of a new creation, following the disappearance of the old heaven and earth.[65] The whole image is of a kind of 'utopia' or image drawn from a different world, in which heaven and earth are fused; God's throne is no longer in heaven but within the New Jerusalem and among his people.

In the present text,[66] vv. 1-8 depicts a general scene before the detailed description of the New Jerusalem (vv. 9-27). This passage marks the dramatic climax of the whole work, since it is the only visionary text in Revelation in which words uttered by God himself are recounted (vv. 5-8).[67] Thus the message of Revelation, including its ethical dimension (v. 8), is ascribed the highest possible authority. The sequence of sayings draws heavily on eschatological texts from the book of Isaiah. After the prophecy of a new heaven and a new earth (cf. Isa 65.17; 66.22) and the mention of 'Jerusalem, the holy city' (Isa 52.1b) linked to the image of a bride (Isa 61.10 LXX; cf. Isa 61.5), it promises the removal of tears from every face (Isa 25.8), the defeat of death (cf. Isa 25.8), and the renewal of all things (Isa 43.19).[68] As with many passages in Revelation, this one

---

64 See generally the works by Sim, *Das himmlische Jerusalem*; Söllner, *Jerusalem*; Lee, *The New Jerusalem*.

65 See especially Pezzoli-Olgiati, *Täuschung und Klarheit*, p.163, and, differently, Lee, *The New Jerusalem*, pp.267–9, who tries to construct a greater continuity, though this approach is in my view mistaken and does too much violence to the text.

66 The various suggestions concerning an earlier stratum of composition cannot be discussed here; see, e.g., David E. Aune, *Revelation 17–22* (WBC 52C; Nashville: Thomas Nelson, 1998), p.1115.

67 Rev 1.8 is not part of the vision. Only Rev 21.3-4 is said to be uttered 'from the throne' (cf. 7.15-17).

68 Cf. the commentaries, especially Pierre Prigent, *Commentary on the Apocalypse of St. John* (trans. Wendy Pradels; Tübingen: Mohr Siebeck, 2004), pp.589–99;

largely appears to be a 'bricolage' of scriptural passages, with a strong focus on the eschatological perspective found in the book of Isaiah.

It is therefore remarkable that Rev 21.3 draws on different scriptural contexts. After the vision of the New Jerusalem coming down from heaven, dressed and adorned like a bride (cf. Ezek 16.11-13; *4 Ezra* 10), a voice 'from the throne'[69] comments on the scene and highlights the relevance of the New Jerusalem:

> And I heard a loud voice from the throne:
> 'Behold the *"tabernacle"* of God is with people,
> and he will 'tabernacle' with them,
> and they will be his people,
> and God himself will be with them as their God...'
>
> καὶ ἤκουσα φωνῆς μεγάλης ἐκ τοῦ θρόνου λεγούσης,
> ἰδοὺ ἡ σκηνὴ τοῦ θεοῦ μετὰ τῶν ἀνθρώπων,
> καὶ σκηνώσει μετ' αὐτῶν,
> καὶ αὐτοὶ λαοὶ αὐτοῦ ἔσονται,
> καὶ αὐτὸς ὁ θεὸς μετ' αὐτῶν ἔσται αὐτῶν θεός.

This passage alludes to phrasing in Ezekiel: for example, 43.7: 'I will tabernacle in the midst of the people of Israel forever', 43.9: 'I will tabernacle in their midst forever', but even more clearly 37.27: 'My tabernacle shall be with them, and I will be their God, and they shall be my people'. Here the notion of God's dwelling is linked to the bipartite covenant formula, 'I will be their God, and they shall be my people'.[70] This combination is also paralleled in texts from the Priestly codex, such as Lev 26.11-12: 'I will make my dwelling (מִשְׁכָּנִי) in your midst... And I will walk among you and will be your God, and you shall be my people'.[71] Revelation 21.3 evidently draws on an eschatological and universalistic type of exilic *Shekhina*-theology, as originally developed in Zech 2.10-11 (LXX: 2.14-15): 'Sing and rejoice, O daughter of Zion, for behold, I come and I will dwell in your midst, declares the LORD. And many nations shall join themselves to the LORD in that day, and shall be my people. And I will dwell in your midst, and you shall know that the LORD of hosts has sent me to you.'

Gregory K. Beale, *The Book of Revelation: A Commentary on the Greek Text* (NIGTC; Grand Rapids: Eerdmans; Carlisle: Paternoster, 1999), pp.1039–54.

69   It cannot be the voice of God himself, because God is mentioned in the third person.

70   Cf. also Ezek 34.30; 36.28.

71   Cf. Exod 29.45 with only one part of the formula: 'I will dwell...among the Israelites, and I will be their God'.

Revelation 21.3 betrays almost no ties to the sapiential pattern of the 'tabernacle' tradition so prominent in John 1.14. Rather, it combines the notion of God's eternal 'tabernacling' in the midst of his people (Ezek 43.7) with the covenant formula (as, e.g., in Ezek 37.27 and Lev 26.11-12) and presents the promise within an eschatological context, something which had already been developed in Ezekiel 37 and Zech 2.10-11, but also in the sanctuary-oriented reception of the tradition in the *Temple Scroll* and in *Jubilees* 1. With regard to its content, Rev 21.3 foreshadows the description of the New Jerusalem in 21.9–22.5, anticipating its character as a holy city without a sanctuary, a city which is itself a sanctuary, where God's eschatological people from among all nations can enjoy communion with God and the Lamb (Rev 21.22).

Notably, Rev 21.3 possesses a very universalistic tone: ἡ σκηνὴ τοῦ θεοῦ μετὰ τῶν ἀνθρώπων – 'God's tabernacle among humans'. The scope of this eschatological vision is therefore much wider than its biblical precedents, which limit God's presence to 'his people', the Israelites. The universal people of God consists of humans from all nations, as indicated by the remarkable plural form, αὐτοὶ λαοὶ αὐτοῦ ἔσονται. In the New Jerusalem the covenant from Mt. Sinai, once established in the 'tabernacle' in the wilderness, is fulfilled in an eschatological communion between God and his (universal) people and in the immediate and eternal presence of God among them.

6. Conclusion: Different Receptions within a Different Eschatological Framework

We can now return to the comparison of John 1.14 and Rev 21.3 and their respective receptions of the biblical *Shekhina*-motif.

(1) Both texts use the same vocabulary, namely words belonging to the Greek family σκηνόω / σκηνή, and both quite clearly adopt the notion of 'dwelling' or 'tabernacling' (שׁכן). Of all the New Testament writings, the two 'Johannine' texts – the Gospel of John with its Prologue, and Revelation with its final vision – provide the only clear reception of the biblical *Shekhina*-theology, the idea of God's 'dwelling' with his people.

(2) Despite this common general background, the two texts appropriate the motif from different lines of tradition by referring to different scriptural contexts. Whereas the Johannine Prologue is heavily dependent upon the wisdom tradition, primarily Sirach 24 where the idea of 'dwelling' is transferred from God to Wisdom, the scriptural context of Rev 21.1-8 is shaped by a number of eschatological texts, drawn primarily from the books of Isaiah and Ezekiel, so that the motif of

God 'dwelling' in the midst of his people appears in its modified eschatological and universalistic form.

(3) The application of the *Shekhina* motif in John 1.14 and Rev 21.3 does not allow us to posit direct dependence between them. Rather, it points to their appropriation of different biblical and post-biblical traditions in which the common 'tabernacle' motif was transmitted.

(4) Both passages display a markedly different temporal perspective, which underlines the contrast between the eschatological orientation of the Fourth Gospel and Revelation.

(a) Revelation knows of the completed work of Christ and praises the enthronement of the Lamb and the heavenly kingdom of God (cf. 5.12), but the accent lies on the hope for the inauguration of God's kingdom on earth, which presupposes the fall of Babylon and the defeat of the blasphemous reign and its pseudo-divine powers. The indwelling of God and the ultimate state of peace and salvation for the followers of the Lamb is therefore still awaited. Those who preserve God's word amidst the temptations of contemporary society and the coming crisis will become citizens of the New Jerusalem; they will be comforted and freed from all suffering, danger and death, and they will experience eschatological communion with God and the Lamb. God's dwelling or 'tabernacling' on the new 'earth', in a place to be created after the earth's disappearance, is an aspect of the future, final completion.

(b) Although the Gospel of John does not advocate a purely 'realized' eschatology which cannot accommodate future expectation, it does stress the present reality of salvation and judgement, as well as the presence of God himself in the person of Jesus, the incarnate word, in whom eschatological salvation is realized. Its few references to end-time resurrection cannot easily be removed from the text; indeed they have their place within Johannine thought.[72] In particular there is an expectation of final communion between Jesus and his followers, in the realm of the Father where he already dwells (cf. John 12.26; 14.3; 17.24; see also 1 John 3.2). However, the Gospel narrative stresses the presence of God himself and the accomplishment of the eschatological expectation in Jesus. According to the Gospel's post-Easter perspective, with its fusion of temporal horizons, the incarnate Jesus already possesses and reveals the divine glory (2.11), although it is primarily given to him through glorification in his 'hour' (cf. 12.28; 13.31-32; 17.1). The post-Easter view of the δόξα and divine authority of the glorified one has shaped the narration about Jesus' earthly way; this is already reflected in the Johannine Prologue when it states that the divine λόγος became flesh

---

72   See Frey, *Eschatologie*, III, passim.

and 'tabernacled' among us. The Gospel emphasizes that God made his dwelling in a human being, even sharing the fate of death, and it stresses that the risen Jesus – or, more strongly, the ultimate image of God himself – is characterized by the signs of the cross. If God's 'tabernacling' is not limited to a short-time episode in human history – from incarnation to exaltation – we must conclude that the permanent dwelling of God (as suggested by the terms σκηνόω or שׁכן) is now and forever located in the image of the crucified and resurrected one, as mediated through the Spirit and through the Gospel narrative. Although final completion is, in some respects, yet to come, God's dwelling within the realm of earthly life is accomplished in the person of the incarnate, crucified and exalted Jesus.

(5) Whereas Revelation still expects direct communion with God and Jesus in the new space of the New Jerusalem, the Gospel shares this hope in a more individualized manner, with no specification of place, as is expressed in the 'last will' of the departing Jesus: 'they shall be where I am' (John 17.24).

Is this an apocalyptic motif turned 'inside out' or 'upside down', as John Ashton has phrased it, or is it rather a different, albeit parallel, concept? In any case, the close comparison of the motif undertaken in this essay demonstrates how difficult it is to make historical connections between Revelation and the Fourth Gospel, and that different versions of the concept could be shared within early Christianity, even within the 'Johannine Corpus'.

Unveiling Revelation:
The Spirit-Paraclete and Apocalyptic Disclosure in the Gospel of John

Catrin H. Williams

One of the most striking features of the narrative schema of John's Gospel is the way in which the narrator reflects openly, at key points in the text, on the distinction between the pre-Easter and post-Easter understanding of Jesus and his earthly mission. After his resurrection, it is claimed, the disciples 'remembered' Jesus' veiled statements and actions as well as scriptural words about him (2.22; 12.16). This 'remembering' does not simply consist of the recollection of past events; it acts as a bridge to a new perception that is inseparable from the disciples' post-resurrection perspective which is necessary for belief and deeper insight. John's Gospel links these two levels of understanding to two different time periods (cf. 7.38-39; 13.7; 20.9) with Jesus' hour forming 'the dividing line' between them.[1] Although no explicit reference to the involvement of the Spirit accompanies the statements about the post-Easter *anamnesis* of the disciples, a connection is strongly suggested by the fact that the teaching and reminding activity of the Spirit-Paraclete, as described in 14.26, is said to fall squarely within the period following Jesus' departure and glorification.[2] New understanding is therefore linked to the activity of the Spirit, who 'brings to remembrance' for the disciples that which they have not fully grasped during Jesus' earthly ministry.

---

1 Birger Olsson, *Structure and Meaning in the Fourth Gospel: A Text-Linguistic Analysis of John 2:1–11 and 4:1–42* (Coniectanea Biblica NT Series 6; Lund: Gleerup, 1974), p.263. See also Jörg Frey, *Die johanneische Eschatologie II* (WUNT 110; Tübingen: Mohr Siebeck, 1998), pp.221–3.

2 Michael Theobald, '"Erinnert euch der Worte, die ich euch gesagt habe…" (Joh 15,20): "Erinnerungsarbeit" im Johannesevangelium', *Die Macht der Erinnerung: Jahrbuch für Biblische Theologie* 22 (2007) (Neukirchen–Vluyn: Neukirchener, 2008), p.126, describes the disciples' post-Easter remembering as the *Außenseite* of a deeper reality: through the Spirit's indwelling (14.16-17) Jesus' words are brought to remembrance (14.25-26).

This assessment of the Fourth Gospel's schema is widely held among scholars. What John Ashton has brought to the table is the proposal that the Johannine distinction between pre- and post-Easter understanding is derived from Jewish apocalyptic thought. He skillfully demonstrates that the motif of revelation in two stages, 'one shadowy and obscure, requiring elucidation, the other plain and straightforward, available to all',[3] is a characteristic feature of apocalyptic traditions. Divine revelation, conveyed cryptically through dreams, visions and riddles, is later subjected to decoding by a divinely authorised emissary.[4] John's Gospel, claims Ashton, may not be an apocalypse, but, as a 'narrative within which heavenly mysteries are revealed',[5] it appropriates the apocalyptic motif of two-stage revelation by assigning the role of interpreter to the Spirit-Paraclete, who elucidates the revelation given by Jesus (cf. 14.25-26; 16.12-15).[6] Thus, Jesus' riddling and unveiled words, spoken 'in figures' (ἐν παροιμίαις) during his lifetime (16.25), are unlocked by the Spirit and made open (παρρησίᾳ) for those with eyes to see.[7] The Spirit-Paraclete enables the disciples, in the post-resurrection period, to comprehend what was previously unknown to them (cf. 4.31-34; 11.7-16; 13.36-38; 14.4-5, 8-9; 16.16-18).

John Ashton is not alone in claiming that the pattern of two-stage revelation in John's Gospel is indebted to Jewish apocalyptic tradition. In fact, a 1963 article translated by Ashton for *The Interpretation of John*[8] is among several studies by Ignace de la Potterie that paved the way for the development of Ashton's own ideas about Johannine 'intimations of

---

3   John Ashton, *Understanding the Fourth Gospel* (Oxford: Oxford University Press, 2nd edn, 2007), p.316. Note that throughout this essay references to Ashton's book are to the second edition.

4   George W. E. Nickelsburg, 'The Nature and Function of Revelation in I Enoch, Jubilees, and Some Qumranic Documents', in Esther G. Chazon and Michael E. Stone (eds.), *Pseudepigraphic Perspectives: The Apocrypha and Pseudepigrapha in Light of the Dead Sea Scrolls* (STDJ 31; Leiden: Brill, 1999), p.112, refers to this second stage as the communication of 'revealed interpretation' and 'secondary revelation'. On 'revelation as interpretation', see John J. Collins, *The Apocalyptic Vision of the Book of Daniel* (HSM 16; Missoula: Scholars Press, 177), pp.74–8.

5   Ashton, *Understanding*, p.310. Cf. Christopher Rowland and Christopher R. A. Morray-Jones, *The Mystery of God: Early Jewish Mysticism and the New Testament* (CRINT 12; Leiden: Brill, 2009), pp.123–31.

6   Ashton, *Understanding*, pp.346–7.

7   Ashton, *Understanding*, pp.321–3, 378.

8   Ignace de la Potterie, 'The Truth in Saint John', in John Ashton (ed.), *The Interpretation of John* (Edinburgh; T. & T. Clark, 2nd edn, 1997), pp.67–82; originally published as 'La Verità in S. Giovanni', *Rivista Biblica* 11 (1963), pp.3–24.

apocalyptic'.[9] De la Potterie similarly characterises the Spirit-Paraclete as the interpreter belonging to the 'second phase of revelation',[10] and, in particular, claims that the ἐν παροιμίαις–παρρησίᾳ contrast (John 16.25) and the striking repetition of the verb ἀναγγέλλω to denote the revelatory activity of the Spirit (16.13-15) neatly fit 'the literary genre of apocalyptic'.[11] Ashton does go further than de la Potterie in concluding that the Spirit-Paraclete in John's Gospel fulfils the apocalyptic function of the *angelus interpres*,[12] the heavenly intermediary whose task it is to expound the mysterious revelation contained in visions and dreams that is beyond human decipherment (e.g. Dan 7.16-28; 8.15-26; *1 En.* 16–36; *4 Ezra* 10.29-58; *2 Bar.* 55.3-76.5).[13] Like the *angelus interpres*, the

9   See also Ignace de la Potterie, 'L'arrière-fond du thème johannique de vérité', in Kurt Aland *et al.* (eds.), *Studia Evangelica 1: Papers Presented to the International Congress on 'The Four Gospels in 1957' held at Christ Church, Oxford, 1957* (Texte und Untersuchungen 73; Berlin: Akademie-Verlag, 1959), pp.277–94, and *La vérité dans Saint Jean: Tome 1: Le Christ et la vérité. L'Esprit et la vérité* (Analecta Biblica 73; Rome: Biblical Institute, 1977), pp.362–78, 445–3.

10   De la Potterie, 'Truth', p.77; cf. *La vérité*, p.448. See further Felix Porsch, *Pneuma und Wort: Ein exegetischer Beitrag zur Pneumatologie des Johannesevangeliums* (Frankfurter Theologische Studien 16; Frankfurt am Main: Josef Knecht, 1974), p.296.

11   See de la Potterie, 'Truth', p.77, and *La vérité*, pp.446–7.

12   Ashton, *Understanding*, pp.318, 346. Robert G. Hall, *Revealed Histories: Techniques for Ancient Jewish and Christian Historiography* (JSPSup 6; Sheffield: JSOT, 1991), stops short of attributing the role of the *angelus interpres* to the Paraclete, although he does remark: 'As the scriptures for the Qumran community contain secrets revealed by the inspired Teacher of Righteousness or the heavens for the apocalyptist hold mysteries to be revealed by a heavenly guide and interpreter, so the words and deeds of Jesus contain everything the Johannine Christian needs to know and the Paraclete comes as heavenly guide and interpreter' (p.218). Earlier Johannine scholarship tends to focus on the possible influence of angelic advocate or intercessory figures (cf. John 15.26-27; 16.8-11), rather than interpreting angels (cf. 14.25-26; 16.13-15), in late Second Temple Judaism; see Otto Betz, *Der Paraklet. Fürsprecher im häretischen Spätjudentum, im Johannes-Evangelium und in neu gefundenen gnostischen Schriften* (AGSU 2; Leiden: Brill, 1963); Hans Windisch, *The Spirit-Paraclete in the Fourth Gospel* (trans. J. W. Cox; Philadelphia: Fortress, 1968), pp.15–25.

13   On the significance of the *angelus interpres* in the Hebrew Bible and later Jewish (and early Christian) apocalypses, see Hansgünter Reichelt, *Angelus interpres – Texte in der Johannes-Apokalypse: Strukturen, Aussagen und Hintergründe* (Europäische Hochschulschriften: Theologie 507; Frankfurt am Main: Peter Lang, 1994), pp.5–20. See also Donata Dörfel, *Engel in der apokalyptischen Literatur und ihre theologische Relevanz am Beispiel von Ezechiel, Sacharja, Daniel und Erstem Enoch* (Aachen: Shaker Verlag, 1998); Karin Schöpflin, 'God's

Paraclete 'is sent from heaven to clarify what could not be fully comprehended without him; he completes a revelation that was previously partial and obscure'.[14] Although there is no indication in *Understanding the Fourth Gospel* that Ashton wishes to claim that the Johannine Spirit-Paraclete is *identified* with the interpreting angel of Jewish apocalyptic tradition, he does, as we shall see, list certain examples from the book of Daniel – where the task of elucidating divine mysteries is assigned to an interpreting angel (9.23; 10.21; 11.2; cf. John 16.13-15) – as partial justification for positing a connection between the two heavenly figures.

In view of John Ashton's claim that 'there is no aspect of John's extremely elaborate theory of revelation for which he is more clearly indebted to the apocalyptic tradition than his explanation of the interpretative role of the Paraclete',[15] whilst also lamenting the fact that this aspect of his work has not been taken up in Johannine scholarship,[16] the possible influence of apocalyptic thought on the Johannine presentation of the Spirit-Paraclete calls for further investigation. Ashton, as a rule, focuses more on conceptual than terminological affinities between John's Gospel and the Jewish apocalypses, but it is striking that, in his discussion of the Paraclete as revealer-interpreter, he does highlight the use of the verb ἀναγγέλλω as a significant verbal link between the two bodies of text. As the evidence adduced by Ashton (and, before him, by de la Potterie) is limited to a few Danielic and later possible Jewish parallels, this essay will examine the use of ἀναγγέλλω in a wide range of apocalyptic traditions and related Jewish material, in order to determine how this vocabulary can illuminate the role assigned to the Paraclete in John 16.12-15.

Nevertheless, the first task of this essay is to examine John 14.25-26, where the revelatory function of the Paraclete is characterised in terms of teaching and reminding, and which, together with 2.19-22 and 12.16, provides the framework for John Ashton's analysis of the two-stage revelation in John's Gospel and its indebtedness to apocalyptic thought. These passages (2.22; 12.16; 14.25-26), as already noted, are closely related to each other, but it does not necessarily follow that the notion of post-Easter 'remembering' is an exclusively Johannine phenomenon

---

Interpreter: The Interpreting Angel in Post-Exilic Prophetic Visions of the Old Testament', in Friedrich V. Reiterer, Tobias Nicklas and Karin Schöpflin (eds.), *Angels: The Concept of Celestial Beings – Origins, Development and Reception* (Deuterocanonical and Cognate Literature: Yearbook 2007; Berlin: de Gruyter, 2007), pp.189–203.

14   Ashton, *Understanding*, pp.346–7.
15   Ashton, *Understanding*, p.347.
16   Ashton, *Understanding*, p.7.

whose origins are to be sought from within the Gospel. Ashton notes that 'reminding' is 'arguably the most important' function of the Paraclete,[17] but he does not ask whether this particular function bears more than a general resemblance to the apocalyptic theme of revelation in two stages. As a result, the possibility that certain conceptual and verbal affinities exist between the Johannine and apocalyptic use of the language of 'remembering/reminding' – particularly with reference to the revelation of divine mysteries – will now be considered.

1. Bringing Revelation to Remembrance (John 14.25-26)

The schema of two stages of revelation, with a temporal division between them, is overtly expressed in John 14.25-26. Jesus begins by noting what he has already said (ταῦτα) to the disciples, referring not so much to his immediately preceding words, but to his whole earthly ministry (παρ' ὑμῖν μένων; cf. 14.26: πάντα ἃ εἶπον ὑμῖν [ἐγώ]). The shift to a new, post-glorification phase of revelation is articulated by the contrastive δέ and by the use of future verbal forms to signify the work of the Paraclete (διδάξει, ὑπομνήσει). Several features in this description point, moreover, to the continuity between the revelatory work of the earthly Jesus and that of the Spirit, particularly the fact that the teaching and reminding activity of the Spirit is said to centre on 'all' that Jesus has said. Although some have argued that the Spirit is described as bringing new teaching (διδάξει πάντα),[18] it is more likely that both activities are inextricably linked together: the Paraclete will teach the disciples everything (πάντα) *in that* (epexegetical καί) he will remind them of everything (πάντα) that Jesus has said to them. Also, in view of the tight structural parallelism between the two clauses, both occurrences of πάντα – once with διδάξει, once with ὑπομνήσει – are qualified by the concluding phrase, '[all] that I have said to you'.[19] The reminding activity of the Paraclete involves the refreshing of the disciples' recall of the past, bringing about a spirit-inspired elucidation and actualisation of the hidden meaning of Jesus' revelation.[20]

---

17   Ashton, *Understanding*, p.343.
18   See especially J. H. Bernard, *A Critical and Exegetical Commentary on the Gospel according to St. John* (Edinburgh: T. & T. Clark, 1928), II, p.553; Windisch, *The Spirit-Paraclete*, pp.6–7.
19   Cf. David Pastorelli, *Le Paraclet dans le corpus johannique* (BZNW 142; Berlin: de Gruyter, 2006), pp.276–9.
20   On the Johannine language of remembering, see especially Otto Michel, μιμνήσκομαι κτλ., *ThWNT* IV, pp.678–87; John Painter, 'Memory Holds the Key:

To what extent can it be argued that the description of the Spirit's activity in John 14.25-26 is drawing on recognised *apocalyptic* modes of divine revelation? 'To teach', on the one hand, strongly connotes the communication of revelation in John's narrative (cf. 7.14, 28, 35; 8.20, 28). However, it is difficult to pin down the origin of this Johannine vocabulary to specific traditions, such as those featuring an *angelus interpres* (cf. *4 Ezra* 4.4; 5.32; 7.49, 90; 10.33), since 'teaching' is so widely attested in a variety of biblical and Jewish texts. The language of 'remembering/reminding', on the other hand, may not be widespread in John's Gospel but it is certainly distinctive, both when used by the narrator (μιμνήσκομαι, 2.17, 22; 12.16) and especially when it is ascribed to the Spirit (ὑπομιμνήσκω, 14.26). Mnemonic vocabulary is undoubtedly prevalent in Jewish traditions from the late Second Temple period and beyond, including numerous apocalyptic writings where it mostly appears with reference to remembering God and his commandments (*2 Bar.* 20.3; 48.38; 78.3; 84.7; *T. Levi* 9.6; *T. Zeb.* 9.7) or key events in Israel's past (cf. *4 Ezra* 2.8; *2 Bar.* 31.4; 75.7; 77.11, 23; 84.2). It also occurs, within a forensic context, for the offering of a memorial prayer of intercession (*1 En.* 13.4, 6; cf. 104.1), for remembering the sins of the wicked (99.16) and to denote God remembering his subjects, past and future (*4 Ezra* 12.47; cf. *2 Bar.* 23.3; 78.7; 84.10).[21] Even in *2 Baruch*, which displays a particular interest in the processes of memory,[22] neither the act of 'reminding' nor the act of 'remembering' is encountered as a mode of imparting or receiving divine revelation.

The theme of Spirit-inspired memory does, nevertheless, occur in the final vision of *4 Ezra*, which describes how Ezra wishes to restore the Law whose content is no longer known because it has been burned (14.21; cf. 4.23). He asks God to send his 'holy spirit' into him so that he can write down 'everything that has happened in the world from the beginning, the things that were written in your Law' (14.22). God answers Ezra's prayer by giving him a fire-like liquid to drink, one that symbolises the bestowal of the spirit upon him (14.39). This signifies that God, through his spirit, becomes the agent of revelation, thus

---

The Transformation of Memory in the Interface of History and Theology in John', in Paul N. Anderson, Felix Just and Tom Thatcher (eds.), *John, Jesus, and History.* Vol. 1, *Critical Appraisals of Critical Views* (Atlanta: SBL, 2007), pp.229–45.

21   On the notion of a heavenly 'book of remembrance', see CD-A 20.19, 20–22; cf. 1QH 9.24; *Jub.* 30.19-20.

22   On the prominence of the language of memory in *2 Baruch*, see Matthias Henze, *Jewish Apocalypticism in Late First Century Israel* (TSAJ 142; Tübingen: Mohr Siebeck, 2011), pp.116–26.

replacing Uriel who has fulfilled the role of revealing angel up to this point in the text. Ezra states that, as a result of taking this fiery potion, 'my heart poured forth understanding, and wisdom increased in my breast, for my spirit retained its memory (*nam spiritus meus conservabat memoriam*), and my mouth was opened, and was no longer closed' (14.40-41). The kind of inspiration envisaged here is one whereby Ezra retains the wisdom and understanding (cf. 14.25) that he acquired as a result of drinking the cup of the spirit, which, in turn, enables him to convey what he remembers.[23] He then dictates to five scribes what has been revealed to him: the twenty-four books of the Hebrew Bible – that is, the revelation already received by Moses (cf. 14.3-5) – and seventy secret books to be disclosed to the wise alone (14.42-48). This scene undoubtedly represents the climax of *4 Ezra*, for what the seer receives during this seventh vision is regarded as full revelation. As in John 14.26, the process of remembering is ascribed to divine initiative through the spirit, although it should be noted that the retentive aspect of memory is more pronounced in *4 Ezra* 14.40-41.[24] Ezra is given the ability to remember the wisdom and understanding now revealed to him, but without the (Johannine) emphasis on the mnemonic illumination of what has previously been disclosed to a human recipient, in veiled form, during an initial stage of revelation.

The act of 'remembering' a dream or vision can be assigned a cognitive as well as retentive function, as happens in Josephus's attempt to justify his surrender to the Romans in Jotapata (*J.W.* 3.350-54). He defends his decision by depicting himself as the recipient of divine revelation in the form of dreams, but also as a skilled interpreter of such

---

23 See further Michael E. Stone, *Fourth Ezra: A Commentary on the Book of Fourth Ezra* (Hermeneia; Minneapolis: Fortress, 1990), pp.120, 439. For the view that Ezra's memory retention represents the rejection of memory loss as a distinguishing mark of ecstasy in the Graeco-Roman period, see Stone, *Fourth Ezra*, p.120; John R. Levison, *Filled with the Spirit* (Grand Rapids: Eerdmans, 2009), pp.198–9.

24 Cf. *2 Bar.* 50.1, where 'the Mighty One' states: 'Listen, Baruch, to this word [new revelation about resurrection] and write down in the memory of your heart all that you shall learn' (cf. 20.4). The retentive aspect of memory is also accentuated in *Jub.* 32.25-26, where an angel causes Jacob to *remember* everything he has seen and heard, enabling him to produce an accurate earthly transcript of the content of the seven heavenly tablets. This passage from *Jubilees* is sometimes cited with reference to John 14.26; see, e.g., Craig S. Keener, *The Gospel of John: A Commentary* (Peabody: Hendrickson, 2003), II, p.979 n.412; cf. however Bernard, *St. John*, II, pp.553–4: 'a literary parallel (but no more)'.

dreams and as one with knowledge of the 'prophecies in the sacred books'. He comments that, as he was about to be captured, 'suddenly there came to him remembrance of the nightly dreams (ἀνάμνησις αὐτὸν τῶν διὰ νυκτὸς ὀνείρων εἰσέρχεται) in which God foretold to him the coming fate of the Jews and the future events concerning the Roman rulers' (3.351). Josephus does not mention angelic mediation or a spirit of prophecy in this particular account,[25] but it is likely that he views his recollection of earlier dreams as having been instigated by God, due to 'the passive way in which he describes the experience of remembering them'.[26] Furthermore, he does overtly claim that, during this hour of crisis, he was 'divinely inspired' (ἔνθους γενόμενος) to interpret these predictive dreams with the aid of Scripture (3.353). The combination and sequence of the features encountered in this description are strikingly reminiscent of the process of revelation envisaged in John's Gospel: a series of elusive dreams which form the revelatory core of Josephus's commission – the first stage of revelation – are subjected to retrospective, divinely inspired illumination, whereby the explanation comes – in a second stage – through *anamnesis* and reflection on scriptural prophecies.

An even closer, but largely overlooked,[27] parallel to John 14.26 can be found in the Lukan empty tomb narrative, in which two angels say to the women: 'Why are you looking for the living among the dead? He is not here, but has risen. Remember how he told you (μνήσθητε ὡς ἐλάλησεν

---

25 In his description of an earlier, similarly life-changing experience in Galilee, Josephus does mention a nameless (angelic?) figure who mediates revelation in the form of a dream-vision, saying to him: 'Do not exhaust yourself, but remember that you must also make war against the Romans' (*Life* 209). This call to 'remember' does not, however, relate to the retention or elucidation of revelation, but is a call to obedience through divine commission.

26 Rebecca Gray, *Prophetic Figures in Late Second Temple Jewish Palestine: The Evidence from Josephus* (Oxford: Oxford University Press, 1993), p.53. Cf. Robert Karl Gnuse, *Dreams and Dream Reports in the Writings of Josephus: A Traditio-Historical Analysis* (AGAJU 36; Brill: Leiden, 1996), p.138.

27 Gary M. Burge, *The Anointed Community: The Holy Spirit in the Johannine Tradition* (Grand Rapids: Eerdmans, 1987), p.212 n.59, is among the few Johannine commentators to remark that the resurrection narratives in Luke 24 display 'similar ideas' to John about the post-Easter understanding of the words of the earthly Jesus. Turid Karlsen Seim, *The Double Message: Patterns of Gender in Luke–Acts* (Edinburgh: T. & T. Clark, 1994), p.152, notes that 'remembering', in both Luke and John, supplies the interpretative key that 'opens otherwise closed doors' and gives 'words and meaning to something that would be unfathomably confusing and difficult without the word of the Lord'.

ὑμῖν), while he was still in Galilee, that the Son of Man must be handed over to sinners and be crucified and rise again on the third day' (24.5-7). The women are then said to have remembered (ἐμνήσθησαν) Jesus' words (24.8), before declaring (ἀπήγγειλαν) all these things to the disciples (24.9). Among the many remarkable aspects of this brief scene is its understanding of the processes of remembrance. As in John 14.26 it is not simply a case of Jesus' followers accurately 'recalling' his words, but of them being exposed, through divine mediation, to a post-Easter understanding of the words pronounced by Jesus during his earthly ministry. Of course, the divine agent in Luke 24.6 is not the Spirit[28] but interpreting angels,[29] which does, nevertheless, provide a significant point of reference for the proposal that the Johannine Spirit-Paraclete fulfils the role of the *angelus interpres*. What is also striking is that the mnemonic process in Luke 24 involves the unveiling of what has previously been viewed as elusive and mysterious. As part of their proclamation, the angels remind the women of Jesus' earlier passion predictions (cf. Luke 9.22, 44; 13.33; 18.31-33), and, although none of these predictions is repeated *verbatim* by the angels in 24.6,[30] the explanatory comment in 9.45 notes specifically that the disciples did not understand Jesus' prediction: 'its meaning was hidden (παρακεκαλυμμένον) from them (cf. 18.34: κεκρυμμένον), so they could not perceive it'.[31] This motif of concealment implies a secret whose meaning is deliberately hidden until it is mnemonically disclosed, following the resurrection, in a second stage of revelation. Admittedly, the empty tomb narrative does not state

---

28   In Acts 11.15-17 Peter's memory of Jesus' words is not brought about directly by the Spirit, but through *events* effected by the Spirit.

29   They are described as 'two men in robes that gleamed like lightning' (24.4). This depiction is suggestive of heavenly figures (cf. Acts 10.30), and they are later explicitly described as angels (Luke 24.23). See further Tobias Nicklas, 'Angels in Early Christian Narratives on the Resurrection of Jesus: Canonical and Apocryphal Texts', in Reiterer, Nicklas and Schöpflin (eds.), *Angels*, pp.293–311 (301).

30   On the relationship between these predictions and Luke 24.6, see especially Maria-Luisa Rigato, '"Remember...Then They Remembered": Luke 24.6-8', in Amy-Jill Levine (ed.), *A Feminist Companion to Luke* (London: Continuum, 2002), pp.272–7; Theobald, '"Erinnert euch der Worte"', p.114.

31   Cf. Richard J. Dillon, *From Eye-Witnesses to Ministers of the Word: Tradition and Composition in Luke 24* (Analecta Biblica 82; Rome: Biblical Institute, 1978), p.24: 'The restated passion formulas seem to suggest that *Easter revelation is essentially the unlocking of the mystery of the messiah's passion*, which his followers were prevented from understanding until this point'. See also Hall, *Revealed Histories*, pp.173–5.

that the reminding activity of the angels leads to full insight and belief on the part of the women,[32] but neither is their remembrance described as accompanied by confusion or fear (cf. 24.22-23). The women clearly function as the first important link in Luke 24 and its pattern of transition from confusion to understanding, from concealment to disclosure.

These examples, drawn from apocalypses and from other Jewish and early Christian texts displaying recognizable apocalyptic features, provide varied evidence for the use of the language of memory in relation to the reception of revelation. Mnemonic inspiration can bring about the transmission of divine revelation (*4 Ezra* 14.40-41; cf. *Jub.* 32.25-26) and it can play a key role in the elucidation of that revelation (*J.W.* 3.351; Luke 24.6-8). The available evidence also alerts one to the importance of *recall* in the description of the Spirit-Paraclete's reminding activity in John 14.25-26, though not in the sense of bringing to remembrance what has been forgotten; the emphasis falls on the disciples' subsequent recollection of Jesus' words in the light of the Easter events, a process that enables them, with the aid of the Spirit, to gain a deeper level of understanding. Nevertheless, it must be acknowledged that the examples examined in this part of the essay are far from numerous, nor do they exhibit sufficiently stable conceptual affinities to allow one to claim that, together with the presentation of the Paraclete in John 14.26, they bear witness to a 'fixed' apocalyptic motif.[33] Of all the possible parallels, the one bearing closest resemblance to John 14.26 is Luke 24.6-8, a passage that deserves greater prominence in scholarly attempts to argue for John's familiarity with the Lukan resurrection narratives.[34] Noting certain affinities between the reminding activity of the Lukan *angeli interpretes* and that of the Johannine Spirit–Paraclete certainly sheds light on their understanding of the mechanics of interpretative *anamnesis* as mediated by heavenly agents within a two-stage revelatory process.

---

32   For the view that 'the mystery is kept intact' for the time being, only for it to be revealed later in the narrative (cf. 24.31, 45), see Dillon, *From Eye-Witnesses to Ministers of the Word*, pp.31–50. See, however, Seim, *The Double Message*, pp.154–6.

33   See further Hall, *Revealed Histories*, p.106.

34   Several scholars posit a literary relationship between John 20 and Luke's resurrection narratives. For a recent assessment, see Andrew Gregory, 'The Third Gospel? The Relationship of John and Luke Reconsidered', in John Lierman (ed.), *Challenging Perspectives on the Gospel of John* (WUNT 2/219; Tübingen: Mohr Siebeck, 2006), pp.109–34.

2. Disclosing Revelation (John 16.12-15)

If John 14.25-26, together with 2.22 and 12.16, have largely formed the basis of earlier efforts to delineate the contours of a Johannine schema of revelation, it is 16.12-15 – the second passage depicting the revelatory work of the Spirit-Paraclete – that has so far been the focus of attempts to characterise its two-stage pattern as an *apocalyptic* phenomenon. In 16.12-15 the temporal distinction between the pre- and post-Easter reception of Jesus' revelation takes the following form:[35] Jesus has much to say to the disciples, but they cannot bear his words at present (ἀλλ' οὐ δύνασθε βαστάζειν ἄρτι, 16.12), either due to their sorrow at his impending departure (cf. 16.6)[36] or, more likely, because of their general lack of capacity to understand his earthly revelation. However, when (ὅταν δὲ) the Spirit of truth comes, he will guide (ὁδηγήσει) the disciples into all truth, not through uttering his own words, but by disclosing (ἀναγγελεῖ) what he hears from Jesus, namely 'the things to come' (τὰ ἐρχόμενα, 16.13). The fact that the phrase ἀναγγελεῖ ὑμῖν is repeated at the end of the two subsequent declarations (16.14, 15) suggests that it forms the focal point of this second description of the Paraclete's activity, and, because of its purported apocalyptic links, warrants closer examination.

The verb ἀναγγέλλω is widely attested, especially in the Old Greek translations, where it often means 'to proclaim/announce/report'.[37] Paul Joüon proposes a narrower semantic range, particularly for its Johannine usage,[38] although his suggestion that ἀναγγέλλω means 'to repeat/re-announce (what has been heard)' fits the context of John 16.12-15 far better than its usage elsewhere in the Gospel. Ignace de la Potterie is among several scholars to highlight the widespread use of ἀναγγέλλω in

---

35   For the view that John 16.12-15 is a reworking of the promise found in John 14.25-26, see, e.g., Ulrich B. Müller, 'Die Parakletenvorstellung im Johannesevangelium', *ZThK* 71 (1974), pp.66–77; Walter Rebell, *Erfüllung und Erwartung: Erfahrungen mit dem Geist im Urchristentum* (Munich: Chr. Kaiser Verlag, 1991), p.74.

36   Levison, *Filled with the Spirit*, p.401, notes that John 16.4b-33 is framed by references to the disciples' 'sorrow' and 'persecution'. BAGD, βαστάζω §2bβ, p. 137, notes the figurative use of the word with reference to 'divine mysteries' in John 16.12 (cf. also Herm. *Vis.* 1.3.3).

37   See Johan Lust, Erik Eynikel and Katrin Hauspie (eds.), *A Greek–English Lexicon of the Septuagint* (Stuttgart: Deutsche Bibelgesellschaft, 1992), I, pp.26–7; and BAGD, ἀναγγέλλω §§1–2, p.51.

38   Paul Joüon, 'Le verbe ἀναγγέλλω dans Saint Jean', *Recherches de Science Religieuse* 28 (1938), pp.234–5.

the sense of 'reveal/disclose/unveil',[39] although he remarks that in apocalyptic texts, notably in Theodotion's translation of the book of Daniel, it occurs 'in the special sense of "revealing the hidden meaning of a dream or mystery"'.[40] This, he claims, is the precise nuance of ἀναγγέλλω in John 16.13-15, in 4.25 (with reference to the Messiah who will 'reveal all things') as well as in 16.25[41]: it does not imply the proclamation of a completely new revelation, but points to the explanation of a revelation that was previously mysterious and obscure.[42] Ashton likewise views ἀναγγέλλω in John 16.13-15 as denoting a revelation requiring subsequent explication and, in a similar vein to de la Potterie, claims that the role of the Spirit-Paraclete in this passage is to *expound/explain* the revelation of Jesus.[43] To investigate this proposal further, the use of ἀναγγέλλω in the book of Daniel and other apocalyptic traditions must be examined and the results of that examination weighed against the relevant Johannine evidence.

2.1. The Use of ἀναγγέλλω in the Book of Daniel and Other Apocalyptic Traditions

In Theodotion's version of Daniel,[44] the verb ἀναγγέλλω is frequently used to signify the disclosure of (the meaning of) a dream (θ' Dan 2.2, 4, 7, 9, 11, 16, 24, 25, 26, 27; cf. 2.2, 6 OG). In the opening scene of Daniel 2, Babylonian enchanters and magicians are described as being

---

39 De la Potterie, 'Truth', p.76. Cf. Porsch, *Pneuma und Wort*, pp.295–7; Michel Gourgues, 'Le paraclet, l'esprit de vérité: Deux designations, deux fonctions', in Gilbert Van Belle, Jan G. van der Watt and Petrus Maritz (eds.), *Theology and Christology in the Fourth Gospel: Essays by the Members of the SNTS Johannine Writings Seminar* (BETL 184; Leuven: Leuven University Press, 2005), pp.98–100.

40 De la Potterie, 'Truth', p.77.

41 See de la Potterie, *La vérité*, pp.445–49 (especially p.447 n.30), where he argues that, in 16.25, ἀναγγέλλω should be read instead of ἀπαγγέλλω ($\mathfrak{P}^{66}$, B, D, W, Θ). However, note my comments below (nn. 53, 65) on the interchangeability of these two verbs; cf. C. K. Barrett, *The Gospel According to St John* (London: SPCK, 2nd edn, 1978), p.495; Jörg Frey, *Die johanneische Eschatologie III* (WUNT 117; Tübingen: Mohr Siebeck, 2000), p.192.

42 De la Potterie, *La vérité*, p.448.

43 See Ashton, *Understanding*, pp.318, 345–6.

44 For the view that the Old Greek translation of Daniel was being supplanted by Theodotion's version by the first and second centuries CE, see Alexander A. DiLella, 'The Textual History of Septuagint-Daniel and Theodotion-Daniel', in John J. Collins and Peter W. Flint (eds.), *The Book of Daniel: Composition and Reception* (VTSup 83/2; Leiden: Brill, 2001), pp.593–7; cf. John J. Collins, *Daniel: A Commentary on the Book of Daniel* (Hermeneia; Minneapolis: Fortress, 1993), pp.3, 9–11.

summoned to the court to 'tell the king his dreams' (2.2; MT: לְהַגִּיד; OG and θ': ἀναγγέλλω). T. J. Meadowcroft, who has produced a detailed study of the vocabulary of Daniel 2,[45] notes that at this stage of the narrative there appears to be no distinction in the king's mind between dream and interpretation.[46] The king, in Hebrew, is requesting the recitation and the interpretation of the dream (2.2),[47] both of which Theodotion combines with the aid of ἀναγγέλλω. However, the Babylonian wise men seek to separate interpretation from recitation when they ask the king for an account of the dream: 'Tell the servants your dream (MT: אֱמַר; OG: ἀναγγέλλω; θ': εἰπόν) and we will disclose (MT: *pael* of חוה; OG: φράζω; θ': ἀναγγέλλω) the interpretation' (2.4). Different connotations of ἀναγγέλλω emerge in the Greek versions of Dan 2.4: whereas the OG translation uses the verb in the sense of 'declare/tell' for the *recitation* of the dream, the translational procedure adopted by Theodotion, whose version is characterised by greater formal equivalence to its source,[48] is to use ἀναγγέλλω for the *disclosure* of the dream's interpretation (cf. θ' Dan 2.7). Up to this point in the narrative, suggests Meadowcroft,[49] the two parties appear to have been talking at cross-purposes, heightened by the ambiguity of the king's initial statements.[50] Only in 2.9 does the king, in Aramaic, begin to distinguish clearly between the process of 'telling the dream' and 'disclosing the interpretation': 'Therefore tell (אֱמַר; θ': εἰπόν) me the dream and I shall know that you can disclose to me its interpretation (*pael* of חוה; θ': ἀναγγέλλω)'.[51] Later in the chapter, it becomes clear that the dream and its interpretation constitute 'the mystery' (רז; 2.27-29) that God alone can

---

45   T. J. Meadowcroft, *Aramaic Daniel and Greek Daniel: A Literary Comparison* (JSOTSup 198; Sheffield: Sheffield Academic, 1995), pp.175–81.

46   Meadowcroft, *Aramaic Daniel and Greek Daniel*, p.175.

47   Collins, *Daniel*, p.156, notes the use of dream reports as a kind of 'telepathic test' (n. 42): 'The rationale of the king's demand that they tell the dream becomes clear in v 9: it is a way of checking the reliability of the interpretation'.

48   See Timothy R. McLay, 'Daniel: To the Reader', in Albert Pietersma and Benjamin G. Wright (eds.), *A New English Translation of the Septuagint and the Other Greek Translations Traditionally Included under that Title* (Oxford: Oxford University Press, 2007), pp.992–3.

49   Meadowcroft, *Aramaic Daniel and Greek Daniel*, p.176.

50   This ambiguity is not as consistently portrayed in the OG translation, where 'dream' and 'interpretation' are distinguished as the objects of different verbs. Theodotion is closer to MT, using only one verb on each occasion: v. 5: γνωρίζω; v. 6: γνωρίζω; v. 6: ἀπαγγέλλω; v. 9: ἀναγγέλλω.

51   ἀναγγέλλω [or ἀπαγγέλλω in 2.6] is Theodotion's usual translation of the *pael* or *haphel* of חוה (2.4, 7, 9, 11, 16, 24, 27); it is also used to render the *haphel* of ידע (2.9, 25, 26).

reveal (ἀποκαλύπτω; cf. θ' Dan 2.19, 22, 28, 29, 30, 47), namely the events that will take place 'at the end of days' (2.28; cf. 2.29, 45).

The consistent manner in which ἀναγγέλλω is used in Theodotion's version of Daniel 2 raises the question whether the most appropriate rendering of its occurrences – as suggested by John Ashton – is 'expound' or 'explain'. The verb is certainly used in this Danielic context to convey the communication of dream interpretation. However, the emphasis appears to fall more on *disclosure* rather than specifically on interpretation, on the making known of that which was previously concealed. It should be noted in this respect that the noun 'interpretation' (θ': σύγκρισις; MT: פשרא) is predominantly the object of the verb ἀναγγέλλω in Daniel 2 (vv. 4, 7, 9, 16, 24, 25, 26), which, if one follows Ashton's proposal, would produce the rendering 'expound the interpretation'. Nevertheless, the topic of discussion is not so much the explanation of a previously revealed interpretation, but the *unveiling* of Nebuchadnezzar's dream and of its hidden meaning ('to disclose the interpretation'). In other words, the Babylonian wise men and Daniel offer to recite the king's dream and then to reveal its interpretation. Thus, while the process of dream interpretation in Daniel 2 undoubtedly belongs to the second stage of revelation as envisaged by Ashton and de la Potterie, it does not follow that the interpretative aspect is somehow embedded in the meaning of the verb ἀναγγέλλω.[52]

When Daniel's skills as the interpreter of 'hidden things' are again illustrated by his decoding of the writing on the wall (Dan 5), the possible explanatory connotation of ἀναγγέλλω becomes more apparent. The queen mother says to Belshazzar that Daniel will be able to decipher the meaning of the writing because he has an 'excellent spirit, knowledge and understanding to interpret dreams (מפשר חלמין), to unlock riddles (ואחוית אחידן) and to solve problems' (5.12a). The verb used to denote the unlocking of riddles is the same as the one used for dream interpretation in Daniel 2 (חוה), one which Theodotion again renders as ἀναγγέλλω and whose object, 'riddles', is represented by the otherwise rarely attested κρατούμενα (lit. 'things controlled'). The context of the queen's statement, with its emphasis on elucidation, suggests that Daniel is perceived as doing much more than reciting riddles but also as disclosing their meaning,[53] a connotation picked up by Theodotion in his

---

52 This gains support from the much later *Testament of Abraham* (Rec. A), where it is stated that Isaac will disclose his vision of Abraham's death (ἀναγγελεῖ τὸ ὅραμα) while Michael will interpret it (σὺ δὲ διακρινεῖς) for Abraham (4.8).

53 Cf. *4 Ezra* 4.3-4, where the angel Uriel tells Ezra that he has been sent to present him with three riddles: 'If you can solve/unlock one of them for me (*de*

translation of the queen's next statement (5.12b): 'Now let him be called and he will disclose the interpretation to you (καὶ τὴν σύγκρισιν αὐτοῦ ἀναγγελεῖ σοι)'.[54]

The verb ἀναγγέλλω occurs on three further occasions in Theodotion's translation (θ' Dan 9.23; 10.21; 11.2), with Daniel no longer the interpreter of dreams but the recipient of revelation in the form of apocalyptic visions. And yet, as John J. Collins has noted, the understanding of revelation is similar in both halves of the book: 'Revelation is given in a veiled symbolic form, which must then be decoded by a wise interpreter. In chs. 1–6 the interpreter is human, in chs. 7–12 angelic; but in each case the process is the same.'[55] If Daniel serves as the agent of God's revelation by unlocking the mystery of the king's dream (cf. 2.19-23, 30), the angelic figures later act as intermediaries of God's revelatory message. Consequently, after the scenes in chs. 7–8 where an unnamed angel explains to Daniel the symbolic visions he has just experienced, ch. 9 opens with Daniel's attempt to establish the meaning of the mysterious reference to 'seventy years' in Jeremiah's prophecy (25.11-12; 29.10). The first stage of (opaque) revelation in ch. 9, therefore, is not an allegorical vision but a scriptural text. Interpretation of the scriptural revelation follows, in a second stage, when Gabriel, in his role as *angelus interpres*, approaches Daniel and says: 'At the beginning of your supplications a word went out and I have come to declare it (MT: לְהַגִּיד), for you are greatly beloved. So consider the word and understand the vision' (9.23). As in Dan 2.2, Theodotion uses ἀναγγέλλω to translate

---

quibus si mihi renunciaveris unam ex his), I will show you the way you desire to see'. Ashton (*Understanding*, p.318 n.17) suggests that the Latin verb *renunciare* here renders ἀναγγέλλω, as proposed by Adolf Hilgenfeld, *Messias Judaeorum: Libris eorum Paulo ante et Paulo post Christum natum conscriptris illustratus* (Leipzig: R. Reisland, 1869), p.41, in his reconstruction of the lost Greek text of *4 Ezra*. Interestingly, A. F. J. Klijn, *Die Esra-Apokaypse (IV. Esra). Nach dem lateinischen Text unter Benutzung der anderen Versionen übersetzt* (GCS; Berlin: Akademie-Verlag, 1992), pp.11–12, proposes that the Greek equivalent of *renunciare* (4.4) is in fact ἀπαγγέλλω. This is not a very different alternative, because both verbs are often used in strikingly similar ways. For example, in θ' Dan 2.6 ἀπαγγέλλω denotes the disclosure of dream and interpretation that, elsewhere in the chapter, is conveyed by ἀναγγέλλω.

54   Cf. also θ' Dan 5.15: 'And now the sages...came in before me [Belshazzar] to read this writing and make known to me its interpretation (καὶ τὴν σύγκρισιν αὐτῆς γνωρίσωσίν μοι) and they were not able to disclose it to me (ἀναγγεῖλαί μοι)'.

55   John J. Collins, 'The Court-Tales in Daniel and the Development of Apocalyptic', *JBL* 94 (1975), p.230. See further idem, *The Apocalyptic Vision of the Book of Daniel*, pp.75, 83.

the Hebrew verbal form הִגִּיד: 'I have come to disclose it to you (ἀναγγεῖλαί σοι; OG: ὑποδεῖξαί σοι)'. The 'word' in question is the interpretation of Jeremiah's prophecy (cf. Dan 9.24-27),[56] which is issued by God but disclosed (ἀναγγέλλω) to Daniel by Gabriel. Thus, although the declaratory force and auditory aspects of ἀναγγέλλω in 9.23 cannot be denied, the connotation of divine disclosure is again evident, because Gabriel transfers a revelatory message of eschatological significance that, without his intervention, would remain hidden. The emphasis is on the *transmission* of 'revealed interpretation',[57] which this time takes the form of a divine word rather than a dream or a vision.

The two remaining occurrences of ἀναγγέλλω in Theodotion's translation of Daniel, both of which have an *angelus interpres* as subject, attest a similar usage of the verb to 9.23. A man clothed in linen, who is probably Gabriel (as in chs. 8–9), declares to Daniel, 'I will disclose to you (ἀναγγελῶ σοι) what is inscribed in the book of truth' (10.21) and then continues, 'and now I will disclose the truth to you' (ἀλήθειαν ἀναγγελῶ σοι) (11.2). In both cases, as earlier (2.2; 9.23), Theodotion uses ἀναγγέλλω to render the verbal form אַגִּיד (where OG reads ὑποδεῖξαί σοι), and the focus once again is upon the angel's verbal disclosure of what was previously concealed: the mysterious 'truth'. The angel unveils the content of the 'book of truth', namely the predetermined course of history and sequence of eschatological events, which enables Daniel to understand the fate of his people (cf. 10.12-14). The angelic speech itself (11.2–12.13) may not function as a direct explanation of a previously encountered vision, which is what one usually expects from an *angelus interpres* (cf. Dan 7–8),[58] but the prophetic oracle disclosed by Gabriel does, within its wider context, explicate the message of the earlier apocalyptic visions and the revealed interpretation of Jeremiah's prophecy.[59]

The use of ἀναγγέλλω in non-canonical Jewish (and some early Christian) texts, many of which are apocalypses or texts with clear

---

56 See, e.g., Louis F. Hartman and Alexander A. DiLella, *The Book of Daniel* (AB 23A; Garden City, NY: Doubleday, 1978), pp.243, 249.

57 Nickelsburg, 'The Nature and Function of Revelation', p.112.

58 Interpreting angels most often explicate what has been *seen* (cf. Zech 1.9, 14, 19; Dan 8.16; *2 Bar.* 55.3). However, as far as the transmission of revelation is concerned, the apocalyptic scenario outlined in Dan 10–12 bears closer resemblance to the 'dialogic revelations' in *4 Ezra*, where Uriel communicates 'new' revelation before acting as the *angelus interpres* of visions containing eschatological secrets (cf. 10.59). See Stone, *Fourth Ezra*, pp.134, 425–6; Dörfel, *Engel in der apokalyptischen Literatur*, pp.175–6.

59 See further Schöpflin, 'God's Interpreter', p.201.

apocalyptic features, relates closely to the evidence gathered from Theodotion's version of Daniel.[60] Of course, the task of conducting a comparative analysis – in order to determine whether the verb can operate as a 'technical' apocalyptic term – is hindered by the fact that several potentially fruitful lines of enquiry cannot be pursued. This is because a number of the apocalypses were not written in Greek or have only survived in languages other than the original Greek text.[61] Nevertheless, some key features of the use of ἀναγγέλλω can be identified on the basis of the extant evidence.

First, it can be claimed that, apart from a few exceptions,[62] the verb ἀναγγέλλω is predominantly used – as in Theodotion's translation of Daniel – to represent the verbal disclosure of information previously unknown to, or hidden from, the recipient. This applies to the evidence available from Jewish apocalypses, as well as from texts belonging to other genres (including testaments) that exhibit well-known apocalyptic characteristics such as the disclosure of divine secrets by otherworldly beings. In a frequently cited example from *3 Baruch*,[63] the angel of the Lord tells Baruch that he will show him the heavenly mysteries; he has been sent before him so that 'I should disclose and show to you (ὅπως ἀναγγείλω καὶ ὑποδείξω σοι) all things of God' (1.4). In other words, the verb ἀναγγέλλω, like the verb ὑποδείκνυμι (cf. *3 Bar.* 1.6, 7, 8; 2.6; Dan 9.23; 10.21; 11.2 OG), is used to denote the imparting of divine revelation that would otherwise remain unknowable. This connotation of disclosure, particularly unveiling-through-speech, continues when Baruch asks the angel: 'Reveal to me (ἀνάγγειλόν μοι), I pray you, what is the thickness of this heaven in which we have journeyed, and what is its width…so that I may make them known (ἵνα κἀγὼ ἀπαγγείλω) to the sons of men' (2.4). Unless one seeks to claim that *3 Baruch* establishes

---

60 For a list of extant examples, see Albert-Marie Denis (ed.), *Concordance grecque des Pseudépigraphes d'Ancien Testament* (Louvain: Institut Orientaliste, 1987), p.138.

61 For example, the Syriac text of *2 Baruch* contains many references to 'the Mighty One' showing visions (54.6), making known mysteries (81.4; 85.8; cf. 71.2), and revealing the interpretation of a vision (54.20; 56.1; 76.1). Similarly, in the Latin text of *4 Ezra* Uriel 'shows' revelation (4.47; cf. 4.3-4; 5.56; 6.33; 8.62-63; 12.9; 13.15) and 'tells' revelation (5.13; cf. 8.2; 10.38; 13.21) through the interpretation of parables and visions/dreams/signs.

62 The element of disclosure is sometimes absent, with the emphasis solely on reporting/declaring information, not on revealing/transmitting to others what has already been unveiled to the speaker (see *T. Zeb.* 5.1; 7.1; *T. Job* 16.7; *Apocr. Ezek.* 64.70.12; cf. Acts 14.27; 15.4; 2 Cor 7.7).

63 J. Schniewind, ἀναγγέλλω κτλ., *ThWNT*, I, p.63; de la Potterie, 'Truth', p.77.

a distinction between angelic and human modes of communication, it is noteworthy, certainly as far as the Johannine evidence is concerned,[64] that both ἀναγγέλλω and ἀπαγγέλλω are used in a virtually synonymous manner in this passage[65] to signify not so much proclamation and/or interpretation, but the disclosure and transmission of previously hidden information: Baruch requests the angel to unveil to him the mysteries that he will then make known to other humans.

Secondly, although heavenly beings are by no means the exclusive subject of ἀναγγέλλω in Jewish (and early Christian) texts,[66] there is no doubt that the revelatory activity of angelic figures is frequently expressed with the aid of this verb, particularly when the emphasis falls on the auditory rather than the visual aspect of the mediated revelation. Human beings request that an angel discloses (ἀνάγγειλόν μοι) information to them (*Jos. Asen.* 14.7; 15.12), and, particularly in Recension A of the *Testament of Abraham*, the angel Michael is commissioned by God to descend and reveal the heavenly secret to Abraham that he is about to die (ἀναγγέλλω: 1.6; 4.6; 7.11; cf. 17.6; 20.1; 20.3).

The above analysis of the use of ἀναγγέλλω in the book of Daniel (Theodotion), and in other Greek texts bearing apocalyptic features, demonstrates that, in the majority of cases, it denotes the verbal disclosure and transmission of revelation otherwise unknown to the recipient. Although the explication of previously communicated revelation is sometimes implied in the context, it does not follow that ἀναγγέλλω necessarily connotes an *interpretative* form of communication; it can also signify the unveiling of 'new' revelation. Hence, while the *angelus interpres* is frequently depicted in apocalyptic traditions as explaining an already received vision or oracle, on several occasions this heavenly figure takes on the role of a revealing – rather than strictly interpreting – angel, whose task is to disclose what has thus far not been revealed.

2.2. The Use of ἀναγγέλλω in John 16.13-15

In what ways can this examination of various examples of the Jewish attestation of ἀναγγέλλω cast light on its use in John 16.13-15 to denote

---

64   See John 4.25; 5.15; 16.13-15, 25.
65   For further examples, see *4 Bar.* 1.9 and 2.1.
66   E.g. Adam (*L.A.E.* 3.2; 6.2; 31.2); Eve (*L.A.E.* 14.3; 15.1); Enoch (*1 En. [Greek]* 13.10); Aseneth (*Jos. Asen.* 19.4); Levi son of Leah (*Jos. Asen.* 26.6; 28.17); Levi (*T. Levi* 8.19; 10.1); Naphtali (*T. Naph.* 7.4); Abraham (*T. Ab.* [A] 5.12); Isaac (*T. Ab.* [A] 4.8; 7.1). In all these cases the emphasis is on transmitting information previously hidden from the recipient. Cf. also Acts 20.27; Rom 15.21; 1 Pet 1.12; 1 John 1.5.

the revelatory work of the Spirit-Paraclete? Most Johannine commentators opt for the view that in 16.12-15, as in 14.25-26, the primary function of the Paraclete is to *interpret* the already existing revelation of the earthly Jesus; this is often due to scholars' reluctance to entertain the possibility that John ascribes to the Spirit the communication of new, post-Easter revelation.[67] In other words, because revelation must already be 'complete' in the earthly Jesus,[68] all that the Spirit can offer is a deeper and fuller understanding of that revelation.

The description of the Paraclete's activity in John 16.12-15 should, however, be read on its own terms rather than, as often seems to be the case, through the lens of 14.25-26 (cf. 2.22; 12.16). That a new stage of revelation is envisaged in 16.12-15 finds support not only by the use of ἀναγγέλλω in other texts to connote the unveiling of hitherto undisclosed revelation, but also by its immediate context:[69] Jesus has words of revelation that he was unable to communicate to his disciples during his earthly ministry (16.12), but, following his departure, the Spirit will disclose these as-yet-unrevealed words, which the Paraclete will hear in the post-Easter future from the glorified Jesus (ἀκούσει).[70] The content of

---

67 See especially Rudolf Bultmann, *Das Evangelium des Johannes* (Göttingen: Vandenhoeck & Ruprecht, 18th edn, 1964), pp.441–2; Raymond E. Brown, *The Gospel According to John* (AB 29A; New York: Doubleday, 1970), II, pp.708, 714–16; de la Potterie, *La vérité*, pp.449–50; Hans-Christian Kammler, 'Jesus Christus und der Geistparaklet: Eine Studie zur johanneischen Verhältnisbestimmung von Pneumatologie und Christologie', in Otfried Hofius and Hans-Christian Kammler, *Johannesstudien: Untersuchungen zur Theologie des vierten Evangeliums* (WUNT 88; Tübingen: Mohr Siebeck, 1996), pp.137–8.

68 Olsson, *Structure and Meaning in the Fourth Gospel*, p.270.

69 Ernst Bammel, 'Jesus und der Paraklet in Johannes 16', in Barnabas Lindars and Stephen S. Smalley (eds.), *Christ and Spirit in the New Testament: In Honour of C.F.D. Moule* (Cambridge: Cambridge University Press, 1973), p.207, speaks of John 16.13 in terms of 'die Kundmachung neuer Wahrheitselemente'. See further Müller, 'Die Parakletenvorstellung', pp.37, 72–4; Frey, *Die johanneische Eschatologie III*, pp.193–204.

70 B D W Θ read the future tense, but ℵ L have the present tense (ἀκούει). Although ἀκούσει is sometimes viewed as a later attempt at closer alignment with other future verbal forms in John 16.13 (e.g. Brown, *The Gospel according to John*, pp.707–8), ἀκούει could represent a scribal attempt at linking the Paraclete's activity more closely with the revelation of the earthly Jesus; see especially Reimund Bieringer, 'The Spirit's Guidance into all the Truth: The Text-Critical Problems of John 16,13', in Adelbert Denaux (ed.), *New Testament Textual Criticism and Exegesis: Festschrift J. Delobel* (BETL 161; Leuven: Leuven University Press, 2002), pp.190–1, 196–7.

this new revelation is described, at least initially (16.13), as 'the things to come' (τὰ ἐρχόμενα), referring in all likelihood to the Spirit's future disclosure (ἀναγγελεῖ) of eschatological secrets about end-time events rather than to Jesus' death and resurrection as 'future events'.[71] As noted by C. K. Barrett, 'From the standpoint of the evangelist τὰ ἐρχόμενα must be events still future, that is properly eschatological events'.[72] Thus, even if the overarching 'teaching' role of the Johannine Paraclete is to unlock Jesus' revelation after Easter, this role can accommodate both the mnemonic illumination of the words of the earthly Jesus (14.25-26) and the disclosure of what has hitherto remained 'concealed' (16.12-15).

John Ashton concurs that the Spirit is not presented as a 'mere mouthpiece' of Jesus in 16.12-15, and he draws an analogy between this passage and the presentation of the revealing angel Uriel in *4 Ezra*, who not only elucidates dreams and visions but can 'take the initiative in disclosing other mysteries'.[73] Nevertheless, because the angelic unveiling of 'new' mysteries can be conveyed with the aid of ἀναγγέλλω (cf. θ' Dan 9.23; 10.21; 11.2), the most fitting rendering for its occurrences in John 16.13-15 is not 'explain', which implies the elucidation of something already communicated by Jesus to the disciples, but 'reveal' or 'disclose',[74] which convey the Paraclete's role as the divine agent whose task, precisely in his capacity as interpreter, is to communicate 'further revelation' following Jesus' departure.

2.3. The Use of ἀναγγέλλω as an 'Apocalyptic' Motif

The discussion in the second half of this essay has centred on possible links between John 16.13-15 and Jewish apocalyptic traditions in their use of ἀναγγέλλω to denote disclosure. To determine whether this usage

---

71 E.g. Betz, *Der Paraklet*, pp.190–2; Frey, *Die johanneische Eschatologie III*, pp.197–204. For the view that τὰ ἐρχόμενα refers to Jesus' death and resurrection which, from the perspective of the narrative, still lie in the future, see, e.g., Kammler, 'Geistparaklet', pp.148–50; Levison, *Filled with the Spirit*, p.402.

72 Barrett, *The Gospel According to St John*, p.490.

73 Ashton, *Understanding*, p.347.

74 A similar argument can be forwarded regarding the use of ἀναγγέλλω in John 4.25. For the view that its occurrence in 5.15 also denotes the disclosure of otherwise concealed information, see W. C. van Unnik, 'A Greek Characteristic of Prophecy in the Fourth Gospel', in Robert McLachlan Wilson and Ernest Best (eds.), *Text and Interpretation: Studies in the New Testament Presented to Matthew Black* (Cambridge: Cambridge University Press, 1979), p.214; cf. Gourgues, 'Le paraclet, l'esprit de vérité', p.99 n.23, on John 5.15: 'dévoiler quelque chose qu'on ne connaissait pas'.

of ἀναγγέλλω is a distinctively apocalyptic phenomenon, one cannot overlook the striking occurrences of this vocabulary in texts not so far considered, especially the OG translation of Isaiah where, in chs. 40–55, it is frequently used to emphasise the sovereignty of Israel's God as manifested in his unique ability to 'disclose' (Hebrew: הגיד; OG: ἀναγγέλλω) events before they occur (cf. 43.12; 46.10; 48.3, 5). This argument is highlighted in the Deutero-Isaianic trial speeches when God challenges the nations' gods to display their power by disclosing (OG: ἀναγγέλλω) future events (44.7; cf. 41.26; 43.9; 47.13; 48.14).

As well as aptly describing ἀναγγέλλω as an *Offenbarungsterminus* in both John 16.13-15 and OG Isaiah, Jörg Frey proposes that the Isaianic usage provides the interpretative key to the depiction of the revelatory work of the Paraclete. In the same way as Yahweh's unveiling of the future represents a form of divine legitimation over and against all other possible contenders, John 16.13-15 serves to legitimate the work of the Spirit as divinely authorised revelation.[75] This link gains further support from the fact that the Spirit's disclosure of 'the things to come' (16.13: καὶ τὰ ἐρχόμενα ἀναγγελεῖ ὑμῖν) possesses two close verbal parallels, also with strong eschatological overtones, in the OG version of Isaiah (41.23; 44.7; cf. 46.10).[76] Both texts share an emphasis, claims Frey, on the predictive aspect of ἀναγγέλλω, with the result that, in John 16, it relates to the Spirit's prophetic proclamations following Jesus' departure.

Given the wider influence of the prophecies of Isaiah on John's Gospel,[77] the resemblances between John 16.13-15 and the OG translation of Isaiah are certainly striking. However, while there is no doubt that the element of proclamation is prominent in the use of ἀναγγέλλω in OG Isaiah, it is debatable whether its application differs considerably from what is encountered in the book of Daniel (and related literature), particularly if one concedes, as has been argued in this essay, that the notion of 'interpretation' is not necessarily embedded in the verb. Furthermore, the element of disclosure characterises the Isaianic usage more than is

---

75 See *Die johanneische Eschatologie III*, p.194.

76 See Franklin W. Young, 'A Study of the Relation of Isaiah to the Fourth Gospel', *ZNW* 46 (1955), pp.224–7; Porsch, *Pneuma und Wort*, pp.297–8; Frey, *Die johanneische Eschatologie III*, pp.199–202, who notes that John's preference for simple rather than composite verbs explains the replacement of τὰ ἐπερχόμενα with τὰ ἐρχόμενα (p.202).

77 See, e.g., Young, 'A Study of the Relation of Isaiah to the Fourth Gospel', pp.215–33; Catrin H. Williams, 'Isaiah in John's Gospel', in Steve Moyise and Maarten J. J. Menken (eds.), *Isaiah in the New Testament* (London: T&T Clark International, 2005), pp.101–16.

often acknowledged.[78] The trial speeches repeatedly emphasise that Israel's God can reveal his plan for the future because, different from the nations' gods, he is able to disclose new – previously hidden – divine knowledge. This element is particularly evident, for example, when God challenges the nations: 'Who will disclose to you (τίς ἀναγγελεῖ ὑμῖν) the things that were from the beginning (τὰ ἐξ ἀρχῆς)?' (Isa 43.9; cf. 40.21; 41.26; 45.19). The emphasis clearly falls here on the unveiling of things hidden 'from the beginning' rather than on any predictive aspect attached to ἀναγγέλλω.

It should also be noted that, although the phrase τὰ ἐρχόμενα (albeit in the form τὰ ἐπερχόμενα) does occur as the object of ἀναγγέλλω in OG Isaiah (41.23; 44.7 OG) but not in Theodotion's version of Daniel, the hidden revelation disclosed through the interpretation of dreams (Dan 2) and scriptural prophecy (9.23), as well as through the unveiling of mysterious 'truth' (10.21; 11.2),[79] relates specifically in the book of Daniel to future events and to eschatological truths. This aspect is, in fact, symptomatic of the wider influence of Danielic eschatological themes on John's Gospel, including what it has to say about the Son of Man[80] and about the resurrection of the dead.[81]

The one distinctive element that binds together the use of ἀναγγέλλω in John 16.13-15 and several apocalyptic texts, but which is absent from the OG version of Isaiah, is that the hidden, divine revelation or mystery is communicated 'from above' by a heavenly emissary, who, as a result, enables the recipient(s) to gain insight and understanding.[82] The two-stage process of revelation identifiable within the book of Daniel (especially in chs. 2 and 9) and in John's Gospel is not present in the prophecies of Isaiah.

---

78 E.g. Frey, *Die johanneische Eschatologie III*, p.194. Cf., however, Young, 'A Study of the Relation of Isaiah to the Fourth Gospel', p.225; de la Potterie, *La vérité*, p.446; Pastorelli, *Le Paraclet*, pp.181–2.

79 Similarly, the declaration about the Spirit's disclosure of 'the things to come' (John 16.13b) explicates (γάρ) the earlier reference to his 'guiding in(to) all truth' (16.13a).

80 On verbal links between John 5.27 and Dan 7.13-14, see Benjamin E. Reynolds, *The Apocalyptic Son of Man in the Gospel of John* (WUNT 2/249; Tübingen: Mohr Siebeck, 2008), pp.137–40; cf. Ashton, *Understanding*, pp.357–62.

81 On conceptual similarities between Dan 12.2 and John 5.28-29, see Reynolds, *The Apocalyptic Son of Man*, pp.140–2.

82 Note also that the phrase ἐν πάσῃ ἀληθείᾳ in θ' Dan 9.13 offers a verbal parallel to the Spirit's work of guiding in 'all truth' (ἐν τῇ ἀληθείᾳ πάσῃ).

Given that the Greek translations of Isaiah (OG) and Daniel (Theodotion) attest separate but also shared affinities with the description of the Spirit-Paraclete's activity, should one think only in terms of *either* Isaianic *or* Danielic points of contact, or is it possible to envisage the combined influence of both texts, either directly or indirectly, on John 16.13-15? It should be borne in mind in this respect that John's Gospel is more than capable of drawing from more than one scriptural source, both for its explicit quotations[83] and for some of its most salient expressions[84] and motifs.[85] The shared interest in the disclosure (ἀναγγέλλω) of eschatological secrets in both Daniel (Theodotion) and Isaiah (OG) could have inspired John to bring the two traditions into dialogue with each other. Positing the background to ἀναγγέλλω in John 16.12-15 along these lines would, then, allow one to speak of John's appropriation of an apocalyptic motif, insofar as the influence of the concept of two-stage revelation from Daniel (and possibly elsewhere) is combined with a reading of Isaiah through a distinctively apocalyptic lens.[86]

3. Conclusion

Like many other contributions in this volume, this essay has sought to delve deeper into possible 'intimations' of the indebtedness of John's Gospel to Jewish apocalyptic thought, and has done so by focusing on two specific aspects of the revelatory activity of the Spirit-Paraclete: remembrance and disclosure (John 14.25-26; 16.12-15). Comparing

---

83 E.g. John 6.31 (cf. Ps. 78[77].24; Exod 16.4); John 19.36 (Ps 34[33].31; Exod 12.10, 46; Num 9.12). See Maarten J. J. Menken, *Old Testament Quotations in the Fourth Gospel: Studies in Textual Form* (Kampen: Kok Pharos, 1996).

84 So, for example, for the view that the so-called absolute use of ἐγώ εἰμι in John's Gospel is drawn from *both* Deut 32.39 OG and related passages in OG Isaiah (especially 41.4; 43.10; 46.4; 51.12), see Catrin H. Williams, *I Am He: The Interpretation of 'Anî Hû' in Jewish and Early Christian Literature* (WUNT 2/113; Tübingen: Mohr Siebeck, 2000), pp.255–303.

85 See especially Frey, *Die johanneische Eschatologie III*, pp.382–4, who proposes that the reference to two different resurrections in 5.29 (life, condemnation) is due to the adoption of a formulation from Johannine *Gemeindetradition*, which borrows from both Dan 12.2 and Isa 26.19 to proclaim the end-time raising of the dead by the Son of Man.

86 For the view that Isaiah is presented by John as a visionary prophet whose prophecies are disclosures of divine mysteries, see Catrin H. Williams, 'Seeing the Glory: The Reception of Isaiah's Call-Vision in Jn 12.41', in James G. Crossley (ed.), *Judaism, Jewish Identities and the Gospel Tradition: Essays in Honour of Maurice Casey* (London: Equinox, 2010), pp.186–206.

these aspects with Jewish apocalyptic tradition undoubtedly sharpens one's awareness of the distinct ways in which John's Gospel presents the activity of the Spirit-Paraclete in relation to post-Easter revelation. Whether one passage is a reworking of the other, or John 14.25-26 and 16.12-15 attest separate traditions about the work of the Paraclete, this essay has argued that the two passages contain different emphases: John 14.25-26 focuses upon the Spirit's mnemonic illumination of what was revealed in the past, while John 16.12-15 highlights the Spirit's future disclosure of 'new' revelation that has so far remained hidden or unknown.

As well as attempting to bolster the arguments for establishing thematic and verbal points of contact between the Johannine and apocalyptic concepts of two-stage revelation, this essay has sought to highlight the complexity of the task of identifying and evaluating the influence of Jewish apocalyptic traditions on the Gospel of John. The task does not simply involve a search through, and direct comparison of, John and incontrovertibly apocalyptic texts such as Daniel, *4 Ezra* and *1 Enoch*. It also calls for a greater recognition of the already profound impact of apocalyptic thought on the development and reception of other texts with which John engages in a rich and sustained conversation.

'INTIMATIONS OF APOCALYPTIC':
THE PERSPECTIVE OF THE HISTORY OF INTERPRETATION

Christopher Rowland

John Ashton's remarkable contribution to Johannine scholarship has many facets. The one on which we focus in this volume is 'intimations of apocalyptic'. Over the years I have found myself appropriating his words about the Gospel of John as 'an apocalypse—in reverse', as a key to Johannine Christology and its relationship with the book of Revelation. According to Ashton, the divine plan is incarnate, a revelation of God's grand design that is now being realised. John Ashton goes on to assert, however, that during his lifetime Jesus' words remain opaque, a mystery, whose meaning cannot be grasped until the dawn of a new age, when, in a second stage, it will at last receive its authoritative interpretation. Thus the fourth evangelist conceives his own work as 'an apocalypse—in reverse, upside down, inside out'.[1] Those words just quoted form the framework of the treatment of the Gospel of John and its relationship with apocalypticism in ancient Judaism in the book which Chris Morray-Jones and I published in 2009.[2] In it I argued that the Gospel does not offer visions and revelations, by means of an ascent to heaven or communion with the world above (1.51 and 12.28 are solitary exceptions), although it does hint that Jesus has a privileged access to information from, and sight of, God. Jesus claims to offer revelation of God in his person and in his words—from what he has seen and heard in heaven.

Much of what the Fourth Gospel says, however, relates to the theme of the attainment of knowledge of the divine mysteries, in particular the mysteries of God. Jesus proclaims himself as the revelation of the hidden God. He tells Philip, 'He who has seen me has seen the Father' (14.9), and, at the conclusion of the Prologue, the evangelist speaks of the Son

---

1 John Ashton, *Understanding the Fourth Gospel* (Oxford: Oxford University Press, 2nd edn, 2007), p.329.
2 Christopher Rowland and Christopher R. A. Morray-Jones, *The Mystery of God: Early Jewish Mysticism and the New Testament* (CRINT 12; Leiden: Brill, 2009).

in the following way: 'No one has ever seen God; the only Son, who is in the bosom of the Father, he has made him known' (1.18). All claims to have seen God in the past are repudiated; the Jews have 'neither heard God's voice nor seen his form' (5.37): even when, as in Isaiah's case, Scripture teaches that a prophet glimpsed God enthroned in glory, this vision has to be interpreted in the Gospel as a vision of the pre-existent Christ (12.41). No one has seen God except the one who is from God; he has seen the Father (6.46). The highest wisdom of all, the knowledge of God, comes not through the information disclosed in visions and revelations, but through the Word become flesh, Jesus of Nazareth, whose authority relies on the communication he has received from his Father. The goal of the apocalyptic seer and the visionary is the glimpse of God enthroned in glory (e.g. *1 En.* 14). This, according to the fourth evangelist, is to be found in Jesus (1.18; 6.46; 12.41; 14.9) and, to borrow from the letter to the Colossians, it is he 'in whom are hid all the treasures of wisdom and knowledge' (Col 2.3). The Son of Man is the goal of the angels' search for the divine mysteries (John 1.51; cf. 1 Pet 1.11-12). Heavenly visions of God are not on offer in the Fourth Gospel, for claims to see God must be regarded as claims to see Jesus. Hence, the Gospel of John is indeed 'an apocalypse—in reverse'.

This essay takes one of William Blake's *Illustrations of the Book of Job* and seeks to show that Blake's understanding of the Gospel of John evinces an understanding of Johannine themes similar to John Ashton's understanding of the Gospel of John. For Blake, the understanding of God comes as an 'apocalypse—in reverse', in the sense that God appears not as a transcendent being remote in the heavens, but as Christ with him and in him. As such it offers a remarkable anticipation of the kinds of themes that John Ashton and I have treated, albeit in slightly different ways, in our writing.[3] I then go on to consider other 'intimations of apocalyptic' relating to Johannine themes in the Blake corpus.

Exegesis of the Book of Job in his Engravings:
An Epitome of Blake's Approach

Blake turned to the book of Job throughout his life in sketches, watercolours and engravings.[4] While it is easy to see why some commentators

---

3   Ashton, *Understanding*; Rowland and Morray-Jones, *Mystery of God*, pp.123-31; Christopher Rowland, *Blake and the Bible* (New Haven: Yale University Press, 2010), especially pp.58-62.

4   References to Blake's works given in the text are normally to *The Complete Poetry and Prose of William Blake*, edited by David V. Erdman (Berkeley, CA:

have considered Blake's *Illustrations of the Book of Job* (1825) an excuse to parade his theological interests rather than as a real attempt to make sense of the text, I believe we find in this series of illustrations evidence of Blake wrestling with the interpretative problems posed by the book, for example, the relationship between God and Satan and the disappearance of the latter from the book after ch. 2. In MHH Blake had written, 'Know that after Christ's death, he became Jehovah' (*The Marriage of Heaven and Hell*, 6; E35). We see this exemplified in text and image in Plate 17 of *Illustrations of the Book of Job*, which is the product of Blake's last years. In them Blake's artistic creativity is brought to bear on a biblical book in its entirety. As we shall see, Job's words, 'I have heard thee with the hearing of the ear: but now mine eye seeth thee' (Job 42.5), become the defining moment, and for Blake a key way of understanding the book as a whole. Blake's engravings prioritise the images. The engraved images are similar in most ways to those we see in his watercolours, painted for Thomas Butts and John Linnell, but with the addition of the marginal biblical citations and additional illustrations; the surrounding biblical, textual comment is often small. The primary focus of interest, the image, is at the centre surrounded by the various texts.

In one of his early works, *The Marriage of Heaven and Hell* (1790), Blake seeks to show how vision can cleanse 'the doors of perception' (*The Marriage of Heaven and Hell*, 14, E39) and can wean a viewer away from simplistic theological nostrums. For Blake, Job is a victim of habit and lack of awareness of the way in which the 'memory' of received wisdom has informed his life. Blake's understanding of Job's redemption focuses on two key texts: 'I have heard thee with the hearing of the Ear but now my Eye seeth thee' (Blake's version of Job 42.5), and 'And the Lord turned the captivity of Job when he prayed for his friends' (42.10). The first demonstrates an epistemological, the second an ethical, change, and they stand as a paradigm for similar existential change in Blake's readers as they engage with his exegesis. So, Blake's reading of Job's story is one of personal upheaval in which the past is taken up and read differently in the light of the apocalyptic vision.[5] Job (Job 1.1),

---

University of California Press, 2008) (page number prefaced by E). References to Martin Butlin, *The Paintings and Drawings of William Blake* (B), are to the text volume (New Haven: Yale University Press, 1981), with discussion of individual images, *not* to the plates volume. Blake's works are abbreviated as follows: *The Marriage of Heaven and Hell* (MHH); *Jerusalem, The Emanation of the Giant Albion* (J), and *Milton, A Poem* (M).

5   David Bindman, *Blake as an Artist* (Oxford: Phaidon, 1977), pp.209–14.

blameless and upright (cf. Phil 3.6), comes to a new theological understanding on the basis of vision (Job 42.5; cf. Gal 1.12 and 16).

Apocalyptic themes pervade the *Job* series. The Eliphaz and Elihu engravings (Plates 9 and 12), as well as the nightmare experience of Job (Plate 11), in different ways bear witness to the importance of dreams and visions in Blake's reading of the book of Job. This irruption of the imaginative into the habits of religion is of crucial importance. Blake's exegetical insight focuses on the few passages about visions and dreams (Job 4.12-13; 32.8; 33.15), which then become an interpretative framework for his reading of the book of Job as a whole.

The contrast between the earlier images of God enthroned in heaven and the moment when Job and his wife see God face to face *on earth* reflects a major theme of the book of Revelation. At the climax of his vision John sees a new heaven and a new earth, but in the new creation the contrasts of the old creation have gone; heaven is no longer the dwelling place of the holy God separated from humanity, for God now dwells on earth (Rev 21.3). In the *Job* series (as is the case with John 1.14), the recognition of the communion between the human and divine is seen as something which is possible in this life. In Plate 17, God and humanity combine and this is interpreted as a vision of Christ.[6] To use the language of Rev 22.4, not only do humans 'see God face to face' but the divine name is on their heads and they participate in the divine glory: 'we shall be like him', writes the author of 1 John 3.2 (quoted at the top of Plate 17). In the *Job* sequence, Job's understanding of God changes from transcendent monarch exalted in heaven to immanent divine presence, with him and in him, thus reversing the view of God implicit in the opening words of the Lord's Prayer, 'Our Father who art in heaven', printed on Plate 2 of the *Illustrations of the Book of Job*. In the interpretation of the theophany (chs. 38–41) Job discerns the divine as with (and in!) humans (cf. John 14.17, 20; J34.20–21, E180).

The remarkable juxtaposition of Job 42.5 and passages from the Gospel of John comes immediately after an engraving depicting 'The Fall of Satan' (Plate 16). There are ten references to Satan in the opening two chapters of Job; then he is mentioned no more. Blake seems to have attempted to deal with this striking disappearance of Satan at the end of the book. Rather than being tormented by Satan, Job meets the incarnate Christ or, as he puts it in *The Marriage of Heaven and Hell*, Jesus as Jehovah (Plate 6: 'the Jehovah of the Bible being no other than he,

---

6   Bo Lindberg, *William Blake's Illustrations to the Book of Job* (Åbo: Åbo akademi, 1973), pp.86–90.

who dwells in flaming fire. Know that after Christ's death, he became Jehovah'). God is now no longer the tormentor but the divine in human.

There is in *The Marriage of Heaven and Hell* a consistent attempt to take on aspects of Christian orthodoxy, particularly its dualism, and to understand the latter not as one principle negating another but as two contraries in dynamic relationship, without which, writes Blake, there can be no progression (*The Marriage of Heaven and Hell*, 3). As *The Marriage of Heaven and Hell* makes clear, dualism reduces Christianity to a religion of restraint and morality, in which the Spirit, energy, is evacuated of its dynamism and ends up being allied, and subordinated, to the sanction of conventional morality. In an extraordinarily dense passage Blake explores the relationship between Milton's understanding of the relationship between God and Satan in *Paradise Lost* and that found in the book of Job:

> 'Those who restrain desire, do so because theirs is weak enough to be restrained; and the restrainer or reason usurps its place & governs the unwilling.
>
> And being restrain'd, it by degrees becomes passive, till it is only the shadow of desire. The history of this is written in Paradise Lost, & the Governor or Reason is call'd Messiah.
>
> And the original Archangel, or possessor of the command of the heavenly host, is call'd the Devil or Satan, and his children are call'd Sin & Death.
>
> But in the Book of Job, Milton's Messiah is call'd Satan.
>
> For this history has been adopted by both parties.
>
> It indeed appear'd to Reason as if Desire was cast out; but the Devil's account is, that the Messiah fell, & formed a heaven of what he stole from the Abyss.
>
> This is shewn in the Gospel, where he prays to the Father to send the comforter, or Desire, that Reason may have Ideas to build on; the Jehovah of the Bible being no other than he who dwells in flaming fire.
>
> Know that after Christ's death, he became Jehovah.
>
> But in Milton, the Father is Destiny, the Son a Ratio of the five senses, & the Holy-ghost Vacuum!
>
> Note: The reason Milton wrote in fetters when he wrote of Angels & God, and at liberty when of Devils & Hell, is because he was a true Poet and of the Devil's party without knowing it' (*The Marriage of Heaven and Hell*, 5-6).[7]

---

7   The punctuated version is in Geoffrey Keynes (ed.), *Blake: Complete Writings* (Oxford: Clarendon, 1972).

Blake suggests that in Milton's *Paradise Lost* we find an example of this negating of spiritual energy, with the Messiah featuring not as one who bestows the divine spirit, the spirit of prophecy, but as an agent of reason and restraint. Milton, in Blake's view, misidentifies the nature of the messianic energetic principle and evacuates the true power of the messiah by making his Christ a principle of restraint rather than an agent of liberative energy. Nevertheless, Milton unwittingly refers to prophetic energy, desire and the poetic genius, but wrongly identifies them with Satan rather than Christ—hence Blake's comment: 'The reason Milton wrote in fetters when he wrote of Angels & God, and at liberty when of Devils & Hell, is because he was a true Poet and of the Devil's party without knowing it'. The energetic messianic figure *is* there in *Paradise Lost*, but it is not Christ but Satan. Blake points out that there is another side to Jehovah. God is 'no other than he who dwells in flaming fire' (*The Marriage of Heaven and Hell*, 3; cf. Ezek 1; Exod 19.16). It is this flaming Jehovah that Christ became after his death, when he sent out the divine Spirit, according to John 14.16; 15.26; Acts 2.2-3 and Rev 4.5; 5.6.

Plate 17 represents Job coming to see that he shares the divine and that the hitherto remote Jehovah, having descended to earth as Jesus Christ, is now with him and in him. Blake interprets the divine theophany in the whirlwind (chs. 38–41) as a vision of Jesus Christ. Job's understanding of God changes from transcendent monarch to immanent divine presence, epitomised by the words quoted on Plate 17: 'At that day ye shall know that I am in my Father, and you in me, and I in you [John 14.20]. If ye loved me ye would rejoice because I said I go unto the Father' [John 14.28]. What we see in Plate 17 is an apparently divine figure surrounded by a bright halo of light, stretching out both hands to bless Job's wife and Job, the former with hands raised in an attitude of prayer, the latter with hands on his lap. The three comforters have their backs to this event, all with heads in hands, but with the central figure taking a surreptitious glimpse at the event taking place behind him (but only in the engraving, not in the watercolours). The backdrop, vaguely visible, is of mountains, with the glimmer of light coming on the *right* (east). In the margins there is little but a cumulus cloud outline, and at the bottom an angel presiding with eyes closed over open books and a scroll. This is the first time in the sequence that the writing appears in books or scrolls, and also the first time the viewer *sees* what might be written in *any* books. But the important thing to note is that the books are situated in the margins of the image. They function as *marginal* comment on the images, which are central to what Blake wants to communicate. Words are now in their proper place. What is *seen* is given priority. The passages from the Gospel of John transform the interpretation of this scene. 'Now my eye seeth thee' means, according to Blake, that Job has a vision of Christ; as in patristic interpretations of biblical theophanies, a vision of God has become a vision of Christ. Blake's christomonism pervades the interpretation.

Illustrations of the Book of Job, Plate 17
Johannine text interpret Job 42.5
(Image from The Yale Center for British Art,
Illustrations of the Book of Job, B2005.16.18)

The major caption underlines that subordinate place of words to image, of hearing to vision. It is made up of words from Job 42.5: 'I have heard of thee by the hearing of the ear but now my eye seeth thee'. These words are subtly different from the Authorised Version, which has 'I heard of thee with the hearing of the ear'. Crucially, however, Blake omits the words 'and I repent in dust and ashes', thereby indicating that there is no subscription here to the notion of humanity having to grovel before a transcendent deity. This is insight, *not* submission. Above the picture there are quotations from 1 John 3.2 and, above that, 1 Sam 2.6. In the centrally placed scroll below the image are the words, 'At that day ye shall know that I am in my Father & you in me & I in you' (John 14.20) and 'If ye loved me ye would rejoice because I said I go unto the Father' (John 14.28, though omitting, crucially, 'for my father is greater than I' which would conflict with John 10.30).[8] Below this major caption are other quotations from the Gospel of John: 14.9 and 10.30 (above the book on the left in the margin); the verses inscribed on the open book on the left of the page are 14.7, 11, 21b, 17b. This last quotation is a verse about the Spirit-Paraclete, which Blake now links with the indwelling of Christ the Divine Image. Verses inscribed on the book, on the right, are 14.21b and 23, and 16-17a. Blake omits all reference to 'keeping my commandments' (14.21a), which might echo the religion of law which Blake sought to challenge. The quotation of John 14.17 ('for he dwelleth in you & shall be with you') differs from the KJV, which reads 'for he dwelleth with you and shall be in you'.[9] Blake hereby stresses that the Father is *already* in them. Here the mutual indwelling, which is such a prominent feature of the Farewell Discourses (John 14–17), glosses a scene in which Job and his wife are touched by the light of the divine glory.

This Job engraving marks the moment when the contents of the books are actually seen by the reader, and we discover from the words written on the pages that the one whom Job and his wife have seen in the theophany is none other than Christ, the divine in human. Here is the proper ordering of text and image, that is, with the image being given priority and the text illustrating the dominant image. The identification of Old Testament theophanies with the pre-existent Christ resembles a familiar interpretative approach in early Christian writings to be found in the New Testament in John 12.41. In his rewritten Lord's Prayer of 1827

---

8   Lindberg, *William Blake's Illustrations*, p.324.
9   Ibid., p.322.

Blake paraphrases the opening with the words 'Jesus, our Father, who art in thy heaven call'd by thy Name the Holy Ghost'.[10] This indicates a similar identification of Christ with the Father, which is also typical of the Gospel of John. Indeed, a major theme of the Gospel of John is Christ as the image of the invisible God.

The quotation of the Gospel of John in this engraving is apposite. As we have seen, much of what the Gospel says relates to the theme of the Son being the revelation of the invisible Father, the revelation of the hidden God (John 14.9; 1.18; cf. Col 1.15, which is quoted in part in M2.12; E96). The vision of God, the goal of the heavenly ascents of the apocalyptic seers, is in this Gospel related to the revelation of God in Jesus. The vision of God reserved in the book of Revelation for the fortunate seer (4.1), and for the inhabitants of the New Jerusalem who will see God face to face (22.4) is, in the Gospel of John, found in the person of Jesus of Nazareth the Divine in Human. He is the one in whom 'dwelleth all the fulness of the Godhead bodily' (Col 2.9). For Blake (as indeed in the Gospel of John and the Pauline letters), living in God means a particular kind of life. Theology and ethics are indistinguishable. Blake's emphasis on mutual indwelling is not some kind of ecstatic state, for it is above all a way of life, a practice demonstrated in universal brotherhood and forgiveness of sins. Jesus speaks to Albion in *Jerusalem*: 'I am not a God afar off. I am a brother and a friend; Within your bosoms I reside, and you reside in me' (J4.18–19, E146).

Blake's understanding of the relationship between divine immanence and transcendence is complex. Although there are passages which seem to suggest that God is to be identified with the world, and that divinity is a product of the human brain (*The Marriage of Heaven and Hell*, 11), Blake's understanding in *Jerusalem* suggests that the 'beyond' and the 'immanent' are simultaneously active. What is outside coincides with what is inward in Job; the transcendent and the immanent come together. It is not that he sees something other than himself but his true self, as part of the Divine Body that God is, and has always been within, though it is from without, so that he can come to know the glory that is within. Or to put it in John Ashton's suggestive words: 'an apocalypse—in reverse, upside down, inside out'.

---

10   E668; cf. 'Jerusalem' plates 96, 99; J. G. Davies, *The Theology of William Blake* (Oxford: Clarendon, 1948), pp.31–53; Lindberg, *William Blake's Illustrations*, pp.322–3.

Other Johannine Themes Relating to 'Intimations of Apocalyptic' in the Blake Corpus

In his watercolour interpreting John 8.2-11 (1805; Boston Museum of Fine Art, B486), we see Blake capturing the moment in vv. 7-8 when Jesus says, 'he that is without sin among you, let him first cast a stone at her', and stoops to the ground for the second time. The woman's hands are tied. She has her left breast bare and her hair is dishevelled. The accusers retreat and Jesus is left alone with the woman. Jesus stoops to the ground and bows before the woman. This is one of those places where we find Blake exploiting what is implicit in the biblical text in order to make his point about the divine image already being in the woman. Jesus the Divine in Human honours another with the divine image in her by seemingly bowing down before her. Jesus seems to point to the space where the woman can be, which the accusers have vacated.

The following in an excerpt from 'The Everlasting Gospel' (c. 1818 E521):[11]

> Was Jesus Chaste? or did he
> Give any Lessons of Chastity?
> The morning blush'd fiery red:
> Mary was found in Adulterous bed;
> Earth groan'd beneath, & Heaven above
> Trembled at discovery of Love.
> Jesus was sitting in Moses' Chair,
> They brought the trembling Woman There.
> Moses commands she be stoned to death,
> What was the sound of Jesus' breath?
> He laid His hand on Moses' Law:
> The Ancient Heavens, in Silent Awe
> Writ with Curses from Pole to Pole,
> All away began to roll:
> The Earth trembling & Naked lay
> In secret bed of Mortal Clay,
> On Sinai felt the hand divine
> Putting back the bloody shrine,
> And she heard the breath of God
> As she heard by Eden's flood:
> 'Good & Evil are no more!
> Sinai's trumpets, cease to roar!
> Cease, finger of God, to write!

---

11 The punctuated version of this excerpt is found in Geoffrey Keynes (ed.), *Blake: Complete Writings*.

The Heavens are not clean in thy Sight.
Thou art Good, & thou Alone;
Nor may the sinner cast one stone.
To be good only, is to be
A Devil or else a Pharisee.
Thou Angel of the Presence Divine
That didst create this Body of Mine,
Wherefore has thou writ these Laws
And Created Hell's dark jaws?
My Presence I will take from thee;
A Cold Leper thou shalt be.
Tho' thou wast so pure & bright
That Heaven was Impure in thy Sight,
Tho' thy Oath turn'd Heaven Pale,
Tho' thy Covenant built Hell's Jail,
Tho' thou didst all to Chaos roll
With the Serpent for its soul,
Still the breath Divine does move
And the breath Divine is Love.
Mary, Fear Not! Let me see
The Seven Devils that torment thee;
Hide not from my Sight thy Sin,
That forgiveness thou maist win.
'Has no Man Condemned thee?'
'No Man, Lord:' 'then what is he
Who shall Accuse thee? Come Ye forth,
Fallen Fiends of Heav'nly birth
That have forgot your Ancient love
And driven away my trembling Dove.
You shall bow before her feet;
You shall lick the dust for Meat;
And tho' you cannot Love, but Hate,
Shall be beggars at Love's Gate.
What was thy love? Let me see it;
Was it love or Dark Deceit?'
'Love too long from Me has fled;
'Twas dark deceit, to Earn my bread;
'Twas Covet, or 'twas Custom, or
Some trifle not worth caring for;
That they may call a shame & Sin
Love's Temple that God dwelleth in,
And hide in secret hidden Shrine
The Naked Human form divine,
And render that a Lawless thing
On which the Soul Expands its wing.
But this, O Lord, this was my Sin
When first I let these Devils in

>In dark pretence to Chastity:
>Blaspheming Love, blaspheming thee.
>Thence Rose Secret Adulteries,
>And thence did Covet also rise.
>My sin thou hast forgiven me,
>Canst thou forgive my Blasphemy?
>Canst thou return to this dark Hell,
>And in my burning bosom dwell?
>And canst thou die that I may live?
>And canst thou Pity & forgive?'
>Then Roll'd the shadowy Man away
>From the Limbs of Jesus, to make them his prey,
>An Ever devo[u]ring appetite
>Glittering with festering Venoms bright,
>Crying, Crucify this cause of distress,
>Who don't keep the secrets of Holiness!
>All Mental Powers by Diseases we bind,
>But he heals the deaf & the Dumb & the Blind.
>Whom God has afflicted for Secret Ends,
>He comforts & Heals & calls them Friends.'

Blake thus returns to the story of John 8.2-11 in this long section of 'The Everlasting Gospel', a series of verses about events in the Gospels.[12] At several points it starts with questions, for example, 'Was Jesus humble?', or, as in the case of the section we are looking at, 'Was Jesus chaste?'. The answer to the question about chastity is given here by a telling of the story of the woman taken in adultery in John 8, whom Blake identifies with Mary Magdalene (line 4).[13] Blake interprets this as an apocalyptic, 'earth-shattering', event, in which Jesus' actions not only challenge, but also revolutionise, the hegemony of the religion of law (lines 5-14). The setting of the biblical passage in the Temple (John 8.2) makes the climactic focus of the story even clearer—the presence of God is not in the Temple, the Holy Place, but in the act of forgiveness and reconciliation taking place in the environs of Jesus. Blake portrays the Pharisees forcing Jesus to occupy Moses' seat, thereby being asked to make a judgement on the case presented to him (Matt 23.2, in line 7). To describe Jesus' response, Blake evokes the language of cosmic disturbance, such as happened at the crucifixion, to mark the moment (lines 10-14). Echoes of texts like Rev 6.14 may be heard in lines 12-14 ('The

---

12 See Jeanne Moskal, *Blake, Ethics and Forgiveness* (Tuscaloosa: University of Alabama Press, 1994).

13 See Jennifer Wright Knust, *Abandoned to Lust: Sexual Slander and Ancient Christianity* (New York: Columbia University Press, 2006).

Ancient Heavens... All away began to roll'). In the words 'Cease, finger of God, to Write!' (line 23), Jesus pronounces the end of the era of law (cf. Rom 10.4), written on Sinai with the finger of God (Exod 31.18), and condemns the way in which the moral law makes people ashamed, tyrannising human lives (lines 63-68).

Briefly, in the rest of the poem we read of the judgement which Jesus passes on the Angel of the Presence for his part in bringing the woman into the predicament in which she found herself (lines 29-40). After that, Mary's experience of release prompts her to confess her shortcomings (line 45). Her sin turns out to be the pretence to chastity in conformity with a moral law. The conclusion of the poem moves from the particular incident in John 8 to the general question of the mode of redemption and forgiveness, the involvement of Christ in humanity's 'dark Hell' (line 77), and the way in which his death marks the putting off the clothing of Satan's power. It is in effect a meditation on a complex of verses from Col 2.13-15 (particularly in lines 81-83, 91-93). The basis of Blake's remarkable verses is the conviction that Jesus acted 'from impulse not from rules' (*The Marriage of Heaven and Hell*, Plates 23-24, E43) and seems impelled by some higher call.

This appeal to a higher authority is a central assumption of the presentation of Jesus in the Gospel of John, and it becomes the criterion for his action. Jesus claims to offer revelation of God in his person and in his words. There is an authority independent of previous tradition, for 'the Father who sent me has himself given me a commandment about what to say and what to speak. And I know that his commandment is eternal life. What I speak, therefore, I speak just as the Father has told me' (John 12.49-50). It is what Jesus sees with the Father that is the basis of his authority (5.19; 6.46; 8.38).

Cross, Glory and Judgement

One of Blake's depictions of the crucified Jesus ('The Soldiers casting Lots for Christ's Garments' [1800; Fitzwilliam Museum, Cambridge, B495]) puts in the foreground the casting of lots over Jesus' garment. We do not actually see the crucified Jesus, who is a looming presence casting his shadow over the preoccupations of the all too human behaviour in the foreground. Plate 76 from Blake's *Jerusalem* (c. 1821; Yale Center for British Art) illustrates Blake's grasp of Johannine theology. Here Albion (Britain) and Jesus are brought face to face. The radiance proceeding from the crucified Christ touches Albion who by his outstretched arms imitates the crucified Christ. The glory of Christ crucified is an important theme in the Gospel of John (especially John 3.14 and 12.33), and Christ shares this glory with those whom the Father has given him (John 17.22). In the picture 'Angels hovering over the Body of Jesus in the Sepulchre' (c. 1805; Victoria and Albert Museum),[14] there is an attempt to depict the presence of Christ as a meeting place between human and divine, though this time between humanity and God, reflecting on the words:

> And the cherubims shall stretch forth their wings on high, covering the mercy seat with their wings, and their faces shall look one to another; toward the mercy seat shall the faces of the cherubims be. And thou shalt put the mercy seat above upon the ark; and in the ark thou shalt put the testimony that I shall give thee. And there I will meet with thee, and I will commune with thee from above the mercy seat (Exod 25.20-22).

This theme has affinities with the editorial gloss in John 2.19 ('But he spoke of the temple of his body') in reference to the destruction of the Temple by his opponents. Blake's reference to Exodus 25 gives us the one clue that is needed to enable the viewer to see that the body of Jesus is the space where one can meet with God. Here is the Human Form Divine inherent in, and embracing, all people, being given pictorial articulation.

Blake wrote about and illustrated the theme of 'The Last Judgment', for example, in the picture now at Petworth House, Sussex (1808, B642; commentary in 'The Design of The Last Judgment', E552–56). In the Petworth House picture there is movement clockwise indicated by the direction of the bodies and the change in the colours from dark to light. Christ sits impassively and is the point around which the whole picture seems to revolve, a witness to the crisis that has been opened up for those who are part of the picture or would enter into it. The moment of judgement and the awesome consequences are set out. The contrast in colour between the two sides of the picture emphasises the movement of descent into Hades on the right, and the ascent back up to the throne of God on the left. The process of judgement depicted in this picture is always happening, with eternity always ready and available, which is in line with the realised eschatology in parts of the Gospel of John (cf. 5.24). As Blake put it, 'whenever any Individual Rejects Error & Embraces Truth a Last Judgment passes upon that Individual' (*A Vision of the Last Judgement*, E562).

---

14   Bindman, *Blake as an Artist*, p.131; Christopher Heppner, *Reading Blake's Designs* (Cambridge: Cambridge University Press, 1995), pp.197–200, inscribed with 'Exod: cXXV v20', B500.

In a remarkably insightful utterance, Samuel Taylor Coleridge said that Blake was a 'man of Genius—and I apprehend, a Swedenborgian certainly, a mystic *emphatically*. You perhaps smile at *my* calling another Poet, a *Mystic*, but verily *I* am in the very mire of commonplace common-sense compared with Mr. Blake, apo-, or rather ana-, calyptic Poet, and Painter!'[15] In this assessment Coleridge probably picked up on Paul's complex interpretation in 2 Cor 3.14 and 18:

> But their minds were hardened; for to this day, when they read the old covenant, that same veil remains unlifted (μὴ ἀνακαλυπτόμενον), because only through Christ is it taken away... And we all, with unveiled (ἀνακεκαλυμμένῳ) face, beholding the glory of the Lord, are being changed into his likeness from one degree of glory to another; for this comes from the Lord who is the Spirit.

Coleridge suggests either that Blake himself was 'anacalyptic', in the sense that his mind was unclouded and able to discern things that other poets or painters could not see, or that his poetry and paintings enabled those who engaged with them to have that 'anacalyptic' experience, in which the veil is removed from the mind to discern the deeper things about God and the world. Blake would surely have appreciated this insightful judgement by one of his peers.[16]

Notwithstanding that positive assessment by Coleridge, I will not be the last reader and viewer who has come away from Blake's prophetic books perplexed, frustrated at times, confused by the welter of idiosyncratic mythical figures. Indeed, but slowly, the truth dawns that entering his world, probably intentionally, leads to disorientation before it brings illumination. When this paper was read, a member of the audience commented on how repulsive he found the depiction of God as an elderly male with a long beard; indeed, this affected the ability to deal with other aspects of the presentation. In one sense, that reaction is an entirely appropriate response, and one that Blake would have welcomed. Blake's images and words were deliberately allusive, as he regarded 'what is not too Explicit as the fittest for Instruction, because it rouzes the faculties to act' (Letter to Dr Trusler, 1799, E702). Such reaction to images of God remind us that key to Blake's work was questioning the

---

15 Earl Leslie Griggs (ed.), *Collected Letters of Samuel Taylor Coleridge* (6 vols.; Oxford: Clarendon, 1956–71), IV, pp.833–4. On this, see Michael Ferber, 'Coleridge's "Anacalyptic" Blake: An Exegesis', *Modern Philology* 76.2 (1978), pp.189–93; Morton D. Paley, '"Two Congenial Beings from Another Sphere": Blake and Coleridge', *Blake Journal* 10 (2006), pp.26–45.

16 Ferber, 'Coleridge's "Anacalyptic" Blake', pp.189–93.

theological assumptions which depicted God as a rational being who promoted order. Instead Blake sought very deliberately to offer another aspect to the understanding of God rooted in 'enthusiasm', the Spirit of Prophecy and the life of the imagination. To find ourselves repelled by the God 'as an old man' is to be affected in such a way that we are ready to share Blake's questioning of views of theology which do not allow the wind of the divine Spirit to disturb the order of the ancient and conventional.

In Wayne Meeks' now classic 1972 article, 'The Man from Heaven in Johannine Sectarianism', words about the Gospel of John are particularly applicable to Blake's work: 'either he will find the whole business so convoluted, obscure, and maddeningly arrogant that he will reject it in anger, or he will find it so fascinating that he will stick with it until the progressive reiteration of themes brings, on some level of consciousness at least, a degree of clarity'.[17] Similarly, there are some who will find that they are hooked by Blake's textual world, others put off by its obscurity. Blake believed the Bible was in the grip of a theological interpretation which seemed monolithic and unyielding, in which the Bible was used as a rulebook and as a support to quench the Spirit. His myths and text/image juxtaposition were part of a sophisticated attempt on his part to dismantle the monolith.

Blake is one of the premier exegetes of what 'intimations of apocalyptic' might mean in the Bible. The juxtaposition of texts and image in Plate 17 of the *Job* series indicates the link between vision of the divine and the Johannine Christology. The Gospel of John is a key part of Blake's theology of the divine presence in human life, merged with his understanding of the universal divine body based on Colossians and Ephesians which embraces all humanity. John Ashton's suggestive way of enabling us to understand how the Gospel of John relates to 'intimations of apocalyptic' is captured in his words. Blake's *Job* series of engravings anticipates what it is that John's figurative language is aiming to elucidate. As we see in this series, Blake finds in the book of Job an apocalyptic world in which the cosmological dualism of divine world above and human below is turned upside down, as Job comes face to face with the vision of God in Christ; he not only sees this on earth but also in the divine in himself and in the different perspective on the nature of the theological that is opened up to him.

---

17 Wayne A. Meeks, 'The Man from Heaven in Johannine Sectarianism', *JBL* 91 (1972), pp.44–72 (68–9).

Part II

THE GOSPEL OF JOHN AND ITS APOCALYPTIC MILIEU:
SATAN AND THE RULER OF THIS WORLD

WHY ARE THE HEAVENS CLOSED?
THE JOHANNINE REVELATION OF THE FATHER
IN THE CATHOLIC-GNOSTIC DEBATE

April D. DeConick

Years ago when I wrote about ascent traditions and the Gospel of John, I noticed that the author of the Fourth Gospel worked hard to cordon off the heavens and discourage ascent journeys to the Father.[1] Although I had noticed this, I was not able to answer completely the question 'why?' Except for the descent and ascent of Jesus, the heavens are impenetrable in this Gospel (3.13). No one has seen God except through the revelation of the Son who descended and made the Father known (cf. 1.18; 5.37; 6.46). When Jesus ascends back to the Father, humans cannot follow him to the place where he is going, except eschatologically when he returns to take his devotees with him (cf. 7.33-34; 8.21; 13.33, 36; 14.3). It was my curiosity, my desire to answer more fully the question 'why?', that took me back to the Gospel of John to study it anew. Perhaps my years working on other materials had taken me to a different height, a place that might allow me a wider view, a broader horizon to gaze at my subject and penetrate the question.

I was not looking to unearth the secret that I found lurking in the Gospel of John. I was unaware that, within this Gospel, there was a skeleton in the cupboard, a secret so disturbing to mainstream Christians in antiquity that it was silenced by burying it beneath centuries of biblical interpretation and retranslation. I did not know that this secret continued to lie dormant in the modern commentaries whose academic authors claim, like Cyril of old, that 'no one will show us such a reading in the holy and divine scriptures!' Although I had studied the Gospel of John previously, like most members of the academic community I have been trained in a traditional reading of the Gospel, and I did not consider

---

1   April D. DeConick, *Voices of the Mystics: Early Christian Discourse in the Gospels of John and Thomas and Other Ancient Christian Literature* (JSNTSup 157; Sheffield: Sheffield Academic, 2001).

my training to be important methodologically. I did not realise that I was reading the Gospel of John in a certain way because I had been trained to read it that way and no other way. I did not realise that this training was blocking my ability to penetrate the Fourth Gospel and its history.

This time, when I sat down to study the Gospel of John, something had shifted for me. Was it my recent work on the *Gospel of Judas*, which views mainstream Christianity in an unusual way?[2] The author of the *Gospel of Judas* believes that mainstream Christians think they are worshipping the true God, while, in reality, they have been duped by the demonic powers. The god they are worshipping is the god of the Hebrew Bible, a lesser demonic god who rules this world. The true God, they do not know. In the wake of my study of the *Gospel of Judas*, the God-language put into the mouth of Jesus by the Johannine author stood out vividly. In the Fourth Gospel, Jesus consistently calls God '*my* Father' or 'God *the* Father' as if he were making a distinction between his God and someone else's god. This is particularly vivid in John 8, where the author struggles with his self-identity as a follower of Jesus against those he identifies as 'the Jews' who are 'unbelievers'.

John 8 is a painful testament to the emergence of anti-Semitism within the early church at a time when Christianity and Judaism were defining themselves as independent religious traditions, while claiming allegiance to a common scripture and history. The dialogue is racist, dangerous, and painful. It is, I had noticed, the type of argument that the author of the *Gospel of Judas* makes against other Christians whom he thinks are unknowingly worshipping the god of the Jews, a demon, instead of the true God preached by Jesus. Did the author of the Gospel of John have something similar in mind? Was he assuming a tradition that had theologically spliced god so that the real God had become something other than the Jewish god who was viewed as no more than a demon?

These questions resonate more fully when a careful narratological analysis is made of John 8. In this chapter, Jesus explains that his words are trustworthy because he is telling 'the Jews' what he has seen when he was with his Father who resides in a far off heaven. He contrasts his relationship with his Father with their situation: 'and you do what you have heard from *your father*' (8.38). Are we being presented with two fathers, two gods – one the Father of Jesus and the other the Father of the Jews?

This seems to be the logical flow of Jesus' argument, which was set up earlier in the chapter when Jesus tells the Pharisees, 'I bear witness to myself, and the Father who sent me bears witness to me'. They ask

2   April D. DeConick, *The Thirteenth Apostle: What the Gospel of Judas Really Says* (New York: Continuum, rev. edn, 2009).

Jesus, 'Where is your Father?' And Jesus retorts, 'You know neither me nor my Father; if you knew me, you would know my Father also', suggesting that Jesus' Father is not the god whom 'the Jews' worship (8.18-19). Jesus stresses this contrast by arguing in the subsequent narrative that *his* Father God is different from the god that 'the Jews' consider to be *their* father. 'The Jews' refuse this distinction, saying that Abraham is their national father, while their God is the 'one Father'. Jesus disagrees. If they were Abraham's children, he says, they would not be seeking to kill Jesus. Instead of imitating Abraham, they do what their father did. If the God Jesus is preaching was indeed their father, they would have loved Jesus instead of attempting to murder him (8.39-43).

If the God Jesus preaches is not their father, than who is? Jesus replies, according to the standard English translation, 'You are of your father the devil'. The passage, in English translation, goes on to read that 'the Jews' carry out the desires of their father who was a murderer, a liar, and the father of lies (8.44 [RSV]). Or does it? When a careful study of the Greek is made, the reading of the passage is quite different from its standard English translation in two significant places, and both have to do with the issue of two gods:

NA²⁷	RSV	Author's Translation
8.44a ὑμεῖς ἐκ τοῦ πατρὸς τοῦ διαβόλου ἐστὲ	8.44a <u>You are of your father the devil,</u>	8.44a <u>You are from the father of the Devil,</u>
8.44b καὶ τὰς ἐπιθυμίας τοῦ πατρὸς ὑμῶν θέλετε ποιεῖν.	8.44b and your will is to do your father's desires.	8.44b and you want to carry out the desires of your father.
8.44c ἐκεῖνος ἀνθρωποκτόνος ἦν ἀπ' ἀρχῆς	8.44c He was a murderer from the beginning;	8.44c That one was a murderer from the beginning,
8.44d καὶ ἐν τῇ ἀληθείᾳ οὐκ ἔστηκεν, ὅτι οὐκ ἔστιν ἀλήθεια ἐν αὐτῷ.	8.44d and has nothing to do with the truth, because there is no truth in him.	8.44d and he did not stand by the truth, because there is no truth in him.
8.44e ὅταν λαλῇ τὸ ψεῦδος, ἐκ τῶν ἰδίων λαλεῖ,	8.44e When he lies, he speaks according to his own nature,	8.44e When he lies, he speaks from his own characteristics,
8.44f ὅτι ψεύστης ἐστὶν καὶ ὁ πατὴρ αὐτοῦ.	8.44f <u>for he is a liar and the father of lies.</u>	8.44f <u>because he is a liar and so is his father.</u>

In 8.44a, the Greek is clear: ὑμεῖς ἐκ τοῦ πατρὸς τοῦ διαβόλου ἐστὲ. With the article preceding πατρός, the phrase τοῦ διαβόλου is a genitive phrase modifying the nominal phrase ἐκ τοῦ πατρός. Thus: 'You are from the father of the Devil'. If the statement were to mean, as the standard English translation renders it, 'You are of the father, the Devil', then the article preceding πατρός would not be present. In this case the word 'father' would be in the predicate position and could be expanded with an appositional phrase τοῦ διαβόλου, a grammatical decision the author of John makes in 8.56 with reference to 'Abraham, your father' (Ἀβραὰμ ὁ πατὴρ ὑμῶν).[3]

This literal reading is confirmed by 8.44f, which straightforwardly acknowledges the presence of two beings, the Liar and his father: ὅταν λαλῇ τὸ ψεῦδος, ἐκ τῶν ἰδίων λαλεῖ, ὅτι ψεύστης ἐστὶν καὶ ὁ πατὴρ αὐτοῦ. The text reasons that the Devil lies since his nature is that of a liar. Why? Because not only is the Devil a liar but his father is also a liar. The standard English translation is not only peculiar, but strained, reading αὐτοῦ as a genitive 'it' referring to an unnamed singular antecedent such as 'lying' or 'falsehood'. Thus, ὁ πατὴρ αὐτοῦ is rendered in the standard English translation idiosyncratically, 'the father of lies'.

When I turned to the standard modern Johannine commentaries, I noticed that the Greek text is continuously veiled by the scholars, and a straightforward discussion of the passage is sidestepped by them. In the commentaries, the passage generally is translated appositionally and idiosyncratically, 'You are of the father, the Devil', while the literal translation, 'You are from the father of the Devil' (*if* mentioned at all), is trivialised as 'also possible', and then quickly explained away as the purview of the Gnostics.[4]

---

3 R. W. Funk, *A Beginning-Intermediate Grammar of Hellenistic Greek* (SBLSBS 2; 3 vols.; Missoula, MT: Scholars Press, 2nd edn, 1973), 1:§§128; 129.5; 2:§547; BDF, §268; cf. Mark 1.4//Matt 3.1; Acts 12.12; Phlm 3.

4 E.g. J. H. Bernard, *A Critical and Exegetical Commentary on the Gospel According to St. John* (2 vols.; Edinburgh: T. & T. Clark, 1928/1963), II, p.313; D. Walter Bauer, *Das Johannesevangelium* (Handbuch zum Neuen Testament 6; Tübingen: Mohr Siebeck, 1933), pp.127–8; Edwyn Clement Hoskyns, *The Fourth Gospel* (London: Faber & Faber, 1947), pp.343–4; William Barclay, *The Gospel of John* (2 vols.; Philadelphia: Westminster, 1955/1975), II, p.29; C. K. Barrett, *The Gospel According to St John: An Introduction With Commentary and Notes on the Greek Text* (London: SPCK, 2nd edn, 1978), pp.348–9; Rudolf Bultmann, *The Gospel of John: A Commentary* (trans. George R. Beasley-Murray; Philadelphia: Westminster, 1971), pp.318–9; J. N. Sanders, *A Commentary on the Gospel According to St. John* (London: A. & C. Black, 1968), pp.230–1; Rudolf Schnackenburg, *The Gospel According to St. John* (New York: Seabury, 1980), II, p.213; Ernst

Something was going on with this verse, something with a long history that had hidden the simplest reading of the verse. The result of my research on this verse and its extended history has uncovered a strident dispute between two interpretative communities over the meaning of this verse, from our earliest sources on the Gospel of John to the present-day academic commentaries. As I have unraveled this dispute, I have come to reassess the origin of the Gospel of John and its theology, and the relationship of this Gospel to the formation of early orthodoxy and Gnosticism.

1. Four 'Conversations'

The first extant commentaries on the Gospel of John written by Heracleon (*ca.* 160–180) and Origen (*ca.* 230–250) leave the impression that John 8.44, 'You are from the father of the Devil', was a hotly contested passage, and with good reason. For the Gnostic Christian, it was gospel proof – the very words of Jesus – that the God of the Jews was a lesser demonic god different from the Father-God whom Jesus preached. In the Gnostic community, God the Father had been elevated to a transcosmic location, a place beyond the traditional cosmos. At the same time, the God of the Jews had been identified with a lesser demonic god ruling the world. John 8.44 came into play as definitive teaching from Jesus that supported this theology.

The earliest reference to a group of Gnostics using John 8.44 in this way comes to us via Hippolytus (*ca.* 200–230) who quotes from the writings of an unnamed Peratic teacher. The Peratics were an early or

---

Haenchen, *John 2. A Commentary on the Gospel of John Chapters 7–21* (trans. Robert W. Funk; Philadelphia: Fortress 1984), p.29; Raymond E. Brown, *The Gospel According to John* (2 vols.; AB 29/29A; Garden City: Doubleday, 1985), I, pp.357–8.

The only commentary I am aware of that takes seriously the literal translation is by Adolf Hilgenfeld, which led him to develop an argument that the Gospel of John was a Gnostic treatise representing a transition between Marcionism and Valentinianism (Adolf Hilgenfeld, *Das Evangelium und die Briefe Johannis* [Halle: C. A. Schwetschke, 1849], pp.145–77). Gustav Volkmar (*Der Ursprung unserer Evangelien nach den Urkunden, laut den neuern Entdeckungen und Verhandlungen* [Zurich: J. Herzog, 1866], p.76) and Georg Heinrici (*Die Valentinianische Gnosis und die heilige Schrift* [Berlin: Wiegandt & Grieben, 1871], pp.187–90) responded positively to Hilgenfeld. Most twentieth-century commentators, however, have overlooked his work and have upheld the 'authority' of the appositional translation, maintaining an unbroken line in the transmission of catholic tradition.

mid-second-century Gnostic group known to Clement of Alexandria (*ca.* 190–215) and Hippolytus.[5] The Peratic teacher specifically quotes John 8.44, relying on it to demonstrate that Jesus differentiated between gods. He argues that, whenever the Saviour said 'Your Father in heaven', Jesus meant the transcosmic God, the God who was the father of Jesus and who lived outside the traditional universe in another world. Jesus, the Son, was identified with the serpent Draco, the star constellation at the top of the celestial dome. Since Draco's orientation turned regularly so that it appeared that his head was pointed upwards sometimes and downwards other times, the Peratics thought that this constellation functioned mechanically like a revolving doorway, bringing spirits down into the universe at birth from the world of the Father, and at death transferring them out of the universe back into the world of the Father.

The reference to 'Your father was a murderer from the beginning' (John 8.44c) was used by the Peratic teacher as indisputable evidence for the existence of 'the ruler and artificer of matter', who would take the spirits distributed by the Son and reproduce them in the material world. The demiurge was a murderer from the beginning because his work always ended in corruption and death.[6]

The catholic exegete would have nothing of this. So troubling were the implications that the Devil had a father and this father was the Jewish god, that the phrase τοῦ πατρὸς (John 8.44a) was suppressed in some manuscripts of the Gospel of John, leaving the reading 'you are from the Devil'.[7] It is clear, however, that the earliest readings of this passage included the reference to the Devil's father, and that the catholic exegetes had to deal with it. We are fortunate enough to have preserved in the ancient literature four 'conversations' between different Gnostics and their catholic detractors about this verse: Heracleon and Origen; the 'Other Sects' and Epiphanius; the Archontics and Epiphanius; and Mani and the catholics. The evidence from these conversations demonstrates that there existed fairly standard, yet competing, interpretations of John 8.44 that belonged to two emerging interpretative communities: the catholic and Gnostic communities. Not surprisingly, neither agreed with the other.

1.1. Heracleon and Origen
It is clear that the earliest reading of this passage included the reference to the Devil's father. Heracleon, through the writings of his catholic

---

5 Clement of Alexandria, *Strom.* 7.108; Hippolytus, *Haer.* 5.12.1–17.13.
6 Hippolytus, *Haer.* 5.17.7.
7 K sy^s bo^{ms}.

opponent Origen, provides us with our earliest known commentary on this passage. He quotes 8.44, ὑμεῖς ἐκ τοῦ πατρὸς τοῦ διαβόλου ἐστὲ, not only to support a split theology, but also to discuss anthropology.[8] He argues that there is a certain group of people – the choikics (the dust people, those created from the 'earth' or 'dust') – who cannot hear Jesus' word because they are 'from the father of the Devil' made 'from the *ousia* of the Devil (ἐκ τῆς οὐσίας τοῦ διαβόλου)'.[9] He seems to be arguing that, because these people have the same father as the Devil, they are kin. Therefore the choikics are created out of the same *ousia* from which the Devil was created. Their nature is made clear by Jesus, who rebukes them, telling them that they are neither the children of Abraham nor the children of God. Heracleon appears to think that this justifies calling the choikics 'children of the Devil', even though he also thinks that the Devil never sired anyone.[10] The affinity of nature seems to come from the fact that both the Devil and the choikics were sired by the same father, out of the same substance (see Diagram 1 [overleaf]).

The choikics – because they are created of the same *ousia* as the Devil – are of a different nature from two other groups of people identified by Heracleon: the psychics (the soul people) and the pneumatics (the spirit people).[11] The choikics, says Heracleon, are clearly distinguishable in John 8.44a as the group of people that Jesus is addressing.[12] Likewise, the second group of people, the psychics, is distinguishable in 8.44b.

---

8   Origen, *Comm. Jo.* 20.168, 211 (see A. E. Brooke, *The Commentary of Origen on S. John's Gospel* [2 vols.; Cambridge: Cambridge University Press, 1896], II, pp.63, 71). There have been a number of attempts to understand Heracleon's anthropology: Werner Foerster, *Von Valentin zu Herakleon: Untersuchungen über die Quellen und die Entwicklung der valentinianischen Gnosis* (Giessen: Töpelmann, 1928); François Sagnard, *La gnose valentinienne et le témoignage de Saint Irénée* (Paris: J. Vrin, 1947); Gilles Quispel, 'La conception de l'homme dans la gnose valentinienne', *Eranos-Jahrbuch* 15 (1947), pp.249–86; idem, 'Origen and the Valentinian Gnosis', *Vigiliae Christianae* 28 (1974), pp.29–42; Hermann Langerbeck, *Aufsätze zur Gnosis* (Göttingen: Vandenhoeck & Ruprecht, 1967); Elaine Pagels, 'The Valentinian Claim to Esoteric Exegesis of Romans as a Basis for Exegetical Theory', *Vigiliae Christianae* 26 (1972), pp.241–58; Ekkehard Mühlenberg, 'Wieviel Erlösungen kennt der Gnostiker Herakleon?', *ZNW* 66 (1975), pp.170–93; Barbara Aland, 'Erwählungstheologie und Menschenklassenlehre: Die Theologie des Herakleon als Schlüssel der christlichen Gnosis?', in Martin Krauss (ed.), *Gnosis and Gnosticism* (NHS 8; Leiden: Brill, 1977), pp.148–81; Jeffrey A. Trumbower, *Born from Above* (HUT 29; Tübingen: Mohr Siebeck, 1992).
9   Origen, *Comm. Jo.* 20.168 (Brooke, II, p.63; English translation mine).
10 Origen, *Comm. Jo.* 20.218 (Brooke, II, p.72).
11 Origen, *Comm. Jo.* 20.170 (Brooke, II, p.63).
12 Origen, *Comm. Jo.* 20.198 (Brooke, II, p.69).

They are referred to by Jesus in his remark, 'You wish to do the desires of your father' (τὰς ἐπιθυμίας τοῦ πατρὸς ὑμῶν θέλετε ποιεῖν).[13] They are like the Devil who does not have a will, but has desires.[14] People in this group can become the Devil's children, not because the Devil sired anyone (οὐχ ὅτι γεννᾷ τινὰς ὁ διάβολος), but because 'they became *homoiousios* with the Devil by doing his works' (τὰ ἔργα τοῦ διαβόλου ποιοῦντες ὡμοιώθησαν αὐτῷ).[15] They become the Devil's children through adoption (θέσις).[16] These people, by loving the desires of the Devil and doing them, become children of the Devil *like* him in substance.[17] This group appears to be only a portion of the psychics, because Heracleon reasoned that it must follow from this that there also exist children of God by nature and by adoption.[18] He appears to be referring respectively to the pneumatics and the psychics who resist the Devil's desires.

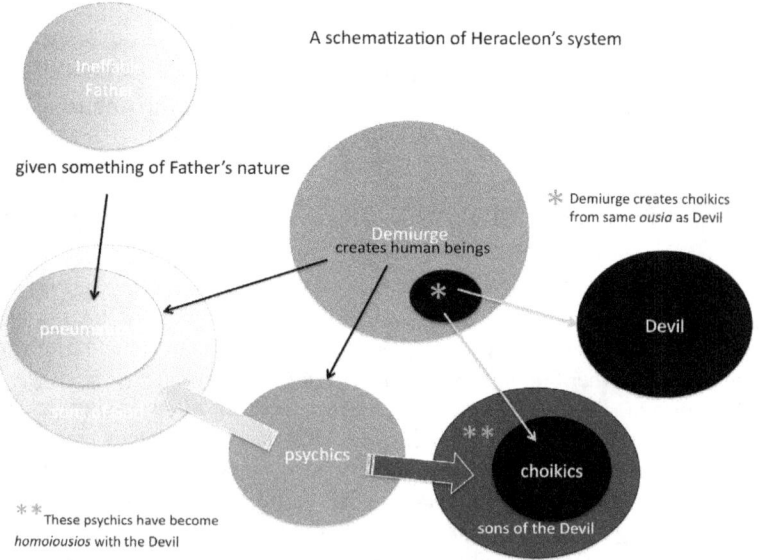

Diagram 1

13   Origen, *Comm. Jo.* 20.211-14 (Brooke, II, p.71).
14   Origen, *Comm. Jo.* 20.211 (Brooke, II, p.71).
15   Origen, *Comm. Jo.* 20.218 (Brooke, II, p.72).
16   Origen, *Comm. Jo.* 20.213 (Brooke, II, p.71).
17   Origen, *Comm. Jo.* 20.214 (Brooke, II, p.71).
18   Origen, *Comm. Jo.* 20.213 (Brooke, II, p.71).

To support his interpretation that some psychics can be called 'children of the Devil', even though the Devil never sired anyone, Heracleon identifies three generic ways that a person can be described as someone's child: the physical generation of a child makes the person a child 'by nature' (φύσει); to do the will of another makes the person a child 'by intent' (διὰ τὴν γνώμην); some people are deemed 'children of darkness' or 'children of lawlessness' by 'value' (ἀξίᾳ) because they have done some of the works of darkness or lawlessness.[19] What he appears to be saying is that the psychics are neither sons of the Devil nor sons of God by nature, but rather by adoption because they have aligned their intentions and their actions correspondingly with the Devil or God.

Heracleon also uses John 8.44 to discuss the nature of the Devil. He reads the passage to assert that the nature of the Devil is falsehood, error and ignorance. Because of his nature, it is impossible for the Devil to 'stand in the truth' or 'have the truth in himself'. His nature, since it is falsehood, makes the Devil incapable of ever speaking the truth. So he is a liar and also the father of falsehood. The Devil is 'unfortunate rather than blameworthy', Heracleon concludes.[20] The one to blame is the Devil's father who invested him with his being and created him.[21]

Origen states that Heracleon also commented on John 4.21, the words that Jesus spoke to the Samaritan woman: 'Jesus says to her, "Believe me, woman, the hour is coming when neither on this mountain nor in Jerusalem will you worship the Father"'. Heracleon identified the mountain with the Devil and his world, which he thinks is only one part of the entire created order. Alluding to Rom 1.25, Heracleon taught that the mountain is 'a deserted dwelling of beasts' which the Gentiles and those who lived before the Law used to worship. The reference to Jerusalem was read to reflect 'the creator whom the Jews served'.[22] Their worship is fleshly and erroneous, paying homage to the Creator who is not the Father.[23] In this passage Heracleon is clearly identifying the allegiance of certain parties to the Devil, the Demiurge, and the Father.

It is obvious from Origen's own commentary on John 8.44 that Heracleon was not the only one interpreting John 8.44 in this direction. Nor was Origen alone in his response, which he presents from four main angles. First, Origen argues that the words ὑμεῖς ἐκ τοῦ πατρὸς τοῦ διαβόλου ἐστὲ are ambiguous. He admits that the literal or plain (δηλόω) reading of the text – Heracleon's view – suggests that 'the Devil has a

---

19   Origen, *Comm. Jo.* 20.215-16, 218 (Brooke, II, pp.71–2).
20   Origen, *Comm. Jo.* 20.252-54 (Brooke, II, p.78).
21   Origen, *Comm. Jo.* 20.202 (Brooke, II, p.69).
22   Origen, *Comm. Jo.* 13.95-97 (Brooke, I, p.262).
23   Origen, *Comm. Jo.* 13.117-18 (Brooke, I, p.266).

father' (ἔχει ὁ διάβολος πατέρα), and that those whom Jesus addresses here appear to be derived from this father. The other meaning, which Origen considers better (βέλτιον), is that the addressees are said to be 'from this father' (ὑμεῖς ἐκ τοῦδε τοῦ πατρός ἐστε), and that the father signified is the Devil.[24]

Origen struggles to give credibility to this second 'better' option, which reads 'of the father' as a predicate and 'the Devil' appositionally. The trouble with this reading is that, if the text were to say 'from the father, the Devil' and not 'from the father of the Devil', the presence of the genitive article preceding 'the father' should not be there (which it is!). To read the sentence as Origen desires – 'from the father, the Devil' – means that he has to stretch the rules of Greek grammar and syntax, something with which he is not completely comfortable. Origen explains in a circular fashion that the presence of the genitive before 'the father' has made the meaning ambiguous. He goes on to say that the true meaning of the passage – 'from the father, the Devil' – would appear much more clearly if the first genitive τοῦ were erased (ἀμφίβολον μὲν οὖν ἂν τὸ λεγόμενον, καὶ εἰ περιήρητο τὸ πρότερον ἄρθρον τὸ τοῦ, πλὴν μᾶλλον ἀνεφαίνετο σαφέστερον τὸ βούλημα τοῦ ῥητοῦ)![25]

Origen knows that he faces opposition to this reading from other Christians who argue that there is no ambiguity. Although Origen does not mention the names of all his opponents, he states that the person who reads the text as 'from the father of the Devil', and thinks that Jesus is addressing the sons of the Devil's father with his words, supports his reading by pointing to Jesus' additional words, 'When he speaks lies, he speaks from his own, because he is a liar and also his father' (John 8.44e–f). The opponent argues, according to Origen, that the liar is the Devil, and another, in addition to the Devil, is the father of the liar.[26] This position assumes that there are two beings mentioned by Jesus: the Devil and his father the liar.

Origen does not respond to his opponent's reading of John 8.44f ('because he is a liar and so is his father') by rendering it: 'because he is a liar and the father of falsehood'. Rather Origen mentions this alternative reading, but discards it, stating that it is an idiosyncratic (ἰδίως) way to read the Greek.[27] He appears to be concerned about this alternative reading because it is one that Heracleon uses to argue that the Devil is an unfortunate character whose father is to blame for evil. So Origen stays

24 Origen, *Comm. Jo.* 20.171 (Brooke, II, p.64).
25 Origen, *Comm. Jo.* 20.172 (Brooke, II, p.64).
26 Origen, *Comm. Jo.* 20.172 (Brooke, II, p.64).
27 Origen, *Comm. Jo.* 20.253 (Brooke, II, p.78).

away from this rereading and argues that 'the lie' refers to the Antichrist, not the Devil, while the Devil is the liar, the father of the Antichrist.

There appears to have been some dispute about this interpretation among catholics, as Origen clarifies his interpretation explaining that the Antichrist is not a lie by nature but by his own choice. There is no need for his colleagues to take offence, nor is it necessary for them to argue that the statement, 'when he speaks a lie, he speaks of his own', refers to all liars. Nor should they assert that the words 'his father is a liar' refer to the fact that everyone who lies is the father of the lies that he speaks. Origen finds his colleagues' argument partially convincing and lets it stand as a testament to the ambiguity of the passage.[28] Elsewhere he relies on this position when he suggests that, because we are human, 'we are liars, just as the father of the lie is a liar'. Therefore we should expediently flee 'to become "gods"'.[29]

Later Origen takes up the discussion again as he investigates further 'what the lie is and its father'. He reassesses the situation and concludes that 'the lie' is 'every evil and deceitful spirit' (including the Antichrist?) whose father is the liar, the Devil.[30] They conduct themselves wickedly like their father, not because these spirits have been spawned by the Devil but because they have acted wickedly like the Devil.[31]

This must have been a popular catholic interpretation, since Clement of Alexandria (*ca.* 190–215) applies John 8.44 to the concept of prophecy, arguing that God is not the author of evil, the Devil is. The false prophets are not from God, but are the prophets of the liar. Tertullian (*ca.* 213) appears to know this interpretation as well, declaring that the Devil is 'a liar from the beginning', as are the men whom the Devil influences, like his opponent Praxeas, who served the Devil in Rome by driving away true prophecy and putting flight to the Paraclete.[32]

The second of Origen's four major arguments against Heracleon consists of a declaration that the passage does not refer to any group or groups of people that are 'by nature' children of the Devil. Because John 8.41 states that the Jews 'do the works' of their father, and 8.44 says that they 'wish to do the desires' of their father, it is demonstrative of the fact that they are children of the Devil because of their sinful actions.[33] For further support, he quotes 1 John 3.8-10:

28   Origen, *Comm. Jo.* 20.173-75 (Brooke, II, p.64).
29   Origen, *Comm. Jo.* 20.266 (Brooke, II, p.78).
30   Origen, *Comm. Jo.* 20.256 (Brooke, II, p.78).
31   Origen, *Comm. Jo.* 20.262 (Brooke, II, p.78).
32   Tertullian, *Prax.* 1.
33   Origen, *Comm. Jo.* 20.97-105, 176-85, 192-94, 219 (Brooke, II, pp.52, 64–67, 68, 72).

> He who commits sin is of the devil, for the devil sins from the beginning. The reason the Son of God appeared was that he might destroy the works of the devil. Everyone who has been born of God does not commit sin, for his seed abides in him, and he cannot sin, because he has been born of God. In this the children of God are manifest, and the children of the devil. No one who is unjust is of God, nor one who does not love his brother.[34]

Third, Origen argues that all souls are created with imaginative capabilities, similar intellectual faculties, and the ability to remember.[35] From this he concludes that they must therefore share the same nature. His opponents disagreed, asserting that dissimilar substances like gold, silver, tin, lead and wax can all be stamped in the same manner by the same seal to make similar impressions. In this case, different natures can be stamped into souls, which all have the abilities to be purposeful, intellectual, and memorial. Although Origen admits that this is a very persuasive argument, he points out that the analogy does not work because the impressions are not identical but distinct since one will be gold, another silver, and so forth.[36]

The fourth defence Origen mounts is his reading of the middle segment of John 8.44, 'He was a murderer from the beginning, and he did not stand in the truth, because truth is not in him'. It appears that both Origen and Heracleon agree that the 'murderer' is to be identified with the Devil. Irenaeus (*ca.* 185) also follows this interpretation of 8.44.[37] According to Origen this identification is clear from the story of Adam and Eve in which the first couple died immediately on the day that the murderous Devil deceived Eve through the serpent, although he modifies this elsewhere in his commentary.[38] He states that the Devil is a murderer not because he killed a particular individual, but because he killed the whole human race insofar as 'in Adam all die'.[39] The Devil as the murderer from the beginning is further identified by Origen with the 'ruler of this world', which he then qualifies: 'I mean, of course, ruler of the earthly region'.[40]

The point of difference between Origen and Heracleon appears to be over what it means to say that the Devil 'did not stand in the truth, because truth is not in him'. As we have seen, Heracleon took this to

---

34   Origen, *Comm. Jo.* 20.97-105 (Brooke, II, pp.52–5).
35   Origen, *Comm. Jo.* 20.203-6 (Brooke, II, pp.70–1).
36   Origen, *Comm. Jo.* 20.208-10 (Brooke, II, p.71).
37   Irenaeus, *Haer.* 5.22.2; 5.23.2.
38   Origen, *Comm. Jo.* 20.221 (Brooke, II, p.72).
39   Origen, *Comm. Jo.* 20.224 (Brooke, II, p.72).
40   Origen, *Comm. Jo.* 20.226 (Brooke II, p.72).

mean that the Devil's very nature was falsehood and ignorance; therefore he was unfortunate rather than blameworthy. The one that should be blamed is the Devil's father who created him in this way.[41] Origen says that he and other catholics do not understand the passage to mean that the Devil was false by nature or that it was impossible for the Devil to have stood in the truth at one time.[42] In fact, the Devil has been deceived by himself and accepts as truth his own lies, making him worse than everyone else who has been deceived by him.[43]

1.2. The 'Other Sects' and Epiphanius

During Epiphanius' discussion of the Cainites, he quotes his own idiosyncratic version of John 8.44 as he tries to argue against the Cainites whom he says taught that people are good or bad by nature not by choice. But as soon as he quotes the passage, he is sidetracked and provides us with a full description of how 'other sects' (αἱ ἄλλαι αἱρέσεις) (not the Cainites) interpret John 8.44.

According to Epiphanius, these other sects assert from John 8.44 that 'the father of the Jews is the Devil' (πατέρα μὲν τῶν 'Ιουδαίων εἶναι τὸν διάβολον) and that 'he has another father' (ἔχειν δὲ πατέρα ἄλλον) and 'his father has a father too' (καὶ τὸν αὐτοῦ πατέρα πάλιν πατέρα).[44] I read Epiphanius' discourse as the slogans of distinct yet unnamed Gnostics who developed them from their enrapture with John 8.44, a text which they interpreted to refer to three characters. They appear to be reading John 8.44a in a multivalent fashion. When read appositionally ('You are from the father, the Devil') it shows that 'the father of the Jews is the Devil'. When read as a standard genitive phrase ('You are from the father of the Devil'), they argued that this proves that the Devil 'has another father'. They understood 'that one' in John 8.44c to refer to the Demiurge (not the Devil) and so were able to read John 8.44f as a reference to the Demiurge (the liar) and his father (the other liar). Thus the slogan repeated by Epiphanius: 'his father has a father too'.

---

41 Origen, *Comm. Jo.* 20.202, 252-54 (Brooke, II, pp.70, 78).
42 Origen, *Comm. Jo.* 20.252 (Brooke, II, p.78).
43 Origen, *Comm. Jo.* 20.244 (Brooke, II, p.77).
44 Epiphanius, *Pan.* 38.4.2-3; see also Karl Holl, *Epiphanius II: Panarion haer. 34–64* (ed. Jürgen Dummer; Berlin: Akademie Verlag, rev. edn, 1980), pp.66–7. All further references to Epiphanius' *Panarion* follow Holl, *Epiphanius* II, and idem, *Epiphanius III: Panarion haer. 65–80* (ed. Jürgen Dummer; Berlin: Akademie Verlag, rev. edn, 1985).

This final slogan is a distinctive teaching: the Demiurge has a father, and if this father is reflected in their reading of John 8.44f, as appears to be the case, then this father is a liar too. In the majority of Gnostic traditions, the Demiurge has a mother, Sophia, but no father. The lack of a father, in fact, is one of the reasons for his deformity. There is only one Gnostic tradition of which I am aware that claims Ialdabaoth has a father. It is the tradition preserved by *Pistis Sophia* in a myth that recounts the activities of Authades, the disobedient ruler of the thirteenth aeon, who brings forth the great lion-faced Ialdabaoth and establishes him in Chaos. By doing this, Authades means to trick Sophia (whom he despises) into leaving his realm. When she peers down into Chaos, she sees Authades' light in the lion-faced beast. Because Sophia is attracted to light, she desires it. So she descends into Chaos where Ialdabaoth captures her and steals her own light from her. This disables her so that she cannot return to her home in the thirteenth aeon, a place outside of the universe but below the Kingdom of Light.[45] Given that *Pistis Sophia* is conventionally dated to the late third century or early fourth century CE, it is quite plausible that Epiphanius (*ca.* 320–403), in his discussion, may be reflecting knowledge of Gnostics familiar with the domain of mythology preserved in *Pistis Sophia*.

Epiphanius elaborates upon his description of the sectarians' interpretation of John 8.44 by explaining (and feigning disbelief) that, when they say, τοῦτον πατέρα τοῦ ἐκείνου πατρὸς εἶναι, they are tracing the Devil's ancestry 'to the Lord of All (ἐπὶ τὸν πάντων δεσπότην), the God of the Jews and Christians and all people (θεὸν Ἰουδαίων καὶ Χριστιανῶν καὶ πάντων)', who is 'the Lawgiver through Moses and he who has done so many miracles'.[46]

Of course Epiphanius considers this interpretation of John 8.44 to be erroneous. He is happy to provide the correct one, along with his own quotation of the disputed passage. It is impossible to know what Epiphanius' Greek version of this verse actually said, because what he quotes is radically different from the version of John 8.44 quoted by Heracleon and Origen. Epiphanius knows that certain groups are arguing that John 8.44a refers to the father of the Devil and he himself admits that the Devil's father needs to be identified. So, one of his strategies to handle this text appears to have been to refashion the passage in such a way that the reference to the father of the Devil is erased. In all the cases where Epiphanius refers to John 8.44a, he does so by stating that the Lord says, 'You are the sons of the Devil', or some like-variation:

45 *Pistis Sophia* 1.30-31, 39, 50.
46 Epiphanius, *Pan.* 38.4.4 (Holl, II, p.67).

John 8.44a	ὑμεῖς ἐκ τοῦ πατρὸς τοῦ διαβόλου ἐστέ,	You are from the father of the Devil.
Pan. 38.4.2.31-32	ὑμεῖς υἱοί ἐστε τοῦ πατρὸς ὑμῶν τοῦ διαβόλου	You are sons of your father the Devil.
40.5.5	ὑμεῖς ἐκ τοῦ Σατανᾶ ἐστε	You are from Satan.
40.6.7	ὑμεῖς τέκνα ἐστὲ τοῦ διαβόλου	You are children of the Devil.
66.63.1	ὑμεῖς υἱοὶ τοῦ διαβόλου ἐστέ	You are sons of the Devil.
66.63.11	ὑμεῖς υἱοί ἐστε τοῦ διαβόλου	You are sons of the Devil.

He then tries to prove that the reference to the Devil in John 8.44a is a reference to Judas, whom Jesus calls 'a devil' and Satan according to the Gospel.[47] Judas, he says, was not the Devil 'by nature (φύσει), but by intent (γνώμην)'.[48] To strengthen this position, Epiphanius quotes Jesus' words from John 17.11-12, although his version differs substantially from the conventional Greek, which says nothing about the Father being the Lord of heaven and earth:[49] 'Father, Lord of heaven and earth, keep those whom you have given me. While I was with them I kept them, and none of them is lost except the son of destruction (ὁ υἱὸς τῆς ἀπωλείας)'.[50] He also refers to Matt 26.24 to show that Judas was a free agent operating on his own volition as the Devil.[51] He says that it is known from every ancient source that the Lord was referring to Judas when he spoke to the Jews in John 8.44.[52]

This allows him to move to his next proposition: because the Jews and Judas were like-minded and they trusted Judas rather than Christ, Judas became the father of the Jews. Epiphanius says that the Jews are like Eve who trusted the serpent and turned away from God. He quotes his reworked version of John 8.44 as foolproof evidence: ὑμεῖς υἱοὶ τοῦ πατρὸς ὑμῶν τοῦ διαβόλου ἐστέ.[53]

Epiphanius then asks: if Judas is the Devil, who is the Devil's father? He reflects on this question, reasoning that the Devil's father has to be the liar who came into existence before Judas (ὁ πρὸ αὐτοῦ ψεύστης ὑπάρχων).[54] In this way he exegetes John 8.44f, which he consistently says refers to the liar (the Devil) and the liar's father:

47 John 6.70; cf. Luke 22.3.
48 Epiphanius, Pan. 38.4.5-6 (Holl, II, p.67).
49 This invocation is from Matt 11.25.
50 Epiphanius, Pan. 38.4.7 (Holl, II, p.67).
51 Epiphanius, Pan. 38.4.8 (Holl, II, p.67).
52 Epiphanius, Pan. 38.4.9 (Holl, II, p.67).
53 Epiphanius, Pan. 38.4.9-10 (Holl, II, p.67).
54 Epiphanius, Pan. 38.4.12-13 (Holl, II, p.68).

John 8.44f	ὅτι ψεύστης ἐστὶν καὶ ὁ πατὴρ αὐτοῦ.	because he is a liar and so is his father.
Pan. 38.4.2.1-2	ὅτι ψεύστης ἐστίν, ὅτι ὁ πατὴρ αὐτοῦ ψεύστης ἦν	because he is a liar, because his father was a liar.
38.4.2.3-4	ὅτι καὶ ὁ πατὴρ αὐτοῦ ψεύστης ἦν	because also his father was a liar.
40.5.5	ὅτι καὶ ὁ πατὴρ αὐτοῦ ψεύστης ἦν	because also his father was a liar.
40.6.7	ὅτι ὁ πατὴρ αὐτοῦ ψεύστης ἐστίν	because his father is a liar.
40.6.7	ὁ πατὴρ αὐτοῦ ψεύστης ἦν	his father was a liar.
66.63.2	ὅτι ὁ πατὴρ αὐτοῦ ψεύστης ἦν	because his father was a liar.
66.63.11	ὅτι ὁ πατὴρ αὐτοῦ ψεύστης ἦν	because his father was a liar.

Who is the father of the Devil according to Epiphanius? He says that this can be no one other than Cain, whom Judas imitated.[55] His interpretation is entirely dependent on the position that Judas is Satan or the Devil not by nature but by intent. He became the Devil by imitating Cain, who was a liar and murderer. Cain too was imitating his father, and it is not Adam whom Epiphanius has in mind. It is the Devil again who appears here to be both Cain's father and son.[56]

1.3. The Archontics and Epiphanius

Epiphanius is not done with John 8.44. The verse turns up two books later in his account of the Archontics, a group which he traces back to the Gnostic teacher and hermit Peter who lived in a village near Hebron during the reign of Constantius and his student Eutactus. According to Epiphanius' account, in the Archontics' scheme of things, the archon Sabaoth was an autocrat, ruling over the lesser archons and their angels from the highest celestial sphere, the eighth heaven.[57] These Gnostics believed that the Devil was the son of Sabaoth, and that Sabaoth was the God of the Jews. His son, the Devil, did not live in the heavens, but on earth where he was more wicked than Sabaoth. They concluded that the Devil did not resemble either Sabaoth or the supernal power they called 'Father', who was inapprehensible. The Devil was a left-hand authority.[58]

---

55 Epiphanius, *Pan.* 38.4.13 (Holl, II, p.68).
56 Epiphanius, *Pan.* 38.5.1-3 (Holl, II, p.68).
57 Epiphanius, *Pan.* 40.2.6 (Holl, II, pp.82–3).
58 Epiphanius, *Pan.* 40.5.1-2 (Holl, II, p.85).

Epiphanius is concerned about the Archontics' persuasive interpretation of John 8.44 and 1 John 3.12, an interpretation which they use to support their anthropogony: Cain and Abel are actually from the Devil's seed (ἐκ τοῦ σπέρματος τοῦ διαβόλου).[59] Their interpretation is layered. First they read John 8.44a and f as proof that 'the father of the Devil is the lying Archon' (τοῦ δὲ διαβόλου εἶναι πατέρα τὸν ἄρχοντα τὸν ψεύστην).[60] This lying Archon is Sabaoth. Secondly, they also appear to have been reading John 8.44a appositionally, because they use it as evidence that Cain's father is the Devil: 'his father was the Devil' (πατέρα αὐτοῦ εἶναι τὸν διάβολον) and 'You are from Satan' (ὑμεῖς ἐκ τοῦ Σατανᾶ ἐστε). They also refer to 1 John 3.12 – 'Cain is of the Devil' (τοῦ διαβόλου εἶναι τὸν Κάϊν) – in order to provide scriptural evidence that Cain was the Devil's seed. This conclusion is further supported with reference to John 8.44c: 'He was a murderer from the beginning' (ἀπ' ἀρχῆς ἀνθρωποκτόνος ἦν). Like the author of 1 John, they identify the 'murderer' in John 8.44c as Cain, who killed his brother according to the Genesis narrative.[61]

So the Archontics were reading the passage as testimony to the existence of Sabaoth as the Devil's father, who is also the father of the liar. The murderer from the beginning was identified as Cain, while the liar was the Devil himself. Cain was the Devil's son. These Gnostics taught that the Devil raped Eve, and from this rape she bore two sons, Cain and Abel.[62] Apparently they assumed that Cain was the primogenitor of a damned race of humans. These Gnostics also taught that Adam and Eve together conceived Seth and that a higher power snatched him up to protect him from Sabaoth. Once he returned, he sired the saved race, those who are 'Strangers' (ἀλλογενεῖς) in this world.[63]

Epiphanius insists that this is nonsense. He reiterates the proof texts that tie Judas to the Devil. He understands these texts to be obvious proof that Judas is the Devil of John 8.44, but by intent, not nature.[64] Cain is the son of the Devil because he copied the Devil's behaviour by lying to Abel and killing him. So Judas and Cain are the liars, and the Devil is their father. He first lied when he spoke through the serpent's mouth to Eve. In fact, Epiphanius thinks that all those who mimic the Devil are sons of the Devil.[65]

59 Epiphanius, *Pan.* 40.5.3-4 (Holl, II, p.85).
60 Epiphanius, *Pan.* 40.5.5-8 (Holl, II, pp.85–6).
61 Epiphanius, *Pan.* 40.5.5-8 (Holl, II, pp.85–6).
62 Epiphanius, *Pan.* 40.5.3-4 (Holl, II, p.85).
63 Epiphanius, *Pan.* 40.7.5 (Holl, II, p.88).
64 Epiphanius, *Pan.* 40.6.2-4 (Holl, II, pp.86–7).
65 Epiphanius, *Pan.* 40.6.5-9 (Holl, II, pp.5–9).

1.4. Mani and the Catholics

According to his opponents, John 8.44 was at the root of Mani's conception of his Gnostic religion. In a (fictional?) 'debate' (*ca.* 326–330) between Mani and Archelaus, the bishop of Carchar, alleged to have been accurately transcribed by Hegemonius, Mani begins his defence of his religion and its central dogma – that an evil god rules the universe and gave the Law – by quoting three biblical passages.[66] The first is Matt 7.18: 'a good tree cannot bear bad fruit, nor a bad tree bear good fruit'. The second is John 8.44: 'the father of the devil is a liar and a murderer from the beginning'. The third is a reference to 2 Cor 4.4, that the god of this world has blinded the minds of people so that they fail to obey Christ's gospel.[67] Later Mani expounds on John 8.44a–b, 'You are from your father the devil and you wish to do the desires of your father', interpreting it as a reference to the god of the Jews, who is a wicked god whose wicked desires were written down and given to Moses in the form of the Jewish Law. Mani then quotes the rest of 8.44 as proof that the ruler of this world is a liar and a murderer.[68]

Archelaus will have none of this. He replies that the passage refers to the Devil who works in us, who wanted to make us the same as himself by the power of his will. God made every individual with free will, established the law of judgement, and appointed in each of us the ability to sin or not to sin. Even some of the angels resisted God's will. The Devil was one of them and fell from heaven like a bolt of lightning. He struts around on earth deceiving people and urging them to become transgressors like him. Those who obey the Devil are those whom the Saviour referred to in John 8.44a–b.[69]

Mani sees the immediate problem with the catholic line of reasoning dispensed by Archelaus: 'If the Devil comes from God, as you say, then you have said that Jesus is a liar'.[70] Why? A father is someone who creates something, and he is called father of whatever he has created.[71] If good proceeds from God, and if this God is the creator (as the catholics say), then you make Jesus out to be a liar when he says in John's Gospel that the Devil has a father, and both are liars. Mani tells Archelaus, 'If

---

66 Mark Vermes and Samuel N. C. Lieu (eds.), *Hegemonius: Acta Archelai* (Manichaean Studies 4; Turnhout: Brepols, 2001).
67 *Acts of Archelaus* 15.6-7 (Vermes–Lieu, p.60).
68 *Acts of Archelaus* 33.1-3 (Vermes–Lieu, p.88).
69 *Acts of Archelaus* 34.1-5 (Vermes–Lieu, pp.94–5).
70 *Acts of Archelaus* 37.1 (Vermes–Lieu, p.96).
71 *Acts of Archelaus* 37.4 (Vermes–Lieu, p.97).

you show me that his father is a liar, and attribute none of this to God, then credence will be granted you on all matters'.[72]

Archelaus is faced with the full weight of the crux of the argument between the catholic and Gnostic communities. Jesus calls the Devil's father a liar in the Gospel of John. If he is a liar, how can he be the just God of truth that the catholics posit? Archelaus does not despair. He tells Mani, 'I will show you the Devil's father'.[73] He explains that the Devil attaches himself to others, like he attached himself to the serpent, Cain and Judas. Through these entities and their actions, the Devil is understood to be a liar and a murderer from the beginning, a point, Archelaus says, even the least intellectual person should be able to discern. Their connection makes Cain and Judas brothers of the Devil as well as fathers of him, since whoever brings forth the Devil from himself and acts according to his desires, has 'sired him and will be said to be his father'.[74] He follows this argument with scriptural support for the multiple meanings of the term 'father', only one of which is 'naturally sired'.[75] He even describes Judas' fathering of his crime as a woman's labour, brought on by eating the morsel of bread after the Devil entered him. The bread caused his belly to swell and labour pains to begin, as he began to birth 'an unrighteous conception'. In the end, he had an abortion rather than a full-term birth, because Judas' life ended in remorse.[76] He then accuses Mani of being the vessel of the Antichrist whose father is Satan.[77]

The conversation between Mani and Archelaus does not end with Hegemonius' record. Epiphanius incorporates long excerpts of the Greek version of Hegemonius' testimony in his description of the Manichaeans. As a result it is not always clear whether the information he relays is from his reading of Hegemonius or from another source. According to Epiphanius, in addition to John 8.44, Mani refers to several texts to demonstrate that the world ruler is evil, rather than the just Lord of the catholic narrative:[78]

> A good tree cannot bring forth evil fruit, neither can a corrupt tree bring forth good fruit; for by its fruit the tree is known (Matt 17.18, 20).
>
> The ruler of this world comes, and finds nothing of his in me (John 14.30).

---

72 *Acts of Archelaus* 37.1-3 (Vermes–Lieu, p.96).
73 *Acts of Archelaus* 37.2-3 (Vermes–Lieu, p.96).
74 *Acts of Archelaus* 37.5-16 (Vermes–Lieu, pp.97–8).
75 *Acts of Archelaus* 38.1-2 (Vermes–Lieu, p.99).
76 *Acts of Archelaus* 37.15-16 (Vermes–Lieu, p.99).
77 *Acts of Archelaus* 40.1-4 (Vermes–Lieu, pp.104–5).
78 Epiphanius, *Pan.* 66.62.1, 66.1, 66.3, 67.5 (Holl, III, pp.99, 106–7).

> The ruler of this world shall be cast down (John 12.31).
>
> The god of this world has blinded the eyes of those who do not believe, lest the light of the glorious gospel of Christ should shine (2 Cor 4.4).
>
> The whole world lies in the evil one (1 John 5.19).

With special reference to John 8.44, Mani liked to say that 'the creator of heaven and earth is the Devil's father'.

Epiphanius' response begins with the assertion, 'but the text cannot possibly refer to this' (μηδαμῶς δυνάμενον ὅλως ἐπὶ τοῦτο τὸ ῥητὸν φέρεσθαι)![79] He makes the argument that the Lord God did not create evil, but that evil is wicked behaviour committed by people. And the source of this evil is the Devil.[80] When Epiphanius quotes John 8.44a, he quotes his own version of it: 'You are sons of the devil' (ὑμεῖς υἱοὶ τοῦ διαβόλου ἐστέ).[81] This version reflects Epiphanius' interpretation of the verse; it is not the version of the Gospel of John to which Mani refers and the one we know today from the manuscript tradition.

Epiphanius falls back on the interpretation of John 8.44 he had reported in his discussion of the 'other sects' and the Archontics. He repeats (with the same string of texts as proofs) that the Devil is Judas, a murderer and a liar, who imitated Cain, who in turn imitated the serpent. The Jews are sons of the Devil because they imitated Judas. This designation has nothing to do with their nature. It has to do with the wicked deeds that they chose to commit, imitating Judas' betrayal of Jesus by their rejection of Christianity.[82]

That John 8.44 was central to Mani's programme is without doubt. Augustine also mentions it. In his own commentary on the Gospel of John, he berates the Jews for changing allegiances; at times they are Abraham's children, at other times God's children. Quoting John 8.44a, he writes that the Jews should listen to the words of the Son of God which identify the Jews as the Devil's children. Then he states that Christians must be wary of this passage because it is used by the Manichaeans to affirm that there exists a certain principle of evil and its family of dark lords who rule this universe. The creator is one of these evil lords, and the Devil and our fleshly bodies originated from him.[83] Based on their understanding of this passage – 'the Lord said it!' – they are accustomed to saying that there are two natures: one good and one

---

79 Epiphanius, *Pan.* 66.63.1-2 (Holl, III, pp.101–2).
80 Epiphanius, *Pan.* 66.62.8-13 (Holl, III, pp.100–1).
81 Epiphanius, *Pan.* 66.63.2 (Holl, III, p.101).
82 Epiphanius, *Pan.* 66.63.9-12 (Holl, III, pp.102–3).
83 Augustine, *Tract. Ev. Jo.* 42.9-10.

evil. The Lord identifies those who cannot hear his message with those people who are not God's.[84]

To argue against the Manichaean reading of John 8.44, Augustine writes that humanity's nature is not evil by design, but has been corrupted by an evil will. He attempts to provide proof for this by stating that the Jews are children of the Devil by imitation, not by birth. The Devil did not come from an evil father, but originated in the same way as the other angels. While the other angels maintained their obedience to God, the Devil did not. This disobedience in fact is what turned him into the Devil.[85]

Delightfully, Augustine preserves the Manichaean response to the catholics. The Manichaeans answer the catholics directly from scripture by asking them, with reference to John 8.44a, 'Let us suppose as you say that the Devil was an angel, and he fell, and with him sin began. But who then was his father?' The catholics reply, 'Who among us ever said that the Devil had a father?', a reply that only makes sense if the catholics are reading John 8.44a appositionally. The Manichaeans know this and therefore they point to the remainder of the Johannine passage, rejoining that the Lord said – and the Gospel declares – that the Devil 'was a murderer from the beginning, and did not abide in the truth, because there is no truth in him. When he speaks a lie, he speaks of his own; for he is a liar, and *his* father'. Augustine complains that the Manichaeans' response is persuasive because of its literalness, which makes sense to those whom Augustine calls 'simpletons'.

But Augustine is not a simpleton. He wants to clear this up once and for all. He says that the meaning can be gained from the words themselves: 'The Lord called the Devil the father of falsehood'. It is apparent that Augustine reads John 8.44f in the same way as Heracleon had done: αὐτοῦ is understood as a reference to an unnamed singular antecedent ('falsehood'), instead of as a straightforward reference to the Devil and *his* father. He argues further against the position that the text refers to anyone who lies as fathering a lie, because people are not responsible for fathering the lie, only for uttering the lie. It is only the Devil who fathers them. In summary fashion he states that God the Father begat him as his son of truth, but the Devil fell and begat his own falsehood, hearing it from no one. The Devil as the serpent is the murderer from the beginning whose first crime was to slay Adam. 'And he did not abide in the truth. There is no truth in him.' This means that he fell away from the truth that he had possessed at one time.

---

84   Augustine, *Tract. Ev. Jo.* 42.15.
85   Augustine, *Tract. Ev. Jo.* 42.10.

2. Interpretative Trends

Much was at stake with the interpretation of John 8.44, and this was recognised very early in the Christian tradition. For obvious reasons, the interpretation of this verse resulted in a debate between the catholic and the Gnostic communities. Both communities appear to have been aware of the various ways in which the Greek text of John 8.44 was being read and then interpreted.

2.1. A Literal Reading of John 8.44a: 'You are from the father of the Devil'

John 8.44a appears to have had a 'plain' or literal reading ('you are from the father of the Devil'), as did John 8.44f ('because he is a liar and so is his father'), from which the Gnostic communities benefited and which the catholic communities needed to explain. The Gnostic communities could (and consistently did!) point to this passage as words of Jesus confirming the existence of a god who fathered the Devil, a god whom the Jews worshipped but which was not the god whom Jesus worshipped. This god was considered to be a wicked deity who fathered the Devil and a certain portion of humanity from the same substance. Heracleon is thus able to argue that the choikics are made from the same *ousia* as the Devil, while also maintaining (true to the Christian tradition) that the Devil never sired anyone. The Gnostic interpreters associated either the Devil or the Demiurge with the 'liar' and the 'murderer from the beginning', and the lying father with the Demiurge or an Authades-type god.

2.2. A Literal Reading of John 8.44f: 'Because he is a liar and so is his father'

None of the early catholics prefers the plain reading of John 8.44a, but, early in the tradition, they do claim the plain reading of John 8.44f, 'because he is a liar and so is his father'. They develop four main explanations of the text. First, the lie/liar is identified with the Antichrist, and the Devil with 'his father'. In this case, the Devil is also 'the murderer from the beginning'. Origen said that the 'lie' that is spoken by the Devil is the Antichrist, so the Devil is the father of the lie as well as the liar and the murderer from the beginning. Origen thinks this identification is clear from the story of Adam and Eve, when the serpent killed the whole human race. Second, the lie/liar refers to any evil spirit whose father is the Devil. Associated with this is Clement of Alexandria's interpretation that false prophets are the prophets of the Devil, the liar. Third, Origen knows of catholics other than himself who argue that the liar is anyone who lies, and the liar's father simply means that the liar has fathered the lie. He is not convinced by this line of reasoning, but lets it stand in his commentary as testimony to the passage's ambiguity. Fourth, there appeared a tradition that associated Judas and Cain with this passage. Epiphanius testifies to it, but his narratives are not consistent. In one narrative, he argues that Judas is the Devil who is the liar, and that his father, who also is a liar, is Cain. In another narrative he says that Cain's father is the Devil, so that Judas and Cain are the liars and the Devil is their father. This confusion may be the result of Epiphanius' knowledge of the *Acts of Archelaus*, which identify the Devil with the liar and the murderer from the beginning. The Devil attaches himself to Cain and Judas. Cain and Judas are brothers as well as fathers of the Devil, because whoever acts out the wishes of the Devil has sired the Devil. Some Gnostics appear to be familiar with these traditions. Epiphanius reports that the Archontics said that the Devil was the liar and Cain, his son, was the murderer from the beginning, the primogenitor of a damned portion of humanity.

These four interpretative strategies are responsive to the Gnostic reading, which claimed, matter-of-factly, that the lie/liar was the Devil and that he had a father who was also a liar. Only Epiphanius' 'other sects' appear to have made the interpretative leap that the Devil's father was the liar; that father had another father who was also a liar. In this latter case, we appear to be seeing a Gnostic tradition similar to that found in *Pistis Sophia*, with Authades as the arrogant father of Ialdabaoth.

2.3. An Idiosyncratic Reading of 8.44a: 'You are from the father, the Devil'

As for the appositional reading of 8.44a, 'from the father, the Devil', this is the one that the catholics use exclusively, even though they confess that this particular reading ('from the father, the Devil' rather than 'from the father of the Devil') would be clearer if the genitive article before 'father' were erased. Their ultimate concern is that the scripture cannot say 'from the father of the Devil', so they plead that another reading of the text is necessary, one that they regard as 'better' than the plain reading. They are so certain that the text means 'from the father, the Devil' that they freely render it as 'You are sons of the Devil', and attribute these words to Jesus instead of the words found in the scripture. They are uneasy about quoting the Greek text in the form it appears in the biblical passage itself. As a result they tend to substitute for it what they think the passage should say by liberally paraphrasing the passage whenever they refer to it.

Heracleon appears to have read 8.44a in a multivalent way, in its plain sense as support for a Demiurge and appositionally as support for his position that a portion of humanity were sons of the Devil. These people were created by the Demiurge from the same substance as the Devil. From this multivalent reading Heracleon could argue that they were created from the same *ousia* as the Devil, even though they were not sired by him. The 'other sects' mentioned by Epiphanius appear to have been reading the text in a similar multivalent fashion: to show that the father of the Jews is the Devil and to prove that the Devil has another father.

2.4. An Idiosyncratic Reading 8.44f: 'Because he is a liar and the father of it'

As for the idiosyncratic reading of 8.44f – 'because he is a liar and the father of it (i.e. falsehood/lies)' – this was not originally developed or favoured by the catholics. It appears to have originated with Heracleon, who used it to argue that the Devil's nature is falsehood, error and ignorance. Because of this we should understand the Devil to be an unfortunate character. We should not blame him for evil. Rather his father, the Demiurge, should be blamed since it was he who created the Devil and invested him with his wickedness. This line of reasoning appears to have been so persuasive that the catholics avoided this idiosyncratic reading until Augustine, who is the first catholic I am aware of who preferred it. He appears to have realised that the force of the Gnostic argument for the existence of the Devil's father was strongly tied to 8.44f ('because he is a liar and *his* father') and the Manichaeans emphasised αὐτοῦ to make this point. Augustine marks this as the 'simpleton' reading and then retranslates it a manner similar to Heracleon. Thus the Devil is the father of falsehood, but, insists Augustine, this falsehood was not begotten by God. Rather the Devil fell and begat his own falsehood.

3. The Secessionists and the Johannine Epistles

How early can we trace the dispute over the 'authentic' reading and meaning of John 8.44? Are Heracleon and the Peratic commentator our earliest sources for the literal or plain reading of the Greek text, that is, for its reference to the Devil's father as a god other than the Father preached by Jesus? It has long been recognised that 1 John 3.11-12a ('For this is the message which you have heard from the beginning, that we should love one another, and not be like Cain who was from the Evil

One and murdered his brother') refers to John 8.44, although most modern commentators consider it to be a casual allusion or an independent use of a shared Johannine tradition.[86] Given what I have learned about the history of interpretation of John 8.44, I have become convinced that 1 John 3.11-12a is neither of these, but an intended reference to John 8.44. In fact, the entire epistle appears to me to have been written as an exposition on John 8.12-55, in order to dispute an interpretation of this passage espoused by the Johannine secessionists. To understand the secessionists' position, it is necessary to read the epistle against the grain and determine the type of exegesis to which the presbyter is responding.

The position of the Johannine presbyter amounts to an early version of the catholic hermeneutic that I have tracked in this essay, a hermeneutic developed in order to tame the plain or literal reading of John 8.44. The epistle opens with a reference to John 8.25: 'They said to him, "Who are you?" Jesus said to them, "Even what I have told you *from the beginning* (τὴν ἀρχὴν ὅ τι καὶ λαλῶ ὑμῖν)".' Keying into this passage, the presbyter declares that he and his supporters (in opposition to the secessionists) testify and proclaim Jesus as the manifestation of eternal life.[87] They know who he is. He is the 'word of life' that they have heard *from the beginning* (ὃ ἦν ἀπ' ἀρχῆς).[88]

The presbyter then unfolds several aspects of this proclamation, the 'truth' that he and his supporters have heard from the beginning. These aspects are summarised by him twice, in 1 John 2.12-22 and 5.18-20, where he addresses his supporters and praises them for correctly understanding certain subjects. From this praise we can reconstruct the subjects that were of concern to him. First, he is anxious about the understanding of the identity of the true God and about God's relationship to evil and the Devil. Second, he is concerned about the problem of sin, particularly whether or not believers are sinners. Third, he wants the identity of the 'liar' to be known. Fourth, he is concerned about different views regarding Jesus' nature and role in salvation. These concerns appear to have been generated by the presbyter's interaction with the secessionists (prior to their secession) and involved a clash of interpretations over John 8.44.

---

86 Cf. Theo C. de Kruijf, 'Nicht wie Kain [der] vom Bösen war…[1 Joh 3,12]', *Bijdragen* 41 (1980), pp.47–63; Georg Strecker, *The Johannine Letters: A Commentary on 1, 2, and 3 John* (trans. Linda M. Maloney; Hermeneia; Minneapolis: Fortress, 1996), pp.108–9; Judith M. Lieu, *I, II, & III John: A Commentary* (Louisville/London: Westminster John Knox, 2008), pp.18, 134–5, 148, 246–7.
87 Cf. John 1.4; 3.16, 36; 5.24.
88 1 John 1.1-3; cf. 5.11-12.

3.1. The Nature of the Father, the True God

The presbyter claims that he and his supporters 'know' the Son and the 'true' God, his Father (1 John 5.19-20). He appears to be touching upon Jesus' conversation in John 8.12-51 where a number of gods are in play. In particular, he is referring to John 8.19 where Jesus tells his opponents: 'You neither know me nor my Father. If you knew me, you would know my Father also.'

Who is the true God? Throughout the epistle, the presbyter wants to make the case that the true God is free from evil. He and his supporters claim to have heard from Jesus that 'God is light and in him is no darkness at all'. This may represent their interpretation of John 8.12, 'I am the light of the world'. In 1 John 2.29, the presbyter claims that God is 'righteous' and that his righteousness assures kinship between himself and those who act piously. God's nature is sinless, as are those people who do not commit sin and are born as his children (3.9). The Father is associated with love and righteousness; he is a just God whose laws are to be obeyed.[89] The presbyter reassures his readers that God's laws are not miserable (βαρύς, 5.3). There will be a judgement, but the believer who is constant in his or her obedience to God's laws has nothing to fear (2.7-11; 4.17-21). Believers can depend on this because God's love was made apparent when he sent his Son into the world as 'expiation for our sins' (4.10). The presbyter is particularly concerned to demonstrate that Jesus' commandment – to love one another – is the central law of God, and that even though it is a 'new' commandment, it is already part of the old law (2.7-11).

The presbyter is concerned with the secessionists' theology. They appear to be claiming that they know about the 'true' Father; he is not the traditional god who gave the laws to the Jews. In all likelihood they were teaching that the Jewish God gave 'miserable' laws that were to be obeyed, because he himself was wicked and associated with the 'darkness' and 'the world'. The secessionists appear to have been emphasising that the God preached by Jesus was to be contrasted with the Jewish God of the Law. Jesus' Father was a God of love who gave a 'new' commandment, to love one another, while the God of the Jews was a malicious god who gave the old Mosaic laws to burden people. The presbyter and the secessionists agree on the loving nature of the Father, while disagreeing over the identity of the god that the Father actually is. The presbyter views the Father as the Mosaic god. The secessionists do not.

---

89   1 John 3.1; 4.7-8, 10-12, 16-17; 5.3.

3.2. Human Nature, Fixed or Not?

The presbyter wishes to make it known that one's affiliation with God or the Devil has nothing to do with a fixed nature. Through a direct reference to John 8.44, and in line with the later catholic interpretation of this passage, the presbyter states that physical parentage does not determine whether a person is born from God and considered a child of God, or is 'from the Devil' (ἐκ τοῦ διαβόλου ἐστίν) and considered a child of the Devil. Rather this is determined by deeds.

Here the presbyter is quoting the appositional reading of John 8.44a ('you are from the father, the devil) to prove his point: the person who does right is righteous, and the person who commits sin is 'from the Devil'. The presbyter then associates the 'murderer from the beginning' (John 8.44c) with the Devil. He thus explains that sinners are the Devil's children 'because the Devil has sinned from the beginning' (ὅτι ἀπ' ἀρχῆς ὁ διάβολος ἁμαρτάνει) and sinners have imitated him (1 John 3.8).

The presbyter continues to reveal the message that he and his supporters 'heard from the beginning' (ἠκούσατε ἀπ' ἀρχῆς, 3.11). We should 'not be like Cain who was from the Evil One and murdered his brother' (3.12). Why did he murder Abel? Because Cain's deeds were evil (3.7-12). Cain's murder is expanded by the presbyter to include any hatred that one brother has for another (3.15).

This reading of John 8.44 is an early version of the catholic hermeneutic that read the text appositionally – 'from the father, the Devil' – and identified the Devil as the murderer from the beginning whom Cain copied. The Devil's children are identified as those, like Cain, who copy the Devil and commit sin (3.8, 10). They do not have the 'spirit of truth' but the 'spirit of error' (4.6). They can be identified because they are liars (like the Devil and Cain), who say they love God but then hate their brothers (2.4; 4.20).

This position is expanded at length in the epistle. The presbyter is concerned about his opponents who appear to have said that believers are not sinners, but have a fixed nature that make them children of God. 'If we say we have no sin, we deceive ourselves, and the truth is not in us' (1.8). He says that such a statement – 'we have no sin' – makes the Son a liar, and his word not part of their community (1.10). This is a clear reference to a clash over the interpretation of John 8.24, where Jesus states, 'I have told you that you would die in your sins unless you believe I am he'. The secessionists appear to have understood this passage to mean that believers were part of a sinless generation, while the presbyter thought that the text meant that even believers had sin, but their relationship with Jesus had absolved them of that sin.

So, a doctrine of expiation is mentioned by the presbyter.[90] The presbyter appears to think that the believer gains God's spirit and is born into God's family through an anointing ritual.[91] This birth means that God's nature now lives within the believer and absolves him or her from sin. The presbyter talks about his followers being 'perfected' and 'purified' (2.5; 3.3). Thus 'he cannot commit sin because he is born of God' (3.9; cf. 2.27; 3.7-12). It also means that the believer is protected from future assaults by the Devil (5.18).

The presbyter's exegetical response to his opponents gives us insight into the position of the secessionists and their reading of John 8.44. The secessionists appear to have been claiming that they knew the 'true' Father preached by Jesus, and were part of a sinless generation connected to him by nature. They appear to have identified this 'pure' and 'perfected' generation with the church. Opposing this generation was another generation that consisted of the children of the Devil, a sinful generation associated with the Devil via a fixed nature. They appear to be assuming that the Devil and his wicked generation were created by the other Father, the miserable god who was the Lawgiver and God of the Jews.

3.3. The Liar Identified

The presbyter wants to be certain in identifying the 'liar' of John 8.44d and f, and, in so doing, he reads 8.44f naturally, as do the other early catholic exegetes: '(8.44d) He did not stand by the truth, because there is no truth in him…(8.44f) because he is a liar and so is his father'. The 'liar', according to the presbyter, is anyone who disobeys God's commandments, including the worst offender, the Antichrist, who denies the Father and the Son (2.4, 22).

The Liar is the person who says that he loves God while hating his brother (4.20). He is the person who claims to 'know' God, but disobeys God's commandments: 'the truth is not in him' (2.4). All of these people have the Devil as their father and walk in darkness, lying and not living according to the truth (2.6). They do not know the true Father or Jesus as they claim they do. They have not overcome the Devil but are his children (cf. 2.12-14).

The presbyter plays with John 8.23, where Jesus contrasts his detractors with himself. It reads: 'You are from below, I am from above. You are of this world, I am not of this world'. The presbyter uses this statement to posit that the secessionists are 'of this world'; they are not 'of the Father' (2.16). He associates 'this world' with lust and pride and

---

90 See 1 John 1.7, 9; 2.2; 4.10; 5.6-7.
91 See 1 John 2.20, 27; cf. 3.24; 4.13.

ignorance of the Father (2.16-17; 3.1). The presbyter also uses John 14.30 against the secessionists. He understands Jesus' allusion to Judas' imminent betrayal – 'the ruler of this world is coming' (ἔρχεται γὰρ ὁ τοῦ κόσμου ἄρχων) – to be a reference to the Antichrist (ἀντίχριστος ἔρχεται) (2.18; 4.3). The presbyter says that his opponents, as antichrists, have finally come into the world.

This is an interesting use of these two Johannine passages (8.23; 14.30), suggesting that the presbyter's opponents likely had other understandings of them. Were the secessionists arguing that Jesus was not 'of this world' which was ruled by the Jewish god? If so, they would have been among the first Christians to have connected the Jewish Lawgiver, the ruler of this world, to Judas, as we now know was the case with the author(s) of the *Gospel of Judas*.[92] Given the presbyter's exegetical tendencies to identify the Liar with a figure other than the Devil, it is very likely that the secessionists were like the later Gnostic exegetes. They were saying that John 8.44f identifies the Liar with the Devil and his father with the malicious Lawgiver. This would be consistent with what we already recovered of their arguments about the nature of the true Father. They were saying that the father of the Devil cannot be the God of truth, but must be the malicious Lawgiver, the god of the Jews.

3.4. Jesus' Nature and Role

The final concern of the presbyter centered on the nature of Jesus and his role. The presbyter wants to tie him tightly to the righteous God, the Lawgiver, who will enact judgement. Jesus Christ is an advocate with his Father on behalf of the righteous, a faithful and just God who hears confessions, forgives sins and purifies.[93] He can do this because he functions as an expiation (ἱλασμός) for sin.[94] He came to teach people God's laws, laws by which they will be judged. The greatest of these laws is love toward one's brother.[95]

The presbyter emphasises that only those who confess that 'Jesus Christ has come in the flesh' (Ἰησοῦν Χριστὸν ἐν σαρκὶ ἐληλυθότα) are to be counted among the children of God (4.2; cf. 2 John 7). Never have there been more misunderstood words than these, taken as solid evidence that the secessionists were docetists.[96] But this is only because our

---

92 DeConick, *The Thirteenth Apostle*.
93 1 John 1.9; 2.1-2; 5.14-15.
94 1 John 2.2; 4.10; 5.6-8.
95 1 John 3.19-24; 4.7-19.
96 For discussion, see Rudolf Bultmann, *The Johannine Epistles: A Commentary on the Johannine Epistles* (trans. R. Philip O'Hara with Lane C. McGaughy and

'academic' histories of early Christology, even today, have been so controlled by the needs, perceptions, and polemics of conventional Christianity, that the traditional Christological categories have not allowed us to see clearly what was going on.[97]

The cry 'in the flesh' was not the presbyter's cry against the docetism of the secessionists, since he is merely referring to the Prologue of the Gospel of John. There is no literary-critical evidence that 'the Word became flesh' is a later addition to the opening hymn, so the secessionists must have been familiar with it. This means that the problem centred on the interpretation of the Prologue. What did it mean that the Logos became flesh? It appears to me that the presbyter took it to mean ensoulment, that the Logos descended into flesh at Jesus' birth and functioned as Jesus' soul. Or to put it another way, the Logos was born as Jesus' *psyche* in flesh.[98] Thus I take 1 John 5.6 to be the presbyter's testimony about Jesus' advent. The Logos did not just come down and possess him at his baptism, 'by the water only' (ἐν τῷ ὕδατι μόνον);[99] rather, Jesus came into being both through water and blood (δι' ὕδατος καὶ αἵματος), the two bodily issues at birth. Jesus' advent through water and blood is proven by the presence of the Spirit, which is one with the water and the blood (5.8). The presbyter's claim is that somehow the Spirit became unified with Jesus' flesh at birth, through the water and blood.

This suggests that the secessionists were arguing that the reference to the Logos becoming flesh should be understood as the possession of the man Jesus by a great Spirit from above, at his baptism, 'by the water only'. This is an entirely different Christological model, and a very old one at that. This model had developed out of the prophetic tradition, which understood that God's Spirit could anoint righteous men, resting in them with every generation (cf. Wis 7.27). This model forms the basis for the Christology in the Gospel of Mark, which uses εἰς to describe

---

Robert Funk; Hermeneia; Philadelphia: Fortress, 1973), pp.62–3; Raymond E. Brown, *The Community of the Beloved Disciple* (New York: Paulist, 1979), pp.147–64; Strecker, *The Johannine Letters*, pp.134–5; Lieu, *I, II, & III John*, pp.10, 23, 169–70.

97 See my full critique and suggestions for a new system in April D. DeConick, 'How We Talk about Christology Matters', in David B. Capes, April D. DeConick, Helen K. Bond, and Troy A. Miller (eds.), *Israel's God and Rebecca's Children: Christology and Community in Early Judaism and Christianity* (Waco: Baylor, 2007), pp.1–23.

98 DeConick, 'How We Talk about Christology Matters', pp.19–20.

99 For a summary of various scholastic readings of this passage, see Lieu, *I, II, and III John*, pp.209–14.

Jesus' possession by the Spirit (1.10). But remnants of it are also found in the other Synoptics and the Gospel of John, which all record the descent of the Spirit at Jesus' baptism and the release of his spirit at the crucifixion.[100] The Gospel of John preserves a saying that must have been of interest to the secessionists: 'This is indeed the prophet-who-is-to-come into this world!' (6.14).

It is also the model used by the Gnostic Christian Cerinthus according to Irenaeus, who states that Cerinthus taught that the primary supreme God, the unknown Father, was separate from the ruler of this world.[101] Tertullian tells us that Cerinthus taught that this lesser god was an angel who represented the god of the Jews and was associated with the Mosaic Law.[102] Irenaeus says that Cerinthus thought that Jesus was born a normal natural child, the son of Mary and Joseph, but he grew to be more righteous than most men. At his baptism, 'Christ descended upon him in the form of a dove'. From then on Jesus proclaimed the unknown Father and performed miracles. At the crucifixion, however, Christ departed from Jesus, so that Jesus the man suffered and rose again, while Christ the Spirit remained impassible.[103]

I mention Cerinthus as a point of comparison, as the type of Christian theological system that would have been very close to the system of the Johannine secessionists. Taking into account the arguments and positions of the presbyter, it appears that the secessionists were arguing from the literal reading of John 8.44 that the god of the Jews, the Lawmaker, was wicked and the father of the Devil. Jesus' Father, however, was the God of love, the true God. Jesus himself was a man possessed by the Spirit of God, born of water only. This recovery of the secessionists' position suggests that the epistles are our first historical testimony to the 'conversation' between the catholic and the Gnostic interpretations over John 8.44.

The skeleton is out of the closet. The plain or literal reading of John 8.44 appears to be primary, while the catholic reading – responsive and secondary – was put into place to tame the beast. This suggests that the Gospel of John may not have been the original property of the proto-orthodox. The proto-orthodox interpretation appears to be superimposed on the Gospel as a way to domesticate it and redirect it.

---

100 Cf. Matt 3.16; 27.50; Luke 3.22; 23.46; John 1.32-33; 19.30.
101 Irenaeus, *Haer.* 1.26.1.
102 Ps.-Tertullian, *Praescr.* xlviii.
103 Irenaeus, *Haer.* 1.26.1.

4. Closing the Heavens

When I wrote my book *The Voices of the Mystics* in 2001, I understood correctly that the Johannine author had sealed tight the open heaven. No one except Jesus and those he would lead at the *eschaton*, when he came again, could pass through the heavens. Individual mystical ascent to the heavenly Father had been shut down. Jesus and the Father could be encountered in the faithful community through the sacraments, through the reception of the Spirit, which had been sent down from the heavens into the cosmos in Jesus' absence.

What I did not know at the time I wrote my book was *why*. Why was the Johannine author so insistent on this point? My study of John 8.44 has clarified this for me. As I have argued in another publication, the theological system assumed by the Johannine author is a 'transitional' system marked by the bifurcation of the Jewish God into a good just Father who lives in the high heaven and a malicious Lawgiver who fathered the Devil and is the ruler of the world – the earth and its atmosphere.[104] What we have in the Gospel of John is a system where the Father of the Devil rules the world with his son, the Devil, just as the righteous Father rules the heavens with his Son, Jesus. The domain of the Lawgiver is 'the world' – the earth and its atmosphere. He is not the astral Lord. The astral Lord is another god. The God of the Heavens is the supreme Father whom Jesus preached. Unlike later developed Gnostic systems, the supreme Father in the Johannine Gospel is still part of this universe. He is not a transtheistic God. He is not living above or beyond the heavens in some distant pleromic world. We see in the Gospel of John the preservation of a panastral system where the God of worship lives in the highest heaven while the Jewish God lives in the lowest. The God of worship is far away, but he is still in the celestial sphere and immediately connected with creation through his Son Jesus. In terms of the development of Gnostic traditions, this represents a crucial step, the 'missing link' between traditional Jewish cosmology and later Gnostic systems.

In later Christian Gnostic texts, it is a common perspective that the great Power Jesus from the Unknown God is the only Power strong enough to move back and forth between the gods and their separate

---

104 April D. DeConick, 'What is Hiding in the Gospel of John: Reconceptualizing Johannine Origins and the Roots of Gnosticism', in April D. DeConick and G. Adamson (eds.), *Histories of the Hidden God* (Gnostika; Durham: Acumen, 2013), pp.13–29.

spheres of dominion. The only way for the faithful to make a similar ascent is through the mediation of Jesus, and this mediation is eschatological or *post-mortem*. Jesus takes the faithful to the Unknown God at the end of time or at death. The individual soul was ignorant, lost, weak, and bound to the rules of a wicked god. Liberation could only come from above through the intervention of a power greater and stronger than the wicked god. This power is Jesus who is the only one who knew and who could hazard the journey across realms and take the faithful souls with him. He also could provide them with specific knowledge and instructions about how to prepare for the journey ritually. Thus, it is true that, eventually, various Christian Gnostic groups do develop series of rituals that allow them to be initiated into the hells and heavens during their lifetimes, rituals that function as trial death journeys. I think that the first inklings of these types of rituals are preserved in the Gospel of John, with its emphasis on new birth through the water and the Spirit, opening entrance into God's Kingdom via a safe and controlled ritual environment.

The people who created the basic metaphysical system preserved in the Gospel of John were panastral theologians. Their theology provides us with the 'missing link' in the formation of later transcosmic metaphysical Gnostic systems. The architects of the foundational theology of the Fourth Gospel were not catholic Christians, but transitional Christians, *bona fide* ancestors of the second-century Gnostics.

THE RULER OF THE WORLD, ANTICHRISTS AND PSEUDO-PROPHETS: JOHANNINE VARIATIONS ON AN APOCALYPTIC MOTIF

Jutta Leonhardt-Balzer

1. Introduction

John Ashton's book is one of the few studies of Johannine literature in which the question of Johannine apocalypticism is examined in more than a cursory manner.[1] He addresses the ways in which the Gospel might be called an apocalypse based on variations of John Collins's definition of the term.[2] The present contribution will approach Johannine apocalypticism not via the question of what constitutes an apocalypse or how to define apocalypticism;[3] instead, it will look at a specific motif that occurs in many apocalyptic writings, and it will examine its use in the Gospel of John and the Johannine Letters. This motif is the 'eschatological opponent', the archenemy who must be overcome for the final victory of God; as such, he is part of the 'eschatological salvation' aspect of apocalypticism.[4] The motif does not only occur in apocalypses, nor can it be found in every apocalypse, but it is a particularly prominent theme in apocalyptic eschatology. Sometimes the opponent is given a name—Belial (e.g. 1QS I–II), Mastema (e.g. *Jubilees*), Satan or the devil (e.g. New Testament)—and sometimes he appears in the texts as a personification of an abstract concept, for example, the Spirit of Darkness in the *Instruction on the Two Spirits* (1QS III.13–IV.26). All of

---

1 Examples of such brief treatments are Ferdinand Hahn, *Frühjüdische und urchristliche Apokalyptik: Eine Einführung* (Biblisch-theologische Studien 36; Neukirchen–Vluyn: Neukirchener, 1998), p.127; Michael Theobald, *Das Evangelium nach Johannes. Kapitel 1–12* (RNT; Regensburg: Pustet, 2009), p.50.

2 Cf. John Ashton, *Understanding the Fourth Gospel* (Oxford: Oxford University Press, 2nd edn, 2007), pp.307–11. Note that in the present study all references to Ashton's book are to the *second* edition.

3 Cf. Ashton, *Understanding*, pp.6–7.

4 See Collins's definition as quoted by Ashton, *Understanding*, p.308.

these terms have their own accompanying myths and therefore their use serves to fulfil a specific function.[5]

In the present essay individual Johannine terms/myths for the archenemy are studied according to their specific function within the Johannine texts (Gospel and Epistles) and their worldview. It is notable that in these writings there is not one *single* term for the archenemy. This in itself shows that the texts work with existing traditions, but also transform them by setting them into their own context. It is therefore necessary to distinguish between the specific terms and myths, and to study their function within the text and the community, before addressing the question of whether they can all be summarised under a single concept.

The terms studied in this essay are the 'Ruler' (ἄρχων) of this world, the most specifically Johannine term for the opponent, after which the more conventional opponents in John's Gospel will be examined: the διάβολος, Satan and 'the evil one'. The focus is not so much on who they are but on what they do, how they function. The results will be compared to the terms used in the Johannine letters: the antichrist and his human representatives, the antichrist(s) and pseudo-prophets. The fundamental question is this: can they be distinguished from each other by their function within the texts (and for the community)? This leads to another question: are these expressions employed to denote one figure or do they represent a host of enemies? This approach will ultimately draw up the apocalyptic battlefield in which the Johannine community finds itself and which it describes with the aid of these particular motifs.[6]

2. Opponents in John's Gospel

Apocalyptic thought does not require a personification of an ultimate enemy, and, even where there is the concept of such a being, it is frequently underlined by an accompanying cosmic dualism. Such an impersonal dualism can be found in the very first reference to evil in the

---

5 For a brief overview of the terms, see the following entries in *DDD*: S. David Sperling, 'Belial', pp.169–71; Jan Willem van Henten, 'Mastemah', pp.553–4; Cilliers Breytenbach and Peggy L. Day, 'Satan', pp.726–32; Greg J. Riley, 'Devil', pp.244–9.

6 The issue of the different functions of dualistic motifs has been raised, for example, in Jörg Frey, 'Licht aus den Höhlen? Der "johanneische Dualismus" und die Texte von Qumran', in Jörg Frey and Udo Schnelle (eds.), *Kontexte des Johannesevangeliums* (WUNT 175; Tübingen: Mohr Siebeck, 2004), pp.117–203, especially pp.170–1, and Ashton, *Understanding*, p.388, but there has been no definitive answer as yet.

Prologue of John: the contrast between light and darkness (John 1.5). In this way the light–darkness dualism – at the very beginning of the Gospel, before any personal representation – serves as background to the figures described within the narrative. The creation contrast of light and darkness at the beginning of the Prologue colours the whole narrative and reappears at key points in the Gospel. It occurs, for example, in John 3.17-21 with reference to the judgement brought into the world, and returns in 12.35-36 with reference to Jesus as the Light who illumines the way of the 'children of light' (υἱοὶ φωτός, 12.36), so that they do not have to walk in the darkness. This is the immediate context of the first reference to the 'ruler of this world'.

Apocalyptic thought does not, moreover, require a metaphysical or cosmic enemy. It is possible to envisage merely human enemies as representatives of ungodly forces, such as the foreign empires in the book of Daniel. In the Gospel of John the human opponents play an important part in the unfolding of the eschatological drama: 'the Jews' in the narrative, and 'the World' in the farewell speeches. The two terms – 'the Jews' and 'the world' – function in an exactly parallel way and possess neutral, positive and negative connotations.[7] The conflict is not a dualism from the outset; the dualism is the result of a dynamic development which begins with Jesus' coming into the world and escalates during the course of his ministry, with the increasing refusal of both 'the world' and 'the Jews' to acknowledge him for who he is. Therefore, although both Jews and world are linked to evil metaphysical forces, and although 'the Jews' in John 8 and in the passion narrative, as well as 'the world' in chs. 15–17, certainly function as enemies of Jesus and the community, they are not irredeemably evil. To the very end the Gospel does not exclude the possibility that Jews come to believe in Christ and that the world becomes the community of believers. In the case of the eschatological opponent, however, we meet a character who is beyond hope: he is cosmic, metaphysical and ethical evil personified. There are three such characters in John: the 'ruler of this world' and the 'evil one' in Jesus' speeches, Satan/the devil in the narrative.

---

[7] This has been demonstrated by Lars Kierspel, *The Jews and the World in the Fourth Gospel: Parallelism, Function, and Context* (WUNT 2/220; Tübingen: Mohr Siebeck, 2006), especially pp.76–110, 214–19. By contrast, in spite of his own admission that more than half the occurrences of the designation 'the Jews' are not negative, Ashton (*Understanding* [2nd edn], pp.64–9) regards the negative meaning as the 'typical use of the term' (p.68).

2.1. The 'Ruler of this World' and 'The Evil One'

The phrase ὁ ἄρχων τοῦ κόσμου [τούτου] appears three times in the Gospel of John, all towards the end of Jesus' ministry. As Jörg Frey has pointed out, the first occurrence in John 12.31 is in a passage no longer directed at outsiders, but at the Greeks who act as a cipher for future believers.[8] The other two occurrences are in the farewell speeches (14.30; 16.11). Therefore all the references to 'the ruler of this world' occur in contexts addressing the situation of the community *after* the glorification of Jesus.

The term ἄρχων denotes a leader or ruler. The term itself does not necessarily have demonic connotations; it merely implies command or power over others.[9] In 1 Cor 2.6, 8 the designation 'rulers of this aeon' probably refers to human rulers. In Dan 10.10-21 the ἄρχοντες are the angels of the nations and thus the opponents of the people of God.[10] There are also references to a ruler over the demons (Matt 9.34; 12.24; Mark 3.22; Luke 11.15), especially Mastema, the chief of the spirits (*Jub.* 10.7), and the 'archon of this aeon' (Eph 2.2).[11] Thus the term ἄρχων conjures up notions of power and rule without always implying a supernatural being. The character of the ἄρχων is defined by the context.

By using 'cosmos' instead of 'aeon', the Gospel of John qualifies the 'ruler' with the aid of a specifically Johannine term.[12] On the first occasion (12.31), in Jesus' last public speech, he is called ὁ ἄρχων τοῦ κόσμου τούτου: 'Now is the judgement over this world, now the Archon of this world will be thrown out' (νῦν κρίσις ἐστὶν τοῦ κόσμου τούτου, νῦν ὁ ἄρχων τοῦ κόσμου τούτου ἐκβληθήσεται ἔξω). It is an instance of irony that the first reference to the 'ruler' of this world does not emphasise his power but rather its demise. This raises the question from where the ruler is expelled. Commentators relate this occurrence of the term ἐκβάλλω to texts such as Luke 10.18-20, where, in the context of the disciples' power over the evil spirits, Jesus says: 'I saw Satan falling from the heaven like a flash of lightning' (εἶπεν δὲ αὐτοῖς· ἐθεώρουν τὸν

---

8 Jörg Frey, 'Heiden – Griechen – Gotteskinder: Zu Gestalt und Funktion der Rede von den Heiden im 4. Evangelium', in Reinhard Feldmeier and Ulrich Heckel (eds.), *Die Heiden: Juden, Christen und das Problem des Fremden* (WUNT 70; Tübingen: Mohr Siebeck, 1994), pp.228–68, especially 256, 263.

9 Cf. David E. Aune, 'Archon', *DDD*, pp.82–5; Gerhard Delling, '"Ἀρχων', *ThWNT* 1, pp.486–8.

10 Delling, '"Ἀρχων', p.488.

11 Aune, 'Archon', pp.83–4.

12 Cf. Frey, 'Licht aus den Höhlen', p.177.

σατανᾶν ὡς ἀστραπὴν ἐκ τοῦ οὐρανοῦ πεσόντα).[13] But in Luke 10 the term used for the adversary is 'Satan' and the verb is πίπτω ('to fall') not ἐκβάλλω in the passive ('to be thrown out').

The other parallel cited by commentators is Rev 12.7-9, which speaks of Michael's and the angels' battle with the dragon and his angels: 'And the great dragon was thrown (down), the old snake, called Devil (ὁ καλούμενος Διάβολος) and Satan (καὶ ὁ Σατανᾶς), who leads the whole world astray (ὁ πλανῶν τὴν οἰκουμένην ὅλην), he was thrown *onto the earth* (ἐβλήθη εἰς τὴν γῆν), and his angels were thrown with him (μετ' αὐτοῦ ἐβλήθησαν)'.[14] As in Luke 10.18-20, the terms for the *world*, for the *direction of the fall* and for the *enemy* are different from those found in John 12.31. Satan is thrown on the earth, implying that he is thrown from heaven. In both texts, Rev. 12.7-9 and Luke 10.18-20, the enemy originates in heaven and is cast out as a sign of the eschatological victory.

Both texts are related to Isa 14.12, the fall from heaven of the morning star (ἐξέπεσεν ἐκ τοῦ οὐρανοῦ), the enemy of God.[15] Originally referring to the king of Babylon, by New Testament times the verse was appropriated as a reference to Satan's fall.[16] The following verse speaks of the enemy's attempt to rise up to heaven. Again, the terminology is different from John 12.31 (ἐκπίπτω, 'to fall out'), and in John there is neither reference to the Archon's fall *from heaven* nor any attempt to raise him *to heaven*. On the contrary, John 12.32 speaks of *Jesus'* ascent that will draw all those belonging to him. This ascent, notably, is not mentioned *before* but *after* the Archon's fall; it cannot be its cause. Furthermore, unlike the enemy in the other traditions, the Archon in John does not try to conquer the world, because he already rules it. Due to the future tense of the verb (ἐκβληθήσεται), traditions about the original fall of Satan cannot be implied here either (e.g. *2 En.* 29.1-6; 31.1-8; *L.A.E.* 15.2–16.4).[17] It is noteworthy that a number of witnesses to John 12.31 read βληθήσεται ($\mathfrak{P}^{66}$, D, a, b, c, e, l, Θ) κάτω (sy-s, b, e, ff-2, l, r, Θ) instead of ἐκβληθήσεται (ℵ, B, L, 892, A, Δ, 574, ff-2, 1, 22, 700, fam. 13) ἔξω ($\mathfrak{P}^{66}$, $\mathfrak{P}^{75}$, ℵ, B, L, 892, A, Δ, D, 1, 22, 700, fam. 13).[18] However, as there is no coherent variant which represents the whole reading, it is

---

13 Cf. Theobald, *Johannes*, pp.812–14; Jürgen U. Kalms, *Der Sturz des Gottesfeindes: Traditionsgeschichtliche Studien zu Apokalypse 12* (WMANT 93; Neukirchen–Vluyn: Neukirchener, 2001), pp.207–34.
14 Cf. Theobald, *Johannes*, pp.812–14; Kalms, *Sturz*, pp.244–73.
15 Cf. Frey, 'Licht aus den Höhlen', p.178.
16 Kalms, *Sturz*, pp.144–9.
17 Kalms, *Sturz*, pp.150–4.
18 Erich Metzing, 'Textkritische Beobachtungen zu ἐκβληθήσεται ἔξω in Joh. 12,31', *ZNW* 88 (1997), pp.126–9.

more likely that this attests the influence of the traditions about the fall of the angels, reinserted into the Johannine text, rather than the original version of John 12.31. The variants show, however, how influential these traditions were in interpreting John 12.31 and, in turn, identifying ἐκβληθήσεται ἔξω as the *lectio difficilior*.

Thus the *language* attached to this motif in John 12.31 does not match either the Isaiah original or its use in other NT texts. This observation is not as indicative for John as it would be for other texts, as the Gospel does not even seek to offer literal renderings of its scriptural references. However, the *function* of the myth needs to match, at least to a certain degree, in order to account for why this tradition was taken up in the first place. The myth explains the victory over the adversary as the fall of the evil spirit from the divine realm and his banishment to earth (or elsewhere). If this were the myth to which John 12.31 refers, the resulting statement would contradict fundamental Johannine tenets: the Johannine writings do not have any concept of hell, and the future tense of the 'throwing out' precludes any use of the myth to explain how the Archon came to be in the world. Furthermore, there is a very limited concept of angels in the Johannine writings. Good angels only occur in the allusion to Jacob's ladder (John 1.51) and in the empty tomb narrative (20.12-13), both using non-Johannine traditions to serve the function of bearing witness to Christ, while the terminology of evil angels does not occur at all in these texts.[19] Furthermore the Johannine writings maintain a very strict separation between 'above' and 'below.' There is only one person who has come from above (John 1.18), and it is impossible for those from below to enter above unless they are γεννηθῇ ἄνωθεν, 'born from above' (John 3.3), and γεννηθῇ ἐξ ὕδατος καὶ πνεύματος, 'born from water and spirit' (John 3.5), references to baptism and the gift of the Spirit.[20] Even of the faithful it is only said that they are 'born from God', not that they are 'from God'.[21] In this context the concept of fallen angels, particularly the one they call 'the ruler of this world' (who is 'from below'), does not fit. Thus the myth of the expulsion of the angels (in the beginning or at the *eschaton*) does not belong to a worldview where heaven is only accessible to those 'from above' or 'born from above'. The myth of the fall functions differently and therefore does not work in the Johannine context.

---

19   In John's Gospel 'Satan', 'the devil' and 'the evil one' are nowhere presented as angels. Angels in John maintain their original function as messengers of God. Therefore the concept of angels cannot be linked with the evil forces.
20   Theobald, *Johannes*, pp.248–52.
21   Cf. Frey, 'Licht aus den Höhlen', p.183.

Is there another way of reading John 12.31? The answer must centre on the place from which the Archon is expelled. The above argument rules out the heavens. Looking at the verse in detail, the immediate – and only – point of reference for the expulsion in John 12.31-32 is the *world*. Commentators have argued that, in the glorification of Christ, the Archon has lost power over the world in principle before being finally overcome at the end, a kind of victory in two stages.²² This does not explain the text, however, since the conflict between the world and the community is depicted as particularly violent in those chapters that refer to the life of the community after Jesus' ascension (John 14–17). Therefore, as the Archon is still very much at work in the world after the cross, it is necessary to look for another explanation. In this respect it is important to note the addition of ἔξω and the fact that the verb ἐκβάλλω can also be used with reference to exorcisms.²³ The verb is used for Jesus' driving out of the demons in Matt 8.31; 12.26-27 and 17.19.²⁴ As in these Matthean passages, the Archon of this world can be viewed as a spirit taking possession of a human being and being driven out by Christ. The present tense of the judgement in John 12.31 then relates to the life and death of Christ in general, while the future tense of ἐκβάλλω in the context of the Gospel narrative links the expulsion of the Archon to the cross and the resurrection, mentioned in the next verse (12.32).²⁵ John 12.31-32, together with the reference to judgement and to the drawing of the faithful to Jesus, refers not only to the exorcism of an evil power but to repossession by another, by the divine spirit. Thus, in response to our earlier question, the Archon is expelled not 'from the world' but 'from

---

22 For a critique of this view, see Ronald A. Piper, 'Satan, Demons and the Absence of Exorcisms in the Fourth Gospel', in David G. Horrell and Christopher M. Tuckett (eds.), *Christology, Controversy and Community: New Testament Essays in Honour of David R. Catchpole* (Leiden: Brill, 2000), pp.253–78, especially 272–4.

23 As suggested in general for John, but not for 12.31, by Theobald, *Johannes*, pp.812–13.

24 Note that the above-mentioned reference to the fall of Satan in Luke 10.18 also occurs in the context of an exorcism.

25 In John 3.17-21 the κρίσις of the world is described in quite parallel terms as the coming of the Son and the refusal of the world to believe: 'For God did not send the Son into the world so that he should judge the world but so that the world might be saved by him. Everyone who believes in him is not judged, but he who does not believe in him is already judged, because he has not come to believe in the name of the only begotten Son of God. But this is the judgement that the light came into the world and men loved darkness more than the light. For their deeds were evil' (3.17-19). Cf. Jörg Frey, *Die johanneische Eschatologie 3. Die eschatologische Verkündigung in den johanneischen Texten* (WUNT 117; Tübingen: Mohr Siebeck, 2000), pp.283–300.

the community'. He represents the irreconcilable aspect of the world and is therefore condemned to vanish altogether. What remains is the community.

The other two references to the Archon in John's Gospel expand upon this theme. In John 16.11 the 'Archon of this world' appears, once again, as already judged, a fact that will be shown by the coming of the Paraclete:

> And when he has come he will bring proof to the world about sin and righteousness and judgement (ἐλέγξει τὸν κόσμον περὶ ἁμαρτίας καὶ περὶ δικαιοσύνης καὶ περὶ κρίσεως); as to sin, that they do not believe in me (ὅτι οὐ πιστεύουσιν εἰς ἐμέ); as to righteousness, that I go to the Father (ὅτι πρὸς τὸν πατέρα ὑπάγω) and you will not see me any longer; as to judgement, that the ruler of this world is judged (περὶ δὲ κρίσεως, ὅτι ὁ ἄρχων τοῦ κόσμου τούτου κέκριται) (16.8-10).

Once more, judgement is directed at the Archon. The three parts of the statement indicate that he is judged on account of his refusal to believe in Christ. This corresponds to what has been defined as judgement in John 3.17-21. Fundamentally the Archon is the representative of the world that refuses to believe in Christ and therefore remains part of the world (instead of becoming 'children of God', cf. John 1.12). This function of judgement is also highlighted in John 5.21-23 and 26-27, in the contrast between bringing judgement and bringing life.[26] Therefore the person who is judged remains in their previous, lifeless state as part of the world that is condemned to perishing.[27] A similar concept of eternal life for the righteous – not life versus eternal damnation, but life versus mortality – can be found in the *Instruction on the Two Spirits* in 1QS III.13–IV.26, where the deeds and lives of the wicked are doomed to perish with this life while only the Sons of Light and their deeds have a future. The eschatological purification of the Sons of Light occurs through the Spirit of God. Similarly, the Archon in the Gospel of John, as the representative of the unbelieving world, is proved wrong and is overcome by the Paraclete's testimony to Christ's truth (John 16.11). The Spirit of God is the one who discloses the judgement of the ruler of this world, another link between the Spirit and the Archon and eschatology.[28]

---

26 Cf. Frey, *Eschatologie*, pp.355–69.
27 Against Ashton, *Understanding*, p.406, who envisages an 'eternal punishment'.
28 Cf. Ferdinand Hahn, *Theologie des Neuen Testaments Band 1: Die Vielfalt des Neuen Testaments: Theologiegeschichte des Urchristentums* (Tübingen: Mohr Siebeck, 2nd edn, 2005), p.659.

A slightly different expression is used at the end of the first farewell speech in John 14.30: ὁ τοῦ κόσμου ἄρχων, 'the Archon of the world'. Jesus says that the Archon is coming (implied is his coming to kill him), but does not have power over him. The Archon is not called 'the ruler of *this* world' but 'the ruler of *the* world'. This is possibly more than a slight variation of expression; rather, it is a deliberate distinction between the Archon's role in Jesus' life, in which the Archon – who is overcome by Jesus – is called the ruler of 'the world' in general, and the Archon's role in the life of believers in the present, for which he is called the ruler of '*this* world', with a certain emphasis on the temporary quality of this realm in order to give comfort to the community in their present situation of fear. What is also different is that there is no reference to the judgement of the Archon in 14.30, only to his lack of power to oppose Jesus. What is the same in both contexts is that the Archon works against Jesus, but does not have the power to succeed. The final call to rise, ἐγείρεσθε ἄγωμεν (14.31), is the same as the phrase used in Mark 14.42, where the words introduce the arrival of Judas before Jesus' arrest; thus John implicitly identifies Judas with 'the ruler of the world'. This is another instance of the Johannine identification of a metaphysical opponent with an actual human being.

A different term for the archenemy is used in the high priestly prayer (John 17.15). Jesus does not pray that the community is taken out of the world but that it is protected 'from the evil one' (ἐκ τοῦ πονηροῦ). The 'evil one' is the representative of the world's threat and hatred towards the community; thus he is clearly associated with 'the world' (17.9-9). Unlike the Archon, the evil one is not explicitly depicted as conquered at this stage, although the adjective πονηρός also occurs in 3.17-21 to characterise the *works* of those who prefer darkness to light and do not believe in the Son; these works are called 'evil' (3.19). This passage, with its reference to the judgement of the world that rejects Jesus, has already been mentioned in this essay with reference to the ruler of this world (12.31). The noun ὁ πονηρός as a term for the opponent of the community (17.15) places 'the evil one' in the context of the refusal to believe. It implies that the 'evil one' is judged in the same way as those who do not believe are judged. It indicates that 'the evil one' has the same function as the Archon in the life of the community. Yet while the references to the Archon span Jesus' life as well as that of the community, the 'evil one' appears only in the context of the latter. A single occurrence does not provide sufficient data to allow one to draw firm conclusions, but, as it stands, it seems to imply a slightly different emphasis.

To summarise: the Archon is the force behind the world in its state of refusal to acknowledge Christ; he is personified unbelief. He persecutes Christ and tries to kill him. But his judgement occurs at the moment when Christ proves that he is who is says he is, that is, in Christ's glorification as believed by the faithful. The ὁ τοῦ κόσμου ἄρχων does *not* – as one might expect – appear in the context of the threat to the present community after Christ's ascension; he is already judged, not merely in principle, but in actual fact. It is, however, a fact of the community's life that it has not been taken out of this world but continues to live in this world, which it regards as an actual danger.

In the context of the threat to the present community, the reference is to the 'evil one', but with no mention of judgement, only his persecution of the faithful. This seems to represent the experience of the community between its own new birth and the persisting expectation of a threat from outside. Unlike 'Archon', the term 'evil one' does not possess connotations of power; in itself it represents *moral* judgement.[29] As a term for a metaphysical being, it implies the superstitious avoidance of pronouncing the name of a negative force, for fear of attracting its attention; there are many instances of its use in the Synoptics (e.g. Matt 13.19), but none in non-Christian sources.[30] As mentioned above, in the Johannine context the term only occurs with reference to the present community. John's narrative about Jesus' life, however, has no inhibitions about giving evil a name, and it is this name that must be examined in order to establish whether there is a coherent concept of a metaphysical adversary in the Gospel of John.

2.2. Satan and the Devil in the Life of Jesus

Σατανᾶς and διάβολος are two terms for the same entity: the former is the Hebrew name, the other the Greek translation used by the LXX.[31] Both appear in the Synoptic Gospels in the temptation narrative and in the context of exorcisms, and in Luke (as in John) in the context of Judas' betrayal.[32] In John's Gospel there is no temptation of Jesus and, at first sight, he does not fight demons either. In the account of Jesus' public ministry (John 1.19–13.30) his enemies are increasingly the

---

29 Cf. Gunther Harder, 'πονηρός, πονηρία', *ThWNT* 6, pp.547–66, especially 546–8.
30 Harder, 'πονηρός', pp.558–9.
31 Cf. Kalms, *Sturz*, pp.139–40.
32 Cf. Jutta Leonhardt-Balzer, 'Gestalten des Bösen im frühen Christentum', in Jörg Frey and Michael Becker (eds.), *Apokalyptik und Qumran* (Einblicke 10; Paderborn: Bonifatius, 2007), pp.203–35, especially 205–25.

Jewish leaders. The more Jesus reveals about himself, the more he antagonises those who do not believe. This is the main battlefield in the Gospel of John. It has repeatedly been noted that Jesus' healings are not described in terms of exorcism, and that there are no exorcisms in the Fourth Gospel.[33] Physical illness is not the main enemy – the main enemy is the refusal to acknowledge Jesus. However, as R. A. Piper points out, passages such as 8.44 and 13.27 demonstrate that John 'has not abandoned an invasionist approach to evil's forces'.[34]

In John 8 the devil is called the father of the Jews because they refuse to accept that Jesus comes from the Father. This is the straightforward reversal of the Synoptic scribes' question about Jesus' authority (Mark 3.22-27 par): the scribes from Jerusalem enquire about the source of Jesus' power over the spirits and suggest that it might be demonic in origin.[35] This passage is hinted at, in the context of a healing, in John 7.19-21. In John 8 Jesus turns the argument around and suggests that anyone who doubts that his authority stems from the Father[36] must be a child of the devil (called διάβολος throughout chs. 7 and 8). Calling the Jews 'children of the devil' (8.44) is another way of denying the truth and authority of their argument. This is shown in 8.48–51 where 'the Jews', in turn, accuse Jesus of being possessed by a demon. As Urban von Wahlde has pointed out, the language of possession is certainly an argumentative device.[37] Ronald Piper also regards this language as related to rivalry, 'reserved for demonising one's opponents'.[38]

---

33 Cf. Wendy E. Sproston, 'Satan in the Fourth Gospel' in Elizabeth A. Livingstone (ed.), *Studia Biblica 1978: Sixth International Congress on Biblical Studies*. Vol. 2, *Papers on the Gospels* (JSNTSup 2: Sheffield: JSOT, 1980), pp.307–11; Eric Plumer, 'The Absence of Exorcisms in the Fourth Gospel', *Biblica* 78 (1997), pp.350–68; Piper, 'Satan', pp.253–78; Graham H. Twelftree, 'Exorcisms in the Fourth Gospel and the Synoptics', in Robert T. Fortna and Tom Thatcher (eds.), *Jesus in Johannine Tradition* (Louisville: Westminster John Knox, 2001), pp.135–43.

34 Piper, 'Satan', p.262.

35 On this Synoptic passage and on the issues of authority for exorcism, see Eric Sorensen, *Possession and Exorcism in the New Testament and Early Christianity* (WUNT 2/157; Tübingen: Mohr Siebeck, 2002), pp.140–2; Clinton Wahlen, *Jesus and the Impurity of Spirits in the Synoptic Gospels* (WUNT 2/185; Tübingen: Mohr Siebeck, 2004), pp.104–5, 124–8, 155–9. Wahlen notes the irony that the impure spirits confess Christ, while the people of God refuse to do so.

36 This is the issue in John 8.13.

37 The argumentative force of the charge of possession has been highlighted by Urban C. von Wahlde, '"You Are of Your Father the Devil" in Its Context: Stereotyped Apocalyptic Polemic in John 8:38–47', in Reimund Bieringer, Didier Pollefeyt, and Frederique Vandercasteele-Vanneuville (eds.), *Anti-Judaism and the*

However, against Piper, the issue in John 8.44-45 is not merely of one party declaring that the other is wrong. The devil is characterised in more serious terms: 'he was a killer of men from the beginning and did not stand in the truth' (ἀνθρωποκτόνος ἦν ἀπ' ἀρχῆς καὶ ἐν τῇ ἀληθείᾳ οὐκ ἔστηκεν), the reason for the latter being that 'he is a liar' (ψεύστης ἐστίν). The devil here represents the force which denies Jesus as Christ. Any person denying Christ belongs to the devil, and in 8.55 Jesus states that if he himself denied that he knows the Father he would be a liar like 'the Jews'. In both passages, John 7.19-21 and 8.37-47, the argument is sparked by Jesus' claim that 'the Jews' are trying to kill him, and in John 8.59 they prove the validity of Jesus' accusation by picking up stones to attack him. Thus their denial of Jesus' origin is more than a mere thought process; the thought is followed by action, the attempt to prove that Jesus is not related to God by killing him. The idea that human action, for good or for bad, is related to a supernatural force has been compared by Urban von Wahlde to the *Instruction on the Two Spirits* in 1QS III.13–IV.26 and similar traditions in the *Testaments of the Twelve Patriarchs* (and 1 John).[39] However, in John's Gospel the link between the devil and the accusation of lies, and especially murder, is stronger than in the other traditions, where the evil spirit incites immoral behaviour but does not actually kill anyone. It must be assumed that the specific accusation is related to matters close to the heart of Johannine thought, and the obvious link is between lies and the denial of Jesus, on the one hand, and murder and his death, on the other.

Therefore it is consistent that Judas Iscariot is called 'a devil' in Jesus' announcement of his treason in John 6.70-71. The devil as an external influence on human actions is mentioned when John attributes Judas' plan to hand over (παραδίδωμι) Jesus to the influence of the διάβολος (13.2); this influence is sealed when, after Jesus permits it, ὁ σατανᾶς enters Judas (13.27). This narrative fits with the argument of John 8: someone who denies Christ and works towards killing him, in order to prove that he is human and mortal, is possessed by the archenemy. This is not changed by the fact that Jesus permits this, and that the cross is part of the divine plan.[40] Consequently, Judas is called 'the son of

Fourth Gospel: Papers of the Leuven Colloquium, 2000 (Jewish and Christian Heritage Series 1; Assen: Van Gorcum, 2001), pp.418–44; see also Sorensen, *Possession*, p.154.

38   Piper, 'Satan', pp.264–5.
39   Cf. von Wahlde, '"You Are of Your Father the Devil"', pp.426–34.
40   The attempt to kill Christ and therefore to deny his relationship with God parallels the Synoptic 'sin against the Holy Spirit' that cannot be forgiven (Mark

perdition' (ὁ υἱὸς τῆς ἀπωλείας, John 17.12), the only one of those given to him whom Jesus does not save. This is the final stop for humanity if they deny Christ, and Judas is the only named example of a human being who is beyond redemption.

As already mentioned, Jesus' farewell speeches to the disciples (John 13.31–17.26) are characterised by a different language. The terms Satan/devil vanish from the text. This is in line with the overall character of these chapters, which no longer refer to Jesus' life but address the community after his death. After the farewell speeches the 'archenemy' vanishes altogether as a separate person and dissolves into the human adversaries of Jesus during the passion. It now remains for this essay to examine the archenemy in the Johannine letters.

3. The Johannine Letters

Early in 1 John a contrast is made between light and darkness: 'God is light and there is no darkness within him' (1.5). Darkness is immediately linked to lies (1.6) and sin (1.8) and later to hatred of one's brother (2.11). The presentation of the adversary in the Johannine letters therefore has a similar background to the one found in the Fourth Gospel. The adversary is first mentioned in the address to the young people in 1 John 2.13, 14: 'you have overcome the evil one' (νενικήκατε τὸν πονηρόν). Here the 'evil one' is encountered as a conquered foe in the context of people who have come to believe in Christ. Immediately after these references the readers are admonished not to love the world (2.15), so here again the 'evil one' appears in the context of the present life of the community and as a representative of the unbelieving world. This is confirmed in 1 John 5.18: 'We know that the one who is born from God does not sin (ὁ γεγεννημένος ἐκ τοῦ θεοῦ οὐχ ἁμαρτάνει), but the one who is begotten from God keeps him, and the evil one does not touch him (ὁ γεννηθεὶς ἐκ τοῦ θεοῦ τηρεῖ αὐτὸν καὶ ὁ πονηρὸς οὐχ ἅπτεται αὐτοῦ)'. The following verse again contrasts those who are from God with those who are of the world. The term used to denote protection from the 'evil one' (5.18) is the same as the one employed in the Gospel (17.12), but what is prayed for there is mentioned as a fact in 1 John. In the letter a close link is also forged between birth from God and the cessation of the influence of the 'evil one' – a thought which is closer to

---

3.28-30 par). Importantly, in Mark this sin is mentioned in the context of the denial of Jesus' authority through the claim that he is possessed by a demon.

the Gospel's depiction of the Archon of this world, thus providing a link between the term Archon and the 'evil one'.

Another term used to describe the enmity of the world is 'the antichrist'/'antichrists' in 1 John 2.18-19:

> Children, it is the last hour, and as you have heard that an antichrist is coming, thus now many antichrists have come, from which we recognise that the last hour is now. From us they have gone forth, but they were not from us. For if they had been from us they would have remained with us.
>
> Παιδία, ἐσχάτη ὥρα ἐστίν, καὶ καθὼς ἠκούσατε ὅτι ἀντίχριστος ἔρχεται, καὶ νῦν ἀντίχριστοι πολλοὶ γεγόνασιν, ὅθεν γινώσκομεν ὅτι ἐσχάτη ὥρα ἐστίν. ἐξ ἡμῶν ἐξῆλθαν ἀλλ᾽ οὐκ ἦσαν ἐξ ἡμῶν· εἰ γὰρ ἐξ ἡμῶν ἦσαν, μεμενήκεισαν ἂν μεθ᾽ ἡμῶν.

A definition of 'antichrist' is given in 1 John 2.22: 'Who is a liar if not the one who denies that Jesus is the Christ? This is the antichrist, who denies the Father and the Son' (Τίς ἐστιν ὁ ψεύστης εἰ μὴ ὁ ἀρνούμενος ὅτι 'Ιησοῦς οὐκ ἔστιν ὁ χριστός; οὗτός ἐστιν ὁ ἀντίχριστος, ὁ ἀρνούμενος τὸν πατέρα καὶ τὸν υἱόν). The expectation of the antichrist is introduced as a concept that the community already knows about.[41] The change from the singular to the plural (2.18) indicates that the expectation relates to the concept of a single figure, which the author then applies to specific opponents, thus implying that apocalyptic teaching about the end of time was practised in the Johannine community.[42] That it is an eschatological opponent can be seen from the reference to his/their coming in the 'last hour'.

At this point it is not clear whether this 'antichrist' is human or superhuman.[43] Linguistically, the closest equivalent to 'antichrist' is ἀντίθεος, which in Homer (Od. 11.117; 13.378; 14.18) means 'godlike' and in Philo (Post. 37, 123; Congr. 118; Fug. 140) signifies 'contrary to God'. In the same way, 'antichrist' could either mean 'false Christ' or 'opponent of Christ'.[44] There is no precedent for the term before 1 and 2 John (Irenaeus, Haer. 5.25-30 is later); a number of passages in the NT predict the appearance of eschatological opponents, but without using this

---

41 Cf. L. J. Lietaert Peerbolte, *The Antecedents of Antichrist: A Traditio-Historical Study of the Earliest Christian Views on Eschatological Opponents* (JSJ Supplement 49; Leiden: Brill, 1996), p.101.
42 Cf. Frey, *Eschatologie*, pp.23–4.
43 Frey, *Eschatologie*, pp.23–4.
44 Lietaert Peerbolte, 'Antichrist', *DDD*, pp.62–4.

particular term. In Mark 13.22 'false Christs' (pseudo-Christs) and 'false prophets' (pseudo-prophets) are said to appear before the end, deceiving people with false signs, as does 'the lawless one' in 2 Thess 2.3-12.[45] The Jewish Belial/Satan traditions (*1 Enoch, Jubilees, Martyrdom of Isaiah, Sib. Or.* 1–2, *Liv. Pro., Pss. Sol.*, 1QS, 1QM, CD, 1QH, 11QMelch) and the expectation of eschatological false prophets may have played their part in the development of the term,[46] but without *the* Christ there cannot be an '*anti*-Christ'. The term's origin, as a result, needs to be sought in the Christian – more precisely, Johannine – tradition.[47] This also accords with the statement that 'they went forth from us' (1 John 2.19). Even if the community's theology cannot acknowledge the possibility that a true member of the community can fall, members have to face the fact that these false teachers – antichrists – were originally part of the community.[48] This distinguishes them from 'the Jews' or 'the world' in the Fourth Gospel, although they function in a similar way by denying the truth about Christ, by deceiving others into believing their falsehoods, and by practising hatred. In view of this activity and the context of deceit and pseudo-prophecy, it is possible that both connotations, 'the one who opposes Christ' and 'the one who tries to introduce a counterfeit Christian message', shape the meaning of the term 'antichrist'.[49] At this point the activity of the antichrist is limited to the refusal to confess Christ. There is no reference to violence and the terms 'antichrist' and 'pseudo-prophet' (unlike the later development of the myth)[50] do not contain any connotation of power, but of (false) prophecy.[51]

Both prophecy and pseudo-prophecy are based on the presence of a spirit. Thus the activity of the antichrist and the pseudo-prophets is fuelled by spiritual powers. Positioned against the Spirit given to the community by God (1 John 3.24) are the other spirits:

---

45   Peerbolte, 'Antichrist', p.63. Gregory C. Jenks, *The Origins and Early Development of the Antichrist Myth* (BZNW 59; Berlin: de Gruyter, 1991), pp.41–8, also lists other passages, e.g., Dan 7, and passages from the prophets (e.g. Isa 14.4-21), but these influenced the later myth, not necessarily the passage in 1 John.

46   Cf. Jenks, *Antichrist*, pp.117–52.

47   Lietaert Peerbolte, 'Antichrist', p.63.

48   Cf. Frey, *Eschatologie*, pp.72–4.

49   Against Frey, *Eschatologie*, p.25; Lietaert Peerbolte, *Antecedents of the Antichrist*, p.110.

50   Cf. Jenks, *Antichrist*, who includes political aspects throughout; for instance, Antiochus and concepts of the 'end tyrant'. See also Kalms, *Sturz*, pp.154–78.

51   Cf. Frey, *Eschatologie*, p.26.

Beloved, do not believe every spirit (μὴ παντὶ πνεύματι πιστεύετε), but judge the spirits whether they are from God (δοκιμάζετε τὰ πνεύματα εἰ ἐκ τοῦ θεοῦ ἐστιν), because many pseudo-prophets (ψευδοπροφῆται) have gone out into the world. From this you shall recognise the Spirit of God: every spirit that confesses Jesus Christ come in the flesh is from God, and every spirit that does not confess Jesus is not from God (πᾶν πνεῦμα ὃ ὁμολογεῖ Ἰησοῦν Χριστὸν ἐν σαρκὶ ἐληλυθότα ἐκ τοῦ θεοῦ ἐστιν, καὶ πᾶν πνεῦμα ὃ μὴ ὁμολογεῖ τὸν Ἰησοῦν ἐκ τοῦ θεοῦ οὐκ ἔστιν). And this is that [the spirit] of the antichrist, of whom you have heard that he was coming and now is already here (ὃ ἀκηκόατε ὅτι ἔρχεται, καὶ νῦν ἐν τῷ κόσμῳ ἐστὶν ἤδη). You are from God (ἐκ τοῦ θεοῦ ἐστε), little children, and you have conquered them (νενικήκατε αὐτούς), because the one who is in you is greater than the one in the world (ὅτι μείζων ἐστὶν ὁ ἐν ὑμῖν ἢ ὁ ἐν τῷ κόσμῳ). They are from the world, wherefore what they speak is from the world and the world listens to them. We are from God; he who recognises God listens to us, the one who is not from God does not listen to us. From this we recognise the spirit of truth and the spirit of deception (τὸ πνεῦμα τῆς ἀληθείας καὶ τὸ πνεῦμα τῆς πλάνης) (1 John 4.1-6).

This idea of two kinds of spirits guiding human behaviour has been linked, once again, to the *Instruction on the Two Spirits* from Qumran, this time by R. E. Brown.[52] As in the context of the *Instruction*, it has been argued that these spirits in 1 John are not personal, and that there are merely hints of demonological traits.[53] This would imply a similar psychological dualism to the one that has been claimed (and rejected) for the *Instruction*,[54] but it is unlikely for the same reasons: the spiritual influence is an actual, personified figure (the 'angel of darkness'/'spirit of deceit' in the *Instruction*, the 'antichrist' in 1 John 4). From 2 John 7 it is clear that this is not simply psychological influence: the many people who lead others astray (πολλοὶ πλάνοι), by denying Jesus' incarnation, are called 'the deceiver and the antichrist' (ὁ πλάνος καὶ ὁ ἀντίχριστος). Here the πλάνος and the ἀντίχριστος are parallel terms, as is also true of the πνεῦμα τῆς πλάνης and the ἀντίχριστος in 1 John 4. The shift from the plural (for actual people) to the singular demonstrates not only that

---

52 Raymond E. Brown, *The Epistles of John* (The Anchor Bible 30; New York: Chapman, 1982), p.487.
53 Frey, 'Licht aus den Höhlen?', p.180, with reference to Hans-Josef Klauck, *Der erste Johannesbrief* (EKK 23/1; Zurich: Benziger; Neukirchen–Vluyn: Neukirchener, 1991), pp.229–30. The same contrast between the 'spirit of truth' and 'the spirit of deceit' can be found in *T. Jud.* 20.1-2, cf. Lietaert Peerbolte, *Antecedents*, p.106.
54 Cf., e.g., John J. Collins, *Apocalypticism in the Dead Sea Scrolls* (London: Routledge, 1997), p.41.

the concept of a single antichrist must have been quite strong,[55] but also that this is the original tradition, while the notion of the 'spirit of the antichrist' as a psychological influence is a secondary application. The context of spirits, however, shows that the antichrist is not merely a human figure either.

Added to the use of the term 'antichrists' for human beings in 1 John 4, there is the more traditional designation 'pseudo-prophets' (in the plural) for human beings who act in the spirit of the antichrist. In Jewish tradition a 'false prophet' is someone claiming to speak in God's name without proper authority (Deut 13.1-5; 1 Kgs 22.6, 13), while in the NT 'the spirit' is more specifically related to 'teaching' (John 14.15–16.26; Acts 2.17; 13.1; 1 Cor 12.28).[56] Thus it is consistent with the overall Johannine approach to refer to someone who speaks and teaches in the spirit of the antichrist as a 'pseudo-prophet'.

While the antichrist is a figure relating to the truth and falsehood of human statements about God, there is also a passage in 1 John that traces not only ideas but human behaviour to an external, personified power. In 3.8 and 10 the same link is made between human behaviour and supernatural spirits as the one found in the *Instruction on the Two Spirits* (1QS III.13–IV.26). In 1 John 3.8 it is beyond doubt that there is an external, not only psychological, influence on human behaviour: 'He who commits sin is from the devil, because the devil sins from the beginning. For this reason the Son of God has been revealed so that he might undo the works of the devil' (ὁ ποιῶν τὴν ἁμαρτίαν ἐκ τοῦ διαβόλου ἐστίν, ὅτι ἀπ' ἀρχῆς ὁ διάβολος ἁμαρτάνει. εἰς τοῦτο ἐφανερώθη ὁ υἱὸς τοῦ θεοῦ, ἵνα λύσῃ τὰ ἔργα τοῦ διαβόλου). The two can be distinguished from each other by their actions (3.10): 'everyone who does not do righteousness is not from God, nor the one who does not love his brother' (πᾶς ὁ μὴ ποιῶν δικαιοσύνην οὐκ ἔστιν ἐκ τοῦ θεοῦ, καὶ ὁ μὴ ἀγαπῶν τὸν ἀδελφὸν αὐτοῦ). The devil is explicitly linked to the practical actions done against others, to sin and to not doing righteousness. This unacceptable behaviour is exemplified by Cain: 'Not like Cain who was from the evil one and slew his brother' (οὐ καθὼς Κάϊν ἐκ τοῦ πονηροῦ ἦν καὶ ἔσφαξεν τὸν ἀδελφὸν αὐτοῦ, 3.12). Again, murder is paralleled with hatred of the community and derived from the devil. Thus, while the antichrist in 1 John is related to transgressions against the first pillar of the community – to confess Christ correctly – Satan is related to transgressions against the second pillar of the community – to love one another. The

---

55 Cf. Frey, *Eschatologie*, pp.23–4.
56 Brown, *Epistles*, pp.489–90.

Cain myth is drawn upon to explain false behaviour. In the same way as Cain killed *his brother*, the 'child of the devil' 'does not love *his brother*'. Like the antichrists who started out from the community, the activity of the devil is to sow discord among the community and to cause people to leave it. It is not an external but an internal attack.

Thus in the Johannine letters the same terminology is used as in the Gospel but in a different way: Satan is not linked to Jesus' life but he is the internal enemy of the community; he guides the actions of the transgressors, while the antichrist guides their thoughts. The question is whether both terms refer to the same being.[57] The variety of terms used to denote the spirit of the antichrist/of deception and the devil clearly refer to different aspects of counter-godly activity, but they function identically to explain deviant thought and action and do not necessarily imply a different being. It is likely that both are comprised in the other term, 'the evil one', who is – in contrast to his presentation in John's Gospel – explicitly said to be overcome by the young people of the community when they came to faith (2.14).

4. Conclusion

The evidence indicates that various motifs are taken up in the Johannine texts. In the Gospel of John the function of the terms for the eschatological opponent can be divided neatly between the life of the community and that of Christ, whereas in the Johannine letters they are related only to the life of the community, in that all attacks seem to come from within. Those who come to faith have conquered 'the evil one', from whose external attacks the community is protected by God; this parallels the depiction of the 'ruler of this world' in the Gospel. In the Johannine letters, the devil, the antichrist and the spirit of deceit act as internal threats, even if this is not acknowledged by the community who prefers to regard those who succumb to their influence as never having been a true part of the community (similar to the Qumran community's reception of the *Instruction on the Two Spirits* in their Covenant liturgy – 1QS I.15–II.12).

The single concept binding together all these enemies seems to be the idea of spirits, good and evil, and their possession of human beings; this theme occurs in virtually every reference to the eschatological adversary. It is the Holy Spirit who discloses that the Archon of this world is

---

57 Cf. Frey, *Eschatologie*, pp.74–5.

judged.[58] The evil Archon is cast out of believers. Satan/the devil enters Judas and drives him to hand Jesus over. As 'the evil one', the enemy continues to threaten the community 'in the world'. The activity of the evil power includes lying, leading people astray about Jesus' origin, denying who Jesus is and, consequently, trying to kill him (in order to prove him wrong) or the community, and leading to discord among the members of the community. In every true believer he has been overcome, although he still leads to hatred within the community and, by lying about the Father and the Son, works as the 'antichrist' whose spirit leads people to deny the truth of Christ and to become pseudo-prophets. The Archon of this world and 'the evil one' characterise the community's conquered, but still active, opponent. Satan and the devil are the figures used to describe the murderous force; this involves drawing on the myth of Cain, on the life of Jesus, and on the experience of certain members' actions against others within the community. Antichrists and pseudo-prophets are those people who have departed from the community in order to return to the world. Their parallel figure within Jesus' life is Judas, the 'son of perdition', who was one of the twelve, evil from the beginning (as shown by his reaction to the anointing), into whom Satan entered to provoke him to hand over Jesus.[59]

The Johannine idea of spirit possession is different from the Synoptics, and, as already noted, resembles that found in the *Instruction on the Two Spirits*. In this non-sectarian apocalyptic wisdom tradition, which develops the Two Ways tradition,[60] the spirit of light rules over the sons of light, while the sons of deceit are ruled by the 'angel of darkness'/ 'spirit of deceit' (two different terms!). The spirit of deceit attacks the sons of light but, at the end, is purged from them by the purifying Spirit of God. Likewise, in the Gospel of John the personification of evil takes possession of human beings in order to deny the truth of Christ and attack those who proclaim it. Unlike the *Instruction*, however, in the Johannine writings this dualistic battlefield does not exist from the beginning of creation, but only from the moment of coming to believe, which is described as a new birth in John 3.5: every person who comes to

58 The fundamental importance of the concept of judgement has also been emphasised by Ashton, *Understanding*, pp.405–11
59 Piper, 'Satan', pp.277–8.
60 Against Ashton, *Understanding*, pp.109–10, 309 who places too much emphasis on the contrast between 'sectarian' and 'establishment'. In Second Temple Judaism there was a much greater variety of views than after 70 CE and there was no such entity as 'establishment'. 'Sectarianism' was not a matter of rejection by a so-called establishment but a self-imposed separation from other contemporaneous Jewish interpretations.

believe in Christ has won the battle against the 'Archon of this world'/ 'evil one'/Satan/Devil/Antichrist. Every person who is born from above (through baptism *and Spirit!*) confesses Christ and follows his commandment to love; the believer is taken out of the Archon's influence and is a person from whom the spirit of this world has been driven out. Therefore it is incorrect to assume that there are no exorcisms in John.[61] Whenever someone comes to believe in Christ, the power behind the denial of Christ and God is driven out, which is an exorcism in itself.[62] Jesus' argument with 'the Jews' in John 8 and their mutual accusation of possession (8.44, 48, 52) provides sufficient evidence that this fundamental trait exists in John's theology. At the same time, this exorcism is the apocalyptic victory of God's spirit over the spirits. The idea of eschatological judgement and the raising of the dead are transformed into the notion of the expulsion of the ungodly spirits from the faithful by the Spirit of God. Judgement is the demonstration that someone preferred this worldly mortal life to that of God. The fate of the ruler of this world is to perish along with that life. This is not only juridical; it is the apocalyptic verdict over all ungodly life. To use another metaphor from John's Gospel: when the light comes, darkness does not merely go away, it ceases to exist.

Yet from this a new problem arises. If the eschatological purification of the sons of light from the *Instruction on the Two Spirits* is thought to happen in the present life of believers, this leaves no future eschatological judgement in the tradition to deal with the continuing reality of evil. In the reception of the *Instruction* in the Qumran community entry into the community purged members from previous sins, similarly to the idea in the Johannine, but the community felt the need to add another tradition containing a future eschatological promise of an apocalyptic battle and victory (1QM) to balance the present eschatology of 1QS. The Johannine community attempted to deal with this problem by taking over the idea of a 'resurrection towards judgement' (εἰς ἀνάστασιν κρίσεως, John 5.28-29), which does not otherwise fit the idea of a judgement that has already taken place. It relates only to human beings, not to metaphysical beings such as the Ruler, and it meets the need to find a final point of closure.

---

61   It is astounding that commentators such as Twelftree, 'Exorcisms', pp.141–2, can emphasise the 'battle with Satan' in John and yet still claim that there are no exorcisms in the Gospel.
62   Cf. Theobald, *Johannes*, pp.812–13.

Evil in Johannine and Apocalyptic Perspective: Petition for Protection in John 17

Loren T. Stuckenbruck

Introduction

Few today would question whether there is a strong socio-rhetorical component to language about evil in the Fourth Gospel and the Johannine Epistles. This has been recognised by many for several decades, especially since the influential studies of Wayne Meeks,[1] Raymond Brown,[2] and J. Louis Martyn.[3] Within such a framework, conditioned as it is by the interaction between groups, the use of an adjective such as 'evil' (φαῦλος, John 3.20; 5.29; πονηρός, 3.19; 7.7),[4] and especially more unambiguously personifying expressions of 'having a demon' (ἔχειν δαιμόνιον, cf. 7.20; 8.48-49, 52; 10.20-21), 'you are from the father the devil' (ὑμεῖς ἐκ τοῦ πατρὸς τοῦ διαβόλου ἐστέ, 8.44) or simply 'the devil' (διάβολος, 6.70; cf. 13.2 – referring to Judas) are ultimately products of polemical perception. To a certain degree, the use of negative labels for detractors also holds for language in the Fourth Gospel about 'the world' (ὁ κόσμος), though references to this term are not so one-sided, so that the text assumes an ability on the part of an audience to discern the difference between 'world' as an arena of God's activity within the created order (1.9-10, 29; 3.16-17, 19; 4.42; 6.14, 33, 51; 8.12, 26; 9.5; 10.36; 11.27; 12.46-47; 16.28; 17.21-23; 18.37) and as an

---

1 Wayne A. Meeks, 'The Man from Heaven in Johannine Sectarianism', *JBL* 91 (1972), pp.44–72 (especially 67–9).
2 Raymond E. Brown, *The Gospel according to John* (AB 29/29A; 2 vols.; Garden City: Doubleday, 1979), and *The Community of the Beloved Disciple* (New York: Paulist, 1979).
3 J. Louis Martyn, *The Gospel of John in Christian History* (New York: Paulist, 1978), and *History and Theology in the Fourth Gospel* (Louisville: Westminster John Knox, 3rd edn, 2003 [1st edn, 1968]).
4 The adjectives here are, except for πονηρός in John 17.15 (see below), always made to characterise 'deeds'.

unwelcoming or even inimical force represented by anything that, in principle, is opposed to God's purposes and is incapable of understanding God's activity through Jesus the Son (especially John 1.10 [3rd occurrence]; 7.4, 7⁵; 13.1; 14.17, 19, 22, 27; 15.18-19; 16.8, 20, 33; 17.6, 9, 11, 14-16, 18, 25).

Another framework within which language about evil in the Fourth Gospel has been interpreted sometimes goes under the category of what is called 'realised eschatology'.⁶ The categorical statement by Jesus that 'I have conquered the world' (ἐγὼ νενίκηκα τὸν κόσμον, 16.33; cf. 1.5), taken in tandem with the uncompromising claims made by the Johannine Jesus about himself and about what he expects of those who adhere and are obedient to him, presupposes that the audience are to imagine themselves as participants in an existence that reflects such a reality. Through identification with the Son, believers place themselves on the side of a victory that has already, in effect, taken place.

Given these rhetorical-sociological and realised eschatological dimensions for interpreting the language of evil in the Fourth Gospel, is there anything in the Johannine tradition that stands outside of this? Is there anything which suggests that the lines are not firmly drawn between the emerging Johannine community and others or between the present state of entrenched ideological certainty and a reality that is yet to be? Since I am not simply asking whether or not the Johannine tradition has any room for eschatology,⁷ it may help to formulate the problem another way, that is, in relation to the persistence of evil: is there anything eschatological or even 'apocalyptic' when it comes to the way evil is dealt with in the text? In one sense, one may be able to answer this question rather

---

5 Significantly, the plural adjective πονηρά describes the 'works' or 'deeds' (ἔργα) associated with the world. Such works are diametrically opposed to ἔργα in all other instances in John where they refer to the allied activities of God and the Son (3.21; 5.20, 36; 6.28; 7.3; 9.3-4; 10.25, 32, 37-38; 14.10-12; 15.24), which Jesus' followers emulate and participate in (6.28; 14.12).

6 See, famously, C. H. Dodd, *The Interpretation of the Fourth Gospel* (Cambridge: Cambridge University Press, 1953), and Rudolf Bultmann, *The Gospel of John: A Commentary* (trans. George R. Beasley-Murray; Oxford: Basil Blackwell, 1971).

7 For strong criticisms of Bultmann's demythologisation project in interpreting John's Gospel, which, at the same time, stress the presence of a Johannine future eschatology, see especially Udo Schnelle, 'Die Abschiedsreden im Johannesevangelium', *ZNW* 80 (1989), pp.64–79, and Jörg Frey, *Die johanneische Eschatologie* (WUNT 96, 110, 117; 3 vols.; Tübingen: Mohr Siebeck, 1997, 1998, 2000), especially *Eschatologie*, I, pp.119–50.

easily: after all, for John, as in Jewish apocalyptic writings, there remains an eschatological judgement in which the wicked will be punished and the righteous rewarded (especially 5.28-29; see further 3.36; 6.54, 57-58; 11.24-27; 12.48[8]; 14.2-4, 15-24; 16.16-33).

However, what about the way evil is expressly combated? Posing the question this way is appropriate on at least three counts. First, there is a general consideration: the notion of realised eschatology, to the extent that it applies to the Fourth Gospel, represents the ideal for a community's self-understanding that includes the hedging of itself off from other groups, especially those with which it is most immediately in tension. In all this, the resulting question would remain: how does one negotiate the undeniable continuing reality of evil wherever it exists, even within the Johannine community? If in the present world the 'already' (cf. 16.33) is a reality that determines and defines socio-religious identity, what does one do with experience that does not fit into or reflect this? An ideal self-perception, whether embraced by a religious community or individuals, still has to reckon with the very means by which counter-experiences are to be interpreted and navigated. Second, not all the vocabulary regarding personified evil in the Fourth Gospel can be reduced sociologically to sectarian and theologically to realised eschatological frames of reference. Nor is evil simply, in my view, a matter of 'ethics'. We may note here a designation such as 'the evil one' in Jesus' prayer at John 17.15 (see on this below) and the several references to 'the ruler of this world' in John 12.31, 14.30 (with 'the world') and 16.11. Third, a reconsideration of evil in the Gospel of John, when placed in conversation with Second Temple Jewish traditions, should caution us from drawing on too narrow a conception of 'apocalyptic'. Since the influential studies on genre and 'apocalypse' in the late 1970s and 1980s,[9]

---

8   Here Jesus claims that 'on the last day the word I have spoken will judge him (i.e. the one who rejects Jesus)'. While this initially appears to be an extraordinary claim, it is the kind of claim that is sustained by the Enochic writer of the *Epistle of Enoch* whose words are not simply denunciatory, but are intended to function as formal testimony at the time of judgement (cf. *1 En.* 96.4, 7; 97.2-7; 99.3, 16; 103.4; 104.1). See Loren T. Stuckenbruck, *1 Enoch 91–108* (CEJL; Berlin: de Gruyter, 2007), p.216, and 'The Epistle of Enoch: Genre and Authorial Presentation', *DSD* 17.2 (2010), pp.387–417 (417): 'In terms of function, the work, which inscribes the "memory" of human deeds (94.8; 96.4, 7; 97.2, 7; 99.3, 16; 103.4; cf. 103.15), imparts irreversible testimony (enhanced by exhortations, disclosure formulae) that guarantees the outcome of eschatological judgement'.

9   See the contributions to David Hellholm (ed.), *Apocalypticism in the Mediterranean World and the Near East: Proceedings of the International Colloquium on Apocalypticism, Uppsala, August 12–17, 1979* (Tübingen: Mohr Siebeck, 1983);

many scholars have made it their business to broaden the scope of what one means by 'apocalyptic' beyond eschatology to, for example, include sapiential and cosmological dimensions as well. My own developing view is that even the provision of a conceptual place for wisdom in apocalyptic thought does not go far enough, and I hope that the consideration of evil in the Fourth Gospel will help to make this more apparent.

The Problem

In dealing with a neglected dimension of evil in the Fourth Gospel, I would like to take Jesus' prayer in John 17.15 as a point of departure: 'I am not asking you to take them out of the world, but to keep them from the evil one'.[10]

There are, at first glance, several observations we may wish to make. (1) The Greek expression behind what I have translated as 'the evil one' is ambiguous. Being in the genitive case, τοῦ πονηροῦ could be either masculine or neuter. The latter sense is *prima facie* a viable option; in general terms it accords more easily with modernist sensibilities, it occurs within a prayer of Jesus that emphasises love and unity among Jesus' disciples and followers (17.11, 21-23, 26), and it is the same term which, in an unambiguous neuter form, describes the 'works' of the world (3.19; 7.7). There are, however, reasons to steer the perspective in the other, more personifying direction. In 17.12 Jesus refers to 'the son of destruction' as the only one whom he did not keep among those God gave to him. This is a reference to Judas Iscariot whose activity to betray Jesus occurs when 'Satan entered him' (εἰσῆλθεν εἰς ἐκεῖνον ὁ σατανᾶς, 13.27); if, as is likely, Jesus' loss of the 'son of destruction' alludes back to the story of Judas as presented in the Fourth Gospel itself, Jesus' prayer assumes the existence of an extra-human force in the world that attempts to detract those who belong to the Son (cf. 17.11, 13). This, in turn,

---

John J. Collins, 'Introduction: Towards the Morphology of a Genre', in idem (ed.), *Apocalypse: The Morphology of a Genre* (*Semeia* 14; Atlanta: Scholars, 1979), pp.1–20, and idem, *The Apocalyptic Imagination: An Introduction to Jewish Apocalyptic Literature* (Grand Rapids: Eerdmans, 2nd edn, 1998), pp.2–11, especially 4–9.

10 A substantial part of the following argument draws on my earlier study, '"Protect Them from the Evil One" (John 17:15): Light from the Dead Sea Scrolls', in Mary L. Coloe and Tom Thatcher (eds.), *John, Qumran, and the Dead Sea Scrolls: Sixty Years of Discovery and Debate* (Early Judaism and Its Literature 32; Atlanta: SBL, 2011), pp.139–60.

makes it more plausible to read Jesus' prayer in conversation with traditions about prayer preserved for us in Second Temple Jewish texts (as below). (2) We may observe that the prayer is a petition for protection uttered by Jesus on behalf of those who are his disciples and, arguably, his later followers in the Johannine community. To be sure, the verb in the petition is not φυλάσσειν ('to guard, protect'), but rather τηρεῖν ('to keep') with which it is interchangeable in the Gospel.[11] As we shall see below, τηρεῖν has its background in the Hebrew term שׁמר (though in the Aaronic blessing of Num 6.24 the available Greek translation reads φυλάξαι σε). We may ask, simply: despite all the so-called realised eschatology at work in the Gospel, why does Jesus find it necessary to ask that, in contrast to what happened to Judas, his followers be protected from demonic power (if we may call it that)? (3) The term 'world' bears a largely negative connotation both here and throughout the prayer. Despite being allied to the evil one, however, it is not treated as the same; though the world 'hates' Jesus' disciples (17.14), it is still considered a place within which they must remain while seeking protection from the evil one who also dwells there. The association between the world and the evil one has to do with cosmology and control. The world is the arena of existence for Jesus' adherents, and the evil one has dominion over it. Thus the main challenge for the believing community in the Johannine perspective is less to escape and relocate out of world's way but, much more, to live in defiance of the grip on power attributed to demonic evil in this world (17.15). This possibility throws up a possible link between the petition being uttered by Jesus and the designation 'the ruler of this world' which has occurred several times in the preceding chapters (12.31; 14.30; 16.11). These references to a being who is deemed to be in control of the present world order occur in words of Jesus that have the defeat of evil in view. In words to the disciples, Jesus has declared, 'Now is the judgement of this world; now the ruler of this world will be driven out' (12.31); 'I will no longer talk much with you, for the ruler of the world is coming' (14.30); and the advocate (i.e. the Spirit) will prove the world wrong 'about judgement, because the ruler of this world has been condemned' (16.11).

Here we return once again to the question: in view of Jesus' assurance that he has overcome the ruler of this world (cf. 16.33), what is the function of a prayer for protection? Before addressing the function of Jesus' prayer, I would like to set the stage for drawing on petitionary prayers

---

11   For φυλάσσειν in the sense of 'to keep' in the Fourth Gospel, see 12.25 and 47, and for τηρεῖν in the sense of 'to protect', see 17.11 and the present text of v. 15.

for protection as they occur in Jewish apocalyptic traditions, especially from those writings preserved among the Dead Sea Scrolls. To appreciate the significance of Jewish tradition for John 17.15, however, two preliminary points require attention: (1) the expression ὁ ἄρχων τοῦ κόσμου in both the wider and Johannine contexts and (2) a more detailed summary of Jesus' prayer in John 17.

The Ruler of this World

The designation 'ruler' (ἄρχων), of course, referred in Greek antiquity to a high official, a person with civic authority or to a military commander. In relation to the non-physical world, Plato made mention of ἄρχοντες in his *Laws* as beings to whom God has given authority over circumscribed areas of the cosmos (*Leg.* 903b). The term also occurs in the Greek text traditions to Daniel, where it refers to the prominent otherworldly beings – Michael ('the first of the rulers', Dan 10.13 OG, Th), 'the ruler of the Persians' (10.13, 20 Th), 'the ruler of the Greeks' (10.21 Th) – who are made to function as protectors of the nations. In this context, the angel Michael assumes such a duty on behalf of Israel.[12] In itself the phrase 'the ruler of this world' is unique in John's Gospel, though it picks up on the notion of one with authority over beings who are inimical to God's purposes, a notion widespread in Jewish apocalyptic tradition.[13] This emphasis on one who acts as an organising power over those who oppose God and God's people also reflects something not developed in Jewish tradition by means of any of the other personalising designations for evil such as 'the devil' or 'demon'.[14] As Jutta Leonhardt-Balzer has observed, neither of these designations serve in the Fourth Gospel to denote God's overarching opponent.[15] The devil (ὁ διάβολος) is presented not so much as one who acts on its own but through people

---

12   See the useful overview of these sources in Jutta Leonhardt-Balzer, 'Gestalten des Bösen im frühen Christentum', Jörg Frey and Michael Becker (eds.), *Apokalyptik und Qumran* (Einblicke 10; Paderborn: Bonifatius, 2007), pp.203–35.

13   See Loren T. Stuckenbruck, 'Demonic Beings and the Dead Sea Scrolls', in Harold J. Ellens (ed.), *Explaining Evil.* Vol. 1, *Definitions and Development* (3 vols.; Santa Barbara, California: Praegers Publishers, 2011), pp.121–44.

14   On the other hand, for the use of 'Satan' as an adversary against God's people and as a chief over an array of demonic spirits, see *Jub.* 10.11 (cf. also 11Q5 xix 13-16), though the relation of 'Satan' to any other entities is not specified. These texts are discussed in more detail below.

15   Leonhardt-Balzer, 'Gestalten des Bösen im frühen Christentum', pp.221–5.

who oppose Jesus. Activity that opposes Jesus comes from the devil and is described through the metaphor of parentage; Jesus accuses his Jewish detractors in John 8.37-45 of being 'from your father the devil' as a way to explain why it is that they reject him. Jesus can even say directly to his own disciples, 'one of you *is* a devil' (6.70-71), by which he refers to Judas who would betray him. 'Being the devil' will, in John 13.2 (see also references to Satan's entry into Judas in 13.27 and Luke 22.3), be re-expressed in terms of Satan putting 'into his heart in order that Judas Simeon Iscariot might betray' Jesus. Similarly, Jesus is accused of having a 'demon' because his teaching and activity make no sense to others (7.20 – to the crowd; 8.48, 49, 52 – to the Jews; 10.20 – some Jews, though in 10.21 other Jews dispute this). This emphasis is picked up in 1 John, in which the devil is held accountable for all human sin and is thus characterised as the one who 'sins from the beginning' (1 John 3.8, 10)

However, the close alignment between demonic and human activity is not ultimately a matter of collapsing the two. Judas' betrayal is, after all, attributed to the *invasive* force of Satan in his heart (13.2); and the charges that Jesus has a demon (8.48-49, 52) presuppose the suspicion, however rhetorical, that a power inimical to God's purposes has taken hold of Jesus, even as Jesus is referring to his death (John 7.19-20) and is being credited with healing those who are blind (10.21). If such language cannot be reduced to metaphor, then 'the ruler of this world' appropriately functions as an overarching designation for a power that controls impulses which, on a profound level, contravene what Jesus declares about himself. In contrast to the terms 'devil' or 'demon' and perhaps even 'Satan' – these terms surface in specific instances of oppositional activity that occurs in particular groups or human beings – the designation 'the ruler of this world' is more comprehensive and wide-ranging. Without referring specifically to 'the ruler', Jesus declares in John 7.7 that the world hates him since he testifies that its works are evil (cf. also 15.18–16.4). As such, 'the world' is personified as an organic conduit for such works. To refer, then, to 'the ruler of this world' is to acknowledge that there is a coherent, organising power behind these deeds and that this organising power is characteristic of the present world order that comes under its sway.[16]

---

16 This is in my view not to be confused with the beings called '*archons*' who, in Gnostic literature from the Nag Hammadi corpus, are credited with creating humanity and are custodians of the cosmos in its material state; see, e.g., *The Hypostasis of the Archons* (NHC II, 4) and *On the Origin of the World* (NHC II, 5; 97.24–127.17 and the fragmentary texts in XII, 2; 50.25-34 and British Library Or.

In one respect, Jesus' announcement of his death in the Fourth Gospel heralds the judgement over 'this world'. In John 12.20-33 Jesus' death is the time, 'the hour', for his glorification (12.23, 27-28). In the text Jesus declares also that *now* 'the ruler of this world' *will* be cast out. This combination of present (now) and future (will) in connection with Jesus' death is striking. Jesus' death marks a defeat, though not fully realised, over demonic evil. In John 14.30-31, Jesus announces that 'the ruler of this world is coming', yet declares that it 'does not have anything in me, so that the world may know that I love the Father, even as the Father has commanded me'. Again this is a pronouncement of both the simultaneous presence and powerlessness of 'the ruler of the world'. Although the ruler of this world plays an essential role in bringing about Jesus' death, Jesus affirms that this 'rule' is not in fact displaying any real power over him. Accordingly, the advocate, the Spirit, reveals the truth about Jesus to the disciples who remain in the world and reveals the condemnation under which 'the ruler of this world' already stands (16.8-11). Thus mention of 'the ruler of this world' is closely bound up with the notion that he already stands under divine judgement, for example, as exposed through Jesus' death.

If by means of Jesus' death 'the ruler of this world' is rendered powerless, one may ask: what kind of defeat is this? Is it a complete removal of that force which coordinates opposition against God, Jesus, and the Johannine community? Does the exorcistic language of 'casting out' (14.30), of being rendered powerless, or of being already judged or condemned bear a finality that leaves little else to be done? In the narrative world of the Fourth Gospel the answer would be 'yes' and 'no'. Insofar as the answer is 'yes', Jesus' death is definitive and, in the Fourth Gospel, functions in *principle* as that which ring-fences or circumscribes the devil's activity as no longer determinative for human existence in the context of faithfulness to God. Much of John's language about evil takes this conviction as its point of departure. That the answer, somehow, can likewise be 'no' is reflected by the fact that Jesus utters petitions for those who will come after him, culminating in their need for divine protection from the evil one (17.15).

4926). While the Johannine tradition may lead to such a worldview, the Gnostic frame does not offer the best point of departure for determining the origin of the ideas it inherited.

John 17: Jesus' Petitions

Jesus' prayer in John 17 is elaborate and can be subdivided into four parts:

1. a series of declarative statements about Jesus' and the disciples' special position and faithfulness in relation to God (17.1-8);
2. petitions for Jesus' disciples (17.9-19);
3. a petition for those who come to faith through the disciples' ministry (17.20-23); and
4. statements that resume and build on selected elements of the prayer (17.24-26).

Limiting our observations to Jesus' petition for his disciples in 17.9-19, we note several points of emphasis: (a) Jesus underlines the enmity or tension between his disciples and 'the world'. This tension manifests itself in the hate that the world shows towards the disciples (v. 14). Jesus' petition unambiguously takes the side of the disciples: he does not pray for the world, but for those whom God has given him (v. 9). However, despite the sharp distinction between the disciples and the world, Jesus does not seek to resolve this tension by requesting that God removes the disciples from the world (v. 15).

(b) Formally, in 17.9-19, Jesus presents God with three petitions. The first occurs in vv. 9-13: God – who is addressed as 'holy Father' – is asked to 'keep (τήρησον) them (i.e. the disciples) in your name which you have given to me' (v. 11). The basis for this request is provided by Jesus, who himself has 'kept' (ἐτήρουν) the disciples 'in your name which you have given me' (v. 12). The notion of 'keeping' is formulated in terms of protection by Jesus, who has guarded (ἐφύλαξα) his disciples so that none of them would be lost.[17] Initially, the petition is concerned with unity among Jesus' disciples – 'in order that they may be one' (v. 11) – a petition which is also brought to bear on later believers (vv. 20-23). At this point, it is not clear from the petition what the protection is supposed to be from. Implied, however, is the perception of a danger that threatens to splinter the community for whom Jesus is praying. Second, in vv. 14-16, Jesus prays again for God to 'keep' (ἵνα τηρήσῃς). Here, there is no doubt that Jesus is asking for protection: 'that you keep them from the evil one' (v. 15). The reason why protection is

---

17 This protection by Jesus echoes the shepherd imagery applied to him in John 10.7-16, though there the protection attributed to him is implied.

requested lies, as we have seen, in a tension between Jesus' followers and 'the world'. Because Jesus is not of the world, those whose unity he has maintained are also not from the world (v. 16), which has 'hated them' (v. 14). Despite this perceived alienation and enmity, Jesus' words refuse to contemplate removal (v. 15); the protection that he requests assumes, instead, that the cosmos, as presently constituted for the disciples, involves an open clash or conflict with 'the evil one' who is 'the ruler of this world'. As in the first request of v. 11, God's protection is bound up with protection by Jesus, who in 14.30 has already declared that 'the ruler of the world has no power over me'. Thus the protection is required if Jesus' adherents are living in an age dominated by 'the evil one'. The third petition of Jesus, in vv. 17-19, is a request for God to sanctify or make his disciples holy (ἁγίασον αὐτούς). Again, as in the first and second petitions of ch. 17, the request is linked with Jesus' own definitive activity: because he has sanctified himself or rendered himself pure for the disciples' sake, they themselves can also be sanctified.

(c) Each of Jesus' petitions to God is a genuine supplication, that is, none merely borrows a petitionary formula in order to accomplish something else. However, because the very basis for the divine response to these requests is already to be found in Jesus' activity, these petitions are replete with statements about him in relation to both God and his followers. On the one hand, Jesus is *the one* sent by God (vv. 3, 21, 23, 25); he is *the one* entrusted by God with the divine name (vv. 6, 12, 26); he is *the one* who is being glorified by God (vv. 1, 5, 10, 22, 24); and he and God are 'one' (vv. 11, 22). On the other hand, the unity between Jesus and God ('just as we are one', vv. 11, 22) and Jesus' origin in God rather than in the world are determinative for Jesus' followers who are aligned with him. Alignment with Jesus makes it possible for his followers to be 'one' amongst themselves and, in their mutual belonging to God through Jesus, to be in tension with 'the world' (v. 14).

The proclamations in ch. 17 – so much of the language attempts to shore up Jesus and his followers' identity – cannot hide the petitionary force of Jesus' prayer. We have been noting that the designation 'the ruler of this world' is of particular relevance here; Jesus asks for protection from the evil one precisely because of the existing, *ongoing* hostility between the disciples and the world. The defeat of this inimical ruler may be assured in Jesus' death to be a reality, at least in principle, but it is not complete. The Fourth Gospel presents Jesus' death as that event which provides assurance of the evil one's essential powerlessness while acknowledging, nonetheless, that the complete destruction of this force lies in the eschatological future.

Several considerations suggest that Jesus' petition in John 17.15 has been shaped by tradition. First, as already noted, 'the evil one' as a designation for the devil occurs only here in the Fourth Gospel and thus seems uncharacteristic of the writer's language which otherwise may have been expected to refer here to 'the ruler of this world'. Second, the phrase 'that you may keep them from the evil one' is reminiscent of language found in the Matthean version of the Lord's Prayer (Matt 6.13: 'but deliver us from the evil one')[18] and in one Pauline writer's declaration about God's faithfulness in 2 Thess 3.3 ('for faithful is the Lord, who will strengthen you and guard you from the evil one').[19] Third, the verb 'keep' (τηρεῖν), which in John 17.11-12 is treated as a synonym for 'protect, guard', may be an echo of the Aaronic blessing of Num 6.24: 'may the Lord bless you and keep you' (MT; Grk. εὐλογήσαι σε κύριος καὶ φυλάξαι σε).

The main difference between the New Testament texts just mentioned and the Aaronic blessing lies in the absence of any reference in the latter to 'the evil one'. Admittedly, the Aaronic blessing simply concludes with the object of the verb ('you') without specifying what it is that Israel is to be kept or protected from. To be sure, in two adaptations of the Aaronic blessing in the Hebrew Bible, 'evil' is added to the equation: (1) 1 Chron 4.10, 'Jabez called on the God of Israel, saying, "Oh that you would bless me and enlarge my border and that your hand would be with me, and that you would *keep me from evil* and harm! (so MT; the Gk. presupposes a

---

18   In the Matthean context of the Sermon on the Mount, the personified meaning of the expression is strengthened by the less ambiguous references to 'the evil one' in Matt 5.37; 13.19, 38.

19   While it is possible to construe the phrase as an abstract reference to 'evil', the foregoing mention of 'the lawless one' in 2 Thess 2.8 strengthens the case for a personified meaning here. In 2 Tim 4.18, on the other hand, the deutero-Pauline writer – though possibly alluding to the Lord's Prayer – is not directly concerned with an evil being when he declares that 'the Lord will rescue me from every evil work (NRSV: attack!) (ἀπὸ παντὸς ἔργου πονηροῦ) and save me for his heavenly kingdom'.

Beyond its semantic overlap with φυλάσσειν, the term 'keep' (τηρεῖν) operates in the Fourth Gospel with a double function: being 'kept' or protected by God from adversity (whether 'the evil one', wickedness, or adversity) varies directly with 'keeping' God's words or commands; this not only occurs in John's Gospel (cf. 17.11 with 17.6 and 12.47; 14.15, 21, 23-24; 15.10, 20), but also in Revelation (cf. 3.10 with 1.3; 3.8; 12.17; 14.12; 22.7, 9). In addition to further references given by Bultmann, *The Gospel of John*, pp.301–2 n. 5, see *y. Pe'ah* 16b: אם שמרתם דברי תורה אני משמר אתכם מן המזיקין ('if you keep the words of the Torah, I will protect you from the demons'). In this formulation the motif of protection from the demonic represents a much earlier tradition that is explored below.

very different text)"'; (2) Ps 121.7, 'The Lord will keep you from all evil; he will keep your life' (NRSV; MT and LXX agree). In neither of these cases, however, do the texts suggest anything about protection from an 'evil one'. The same seems to be the case in the later 2 Macc 1.25, according to which God is addressed as one who rescues Israel 'from all evil', and in Wisdom of Solomon ('you persuaded our enemies that it is you who delivers from all evil', Wis 16.8).

Beyond the Matthean version of the Lord's Prayer and 2 Thessalonians, is there anything which may help one explain the background to the petition for protection from personified evil, and what light might this shed on a Johannine perspective in relation to the defeat and yet persistent reality of demonic evil? What might such a background tell us, more specifically, about the theological framework in which Jesus' petitions in John 17 are formulated? In the following section, we shall explore some petitions, arguing that our closest link between the Aaronic blessing and its adaptations, on the one hand, and the narrative world of John 17 and the Johannine understanding of 'the ruler of this world', on the other, lies in sources preserved in the Dead Sea Scrolls.

Protection from Demonic Power in an Age of Evil: Second Temple Jewish Tradition

Petitions to God for help are attested in abundance in the Hebrew Bible and the Greek translations.[20] Indeed, in line with the few passages we have already considered, there is no single instance in the Hebrew Bible in which God is specifically invoked for deliverance against another

---

20 Such prayers request divine help in relation to one's own shortcomings (Pss 27.12; 39.8; 51.14; 79.9); from dangers coming from opponents or enemies (so, e.g., Gen 32.11; Josh 2.13; Judg 10.15; 1 Sam 12.10; 2 Kgs 21.14; 1 Chron 6.36; 16.35; Pss 6.4; 17.13; 22.20; 25.20; 31.1-2, 15; 40.13; 43.1; 59.1-2; 69.14, 18; 70.1; 71.2, 4; 82.4; 116.4; 119.134, 170; 120.2; 140.1; 142.6; 143.9; 144.7, 11; Isa 44.17); or from premature death or an unwanted afterlife (e.g. Job 33.24 and 28). The material in this section is also discussed in Loren Stuckenbruck, 'Pleas for Deliverance from the Demonic in Early Jewish Texts', in Robert Hayward and Brad Embry (eds.), *Studies in Jewish Prayer* (JSS Supplement 17; Oxford: Oxford University Press, 2005), pp.55–78, and 'Prayers of Deliverance from the Demonic in the Dead Sea Scrolls and Related Early Jewish Literature', in Ian H. Henderson and Gerbern S. Oegema (eds.), *The Changing Face of Judaism, Christianity, and Other Greco-Roman Religions in Antiquity: Presented to James H. Charlesworth on the Occasion of his 65th Birthday* (Gütersloh: Gütersloher Verlagshaus, 2006), pp.146–65.

deity. Prayers seeking divine protection from harm or help in neutralising the effects of demonic power begin to surface, however, in literature from the Second Temple period.

Serek ha-Yahad

Representative of this development is an adaptation of the Aaronic blessing within the Qumran community's covenant renewal ceremony, which, according to the *Serek ha-Yahad*, was to take place year by year (1QS ii 19; the ceremony as a whole is described in 1QS i 16–iii 12). After an opening confession of wrongdoing and affirmation of divine favour by the community (i 23–ii 1a), the liturgy is organised into a short series of blessings to be pronounced by the priests on 'all the men of the lot of God' (ii 1b-4) and two longer series of curses pronounced by the Levites against 'all the men of the lot of Belial' (ii 14-17). The language of both the blessings and curses, though reflecting contemporary concerns of the community, relies heavily on the Aaronic blessing. In particular, the benediction in Num 6.24, 'May the Lord bless you and keep you' (יברכך יהוה וישמרך, LXX: εὐλογήσαι σε κύριος καὶ φυλάξαι σε) is reformulated in 1QS ii 2-3 in terms of contrasting activities of God, thus avoiding the possible implication that the verbs 'bless' and 'keep' are synonymous or complementary: 'May he bless you with everything good, and may he keep you from every evil' (יברככה בכול טוב וישמורכה מכול רע). While in comparison to 1 Chron 4.10 and Ps 121.7 (or even 2 Macc 1.25 and Wis 16.8), the reformulation does not seem to mark much of a conceptual shift from the Aaronic blessing, the larger context makes clear that the blessing is concerned with divine protection from Belial.[21] As the text following the liturgy suggests, it is precisely because the community knows itself to be living during a time of Belial's rule that the ceremony is necessary: 'they shall do thus year by year all the days of the dominion of Belial' (1QS ii 19). Indeed, the ceremony counteracts the reality of life 'during the dominion of Belial' because it is a time when it is possible for members to stray from the covenant on account of 'fear or dread or testing' (1QS i 17-18); likewise, the opening confession of sins is expressly understood as a measure to be taken by

---

21 In this respect, the text's appropriation of Num 6.24 is on a trajectory that leads to the version preserved in Targum Pseudo-Jonathan: יברכינך ייי בכל עיסקך ויטרינך מן לילי ומזייעי ובני טיהררי ובני צפרירי ומזיקי וטלני ('may YYY bless you in all your undertaking, and may he guard you from the night demon, the vile demons, the children of the noon demons, the children of the morning demons, injurious and shadowy beings'; cf. Robert Hayward, 'The Priestly Blessing in Targum Pseudo-Jonathan', *JSP* 19 (1999), pp.81–101.

the community 'during the dominion of Belial' (1QS i 23-24). The expanded benediction that God 'keep you from every evil', therefore, ultimately has protection from demonic power that causes transgression in view. The repetition of the ceremony during the era when Belial exercises dominion implies that there will be a time when it is no longer necessary (cf. 1QS iv 19-21).

Serek ha-Milhamah

A similar perspective is reflected in other Dead Sea documents which, however, do not formulate as explicitly a need for divine protection as part of a blessing or petition. This is, for example, the case in *Serek ha-Milhamah*[22] where the sons of light declare that 'during the dominion of Belial ... you (God) have driven away from [us] his (Belial's) [de]struction, [and when the me]n of his dominion [acted wickedly] you have kept (or: protected) the soul of your redeemed ones (שמרתה נפש פדותכה)' (1QM xiv 9-10 par. 4Q491 = 4QM^a 8-10 i 6-7; cf. further 1Q177 = 4QCatena^a iii 8).

Songs of the Maskil

Of special note here is the document *Songs of the Maskil*, preserved in fragments of 4Q444, 4Q510 and 4Q511. In one of the songs, the sage initially declares the splendour of God's radiance

> in order to terrify and fr[ighten] all the spirits of the angels of destruction, and the bastard spirits, demons, Lilith, owls and [jackals ...] and those who strike suddenly to lead astray the spirit of understanding and to cause their hearts to shudder (4Q510 1.4-6a par. 4Q511 10.1-3a).

This proclamation of divine majesty, which Armin Lange has described as a 'hymnic exorcism',[23] is then followed by an address to 'righteous ones' in which the sage states:

---

22 Thus in the *Two Spirits Treatise*, the Angel of Darkness, who has complete dominion over the sons of iniquity, is made out to be the influence behind the sins, iniquities, guilty deeds and transgressions of the sons of light (1QS iii 21-24); see further 1QS iv 19: 'then truth shall go forth forever (in the) world, for it has been corrupted in paths of wickedness during the dominion of iniquity...'

23 See Armin Lange, 'The Essene Position on Magic and Divination', in Moshe Bernstein, Florentino García Martínez and John Kampen (eds.), *Legal Texts and Legal Issues: Proceedings of the Second Meeting of the International Organization for Qumran Studies, Published in Honour of Joseph M. Baumgarten* (STDJ 23; Leiden: Brill, 1997), pp.383, 402–3, 430–3. Lange also applies this classification to

You have been put in a time of the dominion [of] wickedness and in the eras of the humiliation of the sons of lig[ht] in the guilt of the times of those plagued by iniquities, not for an eternal destruction, [but] for the era of the humiliation of transgression. Rejoice, O righteous ones, in the God of wonder. My psalms (are) for the upright ones (4Q510 1.6b-8; par. 4Q511 10.3b-6).

The *maskil's* declarations about God, told in the third person (i.e. not in the second person in the form of prayer addressed to God), are regarded as potent enough to diminish or counteract demonic powers which are at work in the present order of things ('the dominion [of] wickedness'). While the text does not furnish a prayer for divine protection against these demons, it reflects a framework that holds two concurrent things in tension: (1) the existence of a community of those who are unambiguously 'righteous' and 'upright' and (2) the characterisation of the present age as 'a time of the dominion [of] wickedness'. Analogous to the pronouncement of a benediction in the yearly covenant renewal ceremony in *Serek ha-Yahad*, the song to the righteous functions as an expedient measure that neutralises the threats associated with demonic powers until the present age of wickedness is brought to an end.

Significantly, the documents just considered are arguably sectarian. The hostility between the group behind the writings and other groups may have been felt to such an extent that the world order, as a whole, could not be portrayed as anything other than inimical. This notion, however, of an eschatological tension between divine activity already being realised in a specially elect community and ongoing demonic activity was not entirely unique to the community associated with Qumran. Several prayers come down to us in documents preserved among the texts recovered from the Qumran caves that do not show any obvious signs of having been composed by or for the *Yahad*. Before returning to the Fourth Gospel, we may briefly review prayers for protection from the demonic preserved in Qumran fragments from a 'Prayer of Deliverance (11Q5 xix), the *Aramaic Levi Document* (4Q213a = 4QTLevi[a] 1 i 10 par. *Jub.* 1.19-20), the book of *Jubilees* (10.3-6 and 12.19-20), and the book of Tobit.[24]

1QapGen xx 12-18, *Jub.* 10.1-14; 12.16-21. On the problem of categorising the passage from 1QapGen in this way, see my 'Pleas for Deliverance from the Demonic in Early Jewish Texts', pp.60–2.

24 For a fuller treatment of these and other texts, see my 'Prayers of Deliverance from the Demonic'.

Prayer of Deliverance (11Q5 xix)

The text, which is also extant through two of the six fragments belonging to 11Q6, comes to us as part of a larger manuscript that consists of psalmic texts known through the Hebrew Bible, other hymnic compositions, and a text that attributes a series of compositions to David.[25] Since both 11Q5 and 11Q6 are copied in Herodian hands, they provide evidence for the prayer at the turn of the Common Era, though the compilation itself is surely earlier.[26] The piece, significantly, is composed as a prayer *per se*, showing – perhaps as in 1QS i–ii and the Maskil songs of 4Q510–511 – that we are safe to assume that the text consists of words actually in use during the Second Temple period.

Of the originally 24 or 25 verses of the prayer,[27] some 18 lines of 20 verses are preserved. In the opening extant lines of 11Q5 xix (ll. 1-5), the writer declares that only living creatures can praise God, implying that God should therefore spare him from death (cf. Isa 38.18-19 and Ps 6.4-5). In the next section (ll. 5-12), the writer proclaims YHWH's faithfulness based on his own experience, and for this he offers YHWH praise. This praise of divine activity introduces a plea for forgiveness and purification from iniquity (ll. 13-14), in place of which the one praying seeks to be given a 'spirit of faith and knowledge' so as not to be dishonoured in iniquity. The petition culminates in lines 15-16 as follows:

---

25 For a description of the contents of the six fragments of 11Q5, see James A. Sanders, *The Psalms Scroll of Qumrân Cave 11 (11QPs^a)* (DJD 4; Oxford: Clarendon, 1996), p.5. See further Peter W. Flint, *The Dead Sea Psalms Scrolls and the Book of Psalms* (STDJ 17; Leiden: Brill, 1997), p.190. According to Jan van der Ploeg, 11Q6 is an exact copy of 11Q5; cf. idem, 'Fragments d'un manuscrit de Psaumes de Qumran (11QPs^b)', *RB* 74 (1967), pp.408–13. It is possible, in addition, that 4Q87 (= 4QPs^e) is a copy of the same collection; see Flint, *The Dead Sea Psalms Scrolls*, pp.160–4.

26 Lange argues for a date as early as the first half of the second century BCE; see 'Die Endgestalt des protomasoretischen Psalters und die Toraweisheit: Zur Bedeutung der nichtessenischen Weisheitstexte aus Qumran für die Auslegung des protomasoretischen Psalters', in Erich Zenger (ed.), *Der Psalter in Judentum und Christentum* (Herders Biblische Studien 18; Freiburg: Herder, 1998), p.108. If the treatment of *Aramaic Levi Document* below is correct, however, this prayer may be even go back to the third century BCE.

27 Sanders, *The Psalms Scroll*, p.76, argues that the psalm probably began on the previous column xviii; regarding the end of the prayer, see James A. Sanders with James H. Charlesworth and Henry W. L. Rietz, 'Non-Masoretic Psalms', in James H. Charlesworth *et al.* (eds.), *Pseudepigraphic and Non-Masoretic Psalms and Prayers* (Princeton Theological Seminary Dead Sea Scrolls Project 4a; Tübingen: Mohr Siebeck; Louisville: Westminster John Knox, 1997), p.193 (hereafter referred to as PTSDSS).

אל תשלט בי שטן ורוח טמאה מכאוב ויצר רע אל ירשו בעצמי

Do not let rule (or: have power) over me a satan or an unclean spirit;
may an evil inclination not take possession of my bones.

The first thing to notice is that the petition seeks divine help not to come under the rule or power of a demonic being. Here, that being which would have sway over the one praying is designated as both 'a satan' and 'an unclean spirit'. The latter expression may be an echo of Zech 13.2.[28] However, in the present context it may refer to a disembodied spirit, that is, a being whose origin lies in the illegitimate sexual union between the rebellious angels and the daughters of men which resulted in the birth of the pre-diluvian giants.[29] If the Enochic background, known to us through the *Book of Watchers* (*1 En.* 10 and 15–16) and the *Book of Giants*, lies in the background, the prayer presupposes a wider narrative that negotiates God's decisive intervention against evil in the past (i.e. through the flood and other acts of punishment) and the final destruction or eradication of evil in the future. The petition is therefore one that expresses confidence in God's control over the demonic (i.e. 'do not allow…' *hiphil* vb. + 'satan' and 'unclean spirit' as direct objects), while recognising the very real possibility that such power still leaves its mark in the present. As for the former designation, 'satan', it is not clear whether the writer has a chief demonic ruler in view (i.e. 'Satan', as translated by Sanders and in PTSDSS)[30] or uses the term functionally to refer to a being that plays an adversarial role. Its juxtaposition with 'unclean spirit'

---

28 See Armin Lange, 'Considerations Concerning the "Spirit of Impurity" in Zech 13:2', in Armin Lange, Hermann Lichtenberger and K.F. Diethard Römheld (eds.), *Die Dämonen: Die Dämonologie der israelitisch-jüdischen und frühchristlichen Literatur im Kontext ihrer Umwelt* (Tübingen: Mohr Siebeck, 2003), pp.254–5.

29 For discussions of a wider network of related references in *1 Enoch* (especially chs. 10, 15–16) and the Dead Sea materials (*inter alia* of *Book of Giants*, 4Q444; 4Q510–511; and 11Q11) see, e.g., Philip S. Alexander, 'The Demonology of the Dead Sea Scrolls', in Peter W. Flint and James C. VanderKam (eds.), *The Dead Sea Scrolls after Fifty Years: A Comprehensive Assessment* (2 vols.; Leiden: Brill, 1999), I, pp.331–53, and Loren T. Stuckenbruck, 'The Origins of Evil in Jewish Apocalyptic Tradition: The Interpretation of Genesis 6:1–4 in the Second and Third Centuries B.C.E.', in Christoph Auffarth and Loren T. Stuckenbruck (eds.), *The Fall of the Angels* (Themes in Biblical Narrative 6; Leiden: Brill, 2004), pp.87–118, especially 99–110.

30 See nn.14 and 27 above.

may suggest that 'satan' is not a proper name (see below on the *Aramaic Levi Document* prayer).[31] What is clear, nonetheless, is that the use of the term reflects a development that has gone well beyond its use in the Hebrew Bible, where it denotes an angelic being that is subservient to God (cf. Num 22.22, 32; Ps 109.6; even Job 1–2 and Zech 3.1-2) or functions as a general designation for one's enemies (1 Kgs 11.23, 25; Pss 71.13; 109.20, 29). In the Prayer of Deliverance of 11Q5, 'satan' refers generally to an angelic being whose activity in seeking to rule over the human being runs counter to what the petitioner regards as the divine will.

Though further observations about the petition will be made below when we consider the parallel prayer text in *Aramaic Levi Document*, a more general point about the compilation of psalms in which this petition is found should be made. Whereas James Sanders argued in his edition of the scroll that the compilation in 11QPs^a was produced by the Qumran community,[32] Peter Flint has emphasised that the absence of peculiarly Qumranic expressions and the presence of calendrical affinities with those groups within which the early Enochic works and *Jubilees* were composed suggest that this collection probably predates the formation of the Qumran community and thus enjoyed a wider circulation.[33] If Flint is correct and if the 'Prayer of Deliverance' was in the psalmic compilation, then it is likely that its petition that YHWH acts on behalf of the pious petitioner to disempower 'a satan' and 'an impure spirit' from ruling over him was probably not a single prayer written by and for an individual. It would have enjoyed some degree of circulation, and we are perhaps to imagine that it was written as a model prayer for the pious to recite. This view is strengthened by our consideration of the following text.

---

31   This would, then, be in contrast with *Jub.* 10.11, in which 'Satan' is the named equivalent for Mastema as the ruler of demons on the earth; cf. also *T. Dan* 5.6.

32   James A. Sanders, *The Dead Sea Psalms Scroll* (Ithaca, NY: Cornell University Press, 1967), p.158, designated it the 'Qumran Psalter'.

33   See the discussion by Flint in *Dead Sea Psalms Scrolls*, pp.198–200. While continuing to underscore the consistency between the ideas in the scroll and those of the Qumran community, Sanders has more recently adopted a less narrow view about its origins, arguing that the compilation was acquired by the community; see James A. Sanders, 'Psalm 154 Revisited', in Georg Braulik, Walter Gross and Sean McEvenue (eds.), *Biblische Theologie und gesellschaftlicher Wandel. [Festschrift] für Norbert Lohfink S.J.* (Freiburg: Herder, 1993), pp.301–2.

Aramaic Levi Document

The text in question (4Q213a = 4QTLevi^a 1 i 10) was initially published by Michael E. Stone and Jonas C. Greenfield,[34] and has been dated by J. T. Milik to the late second–early first century BCE.[35] However, the document itself was likely composed during the third or perhaps even the late fourth century BCE.[36] Since the wording of the Aramaic text corresponds closely to that of the more complete Greek manuscript from Mt. Athos (Athos Koutloumous no. 39, at *T. Levi* 2.3), the latter may be used to reconstruct many of the lacunae in 4Q213a.[37]

The text with which we are concerned is part of a prayer spoken by the patriarch Levi just before he is granted a vision of heaven (cf. 4Q213a 2.14-18) and commissioned to become a priest (cf. the later *T. Levi* 2.5–4.6).[38] After Levi makes preparations through cleansing and gestures (4Q213a 1.6-10), a text of his prayer is given (Grk. vv. 5-19; Aram. 1.10–2.10). The prayer, according to Robert Kugler, may be loosely structured as follows: (a) in vv. 6-9 (Grk.; Aram. 1.10-16) Levi prays that God would purify him from evil and wickedness, show him the holy spirit, and endow him with counsel, wisdom, knowledge, and strength, in order that he might find favour before God and give God praise; (b) in v. 10 (Grk.; Aram. 1.17) the patriarch petitions that God protect him from evil; and (c) in vv. 11-19 (Grk.; Aram. 1.18–2.10) the patriarch formulates a series of requests that resume themes touched upon during

---

34 Initially in Michael E. Stone and Jonas C. Greenfield, 'The Prayer of Levi', *JBL* 112 (1993), pp.247–66 (with photograph) and then in George Brooke *et al.* (eds.), *Qumran Cave 4. XVII: Parabiblical Texts, Part 3* (DJD XXII; Oxford: Clarendon, 1996), pp.25–36 and Plate II.

35 So Józef T. Milik, 'Le Testament de Lévi en araméen', *RB* 62 (1955), pp.398–408.

36 See especially the thorough discussion and considerations offered by Henryk Drawnel, *An Aramaic Wisdom Text from Qumran* (JSJSup 86; Leiden: Brill, 2004), pp.63–75 (the early Hellenistic period). Other recent treatments have dated the work to the third and late third–very early second century BCE; so, respectively, Robert A. Kugler, *From Patriarch to Priest: The Levi-Priestly Tradition from Aramaic Levi to Testament of Levi* (SBL Early Judaism and Its Literature 9; Atlanta: Scholars Press, 1996), pp.131–8, and Jonas C. Greenfield, Michael E. Stone and Esther Eshel, *The Aramaic Levi Document* (SVTP 19; Leiden: Brill, 2004), pp.19–22.

37 So, e.g., Stone and Greenfield, 'The Prayer of Levi', pp.257–8 (Aramaic and Greek texts, respectively, from which the citations here are taken); cf. Drawnel, *An Aramaic Wisdom Text from Qumran*, especially pp.99 and 101.

38 Unless otherwise indicted, my present comments follow the line numeration from 4Q213a, rather than the versification derived from the Greek text. However, the content is partially reconstructed by referring to the Greek, as in the eclectic translation of Stone and Greenfield, 'The Prayer of Levi', pp.259–60.

the earlier part of the prayer (a), namely, that God cleanse and shelter Levi from evil (Grk. vv. 12 and 14), that wickedness be destroyed from the earth (Grk. v. 13), and that Levi and his descendants be placed in God's service for all generations (Grk. v. 18; 4Q213a 2.8-9). The wording in the petition for protection in 4Q213a 1.17 is remarkably close to that of the text from 11Q5 discussed above; with the help of the Greek, it reads as follows:

וא[ל תשלט בי כל שטן [לאטעני מן ארחך

And do n]ot let rule (or: have power) over me any satan [to lead me astray from your path.

καὶ μὴ κατισχυσάτω με πᾶς σατανᾶς πλανῆσαί με ἀπὸ τῆς ὁδοῦ σου.

And may no satan rule (or: have power) over me to lead me astray from your path.

The context suggests that the petition here is concerned with demonic threat. Earlier in the prayer, Levi has asked that God 'turn away' (4Q213a 1.7, רחא, Grk. ἀπόστρεψον) to a distance 'the unrighteous spirit (Grk. τὸ πνεῦμα τὸ ἄδικον) and evil thoughts and fornication and hubris'. He then asks, instead, to be shown 'the holy spirit (Grk. τὸ πνεῦμα τὸ ἅγιον) and counsel and wisdom and knowledge and strength'. Moreover, in a further petition not extant in the Aramaic but preserved in the Greek (v. 12), Levi asks for protection as follows: 'and let your shelter of power shelter me from every evil (ἀπὸ παντὸς κακοῦ). Thus, in seeking protection from overpowerment from 'any satan', the writer – as argued above for 11Q5 – is referring to a being belonging to a category of demonic power[39] rather than to a primary power of evil who is called 'Satan'. This is even clearer here than in 11Q5 with the addition of 'any' (כל).

Given the similarity between the petitions in 4Q213a and 11Q5, is there any genetic link? The parallel is strikingly similar to the text that comes down to us in Ps 119.133b: תשלט בי כל און ואל ('and do not allow any iniquity to rule/have power over me, Grk. μὴ κατακυριευσάτω μου πᾶσα ἀνομία, 'may no iniquity rule over me'). It is possible, therefore, that both texts, rather than being directly interdependent in one direction or another, draw on a 'common interpretation' of Psalm 119.[40] This

---

39 See Stone and Greenfield, 'The Prayer of Levi', p.262, who draw attention to the use of the same expression ('every satan') in 1QH isolated fragments 4 and 45.

40 So David Flusser, 'Qumrân and Jewish "Apotropaic" Prayers', *IEJ* 16 (1966), pp.196–97; Kugler, *From Patriarch to Priest*, p.73; Stone and Greenfield, 'The Prayer of Levi', p.263.

view, if correct, (a) underscores that the writers of these texts and of the underlying tradition were personifying traditional references to evil and (b) suggests that such a reinterpretation of biblical prayer was more generally widespread than the evidence preserved in 4Q213a and 11Q5 alone. Lange, however, has argued against a dependence of either text on Psalm 119 and, instead, reasons as follows for a literary dependence between the two documents: (1) it is unlikely that both 4Q213a and 11Q5 xix would have independently substituted the term 'iniquity' of the Psalm with 'Satan' and (2) both texts exhibit 'extensive parallels in demonic thought'.[41] More significantly, Lange admits that there is a parallel between the petition in 11Q5 xix and *Jub.* 1.19-20,[42] in which Moses pleads that God not deliver Israel 'into the control of the nations with the result that they rule over them lest they make them sin against you' and that *'the spirit of Beliar not rule them so as to bring charges against them* before you *and to trap them* away from every proper path so that they may be destroyed from your presence'.[43] The text also shares language with the petition in *Aramaic Levi Document* which, however, lacks the specificity of 'Satan' (= the spirit of Beliar in *Jubilees*) as the inimical demonic power. The wording in *Jub.* 1.20, as in the 'Prayer of Deliverance', has no equivalent for כל and the mention of 'satan' has been replaced by the more proper name in the designation 'the spirit of Beliar' and reformulated as a verb that describes the activity of the demonic Beliar as an accuser of God's people.

These considerations suggest that both Levi's prayer in *Aramaic Levi Document* and Moses' intercession in *Jub.* 1.20 reflect the influence of a tradition that is extant through the 'Prayer of Deliverance'. If this is the case, however, their common concern with the bestowal of a 'holy spirit' in the context of the petition (cf. *Aramaic Levi Document* Grk. v. 8; *Jub.* 1.21), suggests that the underlying tradition was not entirely in line with the petition as preserved in 11Q5. Moreover, if the text of Ps 119.133 is lurking in the background, by the time of *Jubilees*, at least, it lies well behind, and we may infer that the petition for protection from demonic

---

41 Lange, 'Spirit of Impurity', p.262. In favour of literary dependence, Lange argues that one would have expected the Aramaic verb in 4Q213a to be מלך rather than the cognate שלט; this point is not persuasive; cf. Klaus Beyer, *Die aramäischen Texte vom Toten Meer* (Göttingen: Vandenhoeck & Ruprecht, 1984), pp.709–10, and *Die aramäischen Texte vom Toten Meer. Ergänzungsband* (Göttingen: Vandenhoeck & Ruprecht, 1994), p.422.
42 Beyer, *Die aramäischen Texte. Ergänzungsband*, p.262 n. 38.
43 The translation is that of James C. VanderKam, *The Book of Jubilees* (CSCO 511 and Scriptores Aethiopici 88; Leuven: Peeters, 1989), p.5.

power was beginning to acquire a life of its own. If this is correct, then we may offer two observations. First, the writers of these texts have adapted the generally formulated prayer text to suit the purposes of their narrative, doing so in different ways. Whereas the author of *Jubilees* has transformed the ambiguous 'satan', perhaps from 11Q5, into a proper name Beliar while retaining his adversarial function, the author of the prayer of Levi retains 'satan' as a type of demonic being that poses a threat. Second, the existence of the deliverance prayer in 11Q5 demonstrates that the attestation of the petitions for deliverance within larger narratives that have shaped them (i.e. in 4Q213a and *Jub.* 1), does not mean they bear no relation to religious practice. In fact, if the underlying tradition to *Aramaic Levi Document* and *Jubilees* was independent from the petition in 11Q5, then we have to deal with a more widespread prayer than has previously been recognised.

In other words, in 4Q213a and *Jubilees* 1 we do not have prayers formulated in order to enhance a given storyline, so much as an independently circulating petition against demonic power which, due to its popularity, has been narrativised, that is, adapted into new literary settings. The adaptability of the petitionary prayer for protection is illustrated by two further passages in *Jubilees*. Though none of the passages from *Jubilees* discussed here is preserved amongst the fragments of at least fifteen manuscripts of this work among the Dead Sea scrolls, it is the discovery of these materials that gives the considerations here firmer footing when it comes to describing the use of petitionary prayer during the Second Temple period.

Jubilees 10.3-6

This text contains a prayer formulated as the words of Noah spoken after the Great Flood (10.1-2). This prayer comes at the request of Noah's sons, who complain that Noah's grandchildren were being led astray, being blinded and being killed by 'demons'. In response, Noah utters a petition to curb the activities of evil spirits. The text of the prayer is as follows:

> (v. 3) …God of the spirits which are in all flesh,
>   who has acted mercifully with me and saved me and my sons
>   from the water of the Flood
>   and did not let me perish as you did the children of perdition,
>   because great was your grace upon me,
>   and great was your mercy upon my soul.
> Let your grace be lifted up upon my sons,
>   and *do not let the evil spirits rule* over them,
>   lest they destroy them from the earth.

> (v. 4) But bless me and my sons.
> And let us grow and increase and fill the earth.
> (v. 5) And you know that which your Watchers, the fathers of these spirits,
>   did in my days
>   and also these spirits who are alive.
> Shut them up and take them to the place of judgement.
>   And do not let them cause corruption among the sons of your servant,
>   O my God,
>   because they are cruel and were created to destroy.
> (v. 6) And *let them not rule over* the spirits of the living
>   because you alone know their judgement.
> And *do not let them have power over the children of the righteous now
>   and forever*.⁴⁴

Formally, the prayer has a two-fold structure. First, it opens with a declaration of all that God has done on behalf of Noah and his sons to save them from the destruction of the deluge (v. 3). Thus the prayer initially assumes a posture of thanksgiving and praise. The second, more extensive, part of the prayer contains a petition in two parts: (1) Noah asks God to bless him and his sons in order that they might 'grow and increase and fill the earth' (cf. Gen 9.1, 7).⁴⁵ (2) As almost a prerequisite for such a blessing, Noah asks God to punish 'the spirits', the offspring of the fallen angels (v. 5). Because of their destructive activities towards humankind, the prayer asks that the spirits be consigned to a place of judgement. Then, in v. 6, the petition concludes with two reformulations of the initial petition for protection in v. 3, a formula reminiscent of *Jub.* 1.20, 'let not them (i.e. the evil spirits) rule over the spirits of the living' and 'do not let them have power over the children of the righteous now and forever'.⁴⁶

---

44   Here I follow the translation by O. S. Wintermute in *OTP*, II, pp.75–6, because it structures Noah's prayer into stichs (italics my own).

45   Cf. the MT: 'God blessed Noah and his sons, and said to them, "Be fruitful and multiply, and fill the earth"'. In terms of intertextuality, Noah's prayer in *Jubilees* makes God's act of blessing Noah the object of the petition. Significantly, no such command is given in *Jubilees* to the first humans (see Gen 1.28a). This implies that the demons pose an obstacle to the carrying out of God's command to 'be fruitful and multiply' after the Flood; cf. James C. VanderKam, 'The Demons in the Book of Jubilees', in Lange, Lichtenberger and Römheld (eds.), *Die Dämonen. Demons*, p.343.

46   This petition is also similar to texts in *Aramaic Levi Document* and 11Q5 xix mentioned above.

With respect to its specific content, the petition has been recast to reflect the preceding and following narrative in *Jubilees*. The evil spirits referred to are those of the giant offspring of the Watchers and the women they deceived (v. 5; see 5.1-11 and 7.21-24). Though they began as creatures with a human flesh (v. 3; cf. 5.8), they became spirits when they killed one another. And so, after the deluge,[47] Noah's descendants (i.e. his grandchildren) are being threatened by the activities of these impure spirits who are now called 'demons' (v. 2). As for the narrative following Noah's prayer, it describes God's response to the petition. God directs the angels to bind all of the demons (10.7). However, the divine judgement is not achieved with finality. Mastema, the chief of these punished spirits, and mentioned here for the first time in *Jubilees*, begs God to permit him to exercise his (rightful) authority, given that the greatness of human sin is inevitable (v. 8). God responds by having nine-tenths of the spirits consigned to the place of judgement below (v. 9) while a limited number (one tenth) may carry out Mastema's orders (cf. v. 9). In the end, Noah is taught various herbal remedies through which the afflictions brought about by the evil spirits on his offspring could be curbed or at least kept in check (v. 12).

In its position between the ante-diluvian catastrophes and the deluge, on the one hand, and the containment and punishment of malevolent forces, on the other hand, the prayer comes at a pivotal point in the story-line. Because of Noah's great piety, his prayer functions to set on course the temporary position of evil spirits until the eschatological judgement. God's response to his petition ensures that, from now on, the evil that is manifest on earth represents an essentially defeated power whose activity has already been subjected to a preliminary judgement. This strong link to the literary context means that the prayer is here really conceived as *Noah's* prayer, and in its present form does not draw on a prayer that would have been uttered by anyone. Thus the wording of the petition that God punishes the demonic spirits is 'narrativised', that is, it takes into account what the author believed were the specific circumstances faced by the patriarch after the great Flood. However, this is not merely a prayer *composed ad hoc*; the petition that God does not permit evil

---

47 Similar to the *Book of Watchers* (*1 En.* 1–36; especially chs. 6–16), the role of the Flood as divine punishment against the rebellious angels and their progeny in *Jubilees* is unclear; whereas the *Book of Giants* seems to have given the deluge a more prominent role in this respect, *1 En.* 6–16 and *Jubilees* give the impression that when they describe the remaining demonic activity following God's initial judgement against the fallen angels and giants, they have post-diluvian times in view; cf. Stuckenbruck, 'The Origins of Evil', pp.111–12.

spirits to have power over those who are pious was, as we have seen, in use outside the text. It is likely that early readers of *Jubilees* would have been familiar with such a prayer and would have recognised it as it is put into the mouths of Moses in 1.20 and of Noah in 10.3-6.

Not only would ancient readers have recognised the petition for protection, the content of the prayer itself widens the horizon beyond that of Noah and his grandchildren to embrace the implied readers of the author's own time. Two details in the prayer suggest this. First, at the end of the prayer, the plea to curtail the spirits' power no longer simply refers specifically to Noah's grandchildren. Though 'the sons of your servant' could refer to Noah's immediate family, the mention of 'the spirits of the living' and, in particular, 'the children of the righteous *henceforth and forever*' opens the horizon to include all those who are pious after the time of Noah until the very end. In this sense, then, Noah's prayer is also a plea for protection on behalf of all righteous ones who come after him, and readers would have understood themselves to be included in this protection.[48] Second, the brief and conventional form of the conclusion to the prayer presupposes a certain familiarity with this sort of prayer among the readers. To attribute a petition which readers perhaps knew amongst themselves to Noah not only anchors their prayer within a pivotal point of the covenant story of Israel, but also strengthens their confidence in the effectiveness of their prayers for protection against demonic powers: though they lie behind the afflictions and iniquities suffered and carried by God's people, evil spirits are but defeated powers whose complete destruction is assured.

Jubilees 12.19-20

In *Jubilees* yet a third figure is made to offer a petition for protection: Abram, whose prayer is given in 12.19-20:

> (v. 19) ...My God, my God, God most High,
>   You alone are my God.
>   You have created everything;
>   Everything that was and has been is the product of your hands.
> You and your lordship I have chosen.
> (v. 20) *Save me from the power of the evil spirits*,
>   *who rule the thoughts of people's minds.*
>   *May they not mislead me from following you*, my God.
>   Do establish me and my posterity forever.
>   May we not go astray from now until eternity.[49]

---

48   The same may be implied by Moses' intercessory prayer in *Jub.* 1.19–20.
49   The text given follows the translation of VanderKam, *The Book of Jubilees*, p.72 (italics mine).

Abram's petition shares the two-fold structure observed above for 10.3-6. In the first part, the prayer extols God as the only God, and the one who has created all things (v. 19). In the second part, the petition asks for rescue from the rule of evil spirits who would lead humankind astray from showing exclusive devotion to God.[50]

Again, as in the case of Noah's prayer in *Jubilees* 10, it is important to consider Abram's prayer in relation to its immediate literary context. Abram is made to utter his petition just prior to receiving God's promise that he and his descendants will be given a land. The petition, then, associates the promise of the land to Abram with God's power over evil, on behalf of Abram and his descendants. Earlier in the narrative, the path to the story about Abram is laid in ch. 11. After the Flood, Noah's descendants became involved in violent and oppressive activities (v. 2); indeed, they had begun to make idols and thus were coming under the influence of those evil spirits which, under Mastema's rule, were being allowed to lead people astray to commit sin and acts of impurity (vv. 4-5). The introduction of Abram into the narrative, beginning with 11.14, marks a shift in the midst of this post-diluvian corruption among humanity. Abram, at an early age, offers prayers during this time 'to the creator of all' and thus demonstrates the rejection of his father's worship of idols (11.16; 12.2-8, 12-14). At one point, Abram even tells his father, Terah, not to worship idols fashioned by human hands, but rather 'the God of heaven' who has 'created everything by his word' (12.3-4). Therefore, Abram's prayer in 12.19-20, in its focus on God as creator (v. 19), expresses an objection to post-diluvian idolatry behind which lay the activities of malevolent demonic beings. As in the prayer of Noah, Abram's proclamation of God as 'creator' shows how embedded the petition is within the storyline.

If one links the first part of Abram's prayer back to the account of growing post-diluvian evil, it is possible to find the rationale for the petition to counteract the 'evil spirits' in the second part. The reason for the mention of 'evil spirits', however, need be neither so remote nor so implicit. As Lange rightly argues, since the prayer occurs while Abram is gazing at the stars by night (12.16), these spirits must be the stars linked with 'astrology'.[51] Abram, after all, recognises that it is wrong for him to prognosticate on the basis of the stars; this even includes the weather – for example, whether or not it will rain – as the making of such

---

50 As 4Q213a, the prayer in *Jub.* 1.20 and 12.20 refers to demonic activity as 'leading astray', a motif that occurs in the narrative before Noah's prayer in 10.3. The 'Prayer of Deliverance' in 11Q5, however, makes no mention of this.

51 Lange, 'The Essene Position on Magic and Divination', p.383.

predictions distracts from the conviction that meteorological events are to be left in God's control. In sitting alone at night, Abram thus finds himself resisting the temptation to adopt the instruction about 'the omens of the sun and moon and stars within all the signs of heaven' which in the story has been attributed to the fallen angels and which has been rediscovered after the deluge by Noah's great-grandson, Cainan, who 'sinned' because of it (8.1-4).

However, why does the nomenclature of 'evil spirits' occur in the prayer and not a more direct reference to the heavenly bodies which Abram has just seen? Though the 'evil spirits' which originated in the giants are featured in the periods associated with Enoch and Noah, they are nowhere explicitly mentioned in the early part of Abram's story; moreover, though the connection between demonic spirits and idols is mentioned in 11.4-5, the link is not explicitly made here.

Nonetheless, in the subsequent part of the Abraham narrative in *Jubilees*, several passages are illuminative: the angel's explanation of the significance of the law of circumcision (15.30-32); the account about the sacrifice of Isaac (17.15–18.19); and the blessings pronounced by Abraham over Jacob (especially 19.27-29). In 15.30-32, the angel's instruction to Abraham about circumcision is explained as a means by which God rules over his people Israel, over whom 'he made no angel or spirit rule' (v. 32). The rest of the nations, by contrast, are ruled by spirits who lead them astray (v. 31). The link already made in 11.4-5 between evil spirits and the worship of idols (cf. 22.16)[52] suggests that Abram's petition in ch. 12 for the establishment of his 'seed' is one that is ultimately answered when God separates Israel from the nations of the earth to become the people he will protect (15.32). In 17.15–18.19, 'Mastema' is identified as the one who sought to distract Abraham from

---

52 For the association of idolatry among the Gentiles with the influence of demonic powers, Deut 32.16-17 played a formative role: 'They made him [God] jealous with strange gods (בזרים, ἐπ' ἀλλοτρίοις), with abhorrent things (בתועבת, ἐν βδελύγμασιν) they provoked him. They sacrificed to demons (יזבחו לשדים, ἔθυσαν δαιμονίοις), to deities they had never known, to new ones recently arrived, whom your ancestors had not feared' (NSRV). In the Hebrew Bible, the equation of demons and idols is more explicitly made in the Greek translation to Ps 96[95].5a: 'For all the gods of the nations are demons' (δαιμόνια; Heb. אלילים, 'idols'); cf. also Ps 106[105].37 and Isa 65.11. *1 En.* 19.1 picks up this association during the third century BCE, followed in the second century BCE by *Jubilees* (1.11 as well as at 22.16-18) and *Epistle of Enoch* (*1 En.* 99.7). After this, the idea becomes more widespread: see 4Q243 13.2 par. 4Q244 12.2, 'demons of error' (שידי טעותא); *T. Jud.* 23.1; *T. Job* 3.6; *Sib. Or.* 8.47, 381-94 and Frg. 1.20-22; Bar 4.7; 1 Cor 10.20; Rev 9.20; cf. Gal 4.8; *Barn.* 16.7; Ignatius, *Magn.* 3.1 [long rec.]).

obedience to God in the sacrifice of Isaac (17.16; 18.12). In 19.28, Abraham pronounces a blessing over Jacob: 'may the spirit of Mastema not rule over you or over your seed in order to remove you from following the Lord who is your God henceforth and forever...' Abraham's story thus exemplifies how his prayer for deliverance from the rule of 'evil spirits' is answered: his obedience to God thwarts Mastema's plan to test his character; and God's separation of Israel as his elect people is God's response to Abram's prayer of deliverance (and perhaps also the prayers of Moses and Noah).

For all the connections between Abram's prayer in ch. 12 and the narrative, the subject matter of the petition itself remains conventional, that is, it is formulated in a way that is not fully bound into the literary context. The petition for deliverance from the rule of 'evil spirits' (rather than, simply, from the rule of Mastema, as the story bears out) is formulated in general terms. As such, it is a petition by the pious that expresses the desire to stay away from idolatry. Moreover, similar to Noah's petition at 10.6, Abram's plea is concerned with all his progeny 'forever', which includes the implied readers of the story. With perhaps the exception of the Abram-specific phrase 'me and my seed forever', the prayer itself could be uttered by any of Abram's seed, that is, those whom the author regards as pious.

Regarding *Jubilees*, we may, in summary, note that the language of petition for protection from demonic evil occurs in a number of texts: 1.20; 10.3-6; 12.19-20; 15.30-32, and 19.28. As we have been able to note on the basis of 11Q5 xix and the *Aramaic Levi Document*, the recurrence of such language in *Jubilees* picks up on a prayer formula that circulated prior to and independently from the setting within which the communication between its writer(s) and implied readers took shape. In *Jubilees*, to a greater degree than in *Aramaic Levi Document*, a more widely known petition is placed in the mouths of patriarchs to whom formulations are attributed that include the community in relation to whom the work was composed.

From Jewish Tradition to Jesus' Petitions in John 17: Conclusion

In our review of Second Temple Jewish literature preserved in the Dead Sea Scrolls, we have discovered several things that may have an impact on the way one reads Jesus' petitions for his disciples and later followers in John 17. First, analogous to John 17, our Jewish traditions all construe prayer for protection in relation to demonic power, something which marks a development beyond prayers conveyed through the Hebrew Bible. Second, the texts we have looked at are not merely literary; they reflect a piety which, in at least some Jewish circles, was expressed through the offering of prayers for divine protection from the personified forms of evil (cf. 11Q5 xix). Third, such petitions were adaptable. They could be narrativised into stories involving ideal figures from Israel's ancient past (*Aramaic Levi Document*; *Jubilees*). Thus patriarchs would not only be presented as practitioners of the piety familiar to those who read about them, but also would be made to formulate petitions which sought God's protection for their descendants. In such cases – we have been able to observe this in chs. 1, 10, 12, 15 and 19 of *Jubilees* – readers would have been able to find themselves addressed in the unfolding storyline. Fourth, the petitions for divine help against malevolent power were based on a twinfold assumption that (a) the present age is under the dominion of evil (i.e. it is ruled by Belial/r, Mastema, or evil spirits; cf. *Serek ha-Yahad* with the *Two Spirits Treatise*, *Serek ha-Milhamah* and *Songs of the Maskil*) and (b) the powers which hold sway are essentially defeated and await certain eschatological destruction (*1 En.* 10; 15–16; *Jubilees*, *Serek ha-Yahad* with the *Two Spirits Treatise*).

These texts contribute to our understanding of Jesus' prayer in the Fourth Gospel in at least three ways.

First, according to John's Gospel 'the world', which is under the dominion of 'the ruler of the world', is completely opposed to Jesus and his followers because they are not of the world. While the hostility between the present age of wickedness and a future age of restoration has long been known through Second Temple period literature produced by apocalyptic circles, some of the Dead Sea materials express this tension in language that comes closer to what meets us in John's Gospel.

Second, the confidence expressed in the petitionary prayers considered here, based on definitive acts of God in the past and the certain eschatological defeat of demonic power in the future, is re-framed in John's Gospel around Jesus' death through which the world is already judged. Though the inimical world order holds sway, its days are numbered, and it already stands condemned.

Third and finally, the petitions in search of protection are formulated in recognition that, in the meantime, a community which considers itself especially elect needs divine help in order to ward off the unabating influences of evil power. Such prayers would have been known to the pious, whether they were those who recited the 'Prayer of Deliverance' preserved in 11Q5 xix or members of the Matthean and similar communities who prayed to be delivered from 'the evil one' in the Lord's Prayer (Matt 6.13; cf. 2 Thess 3.3). If such a petition was known to implied readers of the Johannine community, then it is not without significance that in John's Gospel the petition that God protect Jesus' disciples 'from the evil one' is placed on the lips of Jesus. In doing this, the writer of the prayer in John 17 would have been providing readers something that we have witnessed in some texts of the Gospel's Jewish predecessors: a prayer which readers may already have been reciting for themselves has been strengthened by having it spoken by the very one in and through whom their religiosity is determined. Therefore, just as the patriarchs' petitions against demonic evil are formulated as prayers for their descendants and spiritual heirs, so also Jesus' petition is concerned with his 'descendants'. And so, the disciples and 'those who believe in me (sc. Jesus) through their word' in the Johannine community find themselves covered in the Johannine text by the force of Jesus' petition.

Post-scriptum

I have one final note for reflection on 'apocalyptic', which I find necessary to sketch as we consider the theme of evil in relation to the Fourth Gospel. So much of the scholarly discussion of an apocalyptic worldview (as well as on 'apocalypse' as a literary genre) during the nineteenth and twentieth centuries has been dominated by a model oriented around the future. Jewish apocalyptic writers, it is made out, had a view of the world conceived in two stages, one about the present as an era of evil and the other as a future time when, after divine judgement, all evil will be held to account as a new world order is established. This way of understanding apocalyptic thought – based primarily on readings of documents such as Daniel, the Apocalypse of John, *4 Ezra* and *2 Baruch* – has served New Testament scholars as a convenient way not only to characterise the novelty associated with the (Jewish) historical Jesus, but also to throw light on adaptations of Jewish tradition in Pauline theology. The emphasis on Jewish apocalyptic eschatology as a background that Jesus and Paul took over and ultimately subverted, while recognising in principle the importance of Second Temple literature for the interpretation of early Christian traditions, does not go far enough in ascertaining the extent of that indebtedness.

Of course, scholarly work on Jewish apocalyptic in conversation with the New Testament has included other dimensions. For some scholars Jewish apocalyptic thought has provided a platform for understanding

Jesus within a 'thoroughgoing eschatology', a view that amounts to an attempt to take seriously Jesus' place within apocalyptic Jewish ideology (as one who focused on the future).[53] For other scholars, in Jesus' activity, both as the Synoptic Gospels present it and in the way Jesus may have understood his mission, God's rule has broken into this world in a definitive way so that 'history' could no longer be the same.[54] Scholars have, of course, observed the shortcomings of such a one-dimensional future orientation of Jewish apocalyptic; after all, the earliest recoverable apocalypses seem just as interested in a spatial understanding of the world made possible through revealed knowledge as in the conversion of

---

53 So the well-known work of Albert Schweitzer, *The Quest of the Historical Jesus: From Reimarus to Wrede* (trans. W. Montgomery; London: A & C Black, 3rd edn, 1954). For a more recent take-up of this perspective, see Dale C. Allison, 'A Plea for Thoroughgoing Eschatology', *JBL* 113 (1994), pp.651–68, and *Jesus of Nazareth: Millenarian Prophet* (Minneapolis: Fortress, 1998), whose argument is formulated against the 'unapocalyptic' reconstruction of Jesus put forth by members contributing to the Jesus Seminar (especially Marcus Borg, John Dominic Crossan, Burton Mack); on the latter, see Robert W. Funk and Roy W. Hoover, *The Five Gospels: The Search for the Authentic Words of Jesus* (New York: Macmillan, 1993), pp.34–8 and 137.

54 See, e.g., C. H. Dodd, *The Founder of Christianity* (New York: Macmillan, 1970); Norman Perrin, *Jesus and the Language of the Kingdom: Symbol and Metaphor in New Testament Interpretation* (Philadelphia: Fortress, 1976), p.204; James D. G. Dunn, *Jesus and the Spirit: A Study of the Religious and Charismatic Experience of Jesus and the First Christians as Reflected in the New Testament* (London: SCM, 1975), pp.41–67, and *Christianity in the Making*. Vol. 1, *Jesus Remembered* (Grand Rapids: Eerdmans, 2003), pp.478–84; Thomas P. Rausch, *Who Is Jesus? An Introduction to Christology* (Collegeville, MN: Liturgical, 2003), pp.77–93.

A similar move is frequently made to underscore the distinctiveness of Pauline theology. Influential advocates of such an understanding of Paul have included Werner Kümmel, 'Paulus', in idem, *Heilsgeschehen und Geschichte: Gesammelte Aufsätze 1933–1964* (Marburg: Elwert, 1965), pp.439–56; Ernst Käsemann, e.g., in *Commentary on Romans* (trans. Geoffrey W. Bromiley; Grand Rapids: Eerdmans, 1980), pp.139–59 (on Rom 5.12-21); J. Christiaan Beker, *Paul the Apostle: The Triumph of God in Life and Thought* (Edinburgh: T. & T. Clark, 1989); and James D. G. Dunn, e.g., in *Jesus and the Spirit*, p.308 ('[t]he most characteristic feature of Christian experience'), and *The Theology of Paul the Apostle* (Grand Rapids: Eerdmans, 1998), pp.461–98 (especially 462–77); cf. recently Thomas R. Schreiner, *New Testament Theology: Magnifying God in Christ* (Grand Rapids: Baker, 2008). For a discussion of these and other Pauline theologians, see my forthcoming piece 'Overlapping Ages and "Apocalyptic" in Pauline Theology' in Jean Baptiste Rey (ed.), *The Dead Sea Scrolls and Pauline Literature* (Leiden: Brill).

the present into a future cosmos.⁵⁵ In addition, some apocalyptic writers demonstrated a concern with divine activity as a constant that shaped the unfolding story of Israel in order to understand and evaluate the present.⁵⁶ Finally, an influential way of understanding the temporal dimension of apocalyptic thought has been the correspondence in apocalyptic literature between *Urzeit* and *Endzeit*, a framework construed as a means to re-enforce eschatology⁵⁷: here the primordial past is understood to have served as a repository of images and symbols that helped apocalyptic writers to imagine the future.

The study above has hinted, however, at another, much neglected dimension, one that is not only overlooked by New Testament scholars but also by those who specialise in Second Temple literature.⁵⁸ In addition to helping to describe deteriorating conditions in the world and how the God of Israel will inaugurate a new age, language about the *Urzeit* also functioned, when adopted, to provide a basis that the faithful can be confident about the future: God's activity in defeating evil is not only a matter to be hoped for in the future; the object of hope has its correlative in the *sacred past* (e.g. at the time of the Great Flood, or at the time of other definitive moments in Israel's story), a past that guarantees an

---

55 So the often repeated definition in the publications by John J. Collins noted above. In addition, the critique by Christopher Rowland of the one-dimensionally eschatological reading of Jewish apocalyptic literature remains valuable; see his *The Open Heaven: A Study of Apocalyptic in Judaism and Early Christianity* (New York: Crossroad, 1982), pp.9–72.

56 So especially N. T. Wright, *The Climax of the Covenant: Paul and the Law in Pauline Theology* (Edinburgh: T. & T. Clark, 1991), and *Jesus and the Victory of God* (London: SPCK, 1996) and *passim*.

57 The most important third- and second-century BCE documents which draw on this correspondence between beginning and end include the Enochic *Book of the Watchers* (*1 En.* 1–36), the *Dream Visions* (*1 En.* 83–84 and 85–90), *Apocalypse of Weeks* (*1 En.* 93.1-10 and 91.11-17), *Exhortation* (*1 En.* 91.1-10, 18-19), *Birth of Noah* (*1 En.* 106–107), *Similitudes* (*1 En.* 37–71), *Book of Giants* and *Jubilees*. Except for the *Similitudes*, the impact of the perspectives upheld by these works in Second Temple literature (including writings among the Dead Sea Scrolls and Jewish literature composed in Greek) was significant.

58 A fine overview of recent scholarship on Jewish 'apocalyptic' thought and literature and its implications for New Testament scholarship is offered by Jörg Frey, 'Die Apokalyptik als Herausforderung der neutestamentlichen Wissenschaft. Zum Problem: Jesus und die Apokalyptik', in Michael Becker and Markus Öhler (eds.), *Apokalyptik als Herausforderung neutestamentlicher Theologie* (WUNT 2/214; Tübingen: Mohr Siebeck, 2006), pp.23–94, though without pointing out the particular suggestion being made here.

outcome in which evil has no place (*1 En.* 10; 15–16; 91.5-10; 106.13–107.1; *Jub.* 5–10; *Book of Giants* at 4Q530 2 ii + 6-7 + 8-12, lines 4-20). Thus in essence, evil, however rampant and overwhelming it may seem to be in the present, is but a defeated power whose time is marked. Since God's rule has asserted itself in the cosmos on a global scale, the present 'era of wickedness' is no time of waiting or despair. One can, even now, proceed confidently enough to deal with demonic power, knowing that although it cannot be eliminated altogether, before the ultimate end of things, it is nevertheless possible to address, curtail or manage its effects. While these reflections range broadly in scope, one may nevertheless ask: how remote is the world of the Fourth Gospel from Jewish apocalyptic tradition in this respect?

Part III

JOHN AND APOCALYPTIC: TEXT AND READERS

TEXT AND AUTHORITY IN JOHN AND APOCALYPTIC

Judith M. Lieu

The work of John Ashton, and the appreciation of it evidenced by this volume, demonstrate the various directions in which the insight can be developed that apocalyptic provides a productive framework within which to think about the Fourth Gospel.[1] This need not presuppose that the author consciously adopted, mimicked, or subverted a recognised apocalyptic genre; it holds true even if the widespread consensus is accepted that there is no single or sufficient overarching blanket definition of apocalyptic and that there will always be the exceptions that prove the rule or that subvert or play with its 'characteristics'.[2] Independent of debates over formal genre, apocalyptic and John share in particular, although not exclusively with each other, first, an imagination, a way of constructing a symbolic universe; secondly, a strategy, particularly rhetorical and literary techniques, by which that universe is reinforced and through which it is used; and thirdly, arguably a social location, which might best be described in terms of socio-historical dislocation and even of an (incipient) sectarian or anti-imperialist consciousness. The concern of this essay is to examine a particular point of intersection between the first two of these, imagination and strategy, namely the epistemological problem and claims inherent in these texts – how the 'knowledge' they profess is defined, achieved, and legitimated. Such questions are readily provoked by apocalyptic, and thus this is another area where apocalyptic can provide a framework for reflection on the Fourth Gospel. It is assumed here that not only overtly 'textual' features but also the description of events, including of the visionary's experience, can be treated as textual strategies, while remaining agnostic about the 'historical' status of those events.

---

1   John Ashton, *Understanding the Fourth Gospel* (Oxford: Oxford University Press, 2nd edn, 2007), pp.328–9: 'Thus the fourth evangelist conceives his own work as an apocalypse – in reverse, upside down, inside out'.
2   See already John J. Collins, *The Apocalyptic Imagination* (New York: Crossroad, 1984), pp.1–32.

Apocalyptic and Textuality

Few would question the importance of text and textuality for apocalyptic literature. At first this might seem counter-intuitive: apocalyptic would seem to be centred on the visual and auditory senses; its discourse belongs to the grammar of the non-logical, the non-linear, the non-syntactical. Such terms, discourse, grammar, syntax, are deliberately taken from the world of textuality, in an apparent exercise in reciprocal deconstruction; however, to use them underlines that widely differing media, both those that are logo-centric and those adopting other forms, are nevertheless open to analysis in terms of their structures of communication.[3] Others would object, in the past, and sometimes still now, that apocalyptic is to be associated with the oppressed, with the non-elite, and therefore with the non-literate 'classes' in society. Even here, however, a cross-cultural approach would invite qualification: revolt, even by the oppressed, has regularly been enflamed by written texts, and has produced its manifesto in them.

More recently, however, the consensus has consolidated that apocalyptic is thoroughly textual; many would associate its production with scribal classes, and/or with certain forms of priestly activity – possibilities that are not mutually exclusive. As transmitted and disseminated, the production of apocalyptic depends on considerable mastery of complex literary strategies; so also the accomplished reader, someone able to respond to those strategies, would also need to have considerable literate competencies. 'Literate competencies' is not intended to suggest that all 'readers' would themselves have to have the skill to compose and to inscribe written texts, nor does it deny that many would have experienced these texts aurally; rather, both readers and hearers must have been thoroughly familiar with the world, or with a particular world, of literary texts. Apocalyptic is a prime candidate for Brian Stock's model of textual communities to which we shall return.[4]

The Apocalyptic Text as Book: Production

The textuality of apocalyptic functions on three levels, although these levels necessarily intersect with each other. The first is the external mode, the level of production – the apocalyptic text as book. Initially this is simply part of the reader's experience, namely the characteristic

---

3   This is true even of those that still make use of material components, art, sculpture.

4   Brian Stock, *Listening for the Text: On the Uses of the Past* (Baltimore: The Johns Hopkins University Press, 1990), pp.140–58.

complex literary patterns and techniques: this might be termed 'objective textuality'.[5] Evidence of this is the fact that apocalyptic has generally invited, if anything, the detection of literary layers and not the imaginative recovery of easily retrievable oral transmission and performance that other, even initially more obviously literary, genres do. Yet apocalyptic texts are also explicitly and self-reflectively written, as *book*, and even so self-designated. This is most obviously a unifying theme throughout *1 Enoch*, and its sub-divisions. It is not simply that readers are made aware that they are encountering a book: '[Book] Five which is written by Enoch, the writer of all the signs of wisdom... (*1 En.* 92.1); Enoch is addressed as 'scribe' and internal narrative references regularly make it clear that it has to be written (*1 En.* 81.6–82.1).[6] In the *Shepherd of Hermas* Hermas encounters an elderly woman carrying a book from which she reads; on their second encounter she instructs him to copy from her book, and he does so, albeit with considerable difficulty, not because of any lack of literate skills but because of his difficulties in understanding (*Vis.* 1.3-4; 2.1).[7] Subsequently the eponymous Shepherd dictates to him, ostensibly the 'Parables' and 'Mandates' that constitute the rest of the book (Hermas, *Vis.* 5.5). In similar fashion Ezra is given detailed instructions for the writing of his visions, while John of the Apocalypse is simply told, 'write what you have seen in a book' (*4 Ezra* 14.24-48; Rev 1.11, 19). In each of these cases the narrator is, in narrative-critical terms, the implied author, but at the same time he is also a character within the narrative. Complicating this, the visionary also reads what he has seen to other characters within the narrative, real or heavenly, or else he passes on the book to a new narrator, as when Enoch tells Methuselah that he has given him 'the book concerning all these things' (*1 En.* 82.1).[8]

---

5 As already noted, in the ancient context many readers were of course hearers, but they would still recognise in such patterns the characteristics of a read text. For the importance of Apocalypses as writing, see Martha Himmelfarb, *Ascent to Heaven in Jewish and Christian Apocalypses* (New York: Oxford University Press, 1993), pp.95–106.

6 It is recognised here that *1 Enoch* as commonly now designated is a composite work. However, from the perspective adopted here it can be treated as a single unit, and what is true of the whole is also true of the parts.

7 See Carolyn Osiek, *The Shepherd of Hermas: A Commentary* (Hermeneia; Minneapolis: Fortress, 1999), p.52.

8 The visionaries in the literature discussed here are male and so 'he' will be used, although at a later date both Aseneth and Perpetua could be added to their number, and many more such women.

This trope answers a number of potential problems that are inherent in the apocalyptic genre. First, it provides legitimation for a mode that is emphatically in need of this. The instruction to write in order to address the gap between the moment of revelation and that of completion is already found in Hab 2.2, but in apocalyptic the identity of the primary visionary and their age, usually in the distant past, immediately create a far greater problem of authenticity and legitimacy – a problem explicitly met by the theme of hiding the books in *4 Ezra* 12.37.[9] Furthermore, visionary or auditory experience is necessarily predicated upon the individual, thus creating a conceptual gap between that experience and the possibility of its immediate reception by a wider audience. Exacerbating this, whereas in other literary genres, including the gospel or apologetic texts, the transmission from the original eyewitness(es) to a new audience, who themselves become part of the authoritative tradition, is easily handled (Luke 1.1-4), apocalyptic presupposes that the visionary is uniquely chosen and has been equipped for an experience that cannot readily be transferred to others.[10] The anxiety this generates is reinforced by the repeated theme of the visionary's imminent death or translation (*2 Bar.* 32.4-9; 76).[11]

Further strategies address but also nuance these inherent problems. So, for example, it is common that vision and writing are not directly contiguous, but are separated by mediating stages. There may be different stages of reception, understanding, and writing, each of which remains under divine control: thus Enoch explains that 'I saw in my sleep what I now speak … he gave me understanding … this book' (*1 En.* 14.1-7).[12] Yet even this process does not give the seer autonomy or control over the transfer from seeing to writing. Enoch has to ask for an explanation of what he himself has already written (*1 En.* 40.8).[13] In Hermas' first vision the woman reads to him, and he is instructed to 'become a listener',

---

9 Cf. also *T. Mos.* 1.10-18.

10 See Michael E. Stone, *Fourth Ezra: A Commentary on the Book of Fourth Ezra* (Hermeneia; Minneapolis: Fortress, 1990), p.374.

11 Consequently there are numerous overlaps between apocalyptic and testamentary literature.

12 The text is difficult to reconstruct; see E. Isaac, '1 (Ethiopic Apocalypse of) Enoch', in *OTP*, I, pp. 5-89, 20; also George W. E. Nickelsburg, *1 Enoch 1: A Commentary on the Book of 1 Enoch, Chapters 1–36; 81–108* (Hermeneia; Minneapolis: Fortress, 2001), p.251.

13 See *1 En.* 93.2, where Enoch is dependent on his vision, on the words of the angels, and on the heavenly tablets (see below).

although even he cannot remember everything that he hears (Hermas, *Vis.* 1.3). Within the visionary's experience the auditory is therefore as important as the visual. Subsequently, however, the difficulty that Hermas had in copying still does not resolve the difficulty of understanding; he only achieves this after ascetic effort – although the account given of what was written seems straightforwardly paraenetic. There is widespread evidence that ascetic practice of various kinds could be the occasion for apocalyptic experience, and even deliberately used to stimulate it (Dan 9.3-4, 20; *2 Bar.* 21.1-3), yet arguably it is no less important for its conveyance in writing.[14] What is evident from these various steps is that the apocalyptic text is forced to address the multiple relationships between 'seeing', speech or hearing, writing, understanding, and further writing, and that it also problematises them.

A different device is adopted by *4 Ezra*: Ezra is told to take five people who 'are trained to write rapidly'; thus equipped they are able to keep up with Ezra's inspiration which itself lasts just long enough for them to write everything. They themselves are also given understanding by God to write, although the script in which they write is one that they do not know. Ezra himself speaks during both day and night, while they stop at night in order to eat: thus the comprehensiveness of the revelation given to Ezra ultimately cannot be constrained even by being written down (*4 Ezra* 14.23-25, 42-43). Through all this, despite human skill, meaning remains exclusively under divine control. Inevitably, this strategy only postpones the question of how the revelatory mode can be maintained through the process of transmission. Within such a framework, the opaque Markan warning 'let the reader understand' should be understood as addressed not to the individual encountering this obscure text, but to the person whose task it is to read out the text to others, and whose reading perhaps is necessarily accompanied by interpretation (Mark 13.14).

Through these strategies of literary production, the processes of communication and dissemination are themselves legitimated. Yet this itself provokes a further question, namely that of the audience – to whom are the texts addressed? The answer to this varies, because once again there is a structural problem. If, as so often, the content of the vision encompasses the whole of human history and the destiny of all humankind, should it not be made available to all? Yet, is it not a primary presupposition of the apocalyptic mode that the true meaning of events is

---

14 See Himmelfarb, *Ascent to Heaven*, pp.104–14.

visible only to the chosen few? Enoch declared that God 'destined and created men to understand the words of knowledge', but whether this in practice refers only to a limited number of the elect is far from clear (*1 En.* 14.1-3). Enoch is 'praised by all people and a leader of the whole earth', who addresses words of warning to sinners, and he anticipates that 'the sons of the earth will contemplate these words of this epistle and they will recognise that their wealth cannot save them when iniquity collapses' (92.1; 100.6). More often, however, it is assumed that the audience who will receive and understand what is written are a narrower circle. *1 Enoch* 81–82, probably an inserted section, explicitly serves to legitimate a particular audience extended through time: Enoch not only addresses his son Methuselah directly but he also puts his revelation in a book which Methuselah is to pass on to his children and to subsequent generations, 'the generations of eternity' – although even for them wisdom does not come automatically.[15] Presumably the fictive audience, Methuselah's offspring, represent the contemporaries of the 'real author', and it is their assent for which the author is contending. Elsewhere the distinction in audiences is made more explicit: of the books Ezra writes, 70 are for the wise, and 24, those of the Scriptures, are for everyone (*4 Ezra* 14.45-48). On the other hand, Revelation, which does not appeal to a seer in the distant past, encompasses an address to 'the seven churches in Asia' within a more general address to 'the one who reads the words of the prophecy' (Rev 1.3-4). An alternative means of sustaining the comprehensiveness of the vision alongside the selectivity of the audience is when the seer does not write down but is only told to write in the memory of his heart (*2 Bar.* 50.1; *4 Ezra* 14.7).

The Apocalypse of John also illustrates another strategy for addressing the problem of the dissemination of the apocalyptic vision to a wider, but still 'constructed', audience, namely the otherwise surprising and widespread use of the letter format. The shape of the book as a whole is loosely presented as a letter, which the author has been instructed to send 'in a book', with an address ('A to B') and with a closing (Pauline) farewell grace (Rev 1.4, 11; 22.21); but it also incorporates seven separate letters, one to each of the named churches, wherein the seer simply conveys a message from the heavenly object of his vision. Although *1 Enoch* 92–105 incorporate a number of different units and types of material, these chapters as a whole loosely take the form of a letter, and they are explicitly so-called in 100.6; it is directed 'to all my sons ... and to the last generations', and its closing recalls the conventional farewell,

---

15 Nickelsburg, *1 Enoch*, pp.334–8.

'And you will have peace'.¹⁶ In *2 Baruch* Baruch first addresses the Elders (*2 Bar.* 31), then an audience consisting of his son, friends and seven elders (44); following a further vision he addresses the people, and at their request he writes a letter, one 'to our brothers in Babylon', those already in exile, and, of his own accord, another to the nine and a half tribes, the Northern Kingdom defeated and dispersed long before the supposed setting of Baruch (77.11-26).¹⁷ This second letter has to be conveyed by an eagle, a heavenly messenger, who is therefore a guarantor of the heavenly authority of what is sent as well as one who is able to reach those who are otherwise scattered and lost. Surprisingly, it is this second letter, and not that to those in Babylon, which forms *2 Baruch* 78–87.¹⁸ According to *2 Bar.* 84.7 this writing then acts as a witness between the visionary and those whom he addresses – although it might be supposed that the destiny of these tribes was not open; they are also instructed to read it in their 'assemblies', particularly on fast days. A similar goal is also achieved in a more prosaic manner by Hermas; he is also told to make two copies of the revelatory book; one is for Grapte to instruct the widows and orphans, the other is to be circulated through Clement 'to the cities outside', while Hermas himself is to read to 'this city' (Hermas, *Vis.* 2.4). In this case it is somewhat more uncertain how these copies relate to the text which recounts this instruction and with which the reader is confronted. However, the involvement of Clement as responsible for sending out the letter, like that of the five scribes in *4 Ezra*, establishes a triangular set of relationships between audience, witnesses or agents, and seer; in *2 Baruch* the people who request the writing of the letter perhaps fulfil a similar function. Such mechanisms do after all generate a 'dynamic of revelation' in which others can participate.¹⁹

The *Shepherd of Hermas* is particularly striking in this regard. The woman who carries the revelatory book and who gives him the command to copy it is revealed to be the church. She also promises to add words to his original compilation before they are circulated, although whether and when she does so is not related. On the one hand, this gives a degree of openness to the revelation. At the same time, Hermas' revelation remains strictly under the authority of 'the church', something that might have

---

16   A subscription 'Epistle of Enoch' is added in the Greek fragment at the end of chapter 107; see Nickelsburg, *1 Enoch*, p.431.
17   See Mark F. Whitters, *The Epistle of Second Baruch: A Study in Form and Message* (JSPSup 42; London: Sheffield Academic, 2003).
18   This is often seen as an example of a Diaspora letter on the grounds that the letter to those in Babylon is said to contain the same things.
19   So Stone, *Fourth Ezra*, p.429, on the role of the people in *4 Ezra* 14.

both positive and negative implications: this is an abstractly conceptualised church, while Hermas is to read 'with the elders who lead the church', a formulation perhaps designed to constrain any personal or institutional authority they might have (Hermas, *Vis.* 2.4).[20]

These various narrative devices effectively create a degree of fluidity between the seer-cum-writer within the text and the writer outside the text, and also between the audience within the text and the audience outside the text. In this way the act of writing mediates between the visionary and the recipients, including different recipients not originally anticipated directly by the vision or by its immediate transmission. Alongside this, such writing also mediates vertically between heaven and earth; usually this operates in a 'trickle down' pattern as the divine truth is transmitted to and among people, although there is also an upward movement when Enoch writes and then reads out a 'memorandum' on behalf of the fallen watchers in the hope that this will bring forgiveness (*1 En.* 13).[21]

Undoubtedly, these legitimating strategies are, at least in some cases, consciously constructed in relation to existing models of 'authoritative book', most obviously to that of Torah. Such undercurrents of, sometimes competing, canonical claims have been traced in particular in the Enochic tradition.[22] As apocalyptic is transformed – if that is the correct model – in later revelatory discourses, as is witnessed in the Nag Hammadi writings, so too is this motif. A common variant is that of an explicit contrast made between the secret book and other books or gospels;[23] likewise, the *Apocalypse of Adam* offers an alternative form of subversion by claiming that the words the elect have kept were not set down in the book or written (*Apoc. Adam* [NHC V, 5] 85). This is reminiscent of *2 Baruch* and it offers a similar challenge to the reader of the text.

The common thread to all these strategies is the attempt to solve the problem of the authority and the reach of the apocalyptic vision, which is understood as the ultimate expression of knowledge of the divine plan. That the vision should take written form in a single text is necessary for that knowledge to be accessible, but it is at the same time inherently problematic, since apocalyptic presupposes the inability of mortals fully

---

20   See Patricia Cox Miller, *Dreams in Late Antiquity: Studies in the Imagination of a Culture* (Princeton: Princeton University Press, 1994), pp.131–47.

21   See Nickelsburg, *1 Enoch*, p.237, for the importance of this as a written document.

22   See David R. Jackson, *Enochic Judaism: Three Defining Paradigm Exemplars* (LSTS 49; London: T&T Clark International, 2004).

23   *Apocryphon of James* (NHC I, 2) 1–2.

to comprehend of their own accord. Indeed, it is this dilemma that explains both why apocalypses tend to grow and why they are so unstable textually.

The Text within Apocalyptic: Heavenly Books

The second level of textuality is already implicated within the first, namely the text within the apocalypse. Although an apocalypse is fundamentally *seen*, it frequently encompasses an existing written text. This is most evident in the common motif of heavenly books, which are made known to the visionary and in some sense are explained in the book then produced by him. The connection between these has already been illustrated when Hermas copies the book carried by the revelatory old woman whom he encounters. An anticipation of the idea may be found in Ezekiel's vision of a scroll covered with words of lamentation, which he has to consume before he can utter his prophecy (Ezek 2.8–3.3); John of Patmos takes up and recasts that motif in a way that heightens the sense of heavenly mysteries and of divine control of the events inscribed (Rev 5). Another biblical precursor is the heavenly figure in human form who is instructed to reveal to Daniel 'what is inscribed in the book of truth', a prefigurement of events to come, and which Daniel is to keep secret until the end of time (Dan 10.21; 12.4, 9). By contrast, Enoch himself 'looks at the tablets of heaven, reads everything on them and came to understand everything'; it is this experience which enables him to recount what will happen after his own time, and in particular to anticipate times of unprecedented suffering or oppression which might otherwise remain an inexplicable 'mystery' (*1 En.* 81; 93; 103.1; 106.19). However, elsewhere Enoch's own account of the stars and their patterns is dependent not only on what the angel Uriel shows to him but also on what he writes down for him (*1 En.* 33). The motif is found more widely: Aseneth is told that some things written in the book of the most high cannot be uttered or known by human beings (e.g. divine or angelic names), although later Levi is said to be able to read letters written in heaven by the finger of God (*Jos. Asen.* 15.22; 22.13).

Such scenes are variants of a widespread ancient topos, one that is not restricted to Jewish and Christian apocalypses, namely that of heavenly tablets.[24] Most frequently, these tablets of heaven are a type of heavenly accounting system containing all the deeds of humanity, identifying the names of the righteous or the sins of the wicked, distinguishing between the fate of good and that of the bad, or 'edited' by the removal from them

---

24 See Nickelsburg, *1 Enoch*, pp.478–80.

of the names of the wicked (*1 En.* 47.3; 108.1-3; *Apoc. Zeph.* 3; 7; *Testament of Abraham*; *2 Bar.* 24; Hermas, *Sim.* 2.9). Even so, the function of such tablets is not only to explain the mechanisms of future judgement: thus, when Aseneth is told that her name is written in the book of the living, her conversion is effectively authenticated before she can act in any way herself (*Jos. Asen.* 15.2).[25]

As this last example demonstrates, an already existing heavenly text provides the assurance that events are not as random as they may appear – despite the unresolved tension this generates with the accounting of deeds for which each individual is responsible. More particularly, the tablets establish the guarantee that oppressor and oppressed, righteous and wicked, will receive the deserts they merit, frequently contrary to the present experience of the author and audience. Yet these heavenly books or tablets are not simply identical to the book that is subsequently written down by the apocalyptic seer: otherwise it would be easier for them simply to be handed over to him. As has been seen, on the one hand they invariably require that a heavenly mediator interpret them for the seer, on the other the visionary has to make a copy, often with considerable difficulty or with other mediation. Necessarily, this copy is bound to contain less than what was recorded in the original. What this device achieves is to address the tension between fixity and flexibility: the heavenly tablets provide for fixity; their opacity, their opening, and their copying allows for the fluidity of interpretation, and perhaps also for repeated reinterpretation in the face of disconfirmation.

The Text behind Apocalyptic: The Reinterpretation of Scripture

The third level of textuality is the important role played within apocalyptic by the reinterpretation of earlier Scripture – the text behind apocalyptic. If apocalyptic is about the shaping of the imagination, the components of such shaping often come out of earlier cultural resources. This reinterpretation of earlier Scripture in apocalyptic is so intrinsic and well documented as to need no elaborate demonstration. Although frequently the underlying Scripture may come from texts already or subsequently deemed canonical, it need not be so; indeed, such reinterpretation may be a mechanism for asserting (alternative) quasi-canonical status.[26] In *1 Enoch* 68 Michael explains to Noah the secret things in the book of Enoch, while a considerable number of other writings from the period appeal specifically to the Enochic literature (e.g. *Jub.* 10.5; 14.1;

---

25 See further Jackson, *Enochic Judaism*, pp.114–15.
26 See above at p.242.

perhaps *4QNoah ar* [4Q534] l. 5); the letter written by Hermas makes an appeal 'as it is written in the Book of Eldad and Modat' (Hermas, *Vis.* 2.4).

Yet this is not simply a matter of the interpretation of Scripture understood as separate from, and indeed superior to, the text under production, a strategy of fulfilment. The text behind apocalyptic is an integral part of the production of the apocalyptic text itself. Indeed, this may be quite precisely so: it has been convincingly argued that the study of the texts was often the stimulus for apocalyptic revelation or for heavenly ascent, perhaps through particular techniques, including meditation.[27] Functionally, this relationship means that apocalyptic is able to address the problem that arises when ownership of the authoritative text becomes contested or when different ways of reading come into conflict. The intrinsic claims of apocalyptic revelation provide a superior, authoritative reading; on the other hand, they can also serve to delegitimise alternative readings. At the most basic level Enoch warns that 'sinners will invent fictitious stories and write out my (?) scriptures on the basis of their own words' (*1 En.* 104.10).[28] Again, this is not a narrowly defined apocalyptic topos: when the third Sibyl complains that Homer wrote falsely but cleverly, a precise (re-)application of the bard's poetry is being prepared for (*Sib. Or.* 3.419). A variety of hermeneutical methods achieve greater sophistication, for example, the pesher exegesis familiar from the Dead Sea Scrolls, which re-identifies the players in unexpected ways.[29] Sometimes the interpretative claims may even result in a collision between the author and the subtext. Thus Scripture is authoritative and yet it also generates a tensive dialectic with the apocalyptic text, with the result that the latter is not for ever dependent on and subordinate to Scripture, as is, for example, the case with commentary.

Apocalyptic and Understanding

Some might here wish to discuss the social realities behind these three literary devices or levels of textuality. It seems likely that just as the solitary reader or interpreter is a familiar trope in the ancient world but was rarely a reality, the same is true of the solitary visionary. Writing and reading are bound up in a social infrastructure and in social networks, as

---

27 David E. Orton, *The Understanding Scribe: Matthew and the Apocalyptic Ideal* (JSNTSup 25; Sheffield: Sheffield Academic, 1989), p.117.

28 The text and its translation are unclear; see Nickelsburg, *1 Enoch*, pp.144–5.

29 On such strategies, see Bruce N. Fisk, *Do You Not Remember? Scripture, Story and Exegesis in the Rewritten Bible of Pseudo-Philo* (JSPSup 37; Sheffield: Sheffield Academic, 2001), pp.82–5.

also is interpretation. Consequently written texts can often legitimate specific communities of interpretation. This is best demonstrated by Brian Stock's analysis of 'textual communities'; such communities are predicated upon the study of particular written texts and upon their distinctive interpretation, they are shaped by the world created by those texts, and their members are equipped with literate skills within that framework. This provides a model that works particularly well for viewing apocalyptic, with reference both to the primary Scriptures, the third level explored above, and to the apocalyptic interpretations and writings generated by their study. It is within such a framework of a community of interpretation that Martha Himmelfarb's suggestion is to be situated, that readers of the text (or some readers) would be enabled to enter into the written apocalypse and to share its vision.[30]

Understood in this way, apocalyptic creates, as it were, its own set of literate skills or a new literacy; it is easy to see how this would implicitly devalue the alternative 'literacy' of the outsiders and thus function as a subversive strategy. Patricia Cox Miller has described Hermas' initiation into salvation as 'literacy', albeit the literacy of understanding dreams.[31] To some extent this generation of an alternative literacy is true of most early Christian as well as Jewish literature, but apocalyptic in particular can be seen as an intensification of what has been observed more generally, namely that early Christian literature 'disenfranchis[es] Roman civilisation through a new form of discourse'.[32] On the other hand, what Richard Gordon has said about Roman religion, namely that writing 'institutionalizes unintelligibility', perhaps also could be said here.[33] It follows that the production and circulation of apocalyptic texts represents participation in a discourse of power and control such as has always been associated with coded wisdom and with anticipation of the future.

Yet it is also evident that apocalyptic belongs within a nexus of hermeneutical and epistemological problems. It is predicated upon the fundamental problem of the inaccessibility (or accessibility) of God and of the impossibility (or possibility) of knowing the divine mind, and of tracing the divine purposes within human history. Apocalyptic explores

---

30   Himmelfarb, *Ascent to Heaven*, pp.106–14, who, against a number of interpreters, emphasises that the framework for participation or imagination was literary and not a mystically or ritually generated one.

31   Quoted by Osiek, *Hermas*, p.52.

32   Stock, *Listening for the Text*, p.3.

33   Richard Gordon, 'From Republic to Principate: Priesthood, Religion and Ideology', in Mary Beard and John North (eds.), *Pagan Priests: Religion and Power in the Ancient World* (London: Duckworth, 1990), pp.179–98 (189).

how such access is possible without detracting from divine sovereignty, and it also seeks to explain how the understanding that has been achieved can be conveyed to others. Yet in doing this it also generates new questions about these dilemmas.

The Fourth Gospel and Apocalyptic Textuality

The Text Behind: The Refiguring of Scripture

This analysis of the textuality of apocalyptic can now serve as a lens for reflecting on the literary strategies of the Fourth Gospel. Here the argument will work backwards through the three levels of textuality that have been identified. Thus, in terms of 'the text behind' it is incontrovertible that John's conceptual and textual world is created by meditation upon Scripture and by the refashioning of Scripture. There can be little doubt that this is a polemical exercise, refuting alternative readings or explorations of the authoritative texts (John 5.39). In part this is achieved by the conventional fulfilment formulae, but these generally play a subsidiary role in John (e.g. John 12.38-40).[34] Much more dominant is the sort of collision between author and subtext that has been seen as characteristic of a pesher-style apocalyptic mimicry. So for example, ch. 6 does indeed overtly reinterpret the focal text, 'he gave them bread from heaven to eat', although it is significant that the scriptural passage is cited not by the author but by the people (John 6.31; see Ps 78[77].24; Exod 16.4; Neh 9.15); more telling, the chapter re-stages the whole scene of sea-crossing, complaining people, and the threat of death for those without belief.[35] Elsewhere in the Gospel, contemporary players find their identity through Cain and the devil (John 8.44), and the Moses who did indeed lift up the serpent in the wilderness is denied any heavenly journeys of his own – such as those on which some may have staked their own claims (John 3.14; Num 21.8).[36]

A seminal role in such scriptural (re-)fashioning is played by John 1.51, where Jacob's dream-vision in Gen 28.12 is evoked. Two modifications of the core text are important, both of which heighten the apocalyptic tone: it is introduced by the plural promise, 'you will see',

---

34 The assertion that Isaiah was the visionary of the divine glory in 12.41 is key to John's reconfiguration of scriptural authority.

35 This is what Birger Olsson, *Structure and Meaning in the Fourth Gospel: A Text-Linguistic Analysis of John 2:1–11 and 4:1–42* (ConBNT 6; Lund: Gleerup, 1974) calls a 'scriptural screen'.

36 Ashton, *Understanding* (2nd edn), pp.251–9.

and it is transformed by the addition of the perfect passive participle 'opened'.[37] It is not, as is sometimes supposed, that the son of man will replace the ladder into the distant and inaccessible heaven, but rather that the heaven has already been opened to visionary view. On a source-critical level, this last motif appears to be transferred from the tradition of the baptismal narratives, which are absent as such from John, although he does retain the tradition of the descent of the spirit (Mark 1.10; Matt 3.16; John 1.33). Such transference reinforces the apocalyptic tone that many have recognised already in the Markan baptismal account, where it is Jesus alone who 'saw'. In this light the questions that in John are left unanswered become yet more insistent: Who is addressed in the plural 'you will see', both within the narrative moment and also beyond it? When and where is this promise fulfilled, or will it be fulfilled? If the perfect participle 'opened' emphasises an abiding situation, and not a temporary opening restricted to the elect visionary or visionaries, is the conclusion to be drawn on any level that the subject 'you' is also without restriction, potentially universal?[38]

As has been seen in the analysis of the first level of textual production in apocalyptic, an answer to these questions should be sought both in terms of the function of the text for readers as well as within its internal unveiling in the narrative. How, then, does the promised 'seeing' relate to the written text in which the promise is made but also in which the apocalyptic events are described? As has often been observed, a similar set of questions is provoked by the mix of first and second person singular and plural in 3.11-12, verses that immediately precede the exclusive revelatory claim regarding the Son of Man in 3.13. Where are the heavenly things that are anticipated here actually spoken ('we speak'), where are they testified (and presumably written), and who is the audience to whom they are spoken and testified, and even written? It would be possible to see 1 John, which is loosely in the form of a letter, as a partial answer to this question, following the model of other 'apocalyptic' letters where seeing does lead to writing and announcing to a new audience; however, that is an avenue that cannot be explored here.

The Text Within: What is Seen and Heard
In this discussion of 3.11-12 there is already an elision with the second level of 'the text within': although the Fourth Gospel does not contain

---

37 Nathanael's sitting under the fig tree recalls Ezra under the oak tree (*4 Ezra* 14.1); see Stone, *Fourth Ezra*, p.410.

38 The promise of the 'greater things' that Nathanael will see is continued from 1.50 to 5.20 and to 14.12.

the concept of a heavenly text or script as in apocalyptic visions, it does work with a surrogate set of ideas. Here John 3.31-36 could well follow after, or serve as an alternative to, the verses just considered (3.11-13). In 3.31-36 the visionary extraordinarily has his true location in heaven, both 'coming from heaven' and being 'above all'. For this reason he is not a stranger to that realm, nor is he in need of an interpreter, and neither is his coming to earth a return to his natural habitat (cf. *1 En.* 90.39): 'What he has both seen and heard that he bears witness to'; 'he speaks the words (ῥήματα) of God' (John 3.32, 34). It is often assumed that 'what is seen' and 'what is heard' in 3.32 refer to two separate things or two separate modes of reception, and that the latter, 'heard', is exclusively oral–aural. However, both 'seeing' and 'hearing' could equally refer to the experience of a heavenly text such as is typical of apocalyptic. This possibility should not be over-pressed, and there may be a deliberate contrast in this claim with those who are dependent on a secondary heavenly text. Thus in John 5 the Son's authority to carry out judgement, including the giving of life, is contingent precisely upon what he sees the Father *doing*, although, even so, this involves the Father himself *showing* – frequently the task of the heavenly guide in apocalyptic – the Son (John 5.19-20). It is significant that the context here is that of divinely guaranteed judgement and life-giving, just as is that of the apocalyptic appeal to heavenly texts.

A key verse in this apocalyptically fashioned textual world is John 1.18, which repeats, or anticipates, the exclusive denial of 3.13 – just as no one has ascended, so no one has seen. The parallel demonstrates that in John 1.18 there is not simply an echo or a reconfiguring of the Exodus and Moses traditions of divine vision (Exod 33.17–34.9). The language locates the claim firmly in the conceptual world of apocalyptic, as a response to the hiddenness or to the inaccessibility of God and of God's ways. However, the verb ἐξηγέομαι, without an immediate object, encapsulates the ambiguity that has just been explored: is it to be translated as 'narrate, give an account of', perhaps suggesting as an implied object a reference to that which (or the one who) has been seen, or does it mean 'exegete, expound', as would be appropriate with reference to a written text?[39]

---

39 For a Mosaic model, see Marie-Émile Boismard, *Moses or Jesus: An Essay in Johannine Christology* (trans. Benedict T. Viviano; BETL 84A; Leuven: Peeters, 1993), pp.94–9. Most commentators supply an object 'him' and compare the use of the verb for making known divine secrets, while also noting that it is used by Josephus for the interpretation of the law.

The ambiguity in the verb points to a 'doubleness' in John's apocalyptic vision which has also been noted elsewhere. In John 1.18 is Jesus represented as the seer, the one who himself experiences the vision of God? Or is he the mediator or interpreter of the mysteries of God for those who can now experience the vision themselves? A third possibility, less obvious here but certainly part of John's broader apocalyptic world, would be that Jesus is the object of the vision, that which or the one who is seen. For Jesus as seer, John 3 has already made clear that Jesus is the one who has seen (3.32); so also when Jesus says, 'I speak what I have seen with the father (παρὰ τῷ πατρί)' and 'I spoke what I heard with [or from] God (παρὰ τοῦ θεοῦ)' (8.38, 40). However, embracing the Jesus who saw (1.18) is the testimony of the 'we' who have themselves seen the glory (1.14): they, it might be suggested, have themselves experienced the apocalyptic vision which includes the person of Jesus himself.[40]

Another verse which destabilises what at first seems straightforward is 6.45, where the one who herself or himself has heard 'from the father' (παρὰ τοῦ πατρός) comes to Jesus. How is such an unmediated hearing made possible? Or, to ask from a different perspective, as earlier was asked of apocalyptic, how is the seeing and the hearing which are properly restricted to Jesus as the exclusive seer transmitted to others, not just to those 'others' who are within the narrative, but also to those who are presumed to stand outside it – a question that anticipates the problem of the written text before us? As if underlining the tension, in the immediately following verse, 6.46, the direct hearing from the father possible for 'anyone' is contrasted with 'seeing the father', which only Jesus as the 'one from God' can experience.

Jesus' farewell promises in John 14 point in the same direction: as is well known, the chapter opens with the conventional image of a heavenly habitation with many resting places, μοναί, kept for the faithful. By the end of the chapter that hope has been radically reinterpreted: father and son come to and create a resting-place, a μονή, with the person who 'keeps' or 'observes my word', a word which is no less that of the father (14.2, 23). Once again, the assurance provokes the question: what form does 'the word' that is to be kept take for those who perform or who receive the Gospel as text? The same question arises as Jesus declares that 'the sayings' (ῥήματα) that God gave to him, he has given to others, and as he goes on to pray that those who believe through 'their word' may themselves experience the divine glory (17.8, 20-21).

---

40 As did Isaiah in John 12.41 (see n. 34 above).

Gospel as Text

Such questions turn our attention to the outermost level, the production of the written text. The references to the disciples as subsequently 'remembering', and to the task of the holy spirit as paraclete of 'reminding' them (John 2.17, 22; 14.26), have often been understood as providing an explanation for the character of the Gospel as the result of spirit-inspired re-remembering and re-telling – which would imply a recognition of the difference between event and interpretation, between 'history and theology'. Yet, as has now become evident, this concept is not, as sometimes supposed, a prophetic or charismatic topos (or not that alone), but is an apocalyptic one: it evokes the visionary who preserves some things in the heart and who, perhaps with the aid of a heavenly mediator or interpreter, comes to an understanding that itself is part of the authoritative experience and of its transmission.

It is with this in mind that the way the Gospel closes becomes important, namely its self-presentation as an emphatically written text. Often unnoticed, the two endings conceptualise this rather differently. Although addressing an unspecified 'you' plural, the ending of ch. 20 conceals the author behind passive verbs '... are written'; at the same time, that passive form strikingly echoes the standard vocabulary of the appeal to Scripture, '(as) it is written' (20.30-31; cf. 6.31; 12.14). Thus the text is accorded authority, even while its personal, direct source is carefully concealed. The self-referential emphasis, '(in) this book', and the claim that is made for what is here written, have their closest parallel in Revelation 22, where the context is a repeated emphasis on the unalterable character of 'the words of this book of (this) prophecy' (Rev 22.18-19). Further, the things that have been written 'in this book' are contrasted with 'the many signs' done by Jesus, which are not written here. What then, for John 20.30-31, is the status of the 'many other signs not written in this book', the Gospel? The conventional answer to this question would be that this was a means of devaluing other non-written traditions, or even of dismissing traditions that were written but in other books – a technique that has been noted elsewhere.[41] An alternative interpretation would be that it leaves open the possibility of further revelations for the elect beyond what is given here, even though this latter is still necessary for belief and for life. In this framework, the 'remembering' by the disciples noted above may carry a different nuance, pointing to this potential surplus, reinforced by the promise of the spirit who will lead them in(to) all truth and who will announce the things to come – not obviously set out in the Gospel (John 16.13). The ambiguity that is implied by these

---

41 See above p.242.

possibilities is exacerbated by the conjunction, or better by the disjunction, between these verses and the preceding verse: 'Blessed are those who have not seen' (John 20.29). Such a macarism neatly deconstructs the previous twenty chapters and their apocalyptic 'visionary' underpinning![42]

The closing verses of ch. 21 produce a markedly different effect (21.24-25).[43] Here an identified outer audience, 'you', is absent, although the previous verse has introduced the otherwise unexplained 'brothers' (21.23). It may be that the readers are expected to see themselves among these 'brothers', but the context is the familiar one of the anxiety generated by the potential departure of the original authority. On this occasion, however, the writer is identified, as 'this man' (οὗτος), and his text is legitimated, 'we know'. However, this legitimation is dependent upon an anonymous group, 'we', whose own authority is left without explanation. Moreover, the extent of what they are authenticating is obscure, first, because the identity of 'these things', both those concerning which he has testified, and those which he has written, is unclear; secondly, because, in contrast to earlier testimony passages (1.34; 3.11; 19.34), here there is no appeal to the certainty, behind the testimony, of what this witness *has seen*. Again (21.25) there is an acknowledgement of the many other things Jesus did: the word 'sign' is missing, and if this verse is imitative of 20.30 it has been deliberately dropped, producing a more comprehensive claim. However, the assertion that the writing of books would never be enough to encompass these many other things curiously deconstructs the written text that we have before us, albeit in a different way from 20.30-31. The consequence is that the routine comprehensive claim of the apocalyptic testimony is radically undermined, and no explanation is given for what is written.

It may be debated whether or not these features of Johannine textuality are deliberate plays on existing apocalyptic motifs, or as sub-themes within the Gospel's 'apocalyptic universe', or merely that they have been reconfigured by the template applied in this essay. Nonetheless, their analysis does highlight various points of disjunction or dis-ease, and these are parts of a broader pattern within John's Gospel. They might be

---

42 There is also an *inclusio* with John 1.50 where Jesus lightly rebukes Nathanael who believes because of what Jesus said he saw, and promises him that he will see greater things. For a comparable closing blessing, see *1 En.* 99.10: 'Blessed will be all who listen to the words of the wise'.

43 Regardless of a decision concerning the origin of John 21 there is an intriguing interplay with the ending of ch. 20.

extended to the pervasive ambiguity of Jesus whose revelation both entails hiddenness and engenders misunderstanding. They are perhaps most clearly evident in the role of the *Word*, there from the beginning, whose divine glory is seen in the midst of the becoming flesh, inscribed in the prologue to a text of many words, which, according to the twofold epilogue, recount not what Jesus said, or saw, but what he did.[44]

---

44 On this see Werner H. Kelber, 'The Birth of a Beginning: John 1:1-18', in Dennis E. Smith (ed.), *How Gospels Begin* (*Semeia* 52; Atlanta: Scholars Press, 1990), pp.120–44.

THE READER AS APOCALYPTIST IN THE GOSPEL OF JOHN

Robert G. Hall

Readers will understand John best when their intellects, imaginations, and longings respond most fully to the ideas, images, and desires that John plays upon. John expects readers who can see the heavens opened and angels descending and ascending on the Son of Man (John 1.51); it expects readers who, by the Paraclete, know what belongs to the exalted Jesus (16.14-15); it expects readers who, though they cannot go with Jesus (13.33), nevertheless stand where Jesus is to see his glory (17.24). Such readers must cultivate apocalyptic skill: John hopes for readers who can respond like apocalyptists.[1]

Ἀποκάλυψις refers to the unveiling of something otherwise hidden: apocalyptic readers uncover mysteries;[2] 'apocalyptic' means 'revelatory'. Apocalyptic readers must respond to ancient revelatory literature that reaches out toward what exceeds the power of a human mind to know, and benefits from some divinity bringing the unknowable into human experience. Therefore, the most responsive readers will long to meet the god who offers knowledge and will stretch every nerve to grasp the incomprehensible.

Ineffable, revelatory knowing is not expressed in propositions, but in dreams, visions, proverbs, likenesses, riddles, signs (*h^{a}lomoth, chazoth,*

---

[1] The term 'apocalyptist' carries with it a divergence between ancient and modern worlds. 'Apocalyptists' are simply the readers and writers of apocalypses – and their disciples. The terms 'apocalypse', 'apocalypticism', and 'apocalyptic' are modern and heuristic, convenient for classifying texts and ideas, although ancient readers and authors would not recognise the terms or the divisions they imply. No ancient, artificial line separated 'apocalyptists' from readers and authors of other revelatory literatures; 'apocalyptists' probably wrote and certainly read other kinds of works. 'Apocalyptists' delighted in compositional and interpretive skills similar to those that pleased authors and readers of other revelatory literatures, whether interpreters of Genesis or of Delphic oracles from Apollo.

[2] For grateful pleasure in revealed mystery, see the *Thanksgiving Hymns* from Qumran (e.g. 1QH 9.21; 10.13; 11.19-23; 15.26-28; 18.4-9; 19.7-14).

maroth, məsalim, chiydoth, parabolai, paroimiai, ainigmata, aporiai, semeia) that serve as multifaceted windows into what is hidden. Apocalyptic authors pose revelatory perplexities; apocalyptic readers ponder the shifting meanings, the switching gestalts,[3] that apocalyptic authors provoke. The most responsive readers will train in themselves an agility of mind to leap from insight to insight as they dwell among the turnings of the parables.

The resulting fullness of meaning flourished in the ancient act of reading. Ancient readers not only read for themselves but read out loud for others, and, since ancient writing lacked punctuation and word division, reading out loud required careful preparation and agile study, allowing meaning to form and re-form. In John 17.24, should the reader choose κἀκεῖνοι ὦσιν, 'and those should be', or κἀκεῖ νοὶ ὦσιν, 'and there in mind they should be'? Ancient reading required alertness to possibility, readiness to see one way, and then another. Since books were too expensive to be read and heard only once, audiences may have heard passages read differently in different performances. Therefore, ancient arts of reading and hearing presupposed meditation and encouraged shifts of perspective. Savvy authors took advantage of the agility ancient reading fostered, and apocalyptists wrote mysteries in riddles and enigmas to shift the viewpoints of readers and hearers back and forth – to give them wisdom. Tom Thatcher asks, 'Why did John write a gospel?' Why move the gospel from an oral to a written setting?[4] Perhaps John was written in part to take advantage of the revelatory fullness of meaning a written text, read and re-read, heard and re-heard, could provoke.

1. Mediterranean Revelatory Literature

Responsive readers of ancient revelatory literature require two qualities: (1) readiness for revelatory experience and (2) agility among the riddles,

---

3 I use this psychological term to remind us how perception re-forms as the mind puts visual clues together first one way, then another. As M. C. Escher draws foreground and background so we see first swans then fish, so revelatory riddles invite seeing first one way, then another.

4 See Tom Thatcher, *Why John Wrote a Gospel: Jesus – Memory – History* (Louisville: Westminster John Knox, 2006), and 'Why John Wrote a Gospel: Memory and History in an Early Christian Community', in Alan Kirk and Tom Thatcher (eds.), *Memory, Tradition and Text: Uses of the Past in Early Christianity* (Semeia Studies 52; Atlanta: Society of Biblical Literature, 2005), pp.79–97. Perhaps the revelation in Jesus can only find perfect expression as written in *meshalim* that can provoke meditation as those in Genesis or Daniel do.

agility among παροιμίαι (cf. John 16.25). Greek drama can illustrate readiness for revelatory experience; Greek oracles can illustrate agility among παροιμίαι.

1.1. Readiness for Revelatory Experience

Modern readers seldom remember the revelatory, mystical, almost apocalyptic, stance of such works as Euripides' *Bacchae* or Sophocles' *Oedipus Rex*. Dionysus is the god of ecstasy, as much poetic, dramatic ecstasy as alcoholic or 'bacchic'. At the Athenian Festival of Dionysus, plays drew worshippers into Dionysian ecstasy, into the presence and experience of Dionysus.

Modern readers of Euripides' *Bacchae* thrill with horror as Dionysus inspires the ecstatic Agave to tear her son limb from limb; ancient Athenian audiences, possessed by the god who possesses Agave, taste Dionysus. The play is theophanic; it reveals the god; it entices audiences into his presence and overwhelms them with his power.

Or again, modern audiences are cut to the quick by their unavailing compassion for Oedipus in *Oedipus Rex*; ancient audiences, rapt in the Dionysian ecstasy, see with divine foreknowledge. They see Oedipus as the gods see us, knowing what Oedipus has done and what he will soon discover. Like Zeus in the *Iliad* weeping over his inability to rescue his son Sarpedon from fated death, so they weep for Oedipus. Dionysus has caught up Sophocles' ancient audience, carrying them off to see the view from Olympus.

Properly understood, the *Bacchae* and the *Oedipus Rex* are theophanic and revelatory. To respond to them fully, readers must worship Dionysus; they must yield themselves to Dionysian ecstasy; they must read the plays prepared, willing, and eager, for revelatory experience.

1.2. Agility among the Riddles: αἰνίγματα, ἀπορίαι, σημεῖα

Plutarch, Priest of Apollo at Delphi, quotes Heraclitus: 'The Lord whose oracle is at Delphi neither tells nor conceals but signs' (οὔτε λέγει οὔτε κρύπτει ἀλλὰ σημαίνει, *Pyth. orac.* 404e-f).[5] Elsewhere, Plutarch concludes that Apollo conceals revelation in enigmas (αἰνίγμασι), injecting perplexities (τὰς ἀπορίας) to inspire his worshippers with longing for the truth and to lure them to investigate it (*E Delph.* 2.385c).

---

5   My own translation; for a Greek and English text of *The Oracles at Delphi* and *The E at Delphi*, see *Plutarch's Moralia*, V (trans. F. C. Babbitt; LCL; Cambridge, MA: Harvard University Press, 1957). Plutarch's understanding of the verb σημαίνει, 'signs', closely mirrors John's use of the noun σημεῖον, 'sign'. Both use the root to issue a call to intuit deeper meaning.

In *The E at Delphi* Plutarch reproduces such an investigation. Like the maxims, 'Know yourself' and 'Nothing too much', an E confronts the worshipper at Delphi (*E Delph.* 385d). Strangers, longing to understand what Apollo reveals, find Plutarch to discuss the E. Their dialogue first considers the E as the letter (spelled ει), then as the number 5, then as 'if', and finally as EI, 'You Are', addressed to Apollo himself (*E Delph.* 393d-e).[6] The E has enticed the visitors to contemplate a vision of Apollo more profound than the sun (*E Delph.* 393d-e); they experience Apollo as eternal unity and simplicity, as beneficent ground of being. Plutarch has illustrated revelatory agility among the riddles: examining meaning on meaning for insight on insight, he has glimpsed the incomprehensible. Apollo has revealed himself.

Long before Plutarch, fifth-century BCE Athenians already recognised a pious duty to investigate oracles for concealed insight. Sophocles bases *Oedipus Rex* on obligation to solve the riddles of oracular speech. Apollo reveals three utterances:

> To Oedipus: 'You will couple with your mother, engendering children no one wants to see; you will kill your father, who engendered you'.
>
> To Thebes on the unavenged murder of Laius:
> 'Drive the corruption from the land
> don't harbor it any longer, past all cure,
> don't nurse it on your soil – root it out'.
>
> To Jocasta and Laius: 'Doom would strike down Laius at the hand of a son born of Laius and Jocasta'.[7]

Oedipus, who once saved Thebes by solving the riddle of the sphinx, now must save Thebes by examining the oracles. His duty is clear: to avert the plague, Oedipus must learn enough to punish the murderer of Laius. Apollo's gracious oracles conceal glimpses of truth; grateful hearers will wrestle with the enigmas, working out their hidden meaning as a pious duty.

Socrates refers to an oracle from Apollo that no one is wiser than Socrates (Plato, *Apol.* 5.21.a).[8] Since he knows he is not wise, Socrates is

---

6   Does Plutarch's speculation on εῖ ('you are') reflect contemporary Jewish speculation on εἰμί ('I am')?

7   Sophocles, *The Three Theban Plays* (trans. R. Fagles; New York: Penguin, 1984), 873–5, 109–11, 786–7. Greek line numbers 791–93, 96–98, 713–14; see Sophocles, *Oedipus Rex* (ed. R. D. Dawe; Cambridge Greek and Latin Classics; Cambridge: Cambridge University, 1993).

8   References to the Apology are from Plato, *Apology of Socrates and Crito* (ed. Louis Dryer; rev. Thomas Day Seymour; London: Blaisdell, 1908), pp.50–2.

perplexed (ἠπόρουν, 'I was at a loss ...', 6.21.b); he assumes that the oracle is a riddle,[9] and launches inquiry. When he reduces to absurdity those he had accounted wise, Socrates is simply trying to decipher the gracious meaning that the god has concealed. And he discovers a probable meaning: the wisest know they are not wise. Socrates pursues the duty imposed by the oracle. He cannot be an atheist; he serves Apollo. Plato's defence of Socrates assumes that Apollo's utterance imposes the duty of discovering its meaning.

In Herodotus, Apollo tells Croesus, 'If Croesus attacks the Persians he will destroy a mighty empire'. Croesus attacks, and his own empire is destroyed. The oracle is a studied ambiguity. Croesus failed to consider all sides of the ambiguity; he only saw one meaning. Herodotus plays with the reader, formally exonerating Apollo, but fostering a lingering doubt about the value of oracles. But his fun presupposes the readers' expectation that oracles require careful investigation into every turn of meaning.

Plutarch leads readers in examining the Delphic E, seeking every sense of E or εἰ, adding meaning on meaning, viewpoint on viewpoint, carefully switching readers' gestalts, to glimpse the divine insight that excels human knowing. Well-known works of Sophocles, Plato, and Herodotus presuppose the solving of oracular enigma as an intellectual duty already hoary with age. Whether long before the Gospel of John (Sophocles, Plato, Herodotus) or contemporary with it (Plutarch), Greeks understood oracular speech as replete with meaning. Agile readers must follow every turn of speech, every switch of gestalt, to glimpse what the god discloses.

What of the Barbarians? In the flood narrative from *Gilgamesh*, Ea makes Utnapishtim his prophet and gives him a riddling oracle for the citizens of the city:

> Ea opened his mouth to speak,
> Saying to me, his servant:
> 'Thou shalt then speak thus to them:
> "I have learned that Enlil is hostile to me,
> So that I cannot reside in your city,
> Nor set my f[oo]t in Enlil's territory.
> To the Deep I will therefore go down
>   To dwell with my lord Ea.
> [But upon] you he will shower down abundance,
> [The *choicest*] birds, the *rarest* fishes.

---

9. 'What then does he riddle?' (αἰνίττεται, 'to riddle, to hint', 6.21.b).

[The land shall have its fill] of harvest riches.
[He who at dusk orders] the husk greens,
Will shower down upon you a rain of wheat".'[10]

The oracle depends on double meaning: 'husk greens', a kind of food, also means 'darkness'; 'wheat' also means 'misfortune'.[11] Read one way, Utnapishtim is cursed by Enlil and will go to Apsu, the subterranean waters; Utnapishtim's hearers will get showers of blessing. Read another way, Utnapishtim will weather Enlil's curse with Ea's protection, as Apsu overwhelms Utnapishtim's hearers by showers of disaster. Ea puts a spin on the prophecy that conceals its meaning, but the wise, like Utnapishtim, might fathom it.

The book of Isaiah systematically understands the children's names first one way, then another. *Shear Jasub*, 'A remnant shall return', promises delight to an exiled people (Isa 11.11, 16) or to a people rejoicing over the destruction of their enemies (14.22; 16.14; 21.17), or to a people once rebellious returning to their God (10.20-21), or to a people cleaving to their God (4.3; 28.5; 37.31-32). But to a rebellious people this name threatens: 'only a remnant shall return' (10.18–19, 22); Shear Jasub likewise threatens the whole earth (24.6).

Immanuel, 'God is with us', sounds like a blessing, as indeed it is: 'Band together, you peoples, and be dismayed ... Take counsel together ... but it will not stand, for God is with us – because Immanuel' (Isa 8.9-10). Yet, because of Israel's sin, living in God's presence is death: 'Because this people has refused the waters of Shiloah that flow gently ... therefore, the Lord is bringing ... the king of Assyria ... He will sweep on into Judah as a flood and ... will fill the breadth of your land, O Immanuel – Oh God is with us!' (Isa 8.6-8).

Immanuel shall eat *yoghurt and honey* (7.15) – surely a blessing reflecting the gift of the land flowing with milk and honey? Yet the next verses turn the milk and honey inside out: in a land desolated by Assyria and uncultivated, only yoghurt and honey are left (7.22-24). Similarly, *Mahershalalhashbaz* is the spoil that Israel takes from his enemies (8.4; 9.2; 11.14) or the spoil Israel steals from his widows (10.2) or the spoil Assyria takes from Israel leaving Israel a land robbed and plundered (42.22).

Probably Isaiah does not simply bear witness to the multivalent meaning of the prophet's riddling speech. The turns of meaning, application and reapplication of the revelatory phrases show responsive readers at

---

10 *Gilgamesh* 11.36-48, trans. E. A. Speiser (*ANET*, p.93).
11 Speiser, *ANET*, p.93 n. 190.

work. Generations of disciples in Isaiah's school have illustrated for later readers the correct way of unpacking the turns of riddling, prophetic speech.

Three centuries before Plutarch (190 BCE), Ben Sira describes how to read Hebrew revelatory literature:

> How different the one who devotes himself to the study of the law of the Most High! He seeks out the wisdom of all the ancients, and is concerned with prophecies; he preserves the sayings of the famous and enters in among the turnings of the parables (ἐν στροφαῖς παραβολῶν συνεισελεύ-σεται); he seeks out the hidden meanings of proverbs (ἀπόκρυφα παροιμιῶν) and is at home with the obscurities of parables (ἐν αἰνίγμασι παραβολῶν) (Sir 38.34–39.3, NRSV altered; see also 39.6-7).

Like Plutarch, like the disciples of Isaiah, Sirach assumes that revelatory writing invites inquiry. The Law, the Prophets, and Wisdom express hidden meanings in parables, riddles, and enigmas; therefore knowledgeable readers will press for deeper insight among the twisting meanings of riddling speech.[12]

Genesis can play with the fullness of meaning inherent in an unpointed text. The Masoretes point Hagar's name for God as אֵל רֳאִי (Gen 16.13) but later point רֳאִי as רֹאִי (Gen 16.13-14), ensuring that the reader appreciates the different possibilities. As אֵל רֳאִי Hagar's name implies 'God who gives vision' or 'the God who appears'. As אֵל רֹאִי it implies 'God who sees me', 'God whom I see', 'The God whom I watch', 'God who looks out for me', or 'God who provides for me'. Does she ask (16.13), 'Have I really seen so far in the direction of the one seeing me (רֹאִי)?' or 'Have I really seen this long after the vision (רֳאִי)?' or (repointing אַחֲרֵי as אֲחֹרֵי, 'hinder part of') 'Have I really seen the hinder part of the one who sees me?'[13] or (repointing רָאִיתִי to רְאִיתִי) 'Am I even so far provided for after the vision?' Hagar's well is named בְּאֵר לַחַי רֹאִי (Gen 16.14). Is חַי רֹאִי 'the living one who sees me' or 'the life I see' or 'the one seeing me is life' or 'the one seeing me lives' or 'the one whom I have seen lives' or even 'the life that makes me see'? The Hebrew word for meditation is הָגָה, 'to mutter'. Muttering Hagar's words, first in one set of vowels then in another, first with one emphasis then with another, brings home the sublimity of Hagar's experience.

---

12 Παροιμία, παραβολή, and αἴνιγμα overlap in sense; each might mean 'riddle'.
13 Do not miss the dialogue with Exod 33.23. Has Hagar seen as much as Moses?

Throughout the formative period for biblical literature, whether Hebrew or Greek, whether prophetic or mantic, philosophical or oracular, authors of revelatory literature wrote for readers eager for revelatory experience and trained to seek fullness of meaning. Such authors and texts hope for readers who will meditate on each utterance, investigating every shift of gestalt, every turn of meaning to fathom its insight. Eventually such readers may express their own insight in new παροιμίαι, αἰνίγματα, παραβολαί, or משלים in whatever genre they chose: dialectic, prophetic, sapiential, or apocalyptic.

2. The Apocalypses

Like their neighbours, authors and readers of ancient Jewish and Christian apocalypses were eager for revelatory experience and agile in revelatory perplexity. Apocalypses are stories of revelatory experience; the shattering transformation of Enoch before God's throne (*1 En.* 71) or Salathiel's wrenching conversion of perspective at the translation of Mother Jerusalem (*4 Ezra* 10.25-31) appeals to those who long to experience revelation. As stories of riddles and clues, apocalypses are like books of mathematical puzzles; those agile among their perplexities will enjoy them most. Apocalypses promise to make their readers apocalyptists like Daniel or Enoch, sharing in revelatory experience, facile among revelatory riddles.

2.1. Apocalypses Promise Visionary Experience
Perhaps the strange and lofty experiences of Daniel, Isaiah, and Enoch seem unattainable. Nevertheless, Daniel, the *Ascension of Isaiah*, and the *Similitudes of Enoch* promise readers apocalyptic insight as deep or deeper than their visionary characters can experience.

Though himself a *maskil*, expert among the riddles, Daniel does not understand the revelation given to him (Dan 12.8-9). However, the *maskilim* of the end shall understand (Dan 11.35; 12.10) and shall give insight to many (11.33). Since Daniel must hide the words until the end (12.4), his perplexities are published for latter-day readers. Their insight into the riddles shall surpass Daniel's. As latter-day *maskilim* their heavenly experience shall match his (12.3).

Likewise, the *Similitudes of Enoch* reproduce Enoch's experience. As Enoch learns wisdom on heavenly journeys, so his followers seek wisdom in heaven (*1 En.* 58.5). As God summons Enoch into his presence (*1 En.* 70.1-2), so God will summon them (*1 En.* 62.8). As Enoch can endure seeing God (71.2) only after Michael shows him further mysteries (*1 En.* 71.1-4), so his followers will drink from wisdom before entering God's presence (*1 En.* 48.1). As Enoch becomes pre-existent Son of Man (*1 En.* 71.14), so his followers become the pre-existent stars of their heavenly names (*1 En.* 43.1-4). Like Enoch, readers of the *Similitudes* will walk with God, and they will not be, for God will take them.

Likewise, the *Ascension of Isaiah* seeks to reproduce the experience of Isaiah. The Angel of the Spirit announces that Isaiah's heavenly experiences – and the knowledge that has stretched his mind – qualify Isaiah for final heavenly ascent (*Ascen. Isa.* 11.34-35). But turning to the readers, Isaiah offers them the same heavenly ascent (11.40). United to the glories of heaven by the descent and ascent of the Beloved and by unity with the descending and ascending Angel of the Holy Spirit, the responsive reader becomes one of the prophets, reproducing Isaiah's experience and attaining Isaiah's reward.

Daniel, the *Similitudes of Enoch*, and the *Ascension of Isaiah* are written to make their readers like their apocalyptic heroes. Their best, and most responsive, readers will seek and find revelatory experience; they may even surpass their heroes in revelatory insight.

2.2. Apocalypses Teach Facility among the Riddles
But apocalyptists are not simply visionaries; they are scholars. Apocalypses do not give answers; they pose riddles. They seek game readers, good students, who are eager to test and improve their agility among the enigmas.

2.2.1. Apocalypses Seek Scholarly Readers. Apocalypses describe their heroes as erudite. God gives Daniel knowledge and insight (הַשְׂכֵּל) in books and wisdom (Dan 1.17). Ezra (7.11-12) and Baruch (Jer 36.32) are scribes. Enoch has studied deeply the heavenly books (*1 En.* 81.1-2) and teaches them to his children (*1 En.* 81.5-6). Apocalypses expect readers to aspire to be like the apocalyptic heroes. To be like their heroes, readers must be good students; they must be scholars.

In the *Ascension of Isaiah* not only scribes but prophets are scholars. Isaiah gathers a school; he instructs the prophets and hears them recite (6.4-5). Student prophets have scribal duties: they write down the words of the senior prophets (1.5). When Isaiah opens a heavenly door Isaiah's school invites everyone to hear the voice of the Spirit, but only prophets and scribes, masters and scholars, hear Isaiah's heavenly trip (*Ascen. Isa.* 6.17). Responsive readers of Isaiah's ascent seek to study in Isaiah's school.

Apocalypses often simply assume scholarly readers. Revelation's description of 'one like a son of man' whose 'hair was white as white wool, white as snow' (Rev 1.13-14) assumes knowledge of Daniel 7. By twisting Daniel into an absurdity, Revelation poses a perplexity for the reader who knows Daniel: how can Jesus be both Ancient of Days and Son of Man? But only the scholarly reader will see the revelatory riddle. Daniel 7 itself assumes scholarly readers: to understand Daniel's perplexity, they must know the Baal myth and Israel's appropriation of it (e.g. Ps 18). The best readers of the *Similitudes of Enoch* will contemplate its rich dialogue with Isaiah (compare *1 En.* 48.1-6 with Isa 49.1-10).

Apocalypses regularly presuppose readers who are well-versed in the apocalyptic books. The *Ascension of Isaiah* draws the reader into Isaiah's apocalyptic prophetic-scribal school. Apocalyptic heroes model for readers the life of apocalyptic training and study. Apocalypses expect scholarly readers.

2.2.2. Apocalypses Pose School Exercises. How does Daniel read the handwriting on the wall? In a delightful article, Wolters traces for us the logic of Daniel's reading.[14] Belshazzar and all his court see the letters מנאתקלפרס, but they cannot decide how to divide the letters into words and vocalise them (5.5-9). Daniel reads a meaning so sophisticated that it is at once convincing. Dividing the enigma into three words of three letters each, Daniel pronounces each of the three words three ways: pointed as nouns of weight – מְנֵא ('mina'), תְּקֵל ('shekel'), פְּרֵס ('half-mina') – the words place the court under standards of judgement. Pointed as verbs the words describe judgement's act: מְנָה ('he has reckoned'), תְּקַל ('he has weighed'), פְּרַס ('he has assessed'). The final re-pointing yields מְנָה ('he has counted out in payment'), תְּקֵל ('you are light in weight'), and פָּרַס ('Persia'). But Daniel does not explain all this; he simply hands down a glimpse of the sentence of the heavenly court:

> This is the interpretation of the matter: MENE, God has reckoned your kingdom and paid it out; TEKEL, you have been weighed on the scales and found wanting; PERES, your kingdom is assessed and given to the Medes and Persians (Dan 5.26-28).

---

14 For the following I am summarising Al Wolters, 'The Riddle of the Scales in Daniel 5', *HUCA* 62 (1991), pp.155–77.

Daniel's interpretation remains a riddle,[15] a school exercise. The reader who traces Daniel's reading will have learned to read as Daniel does. Readers should do their homework; the book of Daniel expects readers eager for further training.

Passage after passage poses new exercises for scholarly readers: Daniel rightly understands Jeremiah's seventy years (Dan 9.2, 23), but Gabriel fills the old riddle with one yet deeper, not seventy years but seventy sevens (9.23-24) – leaving the reader to work out new meaning. *4 Ezra* correlates its vision of the Eagle with Daniel's fourth beast (*4 Ezra* 12.11-12), filling Daniel's complex riddles with deeper perplexities. The *Ascension of Isaiah* cites a detailed bibliography, hoping the reader can enquire more deeply into the descent and ascent of the Beloved (*Ascen. Isa.* 4.19-22). Apocalypses do not give answers; they pose enquiries. They do not solve riddles; they interpret riddles by riddles; they fill one vision with another and they expect their readers to do the same. The reason is clear. An explanation simply kills the riddle; it purges the riddle of that baffling shifting of perspective that leads the responsive reader more and more deeply into revelation. Apocalypses hope for readers who are diligent students, who, like their apocalyptic heroes, are at home among enigmas and thrive among their shifting perspectives, who will investigate them and eventually interpret them by writing new riddles.

2.3. Apocalyptic Experience and Training among the Riddles Qualifies Readers to Experience God's Presence

After seeing Jerusalem, Salathiel is stricken by bewilderment. The mysteries have overpowered him. Only when Uriel explains the mysteries is he ready to see further vision (*4 Ezra* 10.28-38, 55-59). When Enoch cannot approach God, Michael shares with him the mysteries of mercy and righteousness, the mysteries of the stars and the lights, the heavens and the holy ones (*1 En.* 71.1-4); only then, though still overwhelmed and melting in God's presence, can Enoch remain before God long enough for beatification. Transformed into the pre-existent Son of Man, Enoch belongs in God's presence (71.10-14). Enoch's training has qualified him for the heavenly court.

In the highest heaven with Isaiah before the thrones of the Beloved, the Angel of the Spirit and the Great Glory, the Angel of the Spirit tells Isaiah, 'I have saved you...and you shall come here' (*Ascen. Isa.* 11.34-35). He explains how he has qualified Isaiah for the heavenly throne room, 'for these are great things, for you have observed what no one

---

15 Wolters, 'Riddle', p.176.

born of flesh has observed...' (11.34). Insight among the mysteries qualifies Isaiah for the heavenly throne room.

The *Thanksgiving Hymns* exult that God gives knowledge: God raises a worm from dust 'to your knowledge so that he can take his place in your presence with the perpetual host and the [everlasting] spirits' (1QH 19.12-13).[16] Revealed knowledge equips the knower to stand in God's presence.

Conversely, even the highest divinities who depart from God's wisdom are ejected from God's presence:

> You were the signet of perfection, full of wisdom and perfect in beauty... With an anointed cherub as guardian I placed you; you were on the holy mountain of God; you walked among the stones of fire...until iniquity was found in you...so I cast you as a profane thing from the mountain of God, and the guardian cherub drove you out from among the stones of fire. Your heart was proud because of your beauty; you corrupted your wisdom for the sake of your splendor. I cast you to the ground (Ezek 28.12, 14, 16–17).

Only the highest wisdom, the most finely trained discernment, only the mind stretched and stretching to receive God's thoughts, can hope to survive them. Apocalyptists dwell among the riddles and stretch for revelatory experience, not simply to gain insight but in order to enter God's presence.

Therefore, the apocalypses seek readers who long for revelatory experience, who will diligently labour among the riddles, stretching their minds around mystery after mystery until they attain beatific vision. How will an apocalyptist read John?

3. John Summons the Reader to Revelatory Experience

As Jesus comes to the Father (John 17.13), he prays, 'I want them to be with me where I am to see my glory' (17.24). And Jesus' glory is the Father's glory, 'Father glorify me with your own glory, the glory I had with you before the world was' (17.5). John shows responsive readers the glory of God; the Fourth Gospel mediates beatific vision.

Another train of inference yields the same result. The Gospel is written to give the reader eternal life: 'These things have been written that you should believe that Jesus is the Christ, the Son of God, and that by believing you would have life in his name' (John 20.31). Eternal life

---

16 Florentino García Martínez, *The Dead Sea Scrolls Translated: The Qumran Texts in English* (trans. Wilfred G. E. Watson; Leiden: Brill, 2nd edn, 1996), p.353.

is knowing God and Christ: 'This is eternal life: that they should know you, the only true God, and Jesus Christ whom you have sent' (17.3). We know God by seeing Christ: 'Whoever has seen me has seen the Father' (14.9). Therefore, the Fourth Gospel shows Christ to provoke beatific vision and give readers eternal life.

The Fourth Gospel also engenders prophetic, revelatory experience: it promises an interpreting angel. The Paraclete announces what belongs to Jesus and reminds disciples of what Jesus said: 'The Spirit of Truth shall lead you into all the truth…that one shall glorify me, for he will take what is mine and announce it to you' (John 16.13-14). 'The Paraclete, the Holy Spirit whom the Father will send in my name, will himself teach you all things and remind you of everything that I have said to you' (14.26). The Fourth Gospel announces what belongs to Jesus and reminds them of what Jesus says. Therefore, the reader takes the place of the apocalyptic hero; the Paraclete takes the place of the interpreting angel; the Fourth Gospel takes the place of the vision.[17] Readers become Paraclete prophets to understand what Jesus says. Like Philo, they must listen to the divine spirit when seeking to unravel scriptural enigmas (e.g. *Somn.* 2.252; *Cher.* 27–29).[18] Like Daniel, they must have 'an excellent spirit, knowledge, and understanding to interpret dreams, explain riddles, and solve problems' (Dan 5.12).

Therefore, the responsive reader will seek and find beatific vision, will seek and find prophetic insight. As apocalypses seek to reproduce their apocalyptic heroes in their readers, so the Gospel of John seeks to reproduce Jesus (14.12; 17.18; 20.21). As apocalypses recount revelatory vision to foster readers' living among the apocalyptic riddles, so John recounts Jesus' παροιμίαι ('riddles?' – 16.29). The Gospel of John recounts παροιμίαι so that the Paraclete can remind readers of what

---

17 This applies to the reader a metaphor more often applied to the Gospel: the Paraclete acts as an apocalyptic-like interpreting angel toward the Jesus tradition yielding the Gospel. See Hans Windisch, *Johannes und de Synoptiker* (Leipzig: Hinrichs, 1926), pp.135–50; Karlis Kundzins, *Charakter und Ursprung der johanneischen Reden* (Acta Universitatis Latviensis, Theologijas Fakultates Jerija 1.4; Riga: Latvijas Universitates Raksti, 1939), passim; D. Moody Smith, 'Johannine Christianity: Some Reflections on its Character and Delineation', *NTS* 21 (1975), pp.232–3; Robert G. Hall, *Revealed Histories* (JSPSup 6; Sheffield: JSOT, 1991), p.234.

18 John R. Levison, 'Philo's Personal Experience and the Persistence of Prophecy', in Michael H. Floyd and Robert D. Haak (eds.), *Prophets, Prophecy, and Prophetic Texts in the Second Temple Judaism* (LHBOTS 427; New York: T&T Clark International, 2006), pp.202–3.

Jesus said and lead them into all truth. The Fourth Gospel is written to reproduce revelatory experience; the best readers of John read like apocalyptists.

3.1. But Jesus Speaks Riddles: 'I have said these things to you in *paroimiai*' (John 16.25)

Responsive readers of John will dwell among the perplexities (ἀπορίαι). As the gestalts shift, they will know that the Paraclete leads them into all the truth among the richness of Jesus' sayings. Can modern readers of John read as apocalyptists?

3.2. John 3.3, 5

Because they are so well known, the puns on ἄνωθεν, 'from above' or 'again' or 'from the beginning', and on πνεῦμα, 'spirit' or 'wind' or 'breath', from John 3 are a good place to begin considering the perplexities of John's παροιμίαι. Consider 'unless one is born ἄνωθεν, one cannot see the Kingdom of God' (3.3) together with 'unless one is born from water and πνεῦμα, one cannot enter the Kingdom of God' (3.5). Understanding ἄνωθεν as 'from the beginning' and πνεῦμα as 'wind', yields an image of re-creation: 'unless one is born from the beginning, born from water and wind [think Gen 1.2], one cannot enter the Kingdom of God'. Understanding ἄνωθεν as 'from above' and πνεῦμα as 'spirit' yields an image of new life in the Spirit: 'unless one is born from above, born from water [water of life flowing from Jesus who comes from above, John 4.10-15] and Spirit [water from Jesus is the Spirit, John 7.38-39], one cannot enter the Kingdom of God'. 'Water' as death (Lam 3.53; Ps 69.14-15), ἄνωθεν as 'again' and πνεῦμα as 'breath' would yield an image of resurrection: 'unless one is born again, born from water [death] and breath [Ezek 37.9] one cannot enter the kingdom of God'. Even yet the fullness of meaning is not exhausted; water might connote baptism or judgement and the senses of ἄνωθεν and πνεῦμα can combine yet differently. The Gospel of John invites readers to delve for meaning on meaning and expects to awaken their insight as meanings juxtapose and gestalts shift.[19] The responsive reader will see the fullness of meaning that Nicodemus missed.

---

19 Compare Richard's suggestion that John *intends* both 'born again' and 'from above'; see E. Richard, 'Expressions of Double Meaning and their Function in the Gospel of John', *NTS* 31 (1985), p.103.

3.3. John 1.18

The conclusion to John's Prologue is frankly puzzling: μονογενὴς θεὸς ὁ ὢν εἰς τὸν κόλπον τοῦ πατρὸς ἐκεῖνος ἐξηγήσατο, literally, 'the only God, who is in the bosom of the Father, that one has explained' (1.18).[20] Explained what? The common translation offers an initial, satisfying solution: 'The only God who is in the bosom of the Father, that one has made him known'. The Father becomes the object of the verb; Jesus does not simply explain him, he makes him known. Now the word ἐξηγέομαι, at its strongest, refers to the leading out of meaning from oracular puzzles! The translations assume that Jesus for our insight leads out the Father's fullness, as an oracular priest leads out fullness of meaning from an oracular saying. Therefore, the usual translation requires a complex series of metaphorical plays. And it is successful: 'make him known' works in the Fourth Gospel. The goal of the Gospel is the readers' eternal life (20.31), and eternal life is to know (γινώσκειν) God (17.3) and Jesus does make him known (14.7, 9).

However, like oracular speech elsewhere, the saying is carefully crafted to shift under the alert reader's gaze. Responsive readers will seek out the change of gestalt: ὁ ὢν translates naturally as 'who is' in 'who is in the bosom of the Father', but it is also the divine name (Exod 3.14 LXX). The verb ἐξηγέομαι, translated 'make known' above, simply means 'to lead out' and commonly takes εἰς, 'into', followed by the destination. Recognising ὁ ὢν as the divine name, 'THE ONE WHO IS', allows a natural translation of the verb: 'No one has ever seen God; the only God, THE ONE WHO IS, has himself led out into the bosom of the Father' (John 1.18). Led whom? Responsive readers, of course (17.24).

A reader trained among the apocalypses will understand this difficult saying as a call to inquiry, will seek one meaning and then another, and will know the Word made flesh (John 1.14) as the one in the Father's bosom who makes known the Father *and* as the one who leads us out into the Father's bosom. Such a reader will delight in both meanings and leave them in dialogue with each other in the hope of seeing more.

3.4. John 17.20-26

Hagar's speech in Genesis and Daniel's handwriting on the wall attest to oracular texts constructing and exploiting ambiguities in reading unpointed Hebrew or Aramaic. Greek has vowels, yet Greek orthography also has ambiguity: early texts lacked breathing marks, accents, and

---

20 See J. F. McHugh, *A Critical and Exegetical Commentary on John 1–4* (New York: T&T Clark International, 2009), 72–73, 76.

word division. Plutarch exploits orthographic Greek ambiguities when understanding E (as a letter spelled ει) first as εἰ, 'if', then as εἶ, 'You are'. Like ancient readers of Hebrew, ancient readers of Greek would have to determine how to pronounce what they read before they interpreted it. Jewish authors familiar with Jewish revelatory literature might well exploit ambiguities in Greek orthography as their ancestral authors had exploited Hebrew orthography. The conclusion to Jesus' prayer – the last of Jesus' last words (John 17.20-26) – offers a stunning array of orthographic riddling.

3.4.1. John 17.21. The NRSV has Jesus request, 'that they may all be one. As you, Father, are in me and I am in you, may they also be in us, so that the world may believe that you have sent me' (John 17.21). This translation assumes pronouncing EN sometimes as ἐν and sometimes as ἕν. Suppose readers choose to pronounce every EN as ἕν, 'one'. Since Jesus and Father is each masculine, ἕν is the neuter noun, better translated as 'unity'. Reading EN as ἕν yields ἵνα πάντες ἕν ὦσιν, καθὼς σύ, πάτερ, ἕν ἐμοὶ κἀγὼ ἕν σοί, ἵνα καὶ αὐτοὶ ἕν ἡμῖν ὦσιν, ἵνα ὁ κόσμος πιστεύῃ ὅτι σύ με ἀπέστειλας, 'that they should all be a unity, just as you, Father, are a unity with me and I a unity with you, that they should be a unity with us, that the world should believe that you have sent me' (17.21).

Or readers might choose to pronounce EN consistently as ἐν, 'in'. ΕΝΩΣΙΝ then becomes the one word ἐνῶσιν instead of the two words ἕν ὦσιν: ἵνα πάντες ἐνῶσιν, καθὼς σύ, πάτερ, ἐν ἐμοὶ κἀγὼ ἐν σοί, ἵνα καὶ αὐτοὶ ἐν ἡμῖν ὦσιν, ἵνα ὁ κόσμος πιστεύῃ ὅτι σύ με ἀπέστειλας, 'that they should all be in, just as you, Father, are in me and I in you, that they should be in us, that the world should believe that you have sent me' (17.21).

The responsive, oracular reader would allow the two readings ἕν and ἐν, unity and indwelling, to fluctuate back and forth as shifting, revelatory gestalts.[21] Only in the balance between 'unity' and 'indwelling' can disciples intuit their fellowship with the Father and the Son.

---

21   The variant ἐν ἡμῖν ἕν ὦσιν (John 17.21) points out the oscillation between ἐν and ἕν. If original, as Brown suggests, the author clues the reader to read EN both ways. If not, some scribe perceived and pointed out the oscillation (Raymond E. Brown, *The Gospel according to John* (AB 29A; Garden City, NY: Doubleday, 1970), p.772). Neyrey also appreciates the reciprocation between 'one' and 'in' (Jerome H. Neyrey, *The Gospel of John* (New Cambridge Bible Commentary; Cambridge: Cambridge University Press, 2007), pp.286–87.

3.4.2. John 17.20-21

Is not 'in me' (εἰς ἐμέ) interestingly placed? Οὐ περὶ τούτων δὲ ἐρωτῶ μόνον, ἀλλὰ καὶ περὶ τῶν πιστευόντων διὰ τοῦ λόγου αὐτῶν εἰς ἐμέ, ἵνα πάντες ἓν ὦσιν, literally, 'but not concerning these only do I ask, but also concerning those believing through their word *in me* that they should all be one' (17.20-21). But the letters ΕΙΣΕΜΕΙΝΑ, understood as εἰς ἐμέ, ἵνα by modern texts, might be εἷς ἔμεινα:[22] 'But not concerning those only do I ask but also concerning those believing through their word. I have remained one (εἷς ἔμεινα); may they all be a unity (ἕν) as you, Father, are a unity (ἕν) with me and I am a unity (ἕν) with you, in order that they would be a unity (ἕν) with us.' Since εἷς is the masculine adjective, Jesus would be making a divine claim for himself: his followers share unity with Jesus and the Father, but only Jesus is ONE (εἷς).[23] Alert readers will allow gestalts to shift between disciples believing in Jesus to share that unity and Jesus abiding as ONE to ask that they share that unity. Of course, knowledgeable readers, recalling the plays between 'unity' and 'in', will remember to read ἐνῶσιν as well as ἓν ὦσιν: as Jesus has remained ONE, so they should remain IN him as branches in the vine (John 15.4).

3.4.3. John 17.23.

Or consider ΙΝΑΩΣΙΝΤΕΤΕΛΕΙΩΜΕΝΟΙΕΙΣΕΝ, usually understood as ἵνα ὦσιν τετελειωμένοι εἰς ἕν, 'I in them and you in me, *that they may become completely one*, so that the world may know that you have sent me' (17.23, NRSV). Remembering that Jesus frequently uses τελειόω of his own completion of his Father's work (John 4.34; 5.36; 17.4) might suggest, ἵνα ὦσιν τε τελειωμέν οἱ εἷς ἕν, 'and that they may be, let us who are one perfect unity'. In context this reading also makes sense: 'And as for me, the glory that you have given me I have given them, in order that they should be a unity just as we are a unity. And that they may be so, let us who are ONE perfect their unity' (17.22-23).[24] Or is it, 'and that they may be so, let us who are ONE

---

22 Compare John 12.34, ὁ χριστὸς μένει εἰς τὸν αἰῶνα, 'the Christ remains forever', where the crowd probably says more than it knows: ὁ χριστὸς μένει εἷς τὸν αἰῶνα, 'the Christ remains one forever'.

23 Bauckham, probably rightly, understands John 10.30 as an allusion to Deut 6.4. Here in John 17.20 εἷς rather than ἕν makes the allusion even clearer. See Richard Bauckham, *The Testimony of the Beloved Disciple: Narrative, History, and Theology in the Gospel of John* (Grand Rapids: Baker, 2007), p.250.

24 The context is friendly to this rendering. Moloney simply assumes that τετελειωμένοι implies that the Father enables this unity and that Jesus, by completing the task the Father set him, accomplishes it; see Francis J. Moloney, 'To Make God Known: A Reading of John 17.1-26', in *The Gospel of John: Text and Context* (Biblical Interpretation Series 72; Leiden: Brill, 2005), p.305 n. 63.

perfect our unity'? Leading out into the bosom of the Father (1.18), Jesus unites with the Father and unites readers with him.

3.4.4. John 17.24

ὃ δέδωκάς μοι, 'what you have given me' – why the neuter? Most translate it as a masculine plural: Πάτερ, ὃ δέδωκάς μοι, θέλω ἵνα ὅπου εἰμὶ ἐγὼ κἀκεῖνοι ὦσιν μετ᾽ ἐμοῦ ἵνα θεωρῶσιν τὴν δόξαν τὴν ἐμήν, 'Father, I desire that those also, whom you have given me, may be with me where I am, to see my glory' (John 17.24, NRSV). The alert reader will inquire into the perplexity. Perhaps 'what' is 'the unity' (τὸ ἕν):[25] 'Father, as for the unity you have given me, I wish that where I am those also should be with me to see my glory' (17.24). Or, knowing that the unity also includes the Father, a reader might prefer εἰμὶ ἐγώ as 'I AM',[26] the divine name, 'As for the unity you have given me, I wish that where I AM is, those should be with me to see my glory'. Or perhaps the reader, recognising that the unity joins Jesus where he *is going*, prefers εἶμι ἐγώ[27] instead of εἰμὶ ἐγώ: 'As for the unity that you have given me, I wish that where I am going those should be with me'.

Consider ΚΑΚΕΙΝΟΙΩΣΙΝ. Instead of the customary κἀκεῖνοι ὦσιν, try κἀκεῖνο ἴωσιν, 'As for the unity you have given me, I wish that where I am going, they – that very unity – should go with me that they should see my glory'. Or noting the accent on knowledge in the following verses and on the possibility of reading δόξα as 'way of thinking, opinion' in the previous verses, a bold reader might see ΚΑΚΕΙΝΟΙΩΣΙΝ as κἀκεῖ νοῒ ὦσιν μετ᾽ ἐμοῦ, 'and there they should be in mind with me'? The resulting interpretation makes sense, 'The thinking (δόξα) that you have given me I have given them…I wish that where I AM is these also should be in

---

25   Compare Urban C. von Wahlde, *The Gospel and Letters of John*. Vol. 2, *Commentary on the Gospel of John* (Eerdmans Critical Commentary; Grand Rapids: Eerdmans, 2010), pp.293, 736.

26   Catrin Williams, whose careful study *I Am He: The Interpretation of 'Anî Hû' in Jewish and Early Christian Literature* (WUNT 2.113; Tübingen: Mohr Siebeck, 2000), qualifies her to speak, tells me that she does not recollect εἰμὶ ἐγώ (as opposed to ἐγώ εἰμι) used as the divine name. She is quite right. Nothing requires that readers hear the divine name in John 17.24; the echo of Exod 3.14 is much fainter with the reversed word order. Yet readers trained to follow puzzles are not looking for what the wording requires, but for what insight it can give. Alerted to the presence of a puzzle by the surprising neuter, readers can try the divine name, especially in the light of such formulaic passages as Lev 11.44-45 (see also Ps 49.7). Perhaps an initial predicate tends to reverse the word order: ἐγώ εἰμι κύριος ὁ θεὸς ὑμῶν but ἅγιός εἰμι ἐγὼ κύριος ὁ θεὸς ὑμῶν (both clauses from Lev 11.44); John 17.24 has ὅπου as initial predicate with εἰμὶ ἐγώ (see also 7.34, 36; 12.26; 14.3).

27   Brown considers this possibility; see Brown, *John*, II, p.772.

mind with me...I have made your name known to them and I will make it known...' (John 17.22-26). Jesus leads readers out into the bosom of the Father to share fellowship, glory, and thinking in sharing the divine unity.

Modern readers' heads should be spinning, but the apocalyptic reader, the reader trained to read revelatory riddles, 'seeks out the hidden meanings of proverbs (παροιμίαι) and is at home among the obscurities of parables' (Sir 39.3, NRSV). The readers that John hopes for will hear the Paraclete's calling to mind of what Jesus said and his leading them into all the truth among the *paroimiai*, the riddles, that Jesus speaks (John 16.25). Apocalyptic readers trained to respond as John wishes will delight in pronouncing words and phrases first one way, then another, and another. Seeing insight after insight, they will allow insights to spark one another, as in the Spirit they remember what Jesus says and see the things that belong to Jesus (14.26; 16.14-15).

3.5. John 14.31

One last perplexity: John Ashton, probably rightly, joins those who argue that John 14 contained the original 'last discourse' and that 'Arise, let us be going' (14.31) originally changed the scene. In its present position, 'Arise, let us be going' interrupts the speech, forming an *aporia*.[28] But *aporia* echoes Socrates' word for 'perplexity' (Plato, *Apol.* 6.21.b), and responsive readers see perplexity as opportunity.

Remember that Jesus has just said, 'I am going away (ὑπάγω)' (14.28), and that earlier he said, 'Where I am going, you cannot follow me now; but you will follow afterwards' (13.36) and that later he will say, 'Father, I desire that those also, whom you have given me, may be with me where I am, to see my glory' (17.24). Apocalyptic readers, noticing how ἐγείρεσθε, ἄγωμεν ἐντεῦθεν, 'Arise, let us be going', interrupts the context, might try ἐγείρεσθε, ἄγω μὲν ἐντεῦθεν. The μέν implies a contrast: 'Get up! I, at least, am going from here [what about you?]'. Or, remembering that Jesus leads out (ἐξηγήσατο) into the bosom of the Father (1.18), perhaps readers would try ἄγω in its full weight: 'Get up! I at least am leading from here, [but will you follow]?' And now, they can hear the original in different perspective, 'Arise, let us be going'. Jesus is commanding them to come with him to the Father. Let it interrupt; no Johannine editor will excise 'Get up; let's go'.

---

28 John Ashton, *Understanding the Fourth Gospel* (Oxford: Oxford University Press, 2nd edn, 2007), pp.16, 106.

4. Conclusion

Readers trained among the apocalypses approach the Gospel of John with minds carefully honed to seek fullness of meaning, turnings of riddles, changes of gestalt. And they are right to do so, for if the utterances of Apollo at Delphi, or the handwriting on the wall in Daniel, or the revelation of Shamash to Utnapishtim employ shifting fullness of meaning to provoke revelatory insight and mystical experience, how much more so the Gospel of John?[29] John constructs sentences to shift the functions of words: God the only son who is in the bosom of the Father makes him known *and* God the only son, THE ONE WHO IS, leads readers out to the bosom of the Father (1.18). John chooses words as perfect puns or rich connotations to shift meaning: ἄνωθεν is 'again', 'anew', 'from the beginning', and 'from above'; πνεῦμα is 'spirit', 'wind', and 'breath'; 'water' is the water of death, of creation, of life (3.3, 5). John constructs sentences to permit intricate realignments in orthography: ἐν, 'in', or ἕν, 'unity'; εἶμι ἐγώ, 'I am going', or εἰμὶ ἐγώ, 'I am' or perhaps 'I AM'; εἰς ἐμέ, ἵνα, '[believe] in me in order that', or εἰς ἔμεινα, 'I have remained ONE' (17.20-26). The Gospel of John writes *semeia* and *paroimiai*, signs and riddles. Responsive readers must know how to read them. The Fourth Gospel expects the Paraclete to lead receptive readers into all truth and to remind them of what Jesus said. Readers trained among the apocalypses revel among the turnings of the riddles; they follow Jesus to the bosom of the Father; they dwell within the unity of the Godhead; they know the only true God and Jesus Christ whom he sent and so have eternal life (17.3). They are apocalyptists; they are accompanying Jesus on his return to the Father (1.18; 14.31; 17.24). And in their careful reading the Gospel attains its purpose, 'But these [*semeia*] are written so that you may come to believe that Jesus is the Messiah, the Son of God, and that through believing you may have life in his name' (20.31).

---

29 Although Ashton and Thatcher use 'riddling' and 'riddle' more precisely than I do, Thatcher's claim that the Gospel of John structures dialogue as 'riddling sessions' and Ashton's understanding that John uses riddles 'to enclose in a box what is to be revealed' as the 'quintessence of apocalyptic' are friendly to this conclusion. See Tom Thatcher, 'Riddles, Repetitions, and the Literary Unity of the Johannine Discourses', in Gilbert Van Belle, Michael Labahn, and Petrus Maritz (eds.), *Repetitions and Variations in the Fourth Gospel: Style, Text, Interpretation* (Leuven: Peeters, 2009), pp.366, 377; Ashton, *Understanding* (2nd edn), p.130.

APOCALYPTIC MYSTAGOGY:
REBIRTH-FROM-ABOVE IN THE RECEPTION
OF JOHN'S GOSPEL*

Robin Griffith-Jones

1. John's Gospel: Midwife of New Birth from Above

'He came to his own, and his own did not receive him.' Jesus' life was, as John would have it, a revelatory event whose significance almost nobody saw. We should treat John's Gospel as a document whose performance in a ritual setting was designed to be a similarly revelatory event. The performance was to engage the audience as vividly and immediately as the person of Jesus had, according to the story itself, engaged those around him; this performance was to bring the audience in their imagination through a new birth from above, by and in which their awareness of themselves and of the world would be vividly and completely transformed. The revelation that had taken place in Jesus had been opaque. The Gospel respected but did not replicate that opacity; the Gospel was to trigger, deepen or reinforce the listeners' recognition of the revelation that had taken place in Jesus. We will analyse both (1) the techniques that John used and (2) the transformation he sought to effect in his listeners' self-understanding. 'As many as received him, to them he gave the power to become children of God, to those who trust in his name' (1.12); it was the due reception of the Gospel itself that would give the listeners this power to become children of God.

---

* This paper builds on the evidence and argument in Robin Griffith-Jones, 'Transformation by a Text: The Gospel of John', in Frances Flannery, Colleen Shantz and Rodney A. Werline (eds.), *Experientia*. Vol. 1, *Inquiry into Religious Experience in Early Judaism and Early Christianity* (Atlanta: SBL, 2008), pp.105–24. I will speak of the author-editor who would have accepted responsibility for the text in its present form as 'John'; and of those people as the 'listeners' or 'audience' of whom this John would say, if asked, that he had hoped and expected that they, above (and probably before) all others, would read or hear his text.

We are stepping back in this essay from the genre of apocalypse and its instantiations. But they remain in view. The life of John's Jesus had been an apocalyptic event, and its re-performance in John's account was to be such an event in its turn. John Ashton's famous maxim about the Fourth Gospel bears re-interpretation. The Gospel's earthbound listeners, exposed to the performance of this 'apocalypse – in reverse, upside down, inside out',[1] were to be baffled, confused and teased into understanding. This was in itself a transformative process, which John invited his listeners to understand and experience as a new birth from above. The transformation undergone by seers who journeyed to heaven was democratised; it was available to John's earthbound listeners.[2] The Gospel succeeded when it redefined its recipients in their own imagination as the creatures of a new creation. It took them in their imagination to a new Eden where they would see – and be equipped to recognise – the Jesus who was at once (1) the new *adam* of this new paradise and (2) the likeness as the appearance of *adam* seen by Ezekiel on the throne (Ezek 1.26). The Gospel, I will suggest, was itself the midwife of new birth from above; it was a tool of mystagogy, cast as a narrative.

2. Leaning on the Breast of Jesus: Origen and the Listeners' Progress

'No one can understand' the meaning of John 'who has not leaned on Jesus' breast nor received Mary from Jesus to be his mother also' (Origen, *Comm. Jo.* 1.23).[3] Threaded through Origen's *Commentary on*

---

1 John Ashton, *Understanding the Fourth Gospel* (Oxford: Oxford University Press, 2nd edn, 2007), pp.328–9.

2 For the transformation of seers, see, for example, Alan F. Segal, *Paul the Convert: The Apostolate and Apostasy of Saul the Pharisee* (New Haven: Yale University Press, 1990), pp.34–71, and Christopher R.A. Morray-Jones, 'Transformational Mysticism in the Apocalyptic-Merkabah Tradition', *JJS* 43 (1992), pp.1–31. For the relationship between mythical and mystical elements in these traditions, and for the motif of death and of return to life, see V. Daphna Arbel, *Beholders of Divine Secrets: Mysticism and Myth in the Hekhalot and Merkavah Literature* (New York: State University of New York Press, 2003), pp.37–47 (drawing on the classic work of Hans Jonas). To the familiar examples of *2 En.* 22.8-10 [J] and *3 Enoch* passim we should add the *Ascension of Isaiah* (late first century?) 7.25.

3 Text: Origen, *Der Johanneskommentar* in Erwin Preuschen (ed.), *Origenes Werke* (GCS 4; Leipzig: Hinrichs, 1903). Translation: Origen, *Commentary on the Gospel According to John* (trans. Ronald E. Heine; 2 vols.; Washington, DC: Catholic University of America, 1989–93).

John are references to the psychagogic progress of the story's characters in which the readers are invited to share. The Baptist 'who testified now sees Jesus coming to him as he continues to advance and improve. The use of the expression "the next day" [at John 1.29] is a symbol of John's progress and improvement' (*Comm. Jo.* 1.257). 'We have found the Messiah', said Andrew (John 1.41); this statement was to be made by everyone who found the Word of God and was ruled by his divinity (*Comm. Jo.* 2.221). We must acquire the ability to hear Jesus' word; 'one cannot hear insofar as he has not yet had his hearing healed by the word of the one who says to the deaf, "Be opened"' (20.164, from Mark 7.34). 'There are some Lazaruses even now who, after they have become Jesus' friends, have become sick and died [from a return to sin], and as dead persons they have remained in the tomb and the land of the dead with the dead, and later they were made alive by Jesus' prayer, and were summoned from the tomb to the things outside it by Jesus with his loud voice' (*Comm. Jo.* 28.54). Teachers are to become Christs in their turn, praying that their voice be heard to summon their lapsed 'friends' back to life outside the tomb of the gentiles' life (28.54-56). Those still too weak to control their souls are bound hand and feet, but thanks to Christ's second command advance so far that they anticipate that even they themselves may become among those who recline with Jesus (28.59-60). Let us, urges Origen, 'do all things that we may be reckoned in his [Jesus'] choice love; for in this way shall we too recline in the bosom of Jesus' (32.274).[4]

In these observations Origen articulates the design of John's Gospel as it was written to be experienced or rather (as we look for a term that does justice to the Gospel) to be *undergone*. The Gospel (I will argue) was not written to expound eternal life, but – in the listeners' own rebirth from above during and through the Gospel's performance – to engender such life and to be its setting. We will find that the climax of this imaginative and cognitive engagement was to be undergone at John 11: the audience, in their imaginations, were to go through the death of Lazarus and come out the other side, and so *pre-mortem* to live out *post-mortem* blessings. The new and eternal life into which the listeners were to have passed would be lived here on earth, and would offer here on earth what mystics sought to see in their *pre-mortem* journey to the *post-mortem* privileges of heaven. In any performance of the opening chapters – whether within a liturgy or within intra-community catechesis or less formally among

---

4 I adduce the readings of Origen, Augustine and others with due caution, wary of plucking apparent analogies from homiletic settings hundreds of years and miles apart from that of the Gospel's composition.

those known to be sympathetic to John's claims – the tone was set by the hymnic Prologue: here, at its start and as a whole, was a *numinous* text well suited to the solemnity of its function. In the analysis offered by April DeConick in a series of works, the Johannine neophyte did not need the journeys offered to and by the Thomasines,[5] for all that is to be unveiled is unveiled here on earth. John's whole subject was mystical. However, the Gospel was not a text about such mysticism; it was itself a mystical text.[6]

John had in mind, above all, those (perhaps principally catechumens and neophytes) who were attracted by the claims of the Johannine churches and were on their way to commitment to these churches' Jesus. 'We' (1.14) were the communities' leaders and established members such as John himself, speaking from the knowledge they already had and were now imparting to John's audience. Nicodemus speaks for a community (οἴδαμεν, 3.2); so, competitively, does John's Jesus (οἴδαμεν, 3.11), with the words of a Johannine catechist.[7] This is not to suggest that at any one time the text was used by, or of use to, just a small group of initiands; to encounter the text in performance, over and again, will have re-enlivened and reinforced its engagement with and impact on the imagination of any listeners. We might envision one example of the changing relationship between text and its audience: those of long standing within Johannine communities who were encountering the Gospel for the *n*th time were likely to become confident – not least thanks to their deepening awareness of John's ironies and ambiguities – that they had been invested with the spirit to which catechumens were hardly yet encouraged to lay claim. Over time the Gospel itself trained, tested and confirmed its own listeners' progress in understanding.

---

5   April D. DeConick, *Voices of the Mystics: Early Christian Discourse in the Gospels of John and Thomas and Other Ancient Christian Literature* (JSNTSup 157; Sheffield: Sheffield Academic, 2001). I have explored the theme in Robin Griffith-Jones, *Beloved Disciple: The Misunderstood Legacy of Mary Magdalene, the Woman Closest to Jesus* (San Francisco: Harper, 2008), pp.55–9, 68–9.

6   DeConick has defined mysticism as a tradition 'centered on the belief that *a person directly, immediately, and before death can experience the divine, either as a rapture experience or as one solicited by a particular praxis*' ('What Is Early Jewish and Christian Mysticism?', in April D. DeConick [ed.], *Paradise Now: Essays on Early Jewish and Christian Mysticism* [SBL Symposium Series 11; Atlanta: SBL, 2006], pp.1–24 [2, DeConick's emphasis]).

7   Marie-Joseph Lagrange, *L'Évangile selon Saint Jean* (Paris: Gabalda, 1925), p.72.

This *imaginative* engagement for which the text called will be the *Leitmotif* of this essay. Such engagement was not a frothy extra to the intellectual business of understanding John's claims for Jesus. The effects of such engagement *constituted* such understanding. John's Gospel was not a jigsaw puzzle of Christological claims, but a drama into which the author, as it were, scripted the audience. Intellect, imagination and emotion had all to be engaged, if the listeners – empowered by the reception of the Gospel itself to become children of God – were to be born into and then to sustain their new identity.

3. 'Let us hear, and let us rise again!' Augustine's Varying Viewpoints

Origen has illumined for us the character of the Gospel as a whole. With this mystagogic effect in mind, we turn to the processes by which John planned to achieve it. Both Origen and Cyril of Alexandria are of further help here. So vivid was their reading of the text that both would extend, in words of their own, the biblical speeches of Jesus and of other characters.[8] They did so with (generally) clear signposts but without great fanfare; this was just a distinctive deployment of a familiar homiletic device.[9] We naturally ask if they and their readers were the heirs to a similar but more striking device at work centuries before in the gestation of the Gospel itself.

The introductory ἀμὴν λέγω ὑμῖν was surely a dominical idiom, but it has long been suspected that the use of ἀμὴν ἀμὴν λέγω ὑμῖν was extended in the Johannine communities to give to the disclosures of Christian prophets the authority of the exalted Lord in whose name they spoke.[10] It can be argued that almost all the Johannine instances mark the climax of a specifically Johannine line of thought and are (at least in

---

8   Cyril composed words, for example, for Jesus; see Philip E. Pusey, *Cyrilli Archiepscopi Alexandrini in D. Joannis Evangelium* (Oxford: Clarendon, 1873), 331d–2a (on John 6.38-39), 418d–19a (on John 7.21). Origen composed words for the priests and levites, see *Comm. Jo.* 6.59 (on John 1.20-23); for the Baptist, 6.162-63 (on Matt 3.11, etc); and for Jesus, 13.14-16 (on John 4.13-14), 32.87-88 (on 13.6-11), 32.156 (on 13.16-18) and 32.169 (on 13.19).

9   For further consideration of speech-in-character, see Robin Griffith-Jones, 'Beyond Reasonable Hope of Recognition? *Prosopopoeia* in Romans 1:18–3:8', in Christopher Tilling (ed.), *Beyond Old and New Perspectives on Paul* (Eugene: Wipf & Stock, forthcoming).

10 M. Eugene Boring, *Sayings of the Risen Jesus: Christian Prophecy in the Synoptic Tradition* (SNTSMS 46; Cambridge: Cambridge University Press, 1982).

their present form) Johannine rather than dominical.[11] As Boring saw, 'the Paraclete-prophet is an interpreter of the historical Christ-event... bringing its meaning home to the present as the self-interpretation of the risen Christ'.[12] The revelations relayed through the Christian prophets expanded the tradition with words ascribed to Jesus himself. If (and for as long as) ἀμὴν ἀμὴν λέγω ὑμῖν was recognised as a prophetic formula, the added sayings reminded their audiences at every performance of the growing deposit of dominical teaching. The abiding presence of Jesus was realised in the ongoing prophecies uttered in his name, incorporated into the Gospel recited in liturgy, and thereafter recognised by their introductory formulae as the Lord's sayings relayed to the community by his prophets. We are back in that mode of address heard in οἴδαμεν (3.11). We need to recognise how *immediate* was the presence of Jesus in such recitation, and how natural the recognition of old and new prophetic and expository material is likely to have been.[13]

As we train ourselves to listen *well* to the Gospel, Augustine is another reader whose sensibilities and agenda can illumine John's. He alerts us to the suppleness with which we should listen to the Gospel in detail.[14] He ceaselessly shifts and manipulates his own – and so his readers' – viewpoint. At times, of course, he stirs an uncomplicated vividness: 'admirantes audiebamus, tamquam magni miraculi spectaculo ante nostros oculos constituto, cum evangelium legeretur, quemadmodum revixerit Lazarus' ('We heard with wonder, as at the sight of the great miracle taking place before our very eyes, when the gospel was read out, how Lazarus came back to life', *Tract. Ev. Jo.* 49.2). But under the

---

11   Victor Hasler, *Amen: Redaktionsgeschichtliche Untersuchung zur Einführungsformel der Herrenworte "Wahrlich, ich sage euch"* (Zurich: Gotthelf, 1969), pp.146–56.

12   M. Eugene Boring, 'The Influence of Christian Prophecy on the Johannine Portrayal of the Paraclete and Jesus', *NTS* 25 (1978), pp.113–23 (118).

13   The need for such re-presentation of Jesus informed both texts and ministry. For the performance of Matthew (framed by Matt 1.23; 28.20), see Robin Griffith-Jones, *The Four Witnesses. The Rebel, the Rabbi, the Chronicler, and the Mystic: Why the Gospels Present Strikingly Different Visions of Jesus* (San Francisco: Harper, 2000), pp.392–4; and for the role of Paul's own person (Gal 1.16, etc.), idem, *The Gospel according to Paul: The Creative Genius who Brought Jesus to the World* (San Francisco: Harper, 2004), pp.243–64, and 'Looking at Paul, Seeing Christ: Transformation Under Way in 2 Corinthians 1–8', in Reimund Bieringer, Malou Ibita, Dominika Kurek-Chomycz and Thomas Vollmer (eds.), *Theologizing in the Corinthian Conflict: Studies in Exegesis and Theology of 2 Corinthians* (Leuven: Peeters, 2013), pp.255–79.

14   Augustine in D. Radbodus Willems (ed.), *In Iohannis Evangelium Tractatus CXXIV* (CCSL 36; Turnhout: Brepols, 1954), pp.419–33.

influence of the exposition, Augustine's readers are no longer merely spectators. In the condition of themselves and of those around them they are to recognise the condition of Lazarus. They are, as it were, to walk through and round the story under Augustine's tutelage, invited at different moments to hear Augustine exhort themselves and Jesus, to address the story's characters, to recognise in Lazarus' tomb the weight of evil habits, and finally to find hope and determination for themselves in the sight of Lazarus' resurrection. Augustine has already emphasised (49.1) that the resurrection lies ahead, at the last day. But the story has a homiletic value for the present that he naturally deploys: 'omnis qui credit, resurgit...omnis qui peccat, moritur. Qui autem peccare consuevit, sepultus est' ('Everyone who believes, rises again...everyone who sins, dies. And the person who has grown accustomed to sinning, is buried', 49.2). Augustine allies to himself his own reader, in the words which that reader will want to say to the obdurate sinner: 'Dicis ei: Noli facere. Quando te audit quem terra sic premit, et tabe corrumpitur, et mole consuetudinis praegravatur?' ('You say to him, "Don't do it". When does the person hear you, the person whom the earth presses down, who is being corrupted by putrefaction, who is weighed down by the mass of habit?', 49.3). Augustine turns to his own readers or audience: 'audite, fratres, audite quid dicat' ('Hear, brothers, hear what he says'). Then he aligns himself with them to urge them on: 'audiamus et resurgamus!' ('Let us hear, and let us rise again!'). Then he prays for them: 'O Domine, istos resuscita!' ('O Lord, bring them back to life!', 49.14). Augustine makes his most startling manoeuvre in connecting Jesus' groans (John 11.33, 37 Vg) over Lazarus with the groans of the individuals who come to recognise their own burial in sin. 'Quid facio? Quo eo? Unde evado? In voce frementis apparet spes resurgentis. Si ipsa fides intus, ibi est Christus fremens...Quam difficile surgit, quem moles malae consuetudinis premit. Sed tamen surgit' ('What am I doing? Where am I going? What am I escaping from? In the voice of one who is groaning appears the hope of one who is rising again. If faith itself is within, there is Christ, groaning... How hard it is for one to rise, who is pressed down with the weight of bad habit. But nonetheless, he rises', 49.24).

We should at least ask if Augustine's paraenetic style, with its vivid and emotive adoption of different viewpoints, some within and some outside the story's world, reveals an approach to the text close in kind to the approach expected by John: an interpretative fleetness of foot that invites the audience both to surround and to inhabit the story, both to assess and to undergo it.

4. Paradise Regained: Engaging the Listeners' Imagination

Particular themes sustained through the Gospel, whole scenes and the ordering of scenes were all designed to affect the listeners' imagination and intellect together.[15] We can start with such sequential, cumulative uses on a small scale. In John 6 the crowd has eaten and has drawn conclusions about Jesus (6.14-15); they actively seek him out. John as ever has his Gospel's ongoing audience in mind: the crowd, asking Jesus about the works of God (6.28), is picking up on a conversation (4.14, 34) at which the crowd was not present – but John's audience was. Similarly in John 9: the blind man has no reason ever to have heard of the Son of Man (9.35); John is inviting *the Gospel's listeners* to make the confession at this stage of the story.

So we turn to the similar techniques that inform the Gospel's whole first half. The calling and confession of the first disciples at 1.29-51 represent Jesus' invitation to John's audience. 1.38-39 is designed to engage the listeners in the disciples' enquiry and in the Gospel: 'What are you looking for?' 'To see where you are staying.' The characters and listeners together are invited, 'Come and see'. Andrew speaks of the Christ, Philip of the one spoken of by Moses and the prophets, Nathaniel of the son of God and king of Israel (1.41, 45, 49). But to acknowledge the titles proper to Jesus did not ensure an understanding of Jesus. It will be Martha, at the climax to Jesus' public ministry and the centre of the Gospel, who will reveal the import of these titles.

Jesus' insistence to Nicodemus was genuinely baffling. John's listeners themselves had to become familiar with the motifs of John's Gospel (motifs which they will have been encountering as well in the teaching of John's churches); those just starting to encounter such motifs were likely to be as confused as Nicodemus. Already in this early scene Jesus promises eternal life to those who trust in him and come to the light (3.15-21). John's listeners were being primed for rebirth.

---

15 How many days or weeks would have been needed for the recitation of the whole Gospel? For the fullest attempt to match the Gospel's performance to the synagogues' lectionary, see Aileen Guilding, *The Fourth Gospel and Jewish Worship: A Study of the Relation of St. John's Gospel to the Ancient Jewish Lectionary System* (Oxford: Clarendon, 1960); for the Gospel as a fifty-day reading cycle (from the start of Lent to the Sunday after Easter), see Michael D. Goulder, 'The Liturgical Origin of St John's Gospel', in Elizabeth A. Livingstone (ed.), *Studia Evangelica VII* (TU 126; Berlin: Akademie, 1982), pp.205–22.

(We should observe in passing that the listeners' relation to individual characters can evolve over the course of the Gospel. Nicodemus is a teacher of Israel [3.10]; John allowed those in his audience who were baffled by John's own claims to be represented by a figure of authority. The listeners will come to see that they have made clear progress where Nicodemus still lurks in ambiguity. He is brave enough by the end to ask for Jesus' body, but expects it to need anointing or even embalming [19.39-41]. Listeners who were once as baffled as Nicodemus can see by the Gospel's end what uncertainties they have themselves transcended.)

'Is there no salvation henceforth?', asks Cyril of Jerusalem.[16] 'We have fallen. Is it impossible to rise again? We were blinded. Can we never recover our sight? We have become lame. Can we never walk aright? In a word, we are dead; is there no resurrection? Will not he who raised up Lazarus, already four days dead and fetid, far more easily raise you?' Such catechesis might serve us well, as we train our antennae to hear more clearly this catechetical Gospel. Jesus tells the cripple to get up (ἔγειρε, John 5.8) and walk; then we hear that the Father gets the dead up (ἐγείρει, 5.21) and those in their tombs will come out to a rising (ἀνάστασιν, 5.29) of life or of judgement. Cyril of Alexandria knows (and resists) the 'common account' of 5.29, that Jesus is speaking here of the present, be it of Lazarus or of 'the dead' who are not yet called through faith to eternal life; despite Cyril's objection, that account was right. What Jesus promises to the listeners at 5.19-28 he will fulfil in Lazarus – and so in the listeners – at John 11.[17]

This imaginative engagement – the reprise of historical scenes – was not a substitute for the listeners' hard work of typological and exegetical assessment. The listeners were being invited by John to redefine themselves as having been crippled and blind and, when they were finally ready to confront the thought, as having been dead and buried; they were in need of a rescue that only Jesus could offer. This was an ongoing and ultimately radical imaginative re-formation of the self. The cripple and the blind man themselves, then, need to be given only small parts to play in the story; they themselves are signs, pointing beyond themselves. The

16 Cyril of Jerusalem, *Catecheseis* 2.5. Text: PG 33, pp.331–1058. Translation: Leo P. McCauley and Anthony A. Stephenson, *The Works of Saint Cyril of Jerusalem* (Fathers of the Church 61 and 64; Washington, DC: Catholic University of America, 1969–70).

17 Bultmann, characteristically, claimed of 11.25-26: 'I venture the suggestion that we are here dealing with a fragment of the discourse used in 5:19ff' (Rudolf Bultmann, *The Gospel of John: A Commentary* [trans. George R. Beasley-Murray; Oxford: Basil Blackwell, 1971], p.402 n.3). Cyril of Alexandria, *Comm. Jo.* 5.25, insists that Jesus is speaking of the future and final resurrection.

healed man of John 5 is soon ignored. The blind man of John 9 is of interest only as the object of, and one participant in, a debate about the consequences of following Jesus.

By the time of the Lazarus story, the listeners were to be ready to hear the voice of the son of God, and so to be born again from above. Here the emotional tone of the engagement intensifies. The listeners could make for themselves and with due insight the confession made by Jesus' first followers in 1.45-49 and now made in the person of Martha: ἐγὼ πεπίστευκα ὅτι σὺ εἶ ὁ Χριστὸς ὁ υἱὸς τοῦ θεοῦ ὁ εἰς τὸν κόσμον ἐρχόμενος (11.27).[18] The listeners were then ready (John 13–17) to join the innermost circle of Jesus' disciples and to hear Jesus' final teachings; they could, through the private dialogues that followed, stay with Jesus as he stayed with them and could hear the words of Jesus of which the Paraclete – the agent of Jesus' work after his departure[19] – would remind them (14.26), not least in their reception of the Gospel itself.

The listeners' imagination, their emotions and their self-definition were being engaged: in the beneficiaries of Jesus' healings the listeners were learning to see and define themselves as they had not before. We will be tracking the path that John has laid out for the listeners to its destination: to their final self-understanding as new creatures with a new Adam in a new Eden on Easter Day.[20]

5. 'I am'

In this pattern of sustained and evolving themes it is time to recognise John's cumulative and purposefully ambiguous deployment of two terms: ἐγώ εἰμι and ζωὴ αἰώνιος. In the use of ἐγώ εἰμι without a predicate, John's Jesus clearly evokes God's self-declaration ἐγώ εἰμι at

18 Jesus' kingship remains to be clarified. Only at John 18–19 will the contrast become clear between the dominion of Jesus and of earthly kings.

19 'Virtually everything that has been said about the Paraclete has been said elsewhere in the Gospel about Jesus' (Raymond E. Brown, *The Gospel According to John* (AB 29/29A; 2 vols.; Garden City, NY: Doubleday, 1966–70), II, pp.1140–1. For the Paraclete as staying or abiding, see 14.17; for Jesus, see 14.20, 23; 15.4-5; 17.23, 26.

20 This is not to deny that there are other cumulative strategies at work. At 5.16, διὰ τοῦτο ἐδίωκον οἱ Ἰουδαῖοι τὸν Ἰησοῦν, the trial of Jesus is under way: Jesus' enemies began to 'prosecute' him. In the Gospel's largest-scale irony, John invites his audience to sit, through the Gospel, in judgement on the judge of all; upon their verdict on that judge depends his verdict upon them. See Anthony E. Harvey, *Jesus on Trial* (London: SPCK, 1976).

Deut 32.39 LXX, and in Deutero-Isaiah LXX, where it variously renders (1) אני הוא (at 41.4; 43.10²¹; 46.4; 52.6 LXX), (2) אני יהוה (at 45.18 LXX),²² or (3) אנכי אנכי הוא (ἐγώ εἰμι ἐγώ εἰμι, at 43.25; 51.12 LXX; add. αὐτός Aq. Sym. Theod.).²³ Catrin Williams has given valuable nuance and precision to this familiar claim.²⁴ In every one of these Old Testament passages the emphasis is on God's supreme power as the only God (dismissing as illusory any apparent competition from other, supposed gods). The term was a declamatory preface to a substantive claim. And it had a substance and weight of its own; it is likely that אני הוא itself was heard as God's own declaration of his sole supremacy, as a statement of the claim that it was used to introduce and mark. For it gives God's own authority to a declaration of the fundamental truth about God. God confirms, as God alone can, what is true about God. The doubling of ἐγώ εἰμι at Isa 43.25 and 51.12 LXX will have invited the thought that one clause represented God's own self-designation: 'I am "I am"'.

The narratives of the LXX introduce some complexity: ἐγώ εἰμι can render אנכי or אני in the mouth of God²⁵ or of a human actor.²⁶ It is hard

---

21   Isa 43.12c-13 LXX omits the end of 43.12 MT and אני הוא in 43.13a MT, and may have been rendering a defective text; at Isa 48.12 אני הוא is not rendered by LXX, but was said to have been recovered in Aq., Sym., and Theod. See Catrin H. Williams, *I Am He: The Interpretation of 'Anî Hû' in Jewish and Early Christian Literature* (WUNT 2/113; Tübingen: Mohr Siebeck, 2000), pp.60–1.

22   At Isa 45.18-19, אני יהוה ... אני יהוה is rendered ἐγώ εἰμι ... ἐγώ εἰμι ἐγώ εἰμι κύριος [om. the repetition of ἐγώ εἰμι, 45.19, א corr; om. κύριος, A].

23   Williams, *I Am He*, pp.60–1. At Isa 42.8, אני יהוה הוא שמי is rendered ἐγώ κύριος ὁ θεός τοῦτό μού ἐστιν τὸ ὄνομα. At Isa 47.8 and 10, Babylon (in self-divinising delusion) boasts אני ואפסי עוד, ἐγώ εἰμι καὶ οὐκ ἔστιν ἑτέρα; contrast God at 45.5.

24   Williams, *I Am He*; previously, David M. Ball, *"I Am" in John's Gospel: Literary Function, Background and Theological Implications* (JSNTSup 124; Sheffield: Sheffield Academic, 1996); also Alan R. Kerr, *The Temple of Jesus' Body* (JSNTSup 220; London: Sheffield Academic, 2002), pp.321–37.

25   The angel of the Lord (assuring Gideon of his stature by the use of this emphatic form?): ἐγώ εἰμι καθήσομαι ἕως τοῦ ἐπιστρέψαι σε (Judg 6.18). So too, God to David, in 2 Sam 12.7 (*bis*, reported by Nathan; v.l. B, avoiding the first), 24.12 (reported by Gad); 2 Kgs 22.20 (reported by Huldah; v.l. B, avoiding the construction); Ezek 36.36 (A). Not all scribes were comfortable with this strange Greek. For discussion and futher passages in Aquila, see Henry St J. Thackeray, 'The Greek Translators of the Four Books of Kings', *JTS* 8 (1906–1907), pp.262–78 (272–3). Thackeray suggests that אנכי once stood wherever ἐγώ εἰμι is such a subject.

26   Thus, Deborah: ἐγώ εἰμι τῷ κυρίῳ, ἐγώ εἰμι ᾄσομαι (Judg 5.3 B). So too Jephthah in Judg 11.27 B (ἐγώ, A), and Jephthah's daughter in 11.35, 37 B (ἐγώ, A); the relative in Ruth 4.4; Bathsheba in 2 Sam 11.5; Absalom in 2 Sam 13.28

at our distance to assess the impact that such a distinctive and specifically scriptural usage had on John or (whether he expected it or not) on his audience. Even usages familiar to us from the New Testament itself may have sounded *odd*, encouraging the audience to recognise a numinous sense in the idiom, for 'the absolute use of ἐγώ εἰμι is not attested in non-Jewish Greek texts'.[27]

Within the Gospels the term's weight varies. It can be a simple affirmation of identity, in answer to a question.[28] Its ambiguity at Mark 6.50 and 13.6 is surely deliberate; at 14.62, for the first time, the term carries patently heavy freight.[29] The term's use in Mark is cumulative; this leads us to ask once more how the Gospel was performed, in what portions, and with what frequency to what audiences. The effect of such a cumulative use of ἐγώ εἰμι, widely spaced through the Gospel, will have changed as the listeners – perhaps already familiar with the idiom and its use in catechesis – grew familiar with its occurrences. We cannot now know what was the setting of the Gospel's performance; but we cannot for that reason blind ourselves to the likelihood that there *was* a performance, whose circumstances and repetition will have affected the reception of such details.

Our own concern is with the Greek idiom in the setting of John's Gospel, used sometimes with and sometimes without a subject-/predicate-phrase. How would it have been heard? Exodus 3.14 LXX dissolves the mystery of אהיה אשר אהיה (Exod 3.14) into ἐγώ εἰμι ὁ ὤν (followed by ὁ ὤν ἀπέσταλκέν με πρὸς ὑμᾶς), readily interpreted by educated Greek readers as a personalised version of Plato's τὸ ὄν. Where Greek

---

(v.l. B, avoiding the construction); David in 2 Sam 15.28 and 24.17 (*bis*); 1 Kgs 2.2; soldier in 2 Sam 18.12 (B; widespread v.l. avoiding the contruction); Joab in 2 Sam 20.17; Shunemite woman in 2 Kgs 4.13 (ἐγώ εἰμι, A, to avoid the construction?); Jehu in 2 Kgs 10.9; Elihu in Job 33.31 (v.l. A, Cod. Ven., avoiding the construction).

27 Williams, *I Am He*, p.11. In classical Greek we would expect ὅδε εἰμι (Aeschylus, *Cho.* 219; Euripides, *Orest.* 380); cf. the question and answer at 2 Sam 20.17: Εἰ σὺ εἶ Ιωαβ; ὁ δὲ εἶπεν Ἐγώ (rendering אני).

28 John 9.9: 'I'm him' or 'It's me'; cf. 2 Sam 2.20 (rendering אנכי); *T. Job* 29.4; 31.6. See Williams, *I Am He*, pp.184–6, for comparable instances in rabbinic literature. The Hebrew *Vorlage* to *Apoc. Ab.* 8.3 and 9.3 will have carried the weight of God's own self-declaration.

29 The revelation to the Gospel's listeners, Mark 6.48-50, was to be as fleeting and cryptic as it had been to the disciples on the lake. Mark 6.48 (περιπατῶν ἐπὶ τῆς θαλάσσης καὶ ἤθελεν παρελθεῖν αὐτούς) reminds us of God's power at Job 9.8 LXX (περιπατῶν ... ἐπὶ θαλάσσης), and of God's 'passing by' both Moses (Exod 33.19, 22; 34.6 LXX) and Elijah (1 Kgs 19.11). For a full discussion (with due weight given as well to Exod 14–15), see Williams, *I Am He*, pp.214–24.

idiom threatened to dissolve mystery, Philo re-introduced it: λέγεσθαι οὐ πέφυκεν ἀλλὰ μόνον εἶναι τὸ ὄν (*Somn.* 1.230, borne out by reference to Exod 3.14); we can ascribe the name κύριος to God, but the noun is not literal here nor is it a proper personal name (i.e. in two senses it is not a κύριον ὄνομα; *Mut.* 11–13).[30]

We should be aware that the oddity and the significance of the absolute ἐγώ εἰμι may strike us more acutely than it struck the Church fathers who had a far better ear than we have for Greek idiom. (Perhaps, on the other hand, the Father's Being was for Greek theologians so obviously foundational that the Son's needed no particular emphasis. Chrysostom could comment simply on John 8.58:[31] 'as the Father uses this expression, "I am", so also does Christ; for it signifies continuous Being, irrespective of all time'). At John 8.24, ἐὰν γὰρ μὴ πιστεύσητε ὅτι ἐγώ εἰμι, Origen read the text as ὅ τι ἐγώ εἰμι, 'that which I am' (*Comm. Jo.* 19.154).[32] Origen emphasises that the greater, and more perfect, expressions about Jesus are relayed only by John (*Comm. Jo.* 1.22): he then cites five I-am sayings from the Gospel, all with predicates; on John 18.5-8 (at *Comm. Jo.* 28.206-208) Origen does not suggest that ἐγώ εἰμι is any more than an ordinary self-reference. Cyril of Alexandria (*Comm. Jo.* 8.24-25) adduces Isa 43.25 – and Isa 1.16; 40.1, 9-11; Mal 3.1, etc. – but neither draws attention to its doubled ἐγώ εἰμι nor adduces Exod 3.14. He reads John 8.54 to mean 'My father *is*'; the son must share in his father's Being; at 8.58, then, ἐγώ εἰμι is unsurprising.[33]

---

30 Echoes too might have been heard (in the predicated sayings) of Isiac aretalogies. See Garth Fowden, *The Egyptian Hermes: A Historical Aproach to the Late Pagan Mind* (Cambridge: Cambridge University Press, 1986), pp.45–52. For texts, cf. Mary Beard, John North and Simon Price (eds.), *Religions of Rome* (2 vols.; Cambridge: Cambridge University Press, 1998), II, pp.297–300. For the gnostic aretalogies, see George W. MacRae, 'The Ego-Proclamation in Gnostic Sources', in Ernst Bammel (ed.), *The Trial of Jesus: Cambridge Studies in Honour of C.F.D. Moule* (SBT 2/13; London: SCM, 1970), pp.122–34.

31 *Hom. Jo.* 55.

32 Marguerite Harl, *Origène et la fonction révélatrice du verbe incarné* (Paris: Editions du Seuil, 1958), p.174 (cf. John 8.25).

33 We might wonder from the insertions of [ὁ] ᾽Ιησοῦς if scribes found ἐγώ εἰμι unsettling at 18.5-8. At 18.5, B reads ἐγώ εἰμι ᾽Ιησοῦς; the scribe saw no significance (or no clear meaning) in the absolute ἐγώ εἰμι; the repetitions in 18.6, 8 were recapitulatory and more straightforward. Again at 18.5, λέγει αὐτοῖς ὁ [om. ℵ] ᾽Ιησοῦς ἐγώ εἰμι (ℵ A C L Θ M) allowed the sense, 'Jesus: that's me'. 18.6 add. ὅτι C M (cf. 18.8) enabled the following ἐγώ εἰμι to be more easily read as a simple reference back to that previous answer.

We should probably acknowledge in John's usage a loosening of semantic boundaries: the mystery or challenge in these terms will, for John's audience, have resided precisely in the terms' *discernment* at the appropriate (and only the appropriate) moments as God's (self-)designation. Such gradual, progressive but enigmatic unveiling of the terms' significance is wholly characteristic of John's revelation of Jesus to the Gospel's audience. The listeners had to sense and *judge* the freight carried by the terms. So the terms' occurrence is a genuine moment of κρίσις for the listeners as they listen.

Jarl Fossum has shown that the Word of John's Prologue cannot be dissociated from the Divine Name.[34] John's Jesus by his death glorifies the Name of God that he had before all ages and that he *embodies* on earth.[35] Did John then think of ἐγώ εἰμι specifically as a *name* – that is, as the divine Name that Jesus bears or is?[36] The Name made flesh is then speaking the Name that reflexively identifies him *as* the Name.[37] If we were to ask for a crisp, clear answer we might miss the point of John's own careful usage. Ἐγώ εἰμι is exactly suited to John's style and strategy: to tease the audience into seeing what needs to be seen.[38] The revelation is in the person of Jesus; the Word has replaced words. And yet Jesus must be recorded and interpreted by words; John, in his own textual performance, is challenging the authority of all texts. It is only and significantly at the *end* of the private discourse that Jesus hints to his

---

34 Jarl E. Fossum, 'In the Beginning was the Name: Onomatology as the Key to Johannine Christology', in idem, *The Image of the Invisible God: Essays on the Influence of Jewish Mysticism on Early Christology* (Freiburg: Universitätsverlag Freiburg; Göttingen: Vandenhoeck & Ruprecht, 1995), pp.109–34. Discussion of the 'name' must be qualified by the recognition that in English a personal name is that by which the person can be addressed. So, 'You are he' in Ps 102.27: ואתה הוא (σὺ δὲ ὁ αὐτός εἶ, Ps 101.28 LXX). Cf. David's address to God in 2 Sam 7.28: κύριέ μου κύριε σὺ εἶ (אתה הוא) ὁ θεός.

35 On the relationship between the Name and the glory of God and their disclosure, see Jey J. Kanagaraj, *'Mysticism' in the Gospel of John: An Inquiry into its Background* (JSNTSup 158; Sheffield: Sheffield Academic, 1998), pp.219–33 (with reflections on the glory both revealed to and hidden from the mystic [pp.222–3]).

36 Cf. Phil 2.9, and Fossum, 'In the Beginning', pp.125–9; idem, *The Name of God and the Angel of the Lord: Samaritan and Jewish Concepts of Intermediation and the Origin of Gnosticism* (WUNT 36; Tübingen: Mohr Siebeck, 1985), pp.292–321.

37 Williams offers a full and careful survey of the evidence for ἐγώ εἰμι as a divine Name in LXX, *I Am He*, pp.58–62.

38 Matthew similarly *challenges* his audience to recognise – and submit to – the divine authority claimed by Jesus for his own teaching in the antitheses of Matt 5.21-48.

disciples that he, in his person and presence, is the name of God that he himself has made known (17.26). Only now does he offer to the listeners the terms in which they can articulate what he, as the Name, has been expressing and has *been* throughout the Gospel.

As in Mark, then, so in John: we should allow for *development* in the disclosure of the significance of ἐγώ εἰμι, through the course of the story and within individual scenes. We must keep before us, as well, the idiom both with and without a predicate. 'I am', says Jesus, 'the light of the world' (8.12); and, seemingly with less freight, 'I am the one bearing witness about myself' (8.18). John then lets Jesus play with ἐγώ and εἰμι, in naturally emphatic contrasts between 'you' and 'we', before bringing them together.

Ὑμεῖς ἐκ τῶν κάτω ἐστέ, ἐγὼ ἐκ τῶν ἄνω εἰμί· ὑμεῖς ἐκ τούτου τοῦ κόσμου ἐστέ, ἐγὼ οὐκ εἰμὶ ἐκ τοῦ κόσμου τούτου ... ἐὰν γὰρ μὴ πιστεύσητε ὅτι ἐγώ εἰμι, ἀποθανεῖσθε ἐν ταῖς ἁμαρτίαις ὑμῶν. ἔλεγον οὖν αὐτῷ· Σὺ τίς εἶ; (8.23-25)

The Jews' question is quite reasonable, and, whatever we make of 8.25b, Jesus does not obviously answer it. He only teases the Jews with a further use of the clause which may or may not be referring back to 'the son of man' as its predicate: ὅταν ὑψώσητε τὸν υἱὸν τοῦ ἀνθρώπου, τότε γνώσεσθε ὅτι ἐγώ εἰμι (8.28). The use of the term itself informs the debate and leads to its climax: πρὶν Ἀβραὰμ γενέσθαι ἐγὼ εἰμί (8.58).

If as exegetes we weigh the significance of such terms verse by verse and reach clear-cut decisions in each case on its own merits – and still more abruptly, if we require a single such significance to be maintained throughout the Gospel – we empty each passage of its function in the cumulative, riddling whole and may be losing the chance of discerning the *process* through which John sought to take his listeners.[39]

---

39 To see such a progression in the use of 'I am' is to ask whether its occurrences *after* the central John 11.25 are not anticlimactic. Here I suggest only that 14.6 should not be read as an imbalanced triptych, whose second and third elements only expound the first. On the contrary: 'the way' is the subject of 14.8-11; 'the truth and the life', of 14.15-25. The claim of 14.6 controls the rest of the speech that once ended at 14.31. 'I am the true vine' (15.1) re-introduces Jesus as the new Temple (a giant cluster of grapes was on the Temple's façade; cf. Josephus, *Ant.* 15.11.3; *J.W.* 5.5.4), the motif which reaches its climax in the prayer of that new Temple's High Priest and victim (John 17). The double statement at 18.5-6 and its reprise at 18.8 is the climax to the whole series of the 'I am' sayings.

6. The Rising and the Life:
First Lazarus, then the Listeners

So we come to the climactic 11.25-26.[40] Here it is the predicates whose ambiguity is part of the challenge and point of the dialogue. Accepting the longer text, we have an expansion of 11.25a in 11.25b-26:

I am – the rising:	[25b] the person who trusts in me,
	[25c] even if s/he dies,
	[25d] shall live.
I am – the life:	[26a] Everyone who is alive and trusts in me
	[26b] shall not die, not for eternity.

Since we will be dwelling on this passage, it will be as well to clarify some of its terms:

(1) '*I* am – the rising and the life'.[41] The articular ἡ ἀνάστασις καὶ ἡ ζωή carries some of the weight borne by the subject of the sentence. Bultmann described the predicative ἐγώ εἰμι sayings of 6.35, 41, 48, 51; 8.12; 10.7, 9, 11, 14; 15.1, 5 as cases of the 'recognition formula', and so allowed such an emphasis: 'The rising and the life – that is *me*'.[42] Later commentators have perhaps too quickly dismissed Bultmann's point; at issue is the sense that a Greek speaker would have heard in the sentences as they were performed. John, as a native speaker, could of course use the distinction without labouring it: John 8.12, ἐγώ εἰμι τὸ φῶς τοῦ

---

40   Discussing the place of the Lazarus story in the Gospel as a whole, we will acknowledge (1) that the story was placed here late in the Gospel's gestation, (2) that part or all of the Jesus–Martha dialogue was inserted when the story was reaching its final form, and (3) that the dialogue's present form owes much to John or to others who had edited the story ('ein Offenbarungswort des johanneischen Schule', as noted by Jörg Frey, *Die johanneische Eschatologie* [WUNT 117; 3 vols.; Tübingen: Mohr Siebeck, 2000], III, p.434) and (iv) that the Prologue was probably a late addition to the Gospel. All of these developments mark the ongoing refinement and reinforcement of the Gospel's mystagogic function.

41   καὶ ἡ ζωή om. 𝔓⁴⁵, Sinaitic Syriac, two Old Latin mss, Cyprian (*Mort.* 21; cf. *Dom. or.* 13). Origen knew the full text; see *Comm. Jo.* 28.71 (where he quotes as well John 5.21; both resurrection and life are germane here). He more often omits καὶ ἡ ζωή: at *Comm. Jo.* 1.47 and 1.54 ἡ ἀνάστασις is all that his argument requires; at 1.22 he has just quoted John 14.6 ('...and the life'). (Origen will similarly deploy only the term he wants from John 14.6: 'truth' aptly at *Comm. Jo.* 20.240 and 245, 28.156; 'way' very aptly at *Comm. Jo.* 32.80.) These are purposeful abbreviations. On the other hand, at *Comm. Jo.* 1.181 καὶ ἡ ζωή would certainly have been apt; at 1.126, 267, 268 it might have been expected.

42   Bultmann, *John*, pp.225–6 n.3.

κόσμου, 'The eternal light [as introduced at 1.4-5] – that is *me*'; John 9.5, ὅταν ἐν τῷ κόσμῳ ὦ, φῶς εἰμι τοῦ κόσμου, 'I am the temporarily residing *light*'.

(2) 'Everyone who is alive and trusts in me shall not die, not for eternity.' Dodd asserts: 'οὐ...εἰς τὸν αἰῶνα is a strong expression for "never"', invoking 1 Sam 20.15; 2 Sam 12.10; Ps 9.19, etc.; '"will not die eternally" is not a legitimate translation. But the expression is perhaps not uninfluenced by the fact that οὐ μὴ ἀποθάνῃ is felt as the equivalent of ζήσεται εἰς τὸν αἰῶνα.'[43] This calls for a response: (i) Isa 28.28 LXX, for example, οὐ γὰρ εἰς τὸν αἰῶνα ἐγὼ ὑμῖν ὀργισθήσομαι, reveals how close to hand lay the meaning 'not...for ever'. In the Gospel itself, John 8.35 undermines Dodd's principle: ὁ δὲ δοῦλος [Ishmael] οὐ μένει ἐν τῇ οἰκίᾳ εἰς τὸν αἰῶνα [that is, he is thrown out, Gen 21]· ὁ υἱός [Isaac] μένει εἰς τὸν αἰῶνα. Within Jesus' promise at 10.28 lies a hint of Lazarus' rescue in the following scene from the death he has already undergone: κἀγὼ δίδωμι αὐτοῖς ζωὴν αἰώνιον, καὶ οὐ μὴ ἀπόλωνται εἰς τὸν αἰῶνα. (ii) On Dodd's own terms, his final concession is important. A promise that believers 'shall live-for-ever' allows some comparable sense to its mirror image: even if they do die, they 'shall not die-for-ever'. (iii) As we have seen, John was loosening the roots of meaning in such familiar phrases, inviting his audience – who knew that they and those around them were still subject to physical death – to ask themselves what Jesus' promise could or must, if it held good, have signified. John's Jesus promises, with deliberate juxtaposition, κἀγὼ δίδωμι αὐτοῖς ζωὴν αἰώνιον, καὶ οὐ μὴ ἀπόλωνται εἰς τὸν αἰῶνα (10.28; cf 4.14); the unfamiliar sense here of αἰώνιος (of a life at once immediately present and inaccessibly future) unsettles the meaning of the following familiar phrase οὐ...εἰς τὸν αἰῶνα.

So we turn to the role of the dialogue in the scene and in the Gospel as a whole. The oddity of Jesus' claim is familiar; but not, I will suggest, its explanation. Jesus challenges Martha to reassess her expectations. He does so with a deliberately riddling ambiguity. John's listeners were confronted here with a double challenge. First, of credibility: Jesus' followers had, by the time of the Gospel's completion, been disabused of any hope or expectation that Jesus would return before the death of his closest followers (cf. 21.20-23); still to believe oneself beyond the reach of death was to believe in a continuity – even if also a transformation – of life through and beyond dying. Secondly, a challenge of consistency: those who are alive and trust in Jesus (11.26) shall not die; how then can

---

43 C. H. Dodd, *The Interpretation of the Fourth Gospel* (Cambridge: Cambridge University Press, 1953), p.148 n.1.

the possibility of death confront (11.25) those listeners who (are alive and) trust in Jesus?[44] One can credit 11.25 and 11.26 together only if 'dying' in 11.26b has an unfamiliar sense; this raises the question whether 'living' in 11.26a has a special sense too; and this in turn casts into question the sense of 'living' in 11.25. Thus, for any listeners not already prepared for these oddities, the senses of 'living' and 'dying' through 11.25-26 become *retrospectively* ever more unsettled. We might see here evidence that the Johannine audience was expected to be already fully versed, as they heard, in such multivalence; but we do well to air the possibility that John is making deliberate use here of a vertiginous ambiguity.[45]

We may denote the dying and death that are defined and constituted by a failure to trust in Jesus by *die* and *death*, and the life and living that are defined and constituted by trust in Jesus, as *life* and being *alive*. Then Jesus might be saying,

25   The person who trusts in me, even if s/he dies, shall *live*;
26   and everyone who is *alive* and trusts in me shall not *die*, not for eternity.

Such a *segue* might seem smooth and felicitous. However, the pairing 'is alive and trusts in me' is arguably pleonastic and wrongly ordered; it must be presumed that anyone living such life has come to it by and through trust in Jesus. Is Jesus, then, reverting at v. 26a to the mundane life which our ordinary death brings to a close? We then have a nice pair of parallel promises:

25   The person who trusts in me, even if s/he dies, shall *live*;
26   and everyone who is alive and trusts in me shall not *die*, not for eternity.

---

44   There is the more mundane reading: that 11.25 and 11.26 are no more than parallel variants on the same claim, that there shall be life after death for those who trust in Jesus; but the life in 11.26a is then confusingly distinct from the life of 11.25d. Along such simplifying lines, it might be more likely that the couplet was originally addressed to congregations expecting that some believers would not die before Christ's return; by the time, then, of the Gospel's arrival at its present form, the couplet's significance will have changed.

45   See Frey, *Die johanneische Eschatologie*, III, p.435, against Bultmann's followers: '[Der soteriologische Nachsatz V. 25b–26] ist – wie alle Ich-bin-Worte – kein "Ruf zur Entscheidung", sondern eine bedingte Heilzusage an die Glaubenden'. The alternatives are not exhaustive; Jesus' promise and question are just one – important – moment in the psychagogy informing the whole Gospel.

Commentators rightly draw out this distinction between *life* and life; but it is arbitrary, at our distance, to claim that John meant one rather than another. And worse, perhaps, than arbitrary: it might well occlude John's purpose in writing as he does. We should allow the possibility that the primary listeners were being trained *as they listened* to discern the analogy and the contrast between *life* and life, and so to see themselves as living both lives at once. The new birth from above could only be lived through, and was in part constituted by, a transformation in self-understanding which the text itself – and the ambiguities in the text's own central terms – would bring about.

If this is right, John was stretching the minds of his audience, necessarily using the terms he had available in order to speak of that for which (as he might reasonably claim) no specific terms had previously been coined. He will use 'death' and 'life' of conditions with which his audience was – precisely in their membership of and catechesis within the communities in which his evolving Gospel was being used – becoming familiar.

At 11.26c-27 Martha does not – despite the expectations raised by ναί, κύριε – obviously amplify her trust in his promises.[46] The dialogue, then, is a climax of a strange kind: Martha interprets Jesus' promise into the more familiar terms already used at the Gospel's start. Scholars ask whether Martha's confession reveals a complete or incomplete faith, adequately or inadequately understood; and they ask in turn how highly John wanted his audience to assess her apparently less trusting sister, Mary. As the early commentators saw, the contrast between the women does matter. Such commentators had, of course, Luke 10.38-42 in mind; so Mary comes out of the comparison well. Origen (*Comm. Jo.*, fr. 80) viewed Martha as ὑποδεεστέρα, Mary (with a virtue Origen will have valued) as χωρητικὴ τῆς αὐτοῦ ἐπιδημίας; Mary is a symbol of the contemplative life, Martha of the practical life, and Lazarus of those who after faith have fallen into sin. Chrysostom (*Hom. Jo.* 62–63) praises the heavenly wisdom of the two women (62.3). Mary, nonetheless, was more fully believing than Martha: Martha when asked one thing answered another; Mary was more ardent than her sister, and was given up only to one thing, the honour of her master. Cyril (*Comm. Jo.* 11.20, 32) interprets Mary as having a more sensitive soul, and as more accurate and

---

46 John took care to bring into close juxtaposition three relationships in which a believer can stand to an object of belief: to believe or trust in a person (πιστεύειν εἰς + acc. pers.), 25b, 26a; to believe or trust a promissory claim which amounts to a claim of fact (πιστεύειν + acc. *in re*), 26c; and to believe or trust a factual claim which involves the believer in a life-determining response (πιστεύειν ὅτι).

intelligent (συνετωτέρα, αἰσθητικετέραν ἔχουσα ψυχήν, ἀκριβεστέρα) than Martha, without Martha's double-mindedness. At our distance, we might hear the distinction differently: the two sisters start with almost exactly the same sentence; from Martha's words, a dialogue follows; from Mary's, the action of which that dialogue has spoken. In place of speech about resurrection and life, Mary's silence is filled with their *enactment*.

The dialogues of dispute have ratcheted up the objections to faith. By the time the Gospel's performance reached John 11, the listeners knew everything, doctrinal and practical, that could be argued against faith in Jesus and – if the performance was succeeding – were ready to make with Martha, and with her understanding, the confession of that faith. The sisters speak for their brother who cannot speak for himself; the declaration of faith precedes the miracle and satisfies the conditions for it. Cyril of Jerusalem taught in his baptismal catechesis: 'The Lord said, "If you believe, you shall see the glory of God". This was tantamount to saying: "Wake up what is wanting in your dead brother's faith". And the sisters' faith, in fact, availed to recall the dead man from the gates of hell' (*Catecheseis* 5.9).

Cyril was, as ever, a good reader; but there is a further step to be taken. Martha and Mary together speak for their brother, and the three siblings together represent an individual listener of John's Gospel. Cyril of Alexandria interprets Lazarus, Martha and Mary in terms of mind, flesh and soul: if our mind – that is, he says, Lazarus – dies, then the corporeal flesh and holier soul must, as Martha and Mary, approach Christ and beg him; and he will call out with the great voice of the Gospel's trumpet, 'Come out, hither, from the distractions of the flesh'.[47] Even if Cyril's ascriptions are too specific – and even if he must give an awkwardly implausible role to his character's different parts – he is right to see, in the three siblings, the entirety of one person. Such trust, displayed by the tripartite unity of the listener, would be *enough* to bring that listener through new birth from above. Such listeners would hear as neophytes the rest of the Gospel, written for neophytes and offering them some account of the life they now led. John 11.25-26, then, is the moment at which the listeners were challenged to accept the consequences of all the arguments for Jesus that they had heard. The listeners had been called

---

47 Cyril (perhaps Pseudo-Cyril; see Maurice Wiles, *The Spiritual Gospel: The Interpretation of the Fourth Gospel in the Early Church* [Cambridge: Cambridge University Press, 1960], p.36 n. 5) 691a, at John 11.44. Francis J. Moloney asked, 'Can Everyone be Wrong? A Reading of John 11:1–12:8', *NTS* 49 (2003), pp.505–27. No; if Moloney is indeed right, then not everyone had been wrong.

to see themselves as among the crippled and the blind and were – now that they should be ready to do so – to see themselves as among the dead. They would now hear, as Lazarus did, the voice of the son of God, and, hearing it, would come out of their graves and be born again from above and from the beginning. John built up the public ministry of Jesus to a mystagogic climax in which John's listeners as they listened underwent in their imagination the raising of Lazarus. 'Awake, you sleeper, and arise from the dead; and Christ shall shine upon you' (Eph 5.14): it was just such a rising that John's Gospel was designed to effect.[48]

Envisioning themselves as reborn from above and as members of the innermost circle of Jesus' disciples, the listeners were then ready for admission to the final discourses: they were to share the ascent of Jesus at John 17, and, with the understanding of initiates, to watch the new creation's completion at the death of Jesus on the afternoon of the sixth day (τετέλεσται, 19.30; compare, at the end of Day Six of creation [Gen 2.1-2 LXX], συνετελέσθησαν, συνετέλεσεν). With the Beloved Disciple they become the children of Jesus' mother, and so the brothers and sister of Jesus, and so the children of God (1.12). The Word came εἰς τὰ ἴδια (1.11), of whom only few received him (ἔλαβον); the Beloved Disciple received Jesus' mother (19.27: ἔλαβεν αὐτὴν εἰς τὰ ἴδια). Reciprocal receiving is at last attained. The other disciples, meanwhile, have been scattered εἰς τὰ ἴδια (16.32); once more the listeners transcend their earlier models.

As Eve was made from a rib of Adam (πλευρά, Gen 2.22), so the blood and water from the side of Jesus (πλευρά, John 19.34) are the fluids of childbirth from which a new creation is born. The allusion – to an inescapably physical and gynaecological process – was rarely and faintly heard. According to Tertullian, *De Anima* 43: Christ's sleep in death was like the sleep of Adam (Gen 2.21), 'so that from the wound in his side the true mother of the living might be symbolised [figuraretur]: the church'. Rufinus, *In Symbolum Apostolorum* 23, comments: 'I think that the woman is indicated in the side through the rib. And so because the fountain of sin and death issued from the first woman, who was a rib

---

48 Clement of Alexandria (*Protr.* 9.84.2) quotes Eph 5.14 with further lines reminiscent of Jesus as the light of the world: '... the sun of the resurrection, the one begotten before the morning star, he who bestows life through his own rays'. Do we have here a baptismal hymn? Alexander J. M. Wedderburn is unconvinced; see *Baptism and Resurrection* (WUNT 44; Tübingen: Mohr Siebeck, 1987), pp.80–2. I make no claim that the performance of John 11 was linked with baptism; but the story must clearly be brought into relation with Rom 6.1-11.

of the first Adam, the fountain of redemption and life is made to issue from the rib of the second Adam.'[49]

The listeners were finally to see themselves in Eden as part of the new world (cf. John 20.1, 11-18), as the light rises on Day One.[50] Cyril of Jerusalem, with his rich typological imagination and his local knowledge, saw (*Catecheseis* 14.5–6, 9, 11-12; 3.1-4; 8.7) the connections between the resurrection-stories and paradise/creation (14.10). 'It was a garden', said Cyril, 'where he was crucified. Though now richly adorned with kingly gifts, it was formerly a garden, and tokens and traces of this still remain' (14.5). Cyril rightly saw further links with the Song of Songs (2.10-14 LXX; 3.1; 4.12-14; 5.1; 6.11).[51]

Mary Magdalene sees the gardener (cf. Gen 2.15). He asks her, 'Who are you looking for?' Mary is on the point of finding what the listeners have been looking for throughout the Gospel (cf. John 1.38); even to search could only dumbfound and never illumine the posse sent to arrest Jesus (18.4). As the High Priest bore the Name of God on his frontlet, so Jesus, the Name of God, is both the new High Priest (John 17) and the sacrifice in the new Passover (19.14) which is the new creation in the new temple that is his body (2.21).[52] The old Adam had been a priest;[53] so is the new. The Temple's sanctuary was designed to recall Eden, the intersection of heaven and earth where God and humanity had once been

---

49 Brooke Foss Westcott, *The Gospel according to St John* (London: John Murray, 1889), pp.284–6, drew attention to both passages.

50 On this, see Griffith-Jones, 'Transformation', pp.117–19.

51 Cyril connected the story as well with Zeph 3.7-8 LXX ('Therefore wait for me, says the Lord, εἰς ἡμέραν ἀναστάσεώς μου εἰς μαρτύριον, for the day of my rising at the martyrion') and Isa 27.11 LXX ('You women who are coming from the vision, come hither; for my people have no understanding'). Cyril pointed out to his catechumens at the Holy Sepulchre that Golgotha, the sepulchre and the stone were all still visible (*Catecheseis* 13.39); he could himself, as a boy, have seen the cave when it was uncovered. See Martin Biddle, *The Tomb of Christ* (Stroud: Sutton, 1999), p.65.

52 For Passover as the time of creation, see the Song of the Four Nights, inserted into Targum Neofiti of Exod 12.42.

53 Margaret Barker, *The Gate of Heaven* (Sheffield: Sheffield Phoenix, 2008), pp.69–70. On Adam's glorious garments as priestly, see Louis Ginzberg, *Legends of the Jews* (7 vols.; Baltimore: The Johns Hopkins University Press, 1998), V, p.103 (n.93). For Jewish traditions that the dust for the formation of Adam was taken from the place of the altar in Jerusalem and that the Temple was built on the site of Adam's grave, see Ginzberg, *Legends of the Jews*, V, pp.73, 117, 125 (nn.16, 109, 137).

at one.⁵⁴ On Easter morning Mary Magdalene sees angels at the head and foot of the place where Jesus had been laid, with an empty space between them (20.12) just as angels flanked the throne in the Holy of Holies of Solomon's Temple (cf. Exod 25.22; 1 Sam 4.4; 2 Sam 6.2; Pss 80.1; 99.1).⁵⁵ The sanctuary is once more, thanks to a sacrificial death, supremely the place of life.

When Mary sees Jesus in this newly created Paradise, she sees him in the sanctuary which he himself – the intersection of heaven and earth, divine and human – *is*. This Adam is not simply the occupant of Eden. He is the figure who belonged between the cherubim in the Holy of Holies, the likeness as the appearance of *adam* on the throne of God (Ezek 1.26); he has left the *merkavah* and walks with humankind in the cool of a new day. The earthbound Johannine neophyte, with Mary, reaches the sanctuary on earth, whose heavenly counterpart was the destination of the seers who journeyed to heaven and were transformed by their journey; the neophyte too, through the reception of the Gospel and the sight of Jesus there, has been transformed.

We have, throughout this essay, kept the likely liturgical use of John in mind. The earliest Greek lectionary system (probably contemporary in origin with the first monasteries) had the New Year start on Easter Day, on which John's Prologue was read. Was this independence from the resurrection stories evidence of a late, formal system? On the contrary: it feels 'early and almost primitive'.⁵⁶ At Easter, through the Word of God, the new creation came to be.⁵⁷ John's audience was to be born again ἄνωθεν, that is, from above, and from the beginning.

The link between Lazarus and the Disciple whom Jesus loved is the link between the listeners undergoing rebirth from above and the same listeners reborn. Lazarus was not a symbol of a renewal already otherwise understood; his rising, undergone by the listeners, instantiated and so defined the resurrection and the life. In the performance of the text we should be exploring and describing, in John's audience, a cognitive and

---

54   1 Kgs 6.18 (Hall), 29 (Holy of Holies; the exact sense is obscure, 6.29-30 is an ancient addition); 2 Chron 3.5-6 (Hall), 16 (Holy of Holies). For emphasis upon the hall as Eden/creation, the Holy of Holies as God's heaven beyond, see Barker, *Gate of Heaven*, pp.57–103. For emphasis upon the edenic Holy of Holies, see Rachel Elior, *The Three Temples: On the Emergence of Jewish Mysticism* (trans. David Louvish; Oxford: Littman, 2004), pp.244–50.

55   Westcott, *John*, 291.

56   Harry Merwyn Buck, *The Johannine Lessons in the Greek Gospel Lectionary* (Chicago: Chicago University Press, 1958), p.2.

57   As the final act in this new creation, Jesus beathes life into his disciples (ἐνεφύσησεν, 20.22) as God had breathed life into Adam (ἐνεφύσησεν, Gen 2.7 LXX).

imaginative – and in John 11 an emotional – engagement that is alien to us now: the story of the raising of Lazarus was designed to realise the rising of the listeners from the dead. Was Lazarus the 'Beloved Disciple'?[58] Yes; inasmuch as both Lazarus and the Beloved Disciple represented John's listeners, his neophytes. This maieutic, mystagogic Gospel has brought its listeners from womb and tomb alike.

7. Life after Death, Here and Now

We have been surveying one small part of John's sustained attempt to convey to his listeners a claim which, so the claim's nature and the world's resistance suggested, was beyond normal human apprehension. John's audience must be taken through a revolution in their cognitive and imaginative capacities; and this was the process which John designed his Gospel to enable his listeners, as they listened, to undergo. This reading of John confronts the modern exegete with some particular challenges.

It is easy enough to spot the patterns picked out in this essay; far harder is to acknowledge and analyse – at a properly critical distance – the process of transformation through which that discernment was intended to lead the listeners. For as exegetes we deal in words: in the cool expository analysis that lays out ('expounds') the meaning of the text. We occupy and map a universe of discursive understanding. Such exposition is not yet doing justice to the text's function: to effect the *re-formation* of its recipients' identity.

There is a danger that the Gospel becomes in scholars' hands a mere puzzle of doctrinal and biographical gobbets to be assembled (as nearly as possible) into a single coherent picture. Exegetes have in front of them the Gospel as a whole, any part of which can be surveyed in connection with any other at any one time; gone is the *sequence* of the scenes' cumulative challenges and disclosures. In their analysis of the Gospel, exegetes study a map; its listeners walked through the terrain. It is particularly striking that John expected his listeners to have to undergo his Gospel and the rebirth it would trigger before they could understand the death of Jesus which opened the way to that rebirth.

---

58   Jesus loved Lazarus; Lazarus was among those reclining with him at the supper of 12.2; and Lazarus had good reason to pay attention to the σουδάριον in Jesus' tomb (20.7, cf. 11.44). Is the anonymous disciple of 19.15-16 the Beloved Disciple? Why then is the identification not made clear? Because his role at 19.15-16 has no psychagogic value.

The text was not self-contained; it was part of the catechetical and liturgical life of a society whose members' social, domestic and inner lives were informed by their membership. We face here the difficulties to which such a text as the *Songs of the Sabbath Sacrifice* notoriously gives rise: a text uprooted from its own performance and from the liturgies, life and shared commitments of the communities in which it was valued. Extended over thirteen Sabbaths, the *Songs*' performance enabled its participants to move onwards each week from the place in the heavenly Temple that they had attained the week before. It is hard for us now even credibly to describe such an effect, let alone to analyse it. We can hope only to pick up and interpret aright the glimpses afforded by the (now lifeless, desiccated) text into such liturgies, life and commitments.[59]

John offers to his listeners the terms – new strength, new sight and new life – in which to recognise and realise the fundamental change through which their growing insight should (as he would claim) be taking them. In the case of Lazarus himself we might well ask if the performance of an actual ritual accompanied and was interpreted by the performance of the text. Pauline baptism focused on the death through which initiands were taken to free them from the death of sin; it is a famously delicate question, how fully they were introduced thereby, *pre-mortem*, to the newness of life in which as initiates they were to walk (Rom 6.4).[60] A ritual informed and interpreted by the story of Lazarus would have focused on the death from which the initiands were raised into the life of the last day; but a death still lay ahead, and the last day was still to come (John 12.48). John, throughout his Gospel, is working to provide neophytes with a *sustainably robust* understanding and experience, *pre-mortem*, of the new life in the new creation, a life whose time within their present body would come to an end in that body's death.[61]

---

59 In 'Transformation', pp.113–15, I explore the analogy between John's Gospel and Reitzenstein's *Lesemysterium*; see Richard Reitzenstein, *The Hellenistic Mystery-Religions: Their Basic Ideas and Significance* (Pittsburgh: Pickwick, 1978), pp.52, 243. Tage Petersen has suggested a similar function for the *Gospel of Judas* in 'From Perplexity to Salvation: The *Gospel of Judas* Read in Light of Platonic Didactic Strategies', in April D. DeConick (ed.), *The Codex Judas Papers: Proceedings of the International Congress on the Tchacos Codex* (Leiden: Brill, 2009), pp.413–34.

60 Col 3.1-3 dissolves the ambiguity (συνηγέρθητε), but admits that the new life is currently hidden. Was it hidden even from those who were told they were living it?

61 Other early Christian texts were written as well to engender, articulate or guide a spiritual journey in the listener. I have explored some of them in Robin Griffith-Jones, 'Going Back to Galilee to See the Son of Man: Mark's Gospel as an

'A woman proclaims Christ to the Samaritans', observes Origen, 'and at the gospel's end the woman who saw him before all the others tells the apostles of the resurrection'.⁶² Once we recognise a pattern of instruction and progress underlying the whole Gospel, we will be bound to notice the prominence John gives to the women of his story: the Samaritan woman, near the Gospel's start, is more perceptive than Jesus' own disciples; Martha and Mary, at the Gospel's centre, lead into the climactic event of resurrection; Mary Magdalene, at the Gospel's end, is the first to see the risen Jesus on Easter Day. We must do justice too to the two appearances of Jesus' mother, both times addressed as γύναι (2.4; 19.26), once at the Gospel's beginning and once at its end: she is a witness to the start of the new creation (the wine of the old had been brought to its purposed end, John 2.3 ℵ*: συνετελέσθη) and to its completion (19.30: τετέλεσται). We cannot here study the sensibilities best adapted, in John's view, for the rebirth and new life to which the Gospel was designed to introduce its audience, but we must put down a marker: the pattern of privileged women is too striking to be ignored.

As I end this essay, I am aware that it has only started the survey of a landscape that needs to be cleared and charted, inch by inch. The tools we need are offered by the study of apocalyptic texts and of the claims made for the transformation of their *pre-mortem* seers in access, otherwise granted only *post-mortem* or post-judgement, to the courts of heaven. If I am right, there lies ahead of Johannine scholarship a large and vital agenda: to do justice to the long-neglected function that informed the Gospel – a democratised, earthbound apocalypse of the figure on God's throne – from beginning to end.

Upside-Down Apocalypse', in Elizabeth Struthers Malbon (ed.), *Between Author and Audience in Mark: Narration, Characterization, Interpretation* (Sheffield: Sheffield Phoenix, 2008), pp.82–102, and in *Beloved Disciple*, pp.109–72 (*Gospel of Philip, Gospel of Mary* and *Pistis Sophia*).

62   Origen, *Comm. Jo.* 13.179. For the Samaritan woman in the exegesis of the gnostic Heracleon, see Elaine H. Pagels, *The Johannine Gospel in Gnostic Exegesis* (Atlanta: Scholars, 1989), pp.86–93. Origen deftly interprets the Samaritan woman as just the Gnostic that Heracleon wants her to be: that is, in Origen's terms, as one of the heterodox that busy themselves with scripture; her sixth husband represented her misguided attempts to be spiritual (*Comm. Jo.* 13.6, 39, 51). For the capacities and roles of Mary Magdalene in gnostic texts as informed by John 20, see Griffith-Jones, *Beloved Disciple*, pp.75–169.

Epilogue

Adela Yarbro Collins

This volume is refreshing in several ways. First, the contributors seem to have little fear of 'apocalypticism', an unfortunately widespread fear that a scholar's canonical hero, favourite work, or the canon in general may be seen to have a significant affinity with a perspective deemed to be bizarre or incredible in this day and age. The courage needed to tackle such prejudices is no doubt inspired, at least in part, by John Ashton's example in finding 'intimations' of apocalypticism in the Gospel of John. The editors also contributed to such openness by putting at the centre of this volume the question of the relation of the Fourth Gospel to apocalypticism and mysticism.

Another laudable aspect of this collection is methodological diversity. Some essays engage in what we may call 'genre criticism', which includes reflection on the genre 'apocalypse', comparison of genres, and notice of the similarities and overlaps that instances of one genre (the Gospel of John) has with other genres and practices (e.g. the genre apocalypse and the practice of initiation into the ancient mysteries). John Ashton, for example, explores the affinities of the Gospel with apocalypses, especially Daniel and *1 Enoch*. Benjamin Reynolds attempts to explain such affinities with the hypothesis that John has 'the framework of an apocalypse'. It is not quite clear what he means by 'framework'. His proposal that John is an 'apocalyptic Gospel', however, is promising.

Christopher Rowland's essay emphasises the revelation of secrets (as a typically apocalyptic theme) and the history of interpretation. Both represent important aspects of his own scholarly contributions and are particularly appropriate for the Gospel of John. Judith Lieu compares the epistemology of apocalyptic texts with that of John and concludes that typically apocalyptic testimony to the true and the real is undermined by the open-endedness of the Gospel of John and its pervasive ambiguity.

The classic apocalypses consist of a narrative account of how a human being, a visionary or traveller to normally inaccessible places, receives revelation from a heavenly being, usually an angel. The revelation in these texts has two dimensions: secrets about the heavenly world and secrets about the future. The Gospel of John is not an apocalypse because it is not that sort of narrative.

In what sense, then, may we talk about John as 'an apocalyptic Gospel'? The Prologue is not really about revelation of secrets. It is about the coming into the world of one through whom the world was made. The proper response to his coming is 'believing through him' (1.7). Those who respond in this way 'see his glory' (v. 14) and become 'children of God' (v. 12). The last verse of the Prologue seems to be anti-apocalyptic, or at least anti-visionary. It excludes the claims of Moses, Ezekiel, Isaiah, Daniel, Enoch, and John, the author of the book of Revelation, to have seen God enthroned in heaven. Yet the one who has come somehow tells about, reports concerning, or describes God (v. 18). In the rest of ch. 1, and throughout the Gospel, the one who has come into the world is identified as the Messiah.[1] A messianic text, however, is not necessarily an apocalyptic text.

The last verse of ch. 1 moves from talk about the Messiah, king of Israel, and (royal) son of God to something more like revelatory language: 'You (plural) will see heaven opened and the angels of God ascending and descending upon the Son of Man' (1.51). The significance of this concluding statement seems to be that Jesus is not an earthly Messiah who will conquer the enemies of Israel and become king of an earthly realm. Rather he is to be a heavenly Messiah, like the messianic figures of the Parables of Enoch (*1 En.* 37–72) and *4 Ezra*. The future tense, 'You will see', needs to be taken seriously. Jesus becomes a heavenly Messiah at the point of his crucifixion, an event that creates a bridge – the image is actually a stairway – between earth and heaven. The conclusion that this verse refers to Jesus' death is supported by the preceding identification of him by John the Baptist as 'the lamb of God who takes away the sin of the world' (1.29, 36). This description of his role foreshadows the allusion to the crucifixion in v. 51.

In ch. 2 the narrative moves from portrayal of Jesus as the heavenly Messiah who has taken away sin to his characterisation as revealer. The changing of water into wine at the wedding of Cana is the 'beginning of the signs' performed by Jesus. The narrator summarises this performance by saying: 'he revealed his glory, and his disciples believed in him' (2.11).

---

1 Adela Yarbro Collins and John J. Collins, *King and Messiah as Son of God* (Grand Rapids, MI: Eerdmans, 2008), pp.175–87, 202–3.

Chapter 3 reprises two of the themes of ch. 1. The statement in ch. 1, 'No one has ever seen God', is taken up and elaborated: 'No one has ascended into heaven except the one who has descended from heaven, the Son of Man' (3.13). Then the ascent of Jesus is defined as his death by crucifixion, 'And just as Moses lifted up the serpent in the wilderness, so must the Son of Man be lifted up' (3.14). This lifting up of Jesus is then explained in a different formulation of the other theme picked up from ch. 1, the saying about the lamb of God, 'For God so loved the world that he gave his only son, in order that everyone who believes in him may not perish but have eternal life' (3.16; see also 11.51-52).

In the dialogue with Nicodemus, Jesus is portrayed as a teacher who tries but fails to lead Nicodemus to the truth. In the monologue that follows, Jesus, also the Word and the Son of Man, is characterised as one who descends and then ascends. This arc of descent and ascent, however, is not linked here, at least not explicitly and directly, to the role of revealer. He is portrayed as a descending and ascending redeemer, in the sense that he dies for others in order that they may have eternal life.

In an interlude, the scene about John the Baptist and Jesus baptising, the theme of Jesus as the Messiah is reintroduced (3.28-29). In what is either a continuation of Jesus' monologue or a declaration by the narrator, the arc of descending and ascending is replaced by the contrast between the one who comes from above and the one who is from the earth (3.31). The focus here is on Jesus testifying or bearing witness to what he has seen and heard, presumably in heaven (3.32), and on his role as one sent by God who speaks the words of God and gives the Spirit without measure (3.34). The one who comes from above 'is over all things' (3.31) and has authority over all things (3.35). These activities are better placed in the category of Jesus as authoritative messenger or delegate of God, rather than in the category of revelation, given the language used here.

In ch. 4 Jesus is portrayed once again as a teacher. Unlike the conversation with Nicodemus, Jesus here gives a limited and veiled revelation to the Samaritan woman about who he is: one who is able to dispense 'living water' (4.10). The woman responds with openness, though not with understanding. She is rewarded by a fuller self-revelation, 'The water that I will give will become a spring leaping up for eternal life [in the one who drinks it]' (4.14). As the conversation continues, Jesus reveals the kind of worship that God prefers (4.23-24). The dialogue thus far may be understood as an instance of Jesus testifying 'to what he has seen and heard'. The conversation ends with Jesus' affirmation that he is the Messiah, which is presumably equivalent to the authoritative messenger or delegate of God, as his role is described in the last part of ch. 3. The account of Jesus' time in Samaria ends with the people of Sychar declaring that Jesus is 'the saviour of the world' (4.42). In light of previous characterisation of Jesus, this epithet may be understood in light of 3.16 – Jesus is the son of God (the Messiah), who died so that those who believe in him may not perish but have eternal life.

In ch. 5, Jesus talks about judgement in two ways. Those who hear what Jesus says and believe in the one who sent him already have eternal life and do not come under judgement; they have already passed over from death to life (5.24; see also 8.51). In addition to this 'realised eschatology', the passage includes the traditional picture of the general resurrection, which occurs in apocalypses and other texts that express an apocalyptic type of eschatology. The 'hour is coming when all those in their tombs will hear the voice [of the Son of Man] and will come forth, the ones who have done good things to a resurrection of life, but the ones who have done bad things to a resurrection of judgement' (5.28-29).

As in the monologue at the end of ch. 3, Jesus is portrayed in the discourse on the bread of life as one who has come down from heaven, in this case, to do the will of the one who sent him (6.38). As in the passage on judgement in ch. 5, realised and apocalyptic eschatology are combined. In the present, all who see the son of God and believe in him have eternal life. In the future, the Son will raise these believers on the last day (6.39-40, 44, 47; cf. v. 51, 53-54, 58). In this discourse the ascent of the Son of Man is also mentioned (6.61-62). It is implied that this ascent will cause offence. The reason is most likely that this 'ascent' is equivalent to the 'lifting up', that is, the crucifixion of Jesus. Thus this saying is similar to the scene described in 1.51, where the Son of Man, by being lifted up or crucified, provides a link between heaven and earth for those who believe in him.

The theme of Jesus' Messiahship, this time as a matter of controversy, appears once again in 7.25-31 (also in 7.40-43). It is connected both with the idea of his being sent by God (7.28-29) and also with the signs that he performed (7.31). Jesus refers to his impending ascent in a veiled way, but 'the Jews' do not understand (7.32-36).

In ch. 8, Jesus again speaks of his departure (ὑπάγειν) but is misunderstood (8.21-22). He then picks up the earlier theme of the contrast between those of heaven and those of earth, this time in terms of those who are 'from below' and those who are 'from above' ('the Jews' and Jesus himself respectively). This contrast is equivalent to being 'of this world' and 'not of this world' (8.23; also 17.14, 16). He then declares, 'When you have lifted up the Son of Man, then you will know that I am he' (8.28). Given the discussions about whether Jesus is the Messiah in ch. 7 (and earlier), it is likely that 'I am he' is equivalent to 'I am the Messiah'.

In ch. 12, immediately following the request of 'the Greeks' to see Jesus, he declares to two of his disciples, 'The hour has come for the Son of Man to be glorified' (12.23). The following two verses make clear that the glorification of Jesus begins with his death. The saying of 12.25, about loving one's life and losing it, as opposed to hating one's life 'in this world' and keeping it 'for eternal life', is similar to the saying in Mark 8.35. If John is dependent on Mark's (perhaps re-oralised) text or on oral tradition similar to it, the idea of Jesus being glorified on the cross may be a substitution for sayings like Mark 8.38, 'for whoever is ashamed of me and my words in this adulterous and sinful generation, the Son of Man will also be ashamed of him, when he comes in the glory of his father with the holy angels'.

In the same context, Jesus goes on to speak about his death. I agree with Loren Stuckenbruck's conclusion in his essay in this volume about the statement, 'Now is the judgement of this world, now the ruler of this world will be driven out' (12.31). It should not be taken to mean that in his death on the cross (12.32-33) Jesus triumphs completely and absolutely over the angelic being who rules the world, but that his death is an important first step in that process.

In ch. 12, the theme of judgement treated in ch. 5 is reprised. Jesus says that he does not judge those who hear his words and do not keep them (12.47). Those who reject Jesus and do not receive his words have a judge: the word that he has spoken will judge such people on the last day (12.48). Here again we find a degree of realised eschatology: Jesus has come so that those who believe in him may not remain in darkness (12.46). He has not come into the world in order to judge it but to save it (12.47). Blended with this description of 'realised eschatology', or better 'proleptic fulfilment' of eschatological hopes, is the reference to a judgement 'on the last day', an expression of one of the last events in the traditional apocalyptic and eschatological scenario.

As noted above in the discussion of the dialogue with Nicodemus, Jesus is presented as one who has descended and will ascend. This movement is closely connected to the death of Jesus, through which those who believe in him receive eternal life. The redeemer does not descend and ascend primarily to convey revelation but to save the world. The situation is similar in ch. 13, the opening scene of the Farewell Discourse. The narrator's introduction to this scene makes clear that his coming from God and imminent return to God centre on his death, which is about to occur through the agency of the devil and Judas Iscariot (13.1-3). The rest of the scene interprets that death as service for others, especially those whom he loved as 'his own'. Once again it is striking that the 'myth' of the descending and ascending redeemer is not a Gnostic-type account of the granting and reception of revelation. He comes to be glorified in a death 'for' others and to give a new commandment that his disciples love one another (13.34-35).

A somewhat more typical apocalyptic theme emerges at the end of ch. 13 and the beginning of ch. 14. Jesus says to Simon Peter, 'To the place where I am going you cannot follow me now, but you will follow me later' (13.36). By way of consolation in the face of Jesus' death, he tells all the disciples present, 'In my father's house there are many places to stay' (14.2). 'I will come again and take you to myself, so that where I am you also may be' (14.3). The brief dialogues in which these sayings are embedded seem to be the Johannine equivalent of the prophetic pronouncement of the Markan Jesus, 'And then you will see the Son of Man coming in clouds with great power and glory. And then he will send the angels who will gather [his] elect from the four winds and from the ends of the earth' (Mark 13.26-27). The Johannine sayings just quoted do not simply predict or promise that the disciples will follow Jesus to his 'father's house', to heaven. Rather, he will come again and take them there to be with him (cf. 1 Thess 4.17-18, also in a context of consolation).

Another possibly apocalyptic motif occurs near the end of the monologue that concludes ch. 14, 'I will no longer speak much with you, for the ruler of the world is coming' (v. 30).[2] This ruler is probably an angelic being, equivalent to 'the devil' mentioned in 13.2. It is not clear that the devil is a rebel who has seized power that belongs to God. He may be understood here rather as a being to whom God has given power over the world, at least for a time. Although he 'has nothing in [Jesus]', the Son submits to him in obedience to the Father (14.30-31).

'The ruler of the world', however, has apparently not carried out his duties appropriately, as becomes apparent with the announcement that 'the ruler of this world is judged (or exposed, convicted, or rebuked)' (16.11). It is not clear whether this is an event performed by the Paraclete, the Advocate, or a state of affairs brought to light by him. If the latter, perhaps the 'conviction' takes place as a consequence of Jesus' death.

In the same part of the Farewell Discourse, Jesus says to the disciples, 'A little while and you will no longer see me, and again a little while and you will see me' (16.16). The disciples connect what Jesus has just said

---

2   This saying takes up the one in 12.31; see the discussion above and the essay by Loren Stuckenbruck in this volume.

with his previous statement, 'I am going to the father', but otherwise they do not understand. In the following monologue, Jesus clarifies his statement about the 'little while'. He tells them that they are experiencing pain now, but 'I will see you again, and your hearts will rejoice and no one will take your joy from you' (v. 22).

Jesus illustrates the contrast of pain and joy with the pain a woman feels in labour and the joy she feels at the birth of her child. This image, as well as language about 'a little while', suggests that the topic is the return of Christ at the parousia. In the narrative of John, however, Jesus does see his disciples again, a little while after his death, when he has risen from the dead (20.19-23). In the account of that scene, the narrator remarks, 'The disciples rejoiced when they saw the Lord' (v. 20). That narrative development suggests that the monologue in ch. 16 interprets the tradition about the imminent coming of Christ in terms of realised eschatology: Jesus has come in the resurrection appearances. The ending of the relevant part of that monologue supports this reading (16.23-24). At that point Jesus says, 'On that day you will ask nothing of me. Truly, truly, I say to you, if you ask the father for something in my name, he will give it to you. Until now you have asked for nothing in my name; ask and you will receive, in order that your joy may be complete.' These sayings seem to imply that the status of the disciples will be different after the resurrection. Then they may ask in the name of Jesus and will receive a positive response. The present imperative in v. 24 especially indicates that the new situation applies to their ongoing life in the world after the resurrection of Jesus and before the return of Jesus, which is mentioned in 14.3.

The first part of the prayer in ch. 17 further supports the argument that the speech in 16.16-24 presents a proleptic fulfilment of eschatological hopes. Eternal life, which God gave the Son authority to grant, is defined as knowing God and Jesus Christ (17.3). The glorification of the Son is interpreted as the glory he will have after the resurrection, which is the same glory he had before descending into the world (v. 5). The prayer, however, also seems to refer to a future eschatological fulfilment, 'Father, I want those whom you have given me to be with me where I am [going] and see my glory, which you have given me because you loved me before the foundation of the world' (17.24). This saying, in isolation, is open to a reading that supposes the disciples will see Jesus in his glory when they die and individually ascend to heaven. In light of 14.3, however, the saying is better read in terms of an eventual parousia of Jesus: 'I will come again and take you to myself'.

The Gospel of John does not have the typically apocalyptic narrative framework. It does, however, presuppose apocalyptic tradition. The author includes and maintains certain apocalyptic expectations, such as resurrection and judgement on the last day and the return of Christ to gather the elect. It is the proleptic fulfilment of these expectations, however, that the Gospel emphasises. Expressions of such (partial) fulfilments characterise this Gospel's distinctive employment of apocalyptic-eschatological traditions. A close reading reveals that the themes of revelation and Jesus as revealer are less dominant than Rudolf Bultmann, for example, supposed.[3] While it seems appropriate to say that John is an apocalyptic Gospel, it is much less so than Mark and Matthew.

I would like to close with an expression of gratitude to John Ashton for initiating the current conversation about John and apocalypticism. I would also like to thank Christopher Rowland and Catrin Williams for hosting the conference at which the essays in this volume were presented and for asking me to write an epilogue to it.

---

3   John 2.11; 4.7-26. Rudolf Bultmann, *The Gospel of John: A Commentary* (Philadelphia: Westminster, 1971 from the 1964 German ed. and the 1966 Supplement).

Indices

Index of References

Hebrew Bible/ Old Testament		33.17–34.9	249	*Judges*	
		33.19	285	5.3	284
Genesis		33.22	285	6.18	284
1.2	267	33.23	260	10.15	211
1.28	222	34.6	285	11.27	284
2–9	29	40.34	96	11.35	284
2.1-2	294				
2.7	296	*Leviticus*		*Ruth*	
2.15	295	11.44-45	271	4.4	284
2.21	294	11.44	271		
2.22	294	26.11-12	100, 101	*1 Samuel*	
9.1	222	26.12	92	2.6	135
9.7	222			4.4	296
10–36	30	*Numbers*		12.10	211
16.13-14	260	6.24	204, 210, 212	20.15	290
16.13	260				
16.14	260	9.12	126	*2 Samuel*	
21	290	21.8	247	6.2	296
32.11	211	22.22	217	7.28	287
		22.32	217	11.5	284
Exodus				12.7	284
3.14	271, 268, 285, 286	*Deuteronomy*		12.10	290
		4.6	27	13.28	284
12.10	126	4.8	27	15.28	285
12.42	295	4.11-12	27	18.12	285
12.46	126	4.15-16	27	20.17	285
14–15	285	6.4	270	20.20	285
16.4	126, 247	12.11	88	24.12	284
19.16	133	13.1-5	196	24.17	285
19.17	92	14.23	88		
19.20	92	16.2	88	*1 Kings*	
24.9-10	26	16.6	88	2.2	285
25–40	96	16.11	88	6.12-13	89
25	141	26.2	88	6.18	296
25.8	89	29.29	26	6.29-30	296
25.20-22	141	30.11-14	26	6.29	296
25.22	296	32.16-17	226	8.12	88
29	89	32.39	126, 284	8.31-51	88
29.43-46	89			8.39	89
29.45	100	*Joshua*		8.43	89
31.18	140	2.13	211	8.49	89
33–34	94			11.23	217

11.25	217	17.40-43	69	143.9	211
19.11	285	18	263	144.7	211
22.6	196	22.20	211	144.11	211
22.13	196	25.20	211	*Song of Songs*	
		27.12	211	2.10-14	295
2 Kings		31.1-2	211	3.1	295
4.13	285	31.15	211	4.12-14	295
10.9	285	33.31 LXX	126	5.1	295
21.14	211	34.31	126	6.1	295
22.20	284	39.8	211		
		40.13	211	*Isaiah*	
1 Chronicles		43.1	211	1.16	286
3.5-6	296	51.14	211	4.3	259
3.16	296	59.1-2	211	7.15	259
4.10	210, 212	69.14-15	267	7.22-24	259
6.36	211	69.14	211	8.4	259
16.35	211	69.18	211	8.6-8	259
		70.1	211	8.9-10	259
2 Chronicles		71.2	211	9.2	259
7.7	120	71.4	211	10.2	259
		71.13	217	10.18-19	259
Ezra		74.2	88	10.20-21	259
6.12	88	77.24 LXX	126, 247	10.22	259
7.11-12	262	78.24	126, 247	11.11	259
		79	13	11.14	259
Nehemiah		79.9	211	11.16	259
1.9	88	80	13	14.4-21	194
9.15	247	80.1	296	14.12	184
		82.4	211	14.22	259
Job		95.5	226	16.14	259
1–2	217	96.5	226	21.17	259
1.1	130	99.1	296	24.6	259
2	130	101.28	287	25.8	99
4.12-13	131	102.27	287	26.19	126
9.8	285	105.37 LXX	226	27.11	295
28	28	106.37	226	28.5	259
32.8	131	109.6	217	28.28	290
33.15	131	109.20	217	37.31-32	259
33.31	285	109.29	217	38.18-19	215
38–41	131, 133	116.4	211	40–55	124
42.5	130, 131, 134, 135	119	219, 220	40.1	286
		119.133	220	40.9-11	286
42.10	130	119.133b	219	40.11	68
		119.134	211	40.21	125
Psalms		119.170	211	41.4	126, 284
2	68	120.2	211	41.23	124, 125
6.4-5	215	121.7	211, 212	41.26	124, 125
6.4	211	135	90	42.8	284
9.19	290	140.1	211	42.22	259
17.13	211	142.6	211	43.9	124, 125

Index of References

Isaiah (cont.)		37	101	2.45	117		
43.10	126, 284	37.9	267	2.47	17, 20,		
43.12	124, 284	37.27	100, 101		117		
43.13	284	38.12	265	3	16		
43.19	99	38.14	265	3.25	17		
43.25	284, 286	38.16	265	3.33	17		
44.7	124, 125	38.17	265	4	16		
44.17	211	40–48	90, 99	4.2-3	17		
45.18-19	284	43.1-11	88	4.8	117		
45.18	284	43.7	88, 100,	4.34-35	17		
45.19	125, 284		101	5	17, 117		
46.4	126, 284	43.9	88, 100	5.5-9	263		
46.10	124	47	97	5.7	16		
47.8	284			5.8	16		
47.10	284	*Daniel*		5.12	117, 118,		
47.13	124	1.4	20		266		
48.3	124	1.17	262	5.15-17	16		
48.5	124	1.20	15	5.15	118		
48.12	284	2	15, 16, 19,	5.26-28	263		
48.14	124		116, 117,	6	17, 19		
49.1-10	263		125	6.22	17		
51.12	126, 284	2.2	16, 115,	6.26	17		
52.1	99		116, 118,	7–12	13, 118		
52.6	284		119	7–8	118, 119		
53.1	7	2.2	115	7	13, 17, 18,		
55.1	71	2.4	16, 115–		194, 263		
61.5	99		17	7.9-12	43		
61.10	99	2.5	116	7.9-10	17		
65.11	226	2.6	116	7.13-14	17, 125		
65.17	99	2.6	115	7.15	17		
66.22	99	2.7	115–17	7.16-28	106		
		2.9	115–17	7.16	17, 20		
Jeremiah		2.11	16, 115,	7.17	17, 18		
7.12	88		116	7.21-22	18		
25.11-12	118	2.16	115–17	7.25	18		
29.10	118	2.19-23	118	7.27	18		
		2.19	117	8–9	119		
Lamentations		2.20-22	17	8.1	18		
7.38-39	267	2.22	20, 117	8.15-26	43, 106		
		2.24	115–17	8.15-17	20		
Ezekiel		2.25	115–17	8.16	119		
1	76, 133	2.26	115–17	8.17	18		
1.26	275, 296	2.27-29	116	8.20-21	18		
2.8–3.3	243	2.27	16, 115,	8.23-25	18		
3.26-28	91		116	8.26	18		
16.11-13	100	2.28	16, 117	9	19, 118,		
34.30	100	2.29	16, 117		125		
36.28	100	2.30	117, 118	9.2	264		
36.32	262	2.31-35	15	9.3-4	239		
36.36	284	2.44	16	9.13	125		

Index of References

9.20-23	20	*Zephaniah*		*Baruch*	
9.23-24	264	3.7-8	295	3.37	28
9.23	107, 118–			3.38 LXX	28
	20, 123,	*Zechariah*		4.1	28
	125, 264	1.9	119	4.7	226
9.24-27	119	1.14	119		
10–12	119	1.19	119	*2 Maccabees*	
10	48	2.10-11	90	1.25	211, 212
10.10-21	20, 183	2.10-11	100, 101	14.35	93
10.12-14	119	2.14-15	100		
10.13	48, 205	2.14-15	90	NEW TESTAMENT	
10.14	19	3.1-2	217	*Matthew*	
10.21–11.1	23	8.3	90	1.23	279
10.21	19, 107,	8.8	90	3.1	150
	118–20,	13.2	216	3.11	278
	123, 125,			3.16	177, 248
	205, 243	*Malachi*		4.17	60
10.59	119	3.1	286	5.21-48	287
11.2–12.13	119			5.37	210
11.2	19, 107,	APOCRYPHA		6.13	210, 229
	118–20,	*Tobit*		7.18	164
	123, 125	12.19	45	8.31	186
11.30	19			9.34	183
11.33	261	*Wisdom of Solomon*		11.25	161
11.35	261	7.27	176	12.24	183
11.36-39	19	16.8	211, 212	12.26-27	186
11.40-45	19			13.9	73
12.1	19	*Ecclesiasticus*		13.19	189, 210
12.2-3	19	1.14	27	13.38	210
12.2	125, 126	1.18	27	17.4	86
12.3	261	1.20	27	17.18	165
12.4	19, 243,	4.18	27	17.19	186
	261	20.30	27	17.20	165
12.8-9	261	24	91, 94–6,	23.2	139
12.9	20, 243		101	24.43	72, 73
12.10	20, 261	24.3	94	26.24	161
		24.4	95	27.50	177
Joel		24.7	91	28.20	279
3.17	90	24.8	91, 95		
4.17	90	24.10-12	91	*Mark*	
4.20-21	90	24.11	91, 95	1.4	150
		24.12	91, 95	1.10	177, 248
Amos		24.16-17	27	3.22-27	190
9.11	86	24.16	95	3.22	183
		24.23	27, 95	3.28-30	192
Habakkuk		24.27	95	4.23	73
2.2	238	38.34–39.3	260	6.48-50	285
2.3	18	39.3	272	6.48	285
		39.6-7	260	6.50	285

Mark (cont.)		1.1-2	42	1.45-49	283
7.34	276	1.1	47, 84, 94,	1.45	281
8.35	304		96	1.49	281
8.38	304	1.3	210	1.50-51	42
9.5	86	1.4-5	290	1.50	248, 252
13.6	285	1.4	171	1.51	36, 42, 44,
13.14	239	1.5	94, 182,		48, 97,
13.19	19		201		128, 129,
13.22	194	1.6-13	94		185, 247,
13.24	19	1.6	94		254, 301,
13.26-27	305	1.7	301		303
14.42	188	1.9-10	200	2	97, 301
14.62	285	1.10	201	2.3	299
		1.11	42, 48, 95,	2.4	299
Luke			294	2.11	42, 48,
1.1-4	238	1.12-13	94		102, 301,
3.22	177	1.12	95, 187,		307
9.22	112		274, 294,	2.17	109, 251
9.33	86		301	2.19-22	107
9.44	112	1.13	96	2.19	141
9.45	112	1.14-18	94	2.21	43, 97,
10	184	1.14	42, 44,		295
10.18-20	183, 184		47–9, 80,	2.22	104, 107,
10.18	186		84–6, 93–		109, 114,
10.38-42	292		8, 101,		122, 251
11.15	183		102, 131,	3	250, 267,
12.39	72		250, 268,		302, 303
13.29	73		277, 301	3.2	277
13.33	112	1.16	94, 95	3.3	185, 267,
14.35	73	1.17	25, 95		273
16.9	86	1.18	42, 43, 47,	3.5	185, 267,
18.31-33	112		84, 94, 97,		273
18.34	112		129, 136,	3.8	210
22.3	161, 206		147, 185,	3.10	210, 282
23.46	177		249, 250,	3.11-13	249
24	111-13		268, 272,	3.11-12	248
24.4	112		273, 301	3.11	252, 277,
24.5-7	112	1.19–13.30	189		279
24.6-8	113	1.20-23	278	3.12-13	42, 43
24.6	112	1.29-51	281	3.12	43
24.8	112	1.29	200, 276,	3.13	32, 42, 45,
24.9	112		301		147, 248,
24.22-23	113	1.32-33	177		249, 302
24.23	112	1.33	248	3.14	141, 247
24.31	113	1.34	252	3.15-21	281
		1.36	301	3.16-17	200
John		1.38-39	281	3.16	42, 46,
1–20	82	1.38	295		171, 302,
1	301, 302	1.39	63		303
1.1-5	42, 94	1.41	276, 281		

3.17-21	182, 186–8	5.27	13, 43, 46, 125	7.19-20	206
				7.20	200, 206
3.17-19	186	5.28-29	42, 43, 125, 199, 202, 303	7.21	278
3.17-18	12, 42			7.25-31	303
3.19	188, 200, 203			7.28-39	104
		5.29	126, 200, 282	7.28-29	303
3.20	200			7.28	109
3.21	70, 201	5.36	46, 201, 270	7.31	303
3.28-29	302			7.32-36	303
3.31-36	249	5.37	129, 147	7.33-34	147
3.31	42, 302	5.39	247	7.34	271
3.32	249, 250, 302	5.43	47	7.35	109
		6	247, 281	7.36	271
3.34	42, 249, 302	6.14-15	281	7.37-39	97
		6.14	177, 200	7.37	71
3.36	171, 202	6.27-35	42	7.38	71
3.35	302	6.28	201, 281	7.40-43	303
4	302	6.31	126, 251, 247	8	139, 148, 182, 190, 191, 199, 303
4.7-26	307				
4.10-15	267	6.33	200		
4.10	71, 302	6.35	289		
4.13-14	71, 278	6.38-39	278	8.2-11	139
4.14	71, 281, 290, 302	6.38	303	8.2	139
		6.39-40	42, 303	8.7-8	137
4.21	155	6.41	289	8.12-55	171
4.23-24	302	6.44	303	8.12-51	172
4.23	9, 97	6.45	250	8.12	172, 200, 288, 289
4.25	115, 121, 123	6.46	129, 140, 147		
				8.13	190
4.31-34	45, 105	6.47	303	8.18	288
4.34	46, 270, 281	6.48	289	8.19	172
		6.51	200, 289, 303	8.20	109
4.42	200, 303			8.21-22	303
5	31, 249, 283, 303	6.53-54	303	8.21	147
		6.54	202	8.23-25	288
5.8	282	6.57-58	202	8.23	174, 175, 303
5.15	121, 123	6.58	303		
5.16	283	6.61-62	303	8.24	173, 286
5.17	47	6.62	42	8.25	171, 286
5.18	47	6.70-71	191, 206	8.26	46, 200
5.19-28	282	6.70	161, 200	8.28	46, 47, 109, 288, 304
5.19-24	47	7–9	46		
5.19-20	249	7	190, 304		
5.19	140	7.3	201	8.35	290
5.20	201, 248	7.4	201	8.37-47	191
5.21-23	187	7.7	200, 201, 203, 206	8.37-45	206
5.21	282, 289			8.38	140, 148, 250
5.24	141, 171, 303	7.14	109		
		7.17	71	8.39-43	149
5.26-27	187	7.19-21	190, 191	8.40	250

John (cont.)		11.24-27	202	12.47	204, 210,
8.41	157	11.25-26	282, 289,		304
8.44-45	191		291, 293	12.48	202, 298
8.44	149-53,	11.25	288, 289,	12.49-50	140
	155–71,		291	13–17	283
	173–5,	11.26-27	292	13	304, 305
	177, 178,	11.26	289-91	13.1-3	305
	190, 199,	11.27	200, 283	13.1	201
	247	11.33	280	13.2	45, 200,
8.48-51	190	11.37	280		206, 305
8.48-49	200, 206	11.44	293, 297	13.6-11	278
8.48	199, 206	11.51-52	302	13.7	104
8.49	206	12	304	13.8	70
8.51	303	12.2	45, 191,	13.16-18	278
8.52	199, 206		297	13.19	278
8.54	286	12.14	251	13.23	48
8.55	191	12.16	104, 107,	13.27	190, 203,
8.56	150		109, 114,		206
8.58	286, 288		122	13.31–17.26	192
8.59	191	12.17	210	13.31-32	46, 47,
9	10, 31,	12.20-33	207		102
	281, 283	12.23	46, 207,	13.33	42, 147,
9.3-4	201		304		254
9.5	200	12.25	204, 304	13.34-35	305
9.9	285	12.26	102, 271	13.36-38	105
9.33	42	12.27-28	207	13.36	147, 272,
9.35	281	12.27	191		305
9.39	42, 43	12.28	47, 102,	14–17	135, 186
1.29.36	68		128	14	250, 272,
10.7-16	208	12.31-32	13, 186		305
10.7	289	12.31	13, 166,	14.1-3	42
10.9	289		183–6,	14.2-4	202
10.11	289		188, 202,	14.2-3	79
10.14	289		204, 304,	14.2	250, 305
10.18	68, 69		305	14.3	98, 102,
10.20-21	200				147, 271,
10.20	206	12.32-33	304		305, 306
10.21	206	12.32	184, 186	14.4-5	105
10.25	201	12.33	141	14.6	42, 46,
10.28	290	12.34	270		288, 289
10.30	47, 135,	12.35-36	182	14.7	48, 97,
	270	12.36	182		135, 268
10.32	201	12.37-43	49	14.8-11	288
10.36	200	12.38-40	247	14.8-9	105
10.37-38	201	12.38	7	14.9	43, 97,
11	276, 282,	12.41	43, 47,		128, 129,
	293, 294,		129, 135,		135, 136,
	297		247, 250		266, 268
		12.46-47	200		
11.7-16	105	12.46	304	14.10-12	201

Index of References

Reference	Pages
14.11	135
14.12	201, 210, 248, 266
14.13-17	135
14.15–16.26	196
14.15-25	288
14.15-24	202
14.15	210
14.16-17	97, 104
14.16	133
14.17	131, 135, 201
14.19	201
14.20	131, 133, 135, 283
14.21	135, 210
14.22	201
14.23-24	210
14.23	97, 135, 250, 283
14.25-26	104-109, 113, 114, 122, 123, 126, 127
14.26	104, 108–13, 251, 266, 272, 283
14.27	201
14.28	133, 135, 272
14.30-31	13, 207, 305
14.30	165, 175, 183, 188, 202, 204, 207, 209, 305
14.31	188, 272, 273, 288
15–17	182
15.1	288, 289
15.4-5	283
15.4	270
15.5	289
15.10	210
15.18–16.4	206
15.18-19	201
15.20	210
15.24	201
15.26-27	106
15.26	133
16	124, 305
16.4-33	114
16.6	114
16.8-11	13, 106, 207
16.8-10	187
16.8	201
16.11	13, 183, 187, 202, 204, 305
16.12-15	105, 107, 114, 122, 123, 126, 127
16.12	68, 114, 122
16.13-15	106, 107, 115, 121, 123-26
16.13-14	266
16.13	16, 114, 122-25, 251
16.14-15	254, 272
16.14	114
16.15	114
16.16-24	306
16.16-23	202
16.16-18	105
16.16	305
16.20	201
16.21-22	74
16.21	19
16.22	306
16.23-24	306
16.24	306
16.25	8, 105, 106, 115, 121, 256, 267, 272
16.28	200
16.29	266
16.32	294
16.33	19, 201, 202, 204
17	200, 205, 208, 209, 227, 288, 294, 295, 306
17.1-8	208
17.1-5	42
17.1	102, 209
17.3	209, 266, 268, 273, 306
17.4	270
17.5	42, 209, 265, 306
17.6	201, 209, 210
17.8	250
17.9-19	208
17.9-13	208
17.9	201, 208
17.10	209
17.11-12	161, 210
17.11	47, 201, 203, 204, 208-10
17.12	192, 203, 208, 209
17.13	203, 265
17.14-16	201, 208
17.14	204, 208, 209, 303
17.15	69, 188, 200, 202-205, 207–10
17.16	209, 303
17.17-19	209
17.18	201, 266
17.20-26	268, 269, 273
17.20-23	208
17.20-21	250, 270
17.20	270
17.21-23	200, 203
17.21	209, 269
17.22-26	272
17.22-23	270
17.22	47, 141, 209
17.23	209, 270, 283

John (cont.)		20.30-31	43, 46, 49, 55, 251, 252	12–14	77
17.24-26	208			12.28	196
17.24	98, 102, 103, 209, 254, 255, 265, 268, 271–3, 306			14.26-33	77
		20.30	252		
		20.31	265, 268, 273	*2 Corinthians*	
				3.14	142
		21	83, 252	3.18	142
		21.6	71	4.4	164, 166
17.25	201, 209	21.7	48	12.9	86
17.26	203, 209, 283, 288	21.13-15	45		
		21.20-23	290	*Galatians*	
18.4	295	21.20	48	1.12	131
18.5-8	286	21.22-23	83	1.16	131, 279
18.5-6	288	21.23	252	2.20	86
18.5	286	21.24-25	252	4.8	226
18.6	286	21.24	42, 43, 48, 49, 83		
18.8	286, 288			*Ephesians*	
18.37	200	21.25	252	2.2	183
19.9-19	188	22.7	210	5.14	294
19.14	68, 295				
19.15-16	297	22.9	210	*Philippians*	
19.26	48, 299			2.6-11	6
19.27	294	*Acts*		2.9	287
19.29	45	2.2-3	133	3.6	131
19.30	177, 294, 299	2.17	196		
		7.43	86	*Colossians*	
19.31	68	7.44	86	1.15	136
19.34	252, 294	10.30	112	2.9	136
19.35	49	11.15-17	112	2.13-15	140
19.36	126	12.12	150	3.1-3	298
19.39-41	282	13.1	196		
20	113, 251, 252, 299	14.27	120	*1 Thessalonians*	
		15.4	120	1.6	19
20.1	295	15.16	86	3.3	19
20.2	48	20.27	121	3.7	19
20.7	297	22.3	33	4.17-18	305
20.8	49			5.2	72, 73
20.9	104	*Romans*			
20.11-18	295	1.25	155	*2 Thessalonians*	
20.12-13	185	5.12-21	230	1.4	19
20.12	296	6.1-11	294	1.6	19
20.17	42	6.4	298	2.3-12	194
20.19-23	306	8.9	86	3.3	210, 229
20.20	306	10.4	140		
20.21	266	15.21	121	*1 Timothy*	
20.22	296			3.16	6
20.24-29	98	*1 Corinthians*			
20.28	98	2.6	183	*2 Timothy*	
20.29	252	2.8	183	4.18	210
		10.20	226		

Philemon		3.8	173, 196,	1.3	72, 73
3	150		206	1.4	81, 240
		3.9	172, 174	1.5	60
Hebrews		3.10	173, 196,	1.7	60
8.1-2	86		206	1.8	73, 84, 99
9.11	86	3.11-12	170, 171	1.9-11	76, 84
		3.11	173	1.9	49, 81
1 Peter		3.12	163, 173,	1.11	43, 237,
1.11-12	129		196		240
1.12	121	3.19-24	175	1.13-14	263
		3.24	174, 194	1.12–3.22	72
2 Peter		4	195, 196	1.17	71, 73, 84
3.10	72, 73	4.1-6	195	1.18	60
		4.2	175	1.19	237
1 John		4.3	175	1.20	61
1.1-3	171	4.6	173	2–3	75
1.5	121, 192	4.7-19	175	2.2	61, 68, 72
1.6	70, 192	4.7-8	172	2.7	73
1.7	174	4.10-12	172	2.8	60
1.8	173, 192	4.10	172, 174,	2.9	67
1.9	174, 175		175	2.14	61
1.10	173	4.13	174	2.20	61
2.1-2	175	4.16-17	172	2.23	73, 84
2.2	174, 175	4.17-21	172	2.26	73
2.4	173, 174	4.20	173, 174	2.27-28	68, 69, 72
2.5	174	5.3	172	3.1	61
2.6	174	5.6-8	175	3.3	72, 73
2.7-11	172	5.6-7	174	3.8	73
2.11	192	5.6	176	3.9	67
2.12-22	171	5.8	176	3.10	69, 72, 73
2.12-14	174	5.11-12	171	3.15	61
2.13	192	5.14-15	175	4–5	43
2.14	192, 197	5.18-20	171	4.1-2	42
2.15	192	5.18	174, 192	4.1	136
2.16-17	175	5.19-20	172	4.5	133
2.16	174	5.19	166	4.15-17	99
2.18-19	193			5	243
2.18	84, 175,	2 John		5.5-6	60
	193	1	82	5.5	61
2.19	194	7	84, 175,	5.6	133
2.20	174		195	5.9	60
2.22	174, 193			5.12	60, 102
2.27	174	3 John		6.2	60
2.29	172	1	82	6.14	139
3.1	172, 175			7.13-17	61
3.2	102, 131,	Revelation		7.15	85
	135	1–3	84	7.17	62, 68
3.3	174	1.1-6	72	9.20	226
3.7-12	173, 174	1.1	60, 81	10.1	61
3.8-10	157	1.3-4	240	10.11	66

Index of References

Revelation (cont.)		22.4	131, 136	11.40	262
11.1	61	22.6-21	71, 72	10.1	75
11.3	63	22.7	72, 73		
11.8	60	22.8	81	*2 Baruch*	
12	74	22.9	73	14.23-25	239
12.5	60	22.12	72	14.42-43	239
12.7-9	184	22.13	71, 73, 84	15.5	28
12.11	60	22.14	72	20.3	109
12.12	85	22.15	70, 72	20.4	110
12.17	73	22.16	60, 71, 73, 84	21.1-3	239
13	84			22.1	42, 75
13.6	85, 86	22.17-20	72	23.3	109
13.8	60	22.17	62, 71, 72	24	244
13.18	61	22.18-19	251	31	241
14.12	73	22.20	72	31.4	109
14.13	72	22.21	240	32.1	28
15.5	86			32.4-9	238
16.15	72, 73	PSEUDEPIGRAPHA		38.2	29
17.1	61	*Apocalypse of Abraham*		44	241
17.7-18	61	8.3	285	44.13	29
19.7	99	9.1-3	75	46.5	28
19.9	61, 72	9.3	285	48.22	28
19.10	75	10.3-17	46	48.24	29
19.11	42	10.3	46	48.38	28, 109
19.13	60, 84	10.8	46	48.40	28
20.5-6	43	11.1-6	47	48.47	28
20.6	69, 70, 72	17.2	46	50.1	43, 110, 240
20.11-14	43	18	43		
21–22	84	19.4	42	50.2–51.4	43
21	79-81, 84, 98	22.3-5	43	54.6	120
				54.14	28
21.1–22.5	98	*Apocalypse of Zephaniah*		54.20	120
21.1-8	99, 101	3	244	55.3–76.5	106
21.1	99	7	244	55.3	119
21.3-74	99	6.17	43	56.1	120
21.3	85, 86, 97, 98, 100–102, 131	10.2	42	59.2	28
		10.11	43	59.11	28
				66.5	28
21.5-8	99	*Apocryphon of Ezekiel*		71.2	120
21.6	62, 72, 73, 84	64.70.12	120	75.7	109
				76	238
21.8	99	*Ascension of Isaiah*		76.1	120
21.9–22.5	101	1.5	262	77.11-26	241
21.9-27	99	4.19-22	264	77.11	109
21.9	61	6.4-5	262	77.12–87.1	43
21.16-17	99	6.17	262	77.16	29
21.20	63	7.4	75	77.23	109
21.22	101	7.25	275	78–87	241
22	71, 251	11.34-35	262, 264	78.3	109
22.1	62	11.34	265	78.7	109

Index of References

81.4	120	14.8	42	85.3–89.38	29
84.2-5	28	14.24	75	85.3–89.9	29
84.2	109	15–16	216, 228,	89.10-12	29
84.7	109, 241		232	89.13-38	30
84.8-9	28	16–36	106	89.39–90.38	30
84.10	109	16.3	23	90.37	30
85.8	120	19.1	226	90.39	249
85.14	28	21.5	23	91-107	21
		25.1	23	91.1-10	231
3 Baruch		33	243	91.5-10	232
1.4	120	37–72	301	91.11-17	231
1.6	120	37–71	21, 22,	91.18-19	231
1.7	120		231	92-105	240
1.8	120	40.2-3	75	92.1	237, 240
2.1	44	40.8	238	93	243
2.4	120	43.1-4	262	93.1-10	231
2.5	44	47.3	244	93.2	238
2.6	120	48.1-6	263	93.5	30
15–16	43	51.1-5	43	93.6	30
		55.1	75	94.8	202
4 Baruch		55.4	13	96.4	202
1.9	121	58.5	261	96.7	202
2.1	121	62	43, 46	97.2-7	202
		62.1	75	98.1	25
1 Enoch		62.8	261	98.4	25
1–36	21, 223,	68.1	43	98.6	25
	231	69.15	47	99.3	202
1.1	22	70.1-2	261	99.6	25
1.2-5	13	70.1	46	99.7	226
1.2	22, 30	71	53, 261	99.9	70
2	22	71.1-4	262, 264	99.10	252
5.8	23	71.2	262	99.16	109, 202
6–16	223	71.10-14	264	100.6	240
8.2	23	71.14	46, 262	101-108	24
9.6	23	72–82	21, 24, 30,	103.1-4	25
10	216, 228,		43	103.1	243
	232	80.1	75	103.15	202
10.1-22	13	81–82	23, 240	103.4	202
10.7	23	81	243	104.1	25, 109,
13	242	81.1	23		202
13.4	109	81.5-6	262	104.12-13	31
13.6	109	81.6–82.1	237	104.13-105.2	24
13.10	23, 121	81.6	23, 43	104.9-12	24, 30
14–15	30	82.1-3	23	104.9-105.2	24
14	23, 43,	82.1-2	31	104.9	24
	129	82.1	43, 237	104.10	245
14.1-7	238	83–90	21	106-108	25
14.1-3	240	83–84	24, 231	106-107	231
14.1	23	83.8-10	43	106.12	25
14.8-23	43	85–90	24, 231	106.13-107.1	232

1 Enoch (cont.)		10.55-59	264	1.22	46
106.19	243	12.9	120	1.26	43, 46
107	241	12.11-12	264	1.27-29	51
108.1-3	244	12.33	13	1.27	46
108	21	12.37	238	1.29	91
		12.47	109	2.1	43, 46
2 Enoch		13	46	5–10	232
9.9	75	13.2-11	13	5.1-11	223
9.15	75	13.15	120	5.8	223
22.8-10	275	13.21	120	6.17-22	52
22.9-10	53	13.39	13	6.20	46
23.3-6	43	14	241	6.32	46
29.1-6	184	14.1	248	7.21-24	223
31.1-8	184	14.3-5	110	8.1-4	226
40.1-12	43	14.7	240	10	225, 228
68.2	43	14.21	109	10.1-14	214
		14.22	109	10.1-2	221
3 Enoch		14.24-48	237	10.2	223
12.5	47	14.25	110	10.3-6	214, 221,
		14.39	109		224, 225,
4 Ezra		14.40-41	110, 113		227
2.8	109	14.42-48	110	10.3	221-23,
4.1	40	14.44-46	43		225
4.3-4	117, 120	14.45-48	240	10.4	222
4.4	109	14.45-47	29	10.5	222, 223,
4.8	51	81.5	40		244
4.23	109	93.2	40	10.6	222, 227
4.47	120			10.7	183, 223
5.13	120	Joseph and Aseneth		10.8	223
5.31	40, 46	14.7	121	10.9	223
5.32	109	15.2	244	10.11	205, 217
5.38-56	46	15.12	121	10.12	223
5.56	120	15.22	243	11	225
6.11-16	46	19.4	121	11.2	225
6.30-32	46	22.13	243	11.4-6	225
6.33	120	26.6	121	11.4-5	226
7.1-17	46			11.14	225
7.1	40	Jubilees		11.16	225
7.28-26	43	1	221, 228	12	226-28
7.49	109	1.4	51	12.2-8	225
7.90	109	1.5	43	12.3-4	225
8.2	120	1.7	43	12.12-14	225
8.21	51	1.11	226	12.16-21	214
8.63-63	120	1.17	91	12.16	225
10	100	1.19-20	214, 220,	12.19-20	214, 224,
10.25-31	261		224		225, 227
10.28-38	264	1.20	220, 222,	12.19	224, 225
10.29-58	106		224, 225,	12.20	224, 225
10.33	109		227	13.26	52
10.38	120	1.21	220	14.1	244

15	228	2.6-7	43	37.1-3	165
15.25-27	52	2.6	42	37.1	164
15.30-32	226, 227	8.19	121	37.2-3	165
15.31	226	9.6	109	37.4	164
15.32	226	10.1	121	37.5-16	165
17.15–18.19	226			38.1-2	165
17.16	227	*Testament of Naphtali*		40.1-4	165
18.12	227	7.4	121		
19	228			*Barnabas*	
19.27-29	226	*Testament of Zebulun*		16.7	226
19.28	227	5.1	120		
22.16-18	226	7.1	120	Cyril of Jerusalem	
22.16	226	9.7	109	*Catecheseis*	
30.19-20	109			2.5	282
32.10-15	52	*Testament of Abraham*		3.1-4	295
32.25-26	110, 113	1.5	44	5.9	293
33.10-14	52	1.6	121	8.7	295
33.18	46	4.6	44, 121	13.39	295
49.1–50.13	52	4.8	121	14.5-6	295
50.1-2	46	4.9	44	14.5	295
		4.10	44	14.9	295
Life of Adam and Eve		5.12	121	14.10	295
3.2	121	7.1	121	14.11-12	295
6.2	121	7.3	42		
14.3	121	7.8-12	45, 48	Cyril of Alexandria	
15.1	121	7.11	121	*Commentari in Joannem*	
15.2–16.4	184	10.1	43	5.25	282
31.2	121	11–14	43	8.24-25	286
		11–13	43	11.20	292
Prayer of Joseph		17.6	121	11.32	292
9	47	20.1	121		
		20.3	121	Shepherd of Hermas	
Sibylline Oracles				*Similitude*	
1–2	194	*Testament of Job*		2.9	244
3.419	245	3.6	226		
8.47	226	16.7	120	*Vision*	
8.381-94	226	29.4	285	1.3-4	237
Frag 1.20-22	226	31.6	285	1.3.3	114
				1.3	239
Testament of Dan		*Testament of Moses*		2.1	237
5.6	217	1.10-18	238	2.4	241, 242, 245
		10.1	13		
Testament of Judah		10.7	13	5.5	237
20.1-2	195				
23.1	226	APOSTOLIC FATHERS		Ignatius	
25.3	91	*Acts of Archelaus*		*To the Magnesians*	
		15.6-7	164	3.1	226
Testament of Levi		27.15-16	165		
2.3	218	33.1-3	164		
2.5–4.6	218	34.1-5	164		

Index of References

NAG HAMMADI CODICES
Apocryphon of James
1–2 (NHC I, 2) 242

Apocalypse of Adam
85 (NHC V, 5) 242

On the Origin of the World
97.24-127.17
(NHC II, 4)   206

Gospel of Truth
50.25-34
(NHC XII, 2)   206

QUMRAN
1Q477 = 4QCatena[a]
iii 8   213

1QH
4.15   20
5.12   20
9.21   254
9.24   109
10.13   254
11.19-23   254
11.21-23   20
14.12-14   20
15.26-28   254
18.4-9   254
19.7-14   254
19.11-12   20
19.12-13   265
frag   45   219
frag 4   219

1QHab
7.2   16
7.5-6   18

1QM
1.15-19   13
13.10   19
xiv 9-10   213

1QS
1.7-8   20
I–II   180
I.15–II.12   197

i 16-iii 12   212
i 17-18   212
i 23-ii 1a   212
i 23-24   213
ii 1b-4   212
ii 14-17   212
ii 19   212
III.13–IV.26   180, 187, 191, 196
iii 21-24   213
iv 19-21   213
iv 19   213

1QSa
2.8-9   20

1QapGen
xx 12-18   214

4Q181
3-4   20

4Q213a
1.5-19   218
1.6-10   218
1.6-9   218
1.7   219
1.8   220
1.10–2.10   218
1.10-16   218
1.11-19   218
1.12   219
1.13   219
1.14   219
1.17   218, 219
1.18–2.10   218
1.18   219
2.8-9   219
2.14-18   218

4Q243
13.2   226

4Q244
12.2   226

4Q418
81   20

4Q510
1.4-6a   213
1.6b-8   214

4Q511
10.1-3a   213
10.3b-6   214

4Q530
2 ii + 6-7 + 8-12
ll. 4-20   232

4Q534
1.5   245

4QM[a]
8-10 i 6-7   213

4QTLevi[a]
1 i 10   214, 218

11Q5
xix 1-5   215
xix 13-16   205
xix 13-14   215
xix 15-16   215
xix 5-12   215
xix   214, 215, 220, 222, 227, 228

11QT[a]
29.7-8a   90

CD
3.20   20

CD-A
20.20-22   109
20.19   109

TARGUMS
Targum Neofiti Exodus
16.6-7   92
29.45-46   92

Targum of Zechariah
2.5   92

MISHNAH		38.4.5-6	161	5.22.2	158
ʾAbot		38.4.7	161	5.23.2	158
3.3	93	38.4.8	161		
3.6	93	38.4.9-10	161	Justin	
		38.4.9	161	Dialogue with Trypho	
JERUSALEM TALMUD		38.4.12-13	161	81.4	81
Peʾah		38.4.13	162		
16b	210	38.5.1-3	162	Origen	
		40.2.6	162	Commentarii in	
EARLY CHRISTIAN WORKS		40.5.1-2	162	evangelium Joannis	
		40.5.3-4	163	1.22	286, 289
Augustine		40.5.5-8	163	1.23	275
In Evangelium		40.5.5	161, 162	1.47	289
Johannis tractatus		40.6.2-4	163	1.54	289
42.9-10	166	40.6.5-9	163	1.126	289
42.10	167	40.6.7	161, 162	1.181	289
42.15	167	40.7.5	163	1.257	276
49.2	279, 280	51.12.2	66	1.267	289
49.3	280	51.33.9	66	1.268	289
49.14	280	66.62.1	165	2.221	276
49.24	280	66.62.8-13	166	6.59	278
		66.63.1-2	166	6.162-63	278
John Chrysostom		66.63.1	161	13.6	299
Homiliae in Joannem		66.63.11	161, 162	13.14-16	278
55	286	66.63.2	162, 166	13.39	299
62–63	292	66.63.9-12	166	13.52	299
62.3	292	66.66.1	165	13.95-97	155
		66.66.3	165	13.117-18	155
Clement of Alexandria		66.67.5	165	13.179	299
Protrepticus				19.154	286
9.84.2	294	Eusebius		20.97-105	157, 158
		Historia ecclesiastica		20.164	276
Stromata		3.39.1-7	65	20.168	153
7.108	152	3.39.4	82	20.170	153
		7.25.7	65	20.171	156
Cyprian		7.25.14	65	20.172	156
De dominica oratione		7.25.16	66	20.173-75	157
13	289	7.25.22-23	83	20.176-85	157
		7.25.22	65	20.192-94	157
De mortalitate				20.198	153
21	289	Hippolytus		20.202	155, 159
		Refutatio omnium		20.203-6	158
Epiphanius		haeresium		20.208-10	158
Panarion (Adversus		5.12.1-17.13	152	20.211-14	154
haereses)		5.17.7	152	20.211	153, 154
38.4.2-3	159			20.213	154
38.4.2.1-2	162	Irenaeus		20.214	154
38.4.2.3-4	162	Adversus haereses		20.215-16	155
38.4.2.31-32	161	5.25-30	193	20.218	153-55
38.4.4	160	1.26.1	177	20.219	157

Origen
Comm. Jo. (cont.)
20.221	158
20.224	158
20.240	289
20.244	159
20.245	289
20.252-54	155, 159
20.252	159
20.253	156
20.256	157
20.262	157
20.266	157
28.54-56	276
28.54	276
28.59-60	276
28.71	289
28.156	289
28.206-208	286
32.156	278
32.169	278
32.274	276
32.80	289
32.87-88	278
Frag 80	292

Pseudo-Tertullian
De praescriptionem haereticorum
xlviii	177

Rufinus
In Symbolum Apostolorum
23	294

Tertullian
Adversus Praxean
1	157

De Anima
43	294

CLASSICAL WORKS
Aeschylus
Choephori
2.19	285

Euripides
Orestes
380	285

Homer
Odyssey
11.117	193
13.378	193
14.18	193

Plato
Apologia
5.21.a	257
6.21.b	258, 259, 272

Leges
903b	205

Plutarch
De E apud Delphos
2.385c	256
385d	257
393d-e	257

De Pythiae oraculis
404e-f	256

HELLENISTIC-JEWISH WRITINGS
Philo
De cherubim
27–29	266

De congressu eruditionis gratia
118	193

De fuga et inventione
140	193

De mutatione nominum
11–13	286

De posteritate Caini
123	193
37	193

De praemiis et poenis
123	92

De somniis
1.148-49	92
1.230	286
2.252	266

Josephus
The Life
209	111

Jewish Antiquities
15.11.3	288

Jewish War
3.350-54	110
3.351	111, 113
3.353	111
5.5.4	288

INSCRIPTIONS
Gilgamesh Epic
1.36-48	259

INDEX OF AUTHORS

Aland, B. 153
Alexander, P. S. 216
Allison, D. C. 230
Arbel, V. D. 275
Ashton, J. 3, 4, 9–11, 13, 14, 16, 24, 25, 33–40, 43, 45–7, 50, 52–5, 60, 62, 71, 75, 79, 80, 105–8, 115, 118, 123, 125, 128, 129, 180–2, 187, 198, 235, 247, 272, 275
Aune, D. E. 39, 70, 72, 75, 81, 99, 183

Ball, D. M. 284
Bammel, E. 122
Barclay, W. 150
Bardy, G. 65
Barker, M. 27, 295
Barrett, C. K. 5, 59, 115, 123, 150
Bauckham, R. 47, 62, 73, 82, 270
Bauer, W. 150
Beale, G. K. 100
Beard, M. 286
Beker, J. C. 230
Bernard, J. H. 108, 110, 150
Betz, O. 106, 123
Beyer, K. 220
Biddle, M. 295
Bieringer, R. 122
Bindman, D. 130, 141
Blake, W. 129–34, 136–42
Blank, J. 48
Boccaccini, G. 22
Böcher, O. 59, 64
Boismard, M.-E. 249
Borgen, P. 7, 47
Boring, E. M. 278, 279
Bousset, W. 4
Boxall, I. 72, 77
Breytenbach, C. 181
Brooke, A. E. 153–9
Brooke, G. 218
Brown, R. E. 48, 62, 122, 151, 176, 195, 196, 200, 269, 271, 283
Buck, H. M. 296
Bühner, J.-A. 7, 8, 35
Bultmann, R. 5, 14, 31, 34, 39, 45, 55, 122, 150, 175, 176, 201, 210, 282, 289, 307
Burge, G. M. 111

Burridge, R. A. 54
Butlin, M. 130

Ceglarek, M. 86
Charles, R. H. 58, 67
Charlesworth, J. 11, 12
Charlesworth, J. H. 215
Chester, A. 92
Collins, J. J. 9, 15, 37, 39–41, 49, 51, 52, 55, 105, 115, 116, 118, 195, 203, 231, 235, 302
Coloe, M. L. 97
Cullmann, O. 59
Culpepper, R. A. 59

Dahl, N. A. 9
Davies, J. G. 136
Day, P. L. 181
DeConick, A. 147, 148, 175, 176, 178, 277
Delling, G. 183
Denis, A.-M. 120
Deutsch, C. 98
DiLella, A. A. 115, 119
Dillon, R. J. 112, 113
Dodd, C. H. 5, 13, 14, 201, 230, 290
Donahue, J. R. 62
Dörfel, D. 106, 119
Drawnel, H. 218
Dunn, J. D. G. 230

Elior, R. 296
Endo, M. 94
Endres, J. C. 51
Eshel, E. 218
Esler, P. F. 62
Evans, C. A. 94

Fagles, R. 257
Ferber, M. 142
Fisk, B. N. 245
Flint, P. W. 15, 215, 217
Flusser, D. 219
Foerster, W. 153
Fossum, J. E. 44, 287
Fowden, G. 286

Frey, J. 6, 63, 64, 69, 72, 79–85, 93, 98, 102, 104, 115, 122–6, 181, 183–7, 193–7, 201, 231, 289, 291
Funk, R. W. 150, 230

García Martínez, F. 265
Gese, H. 94–6
Gieschen, C. A. 44, 47
Ginzberg, L. 295
Gnuse, R. K. 111
Goguel, M. 4
Goldberg, A. M. 87
Gordon, R. 246
Goulder, M. D. 77, 281
Gourgues, M. 115, 123
Gray, R. 111
Greenfield, J. C. 218, 219
Gregory, A. 113
Griffith-Jones, R. 274, 277–9, 295, 298, 299
Griggs, E. L. 142
Guelich, R. 54
Guilding, A. 281
Gundry, R. H. 44, 45

Haenchen, E. 151
Hahn, F. 180, 187
Hall, R. G. 106, 112, 113, 256, 266, 268
Hamburger, J. F. 61
Harder, G. 189
Hare, D. R. A. 36
Harl, M. 286
Harnack, A. 4
Hartman, L. F. 119
Harvey, A. E. 283
Hasler, V. 279
Hayward, R. 212
Heinrici, G. 151
Hellholm, D. 39, 202
Hengel, M. 54, 80–3, 94
Henten, J. W. van 181
Henze, M. 109
Heppner, C. 141
Herrmann, J. 55
Hilgenfeld, A. 118, 151
Hill, C. E. 81
Hill, D. 60
Himmelfarb, M. 44, 53, 237, 239, 246
Hoek, A. van den 55
Holl, K. 159–63, 165, 166
Hoover, R. W. 230

Hoskyns, E. C. 150
Hurtado, L. W. 46

Isaac, E. 238

Jackson, D. R. 242, 244
Janowski, B. 87–91
Jenks, G. C. 194
Joüon, P. 114

Kalms, J. U. 184, 189, 194
Kammler, H.-C. 122, 123
Kanagaraj, J. J. 287
Käsemann, E. 6, 39, 40, 47, 230
Keener, C. S. 54
Kelber, W. H. 253
Kenner, C. S. 110
Kenny, A. 63
Kerr, A. R. 284
Keynes, G. 132, 137
Kierspel, L. 182
Klijn, A. F. J. 118
Knust, J. W. 139
Koch, K. 55
Kovacs, J. L. 13
Kruijf, T. C. de 171
Kugler, R. A. 218, 219
Kuhn, P. 87
Kümmel, W. 230
Kundzins, K. 266
Kyrtatas, D. 64

Lagrange, M.-J. 277
Lange, A. 213, 215, 216, 220, 225
Langerbeck, H. 153
Lee, P. 98, 99
Leonhardt-Balzer, J. 189, 205
Levison, J. R. 110, 114, 266
Lieu, J. M. 171, 176
Lieu, S. N. C. 164, 165
Lindberg, B. 131, 135, 136
Lust, J. 114

MacRae, G. W. 6, 286
Martyn, J. L. 9, 10, 200
McCauley, L. P. 282
McLay, T. R. 116
McNamara, M. 92, 93
Meadowcroft, T. J. 116
Meeks, W. A. 5, 7, 8, 143, 200

Menken, M. J. J. 126
Metzing, E. 184
Milik, J. T. 21, 22, 218
Miller, P. C. 242
Moloney, F. J. 270, 293
Morray-Jones, C. R. A. 36, 105, 128, 129, 275
Moskal, J. 139
Mühlenberg, E. 153
Müller, U. B. 114, 122

Nagel, T. 81
Neyrey, J. H. 269
Nickelsburg, G. W. E. 23–6, 105, 119, 238, 240–3, 245
Nicklas, T. 112
North, J. 286

O'Day, G. M. 7, 55
Odeberg, H. 36
Olson, D. C. 46
Olsson, B. 104, 122, 247
Orton, D. E. 245
Osborne, G. R. 59
Osiek, C. 237, 246

Pagels, E. 153, 299
Painter, J. 108, 109
Paley, M. D. 142
Pastorelli, D. 108, 125
Peerbolte, L. J. L. 193–5
Petersen, T. 298
Pezzoli-Olgiati, D. 98, 99
Piper, R. A. 186, 190, 191, 198
Plumer, E. 190
Porsch, F. 106, 115
Potterie, I. de la 8, 105, 106, 115, 120, 122, 125
Price, S. 286
Prigent, P. 58, 64, 66, 69, 99
Pusey, P. E. 278

Quispel, G. 153

Rahner, J. 97
Rausch, T. P. 230
Rebell, W. 114
Regul, J. 66, 67
Reichelt, H. 106

Reitzenstein, R. 298
Reynolds, B. E. 13, 41, 80, 125
Richard, E. 267
Rietz, H. W. L. 215
Rigato, M.-L. 112
Riley, G. J. 181
Roetzel, C. J. 33
Roloff, J. 61
Ronning, J. 92
Rowland, C. 36, 37, 46, 47, 49–52, 55, 58, 76, 105, 128, 129

Saffrey, H. D. 76
Sagnard, F. 153
Sanders, J. A. 215, 217
Sanders, J. N. 150
Sandmel, S. 14
Schlegel, J. 79
Schnackenburg, R. 150
Schnelle, U. 42, 81, 201
Schniewind, J. 120
Schöpflin, K. 106, 107, 119
Schottroff, L. 6
Schreiner, T. R. 230
Schulz, S. 6, 8
Schüssler Fiorenza, E. 63, 69
Schweitzer, A. 230
Segal, A. F. 275
Seim, T. K. 111, 113
Sievers, J. 87
Sim, D. C. 62
Sim, U. 98, 99
Smith, D. M. 266
Söllner, P. 98
Sorensen, E. 190, 191
Speiser, E. A. 259
Sperling, S. D. 181
Sproston, W. E. 190
Stehly, R. 66
Stephenson, A. A. 282
Stock, B. 236, 246
Stone, M. E. 21, 41, 51, 55, 110, 119, 218, 219, 238, 241, 248
Strecker, G. 171, 176
Stuckenbruck, L. T. 49, 202, 203, 205, 211, 214, 216, 223, 230
Sturm, R. E. 38
Sullivan, K. P. 44, 45, 47, 53
Swete, H. B. 58, 63, 64

Thackeray, H. St J. 284
Thatcher, T. 34, 35, 255, 273
Theobald, M. 93, 94, 104, 112, 180, 184–6, 199
Thoma, C. 87
Thyen, H. 82
Trebolle-Barrera, J. 21
Trumbower, J. A. 153
Twelftree, G. H. 190, 199

Unnik, W. C. van 123

Van Belle, G. 4
VanderKam. J. C. 220, 222, 224
Vanni, U. 72
Vermes, G. 91
Vermes, M. 164, 165
Volfing, A. 61
Volkmar, G. 151
Vorster, W. S. 54

Wahlde, U. C. von 190, 191, 271
Wahlen, C. 190
Wedderburn, A. J. M. 294
Westcott, B. F. 295, 296
Whitters, M. F. 241
Wiles, M. 293
Willems, D. R. 279
Williams, C. H. 7, 79, 124, 126, 271, 284, 285, 287
Wills, L. M. 54
Windisch, H. 106, 108, 266
Wintermute, O. S. 51, 222
Witherington III, Ben 67
Wolters, A. 263, 264
Wright, N. T. 231

Yarbro Collins, A. 37, 41, 301
Young, F. W. 124, 125

www.ingramcontent.com/pod-product-compliance
Lightning Source LLC
Chambersburg PA
CBHW070013010526
44117CB00011B/1544